Captain Mallom of Wacton Hall

Also by David Large

The Life and Family of Robert Large, Mercer, Mayor of London 1439-1440, First Employer of William Caxton. Foundation for Medieval Genealogy, Vowchurch, Hereford, England, 2008.

Four projects, supervised by Professors Adrian Bell and Anne Curry, published between 2010–2020, in 'The Soldier in Later Medieval England.' Henley Business School & The University of Southampton https://www.medievalsoldier.org/about/soldier-profiles/:

1. Using the Poll Tax to identify Medieval Archers.
2. Men from Stamford, Lincolnshire, commanded by Edmund of Langley, Duke of York (1341-1402): Comparison of names in the Poll Tax and Soldiers' databases.
3. Soldiers named 'LARGE' in the Protection and Attorney database.
4. Soldiers named 'LARGE' in the Garrisons of Lancastrian Normandy, 1415-50.

Captain Mallom of Wacton Hall

and

His Extraordinary Family

David M Large

Poppyland Publishing

Copyright © David M Large.

This edition 2024 published by Poppyland Publishing, Lowestoft, NR32 3BB.

www.poppyland.co.uk

ISBN 978 1 869831 40 0

All rights reserved. No part of this publication may be reproduced, stored in a retrieval system or transmitted by any means, mechanical, photocopying, recording or otherwise, without the written permission of the publishers.

Designed and typeset in 10.5 on 13.5 pt Gilgamesh Pro.

Picture credits are given in the illustrations section, p. ix.

Front Cover: Wacton Hall, today, photograph by Kathy Moyse.
Back cover: author photograph by Philip Price.

Contents

Acknowledgements	vii
Illustrations	ix
Foreword	13
Preface	15
Part 1: The Family and Ancestry of Captain John Mallom	27
Part 2: The Mallom Estates: Growth	49
Part 3: The Mallom Estates: Decline	88
Part 4: The Army Career of John Mallom of Wacton	107
Part 5: Connections by Marriage of Captain John Mallom	159
Part 6: Descendants of Richard Mallom of Wacton	187
Index	217

⁀ To Cheryl ⁀

*And in grateful memory of Emily Cottam and George Bennett
whose enthusiastic teaching of History
first sparked my interest of the study of the past.*

"For whatsoever from one place doth fall,
Is with the tide unto another brought:
For there is nothing lost, that may be found, if sought."

"The Faerie Queene" by Edmund Spencer (1553-1599).

Read by Colonel Brandon to Marianne Dashwood in "Sense and Sensibility" by Jane Austen, who lived from 1775-1817, the main period of interest in this account.

Acknowledgements

Working on a project of this type has involved the help and collaboration of a great many people. I am particularly indebted to Diana Spelman, Genealogist and Record Agent in Norwich, and to Sarah Minney, Genealogist and Record Agent in London, for their unfailing help, advice and encouragement. Without their efforts, this work would never have been completed.

I thank Adrian Soble for our many helpful discussions on aspects of the work.

I am also grateful to the following:

UK: The 8th Marquess Townshend of Raynham Hall, Norfolk; Dr Anthony Smith, Archivist at Raynham Hall; Patrick Palgrave-Moore, Norfolk Genealogist and Antiquary; Kathy Moyse & Andrew Simmonds KC, custodians of Wacton Hall; Dr Julian Litten, Historian & Archaeologist; P. L. Dickinson, Clarenceux King of Arms, College of Arms, London; John Tunesi, Secretary of The Heraldry Society, Baldock, Hertfordshire; David S. Hopkinson, Heraldic Artist, Hertford, Hertfordshire; Geoffrey I Kelly, Historical Research Consultant, Norfolk; Wacton Parochial Church Council, Norfolk; Revd. John Madinda and Aslacton Parochial Church Council, Norfolk; Revd. Clive Wylie, Rector of The Church of the Blessed Virgin Mary and All Saints, Sculthorpe, Norfolk; Clare Oakley & Frances Atherton, Hempnall Group of Churches, Norfolk; Richard Land, Tom Townsend, Archivist, & colleagues at Norfolk Record Office, Norwich; Norfolk Heritage Centre, Norwich; Ellen Carr, Librarian, and Paul White, Look Ups Volunteer, Norfolk Family History Society, Kirby Hall, Norwich; Oliver Bone, Curator, King's Lynn and Thetford Museums, Norfolk; Dr Gudrun Warren, Librarian and Curator, Norwich Cathedral; Marc Morris, Medieval Historian and author, West Sussex; Dr Katharine Keats-Rohan, Historian & Author, Oxford University; Dr Alastair Massie, Robert Fleming, Templer Study Centre Manager and Chris Andrews, National Army Museum, London; Kim Harris, Archives Assistant, Arundel Castle, West Sussex; Michelle Hill, Curator, and Alexander Leese, Assistant Curator, Tameside Museums and Galleries, Ashton-under-Lyne, Greater Manchester; Westminster Abbey Library; Erika Ingham and Mark Lynch, National Portrait Gallery, London; Lily Hosking, UK Parliament; Claudia Thwaites and the Board of Trustees, National Gallery, London; Staff at The National Archives, London, & London Metropolitan Archives, The National Maritime Museum, Greenwich, London; Graham S. Holton, Senior Tutor, Strathclyde Institute for Genealogical Studies, Centre for Lifelong Learning, University of Strathclyde, Glasgow; Dr Callum Watson, Battle Coordinator, The National Trust for Scotland, The Battle of Bannockburn, Stirling; Vicky Hillhouse on behalf of Andrew Hillhouse paintings; Else Churchill, Genealogist, The Society of Genealogists, London; Sam Bryan, Assistant Librarian, Royal Courts of Justice, The Strand, London; Jessica Paterson, Archivist Trainee, Gonville and Caius

College, Cambridge; Julie Harold, Norfolk Co-ordinator of FreeREG; Linda Hodson, Chair of Malhamdale Local History Group; Staff at Ancestry.co.uk, FindmyPast.co.uk, FamilySearch.org, GRO, Southport and the British Newspaper Archive, Jonathan Plunkett, Robert Maidstone, Gary Windeler, Pamela Palgrave, Shirley Howell and Howard Slatter.

USA: Don N. Hagist, Independent Researcher of the American Revolution, and Editor, Journal of the American Revolution, Rhode Island, USA; Professor Jim Piecuch, Kennesaw State University, Georgia, USA; Professor Stanley D.M. Carpenter, US Naval War College, Newport, Rhode Island, USA; Todd W Braisted, The Online Institute for Advanced Loyalist Studies, Mahwah, New Jersey, USA; Dr Nic Butler, Resident Historian, Charleston County Public Library, South Carolina, USA; Cara Delatte, Reference Archivist, The Brooke Russell Astor Reading Room for Rare Books and Manuscripts, The New York Public Library, USA; Ellen M. Clark, Library Director, and Rachel Nellis, Research Services Librarian, The American Revolution Institute of The Society of The Cincinnati, Washington DC, USA; Joseph J. Felcone, Antiquarian Bookseller, Princeton, New Jersey, USA; Julie Stoner, Reference Librarian, Geography and Maps Division, The Library of Congress, Washington DC, USA; John Beekman, The New Jersey Room, Jersey City Free Public Library, Jersey City, New Jersey, USA; Joanne M Nestor, Principal Photographer, New Jersey State Archives, Jersey City, New Jersey, USA; Jayne Ptolemy, Archivist, William L. Clements Library, University of Michigan, Ann Arbour, Michigan, USA; Peter Harrington, Curator, Anne S.K. Brown Military Collection, Brown University Library, Princeton, Providence, Rhode Island, USA; Staff at 19 Archives and Libraries in America & Canada named in the Footnotes, Ira Lund, Cumberland Family Tree, Version 4.10.

Ireland: Staff at the Department of Publications and Images, The National Gallery of Ireland, Dublin.

Australia: Peter Stewart. Researcher into the inter-relationships of medieval people.

Virtually all the institutions who provided illustrations from their collections in the UK, Dublin and the USA waived their fees, and their generosity is gratefully acknowledged.

All royalties from this book are being donated to the Norfolk Record Office and the Norfolk Family History Society in appreciation of the help they have given over several years. I have been fortunate in the advice and help I have received from many sources, but any inadvertent errors in what follows are mine, alone.

I thank Patrick Palgrave-Moore for writing the Foreword, Sue Stephenson for proofreading the text and her valuable comments, and Gareth H.H. Davies of Poppyland Publishing for editorial assistance.

And last, but by no means least, I am glad to acknowledge the constant support and encouragement of my wife, Cheryl, who must have thought at times that I was trying to carve out a new career in retirement.

Illustrations

Part 1

Fig. 01. St Michael and All Angels Church, Great Moulton, Norfolk, author, p. 27.
Fig. 02. St Michael's Church, Aslacton, Norfolk and detail of the armorial on the Mallom ledgerstone, author, p. 28.
Fig. 03 Ledgerstone commemorating the children of John and Phillis Mallom, and Phillis Mallom, with kind permission of Revd. John Madinda and Aslacton Parochial Church Council, p. 29.
Fig. 04. Pastel portrait of John Mallom (d.1761), with kind permission of the Ancient House Museum, Thetford, p. 31.
Fig. 05. St Gregory's Church, Norwich, with kind permission of Diana Spelman. Font photograph by George Plunkett, with kind permission of his son, Jonathan Plunkett, p. 32.
Fig. 06. Church of St Peter Mancroft, Norwich, author. Font photograph by Tom Townsend, p. 33.
Fig. 07. Towards Malham village, within the trees, from the rim of Malham Cove, photograph by Timothy Large, p. 38.
Fig. 08. St Andrew's Church, Bedingham & memorial to Revd. William Copping, author, p. 44.

Part 2

Fig. 09. The Arms of the Family of Mallom of Wacton Hall, Wacton in the County of Norfolk, created and painted by David S. Hopkinson FSHA, Hon FHS, p. 56.
Fig. 10. All Saints Church, Wacton, Norfolk, author, p. 57.
Fig. 11. Ledgerstone to Elizabeth (Stone) Mallom & John Mallom, with kind permission of Wacton Parochial Church Council, p. 58.
Fig. 12. Ledgerstone to Katherine (Mann) Mallom, with kind permission of Wacton Parochial Church Council, p. 59.
Fig. 13. All Saints Church, Woodton, Norfolk, author, p. 63.
Fig. 14. Ledgerstones to John Mallom & to Elizabeth (Suckling) Mallom, with kind permission of Wacton Parochial Church Council, p. 75.

Part 3

Fig. 15. Wacton Hall with the Farm, with kind permission of Kathy Moyse & Andrew Simmonds KC, current custodians of Wacton Hall, p. 88.
Fig. 16. Wacton Hall, today, photograph by Kathy Moyse, p. 89.
Fig. 17. Memorial to Phillis Mallom in St Michael's Church, Aslacton, with kind permission of Revd. John Madinda and Aslacton Parochial Church Council, p. 90.

Part 4

Fig. 18. Sir Armine Wodehouse, 5th Baronet, in 1773 by Thomas Hickey, oil on canvas, with kind permission of the National Gallery of Ireland. Licensed under CC BY 4.0. © Image NGI 653, p. 111.
Fig. 19. Cranmer Hall, Sculthorpe in 1946, with kind permission of Norfolk Record Office (BR 143/152), p. 111.
Fig. 20. George, 1st Marquess Townshend, with The Norfolk Militia by David Morier, c 1758-59, oil on canvas. Image courtesy of the Paul Mellon Centre for Studies in British Art. Photo by Tom St Aubyn. © of the present Marquess Townshend, in whose private possession at Raynham Hall the painting remains, p. 113.
Fig. 21. George Townshend, 4th Viscount, later 1st Marquess Townshend (1724-1807) by James Northcote, RA (Plymouth 1746—London 1831). Oil painting on canvas after Sir Joshua Reynolds PRA (Plympton 1723—London 1792). A half-length portrait in armour, with a mauve sash, holding a baton in his left hand. © The National Trust images. Image No. 1000327. Photograph taken in 2011. Florence Court, with kind permission of the National Trust, p. 113.

Fig. 22.	King George II by George Townshend, 1st Marquess Townshend, pen and ink, 1751-1758, with kind permission of the National Portrait Gallery, London. © NPG 4855(2), p. 113.
Fig. 23.	Rt Hon Charles Townshend PC (1725-1767) by Sir Joshua Reynolds PRA and Studio. Oil painting on canvas, half-length portrait of the sitter set against a plain brown background, turned towards the left and looking out at the spectator. He wears a short brown wig and a generously cut red velvet robe or cloak, a white lace cravat at the neck, Townshend was Chancellor of the Exchequer in the Earl of Chatham's government from 2 August 1766—4 September 1767. © The National Trust images. Image No. 985981, Baddesley Clinton, with kind permission of the National Trust, p. 113.
Fig. 24.	Uniform of men in the 57th Regiment of Foot during the American War of Independence from "The uniform of the several regiments of foot in His majestys service, 1771." Donald Grant. The War Office, London, 1771, with kind permission of The Society of The Cincinnati, Washington DC, p. 115.
Fig. 25.	Militia Soldier by George Townshend, 1st Marquess Townshend, pen and ink, with kind permission of the National Portrait Gallery, London. © NPG 4855(64), p. 115.
Fig. 26.	General Sir Henry Clinton in General Officers' undress uniform, by John Stuart, water colour on ivory, 1777. Ownership © National Army Museum, Out of Copyright, image no: 137836, p. 115.
Fig. 27.	General Sir William Howe, mezzotint, with kind permission of the Anne S. K. Brown Military History Collection, Brown University, Providence, RI, USA, p. 116.
Fig. 28.	Charles Cornwallis, 1st Marquess Cornwallis, by Thomas Gainsborough, oil on canvas, 1973, with kind permission of the National Portrait Gallery NPG 281, p. 116.
Fig. 29.	Disembarkation of Troops at Gravesend Bay under the command of General Sir George Collier RN, hand coloured acquatint from an engraving from The Naval Chronicle vol. 32, London 1814, with the kind permission of The Society of The Cincinnati, Washington DC, p. 117.
Fig. 30.	The British landing at Kip's Bay, New York Island, 15 September 1776 by Robert Cleveley, 1777, with kind permission of the National Maritime Museum, Greenwich, London, 2891, p. 118.
Fig. 31.	Paulus Hook Fort, at the mouth of the North River in 1778, with kind permission of The Library of Congress, Washington DC, p. 119.
Fig. 32.	Work carried out at Paulus Hook Fort in 1777, under the supervision of Lieut. John Mallom of the 57th Regiment of Foot, repairing defences, with kind permission of The Society of the Cincinnati, Washington DC, p. 120.
Fig. 33.	Paulus Hook Monument, Jersey City, New Jersey, USA, photograph by John Beekman, p. 121.
Fig. 34.	Siege of Charleston (1780) from the original painting by Alonzo Chappel, with the kind permission of the Anne S.K. Brown Military Collection, Brown University Library, Providence, Rhode Island, USA, p. 129.
Fig. 35.	Uniforms of the 63rd & 96th Regiments of Foot, by Gerald C. Hudson. Frontispiece in History of the Manchester Regiment (late the 63rd and 96th Foot), by Colonel H.C.Wylly. Vol I: 1758—1883. London, Foster Groom & Co. Ltd. Reprinted by Naval-military-press. Out of Copyright, with kind permission of Tameside Museums & Galleries: The Manchester Regiment Collection. Ashton-under-Lyne, Greater Manchester, p. 129.
Fig. 36.	The Battle of Camden, Death of [American General] Kalb, 16 August 1780, with kind permission of The Society of The Cincinnati, Washington DC, p. 136.
Fig. 37.	Colonel Tarleton, 1782, by Sir Joshua Reynolds, 1723-1792. Bequeathed by Mrs Henrietta Charlotte Tarleton, 1951, with kind permission of © the National Gallery, London, p. 137.
Fig. 38.	Battle of Eutaw Springs, 8 September 1781, with kind permission of The Society of The Cincinnati, Washington DC, p. 146.

Part 5

Fig. 39.	Admiral Horatio Nelson, published by The Medici Society Ltd, Lemuel Francis Abbott, 1912 (1794), with kind permission of the National Portrait Gallery, NPG D38494, p. 161.
Fig. 40.	Stained glass window in St Mary's Church, Shelton, Norfolk commemorating Sir John Shelton & his wife, Lady Anne Boleyn, author, p. 162.
Fig. 41.	Queen Anne Boleyn by an unknown English artist, oil on panel. Late 16th century, based on

	a work of circa 1533-1536, with kind permission of the National Portrait Gallery, NPG 668, p. 164.
Fig. 42.	Queen Elizabeth I, by an unknown continental artist, oil on panel, circa 1575, with kind permission of the National Portrait Gallery, NPG 2082, p. 164.
Fig. 43.	Presumed portrait of Edward I, possibly from the Sedilia, with kind permission of the Dean and Chapter of Westminster Abbey, p. 167.
Fig. 44.	The encounter between Robert the Bruce and Henry de Bohun at Bannockburn, 23 June 1314 by Andrew Hillhouse, with kind permission of Vicky Hillhouse, p. 169.
Fig. 45.	Norwich Castle (the Keep) today, author, p. 173.
Fig. 46.	Bigod Tower, Norwich Castle, George Plunkett, with kind permission of his son, Jonathan Plunkett, p. 173.
Fig. 47.	Bigod Arch, the 12th century Norman entrance to the Keep, George Plunkett, with kind permission of his son, Jonathan Plunkett, p. 173.
Fig. 48.	Thetford Priory, founded by Roger I Bigod, author, p. 174.
Fig. 49.	Norwich Cathedral, author, p. 174.
Fig. 50.	The Presbytery, site of the burial of Roger I Bigod, with kind permission of the Dean and Chapter of Norwich Cathedral. Photograph by Bill Smith, p. 174.
Fig. 51.	Baron Roger Bigod, Earl of Norfolk d. 1221. Fully-rounded cast. Gilding by Thomas Thormycroft. © UK Parliament, WOA S61 heritagecollections.parliament.uk, with kind permission, p. 175.

Part 6

Fig. 52.	Wacton Church font where Richard Mallom was baptised on 6 April 1744, with kind permission of Wacton Parochial Church Council, p. 187.
Fig. 53.	Lozenge carved on the ledgerstone of Mary (Mallom) Wortley illustrating the Mallom coat of arms, author, p. 188.
Fig. 54.	Sculthorpe Church, where baptisms, marriages, and burials of members of the Mallom & Large families took place from the late 1700s onwards, author. Font photograph by Revd. Clive Wylie, p. 201.
Fig. 55.	Gravestone of Laura Elizabeth and Richard William Mallom in Sculthorpe Graveyard, photograph by Revd. Clive Wylie, p. 206.
Fig. 56.	Minnie (Mallom) Woodhouse arriving at St Peter's Church, Dunton-cum-Doughton with Revd. Derrick Wood, to play for Evensong, in the late 1960s, with kind permission of Richard Land and Halsgrove Publishing, p. 206.

Every attempt has been made to ensure that images are correctly attributed: we apologise for any inadvertent errors.

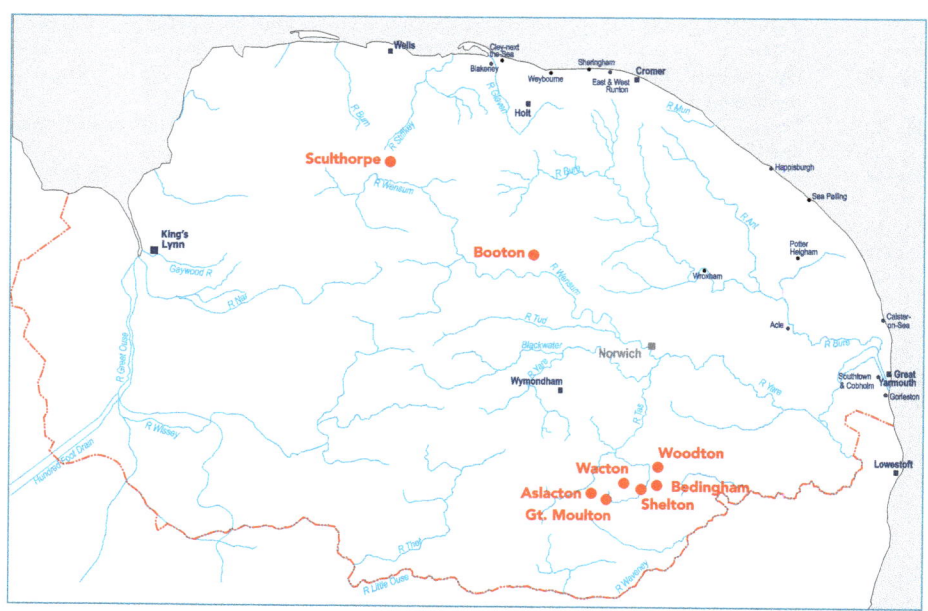

Map of Norfolk showing the approximate positions of the villages in which the key events of the story take place.

Distances: Norwich to Gt Moulton = 15 miles
Aslacton to Bedingham = 11 miles
Norwich to Booton = 13 miles
Norwich to Sculthorpe = 30 miles

Foreword

In the annals of Norfolk history, the Mallom family of Wacton is little known, but there are good reasons for this. An aspiring merchant family anxious to become part of the social hierarchy, becomes after only a comparatively short period of prosperity and influence, embroiled in debt and financial ruin. By the latter part of the 17th century, most of the successful merchant families had already reached their pinnacles of power and influence, whilst the Malloms were only beginning the same process. At the Heralds Visitations of Norfolk in the 16th and 17th centuries, the family is not mentioned as one of sufficient status to be granted arms. Blomefield in his History of Norfolk gives some notice of the family, but Walter Rye in his Norfolk Families makes no mention of the family. It was not until the Antiquary Arthur Campling had his collection of East Anglian Pedigrees published by the Norfolk Record Society that the importance of the Mallom family was brought home to a wider audience. His collection also included pedigrees of the Stone and Raven families, pertinent to this story. There the matter may have rested, but for this book. Through painstaking and methodical research, the author has been able to put flesh on the bones of family members, to such an extent that despite its comparatively short venture into fashionable society, the family has emerged ready to take its place amongst the great and the good.

The number of Yorkshire place names found in Norfolk families, adds credence to the notion that the Norfolk Malloms hailed from that County. Most of these migrants saw in mediaeval Norwich, then the second City in the country, an opportunity to make their fortune. Even by the 17th century, the City's importance and reputation still ensured a steady flow of fortune hunters. The Norwich progenitor of the family became a Freeman of Norwich and served in his civic duty as a constable, but rose no higher in the civic hierarchy. However, he married well and established a trend for his descendants of giving a good education, marrying into minor gentry families and acquiring more land. Towards the end of the 17th century, the head of the family, respected and wealthy, but still not accepted by the higher echelons of society was astute enough to realise that the acquisition of wealth was not in itself a guarantee of social acceptance. A grant of Arms enabled armorial slabs to be erected in all churches where family members were subsequently buried, allowing society to see that the family had 'arrived.' His marriage into a family with ancestries of ancient lineage, power and influence and his purchase of Wacton Hall gave the family that social status it had craved. Had the family continued to achieve its upward aspirations, it could have become one of the great county families, but within a generation, financial ruin affected its prospects. For the latest additions to the family, two young brothers, John and Richard, there was no hope of an inheritance. Were they aware of their illustrious ancestors including Norman nobility and royalty as portrayed by the title description as this Extraordinary Family?

Much of this book centres on the military career of the elder brother John, serving as a Company Commander in the American War of Independence. In those days, commissions were not awarded by merit, but by who you knew and how much you could afford to spend. A display of bravery helped, but by itself illustrious contacts counted more. His enlistment as a young officer was achieved through those same family contacts, seeing in him as the eldest son of a gentleman, a kinsman who needed their support. Most histories of the American War deal with the exploits of senior commanders, but what this book gives is an insight into the war at Company level. The author has meticulously sought references throughout the world to bring detail to his military career which will greatly appeal to all historians of the period. The search for John's brother Richard is equally intriguing. Family historians are only too aware that constructing a pedigree requires proof, and when the evidence is only circumstantial, this is insufficient to draw positive conclusions. However, the author's meticulous and methodical approach to identify Richard, based on circumstantial evidence, is so compelling that few will doubt the success of the conclusion. I would go further and say that as a legal challenge, most jurors would accept this evidence as proof.

David Large is no stranger to historical research having written about Robert Large, Mayor of London, and Soldiers in the Hundred Years War. He has spent many years researching and writing this book often thinking outside the box to achieve this result. His determination to explore all sources no matter where they are located and to unlock the secrets of this extraordinary family, has ensured that his contribution to Norfolk history deserves a wide readership.

Patrick Palgrave-Moore

Preface

The main focus in the account which follows is the life and family of John Mallom (1742–1782), a son of Wacton Hall, Norfolk, whose army career took him across the Atlantic Ocean to fight for the British in the American War of Independence. His ancestry from family who were part of the Merchant Class of Tudor Norwich and before that, in medieval Yorkshire, has been traced, and his connections with some of the most illustrious Norfolk families of the period, including Suckling, Shelton, Wodehouse, Nelson and Boleyn, is highlighted. John Mallom was a direct descendant of Sir Geoffrey Boleyn, Lord Mayor of London from 1457–1478, and through him, a cousin of Queen Anne Boleyn, and her daughter, Queen Elizabeth I. Through his 7th great grandmother, Lady Margaret Butler, who married the mayor's son, Sir William Boleyn, he was descended from the Bigod Earls of Norfolk, who built Norwich Castle and founded Thetford Priory, and the Norman and Plantagenet kings of England. The move of members of the Mallom family from Wacton to Sculthorpe where their descendants lived during the Victorian era, has also been investigated, and where the author's connections to John Mallom's younger brother, Richard, emerged.

It was the period of British History, 1714–1914, which first helped to fire my interest in the study of past, enthusiastically taught by Emilie Cottam and George Bennett, at Todmorden Grammar School, in the West Riding of Yorkshire, as it then was. Every period of history bears witness to great changes, and these two centuries saw the accession of a Hanoverian, George I, to the British throne, Robert Walpole become the first British Prime Minister, the agrarian and industrial revolutions, the Napoleonic Wars, improved transport with the construction of the canals and railways, the Victorian era, with the domestic policies of Gladstone and Disraeli, and particularly for our present purposes, The American War of Independence. All these topics proved fascinating for the 'O' Level student of History, and questions on the likely causes of the war with the American Colonies regularly appeared in the examination. But as I put pen to paper that June morning to attempt an answer, I had no idea that 50 years later, a project would begin to take shape which would bring together research from my paternal ancestry in Norfolk, and the life of a young man called John Mallom, from the Wacton Hall family, 14 miles south of Norwich, who fought for the British in the American War. These two projects gradually, but inevitably, collided, and what follows is the story of how this unfolded.

The Large family lines in Norfolk had been traced back to John Large of Swaffham, saddler and brewer, my 9th great grandfather, who was married for the first time in 1563. Others with the surname lived in nearby villages at the time of the Lay Subsidy Rolls of 1327 & 1332, and the Poll Taxes of 1377–1381. Several of the families of brides who married into the Large line were also researched, including the family of Anne Mary Mallom, who married my 2nd great grandfather, Martin Large, in 1818 in Sculthorpe, then a small village near Fakenham in north-west Norfolk. The groom was the seventh of eight children born to John and Ann Large of nearby Houghton St Giles, and the event in Sculthorpe was almost certainly unremarkable, except to the couple and their families. The surname Mallom proved to be unusual in this spelling in Norfolk, but a pedigree entitled "Mallom of Wacton, Co. Norfolk," by Arthur Campling, was found in the Norfolk Record Office (NRO), which although incomplete in several respects, outlined the descent from Richard Mallom, grocer, of Norwich, made a Freeman in 1605, the award of a Grant of Arms to John Mallom Esq. of Wacton Hall, in 1685, and the name of Elizabeth Suckling, a member of a prominent Norfolk gentry family, who married this John Mallom in 1692. Elizabeth's niece, Catherine Suckling, married Revd. Edmund Nelson, who became Rector of Burnham Thorpe, Norfolk, in 1755, and the whole world knows of the naval exploits of their son, Horatio. It gradually became clear that the apparently inauspicious marriage of Martin Large with Anne Mary Mallom, was a gateway event, so beloved of family historians, and popularised by BBC television programmes, including "Who do you think you are?" The College of Arms in London held a hand-written pedigree, no doubt submitted by John Mallom in support of his 1685 award, which recorded that before their days in Norwich, the Mallom family lived in Malham, Yorkshire, and the area around Skipton during the medieval period: hence the surname. It seems most likely that members of the family migrated south to Norwich, which was rapidly becoming England's second city in the 14th century, and where apprenticeships and business opportunities for young men eager to make progress, held out prospects which were probably more favourable at the time, than in rural Yorkshire.

It was also discovered that three females from the Wacton Mallom family were buried inside Sculthorpe church, in the early-mid 1700s, an indication of their social status. Could there be a connection between them and Anne Mary Mallom who married Martin Large? At about the same time, a letter was found at Norfolk Record Office written by a young army Lieutenant called John Mallom based near Dublin, addressed to Sir Armine Wodehouse, his distant relative in Norfolk, asking for the support of George Townshend, Lord Lieutenant of Ireland. It may be that the letter, written in 1770, had laid unseen for many years, and its likely significance not appreciated. This army officer, John Mallom, a son of Wacton, became the main focus of the research on which this book is based.

In Part 1, we explore the life and ancestry of our subject, John Mallom, who was born in Wacton in 1742, his parents having suffered the tragic experience of seeing their previous eight children all die in infancy or early childhood. They included three boys all baptised John, such was the parents' wish to have an heir named John, as had occurred repeatedly since the 1500–1600s. John had a younger brother, Richard, born in 1744, who also survived the rigors of infancy and childhood, and these two sons of John and Phillis Mallom of Wacton Hall, were their only offspring to reach adult life, and be named in their father's will of 1761.

In Part 2, we look at the growth of the Mallom estates and the granting of a Coat of Arms in 1685, perhaps the highlight of the career of an earlier John Mallom Esq. of Wacton Hall. Many of Captain Mallom's forebears had made considerable progress in life: they had carefully developed their estates, encouraged a good education in their offspring, and they had married well. Unfortunately for our subject, John's father was beset by a succession of disappointments in life, as well as the appalling loss of his children. He failed to graduate from Corpus Christi College, Cambridge, and returned home to Wacton without the coveted degree.

In Part 3, we delve into a sequence of problem cases in the High Court of Chancery which left John Mallom Esq. in serious financial difficulties, such that the family had to sell Wacton Hall in 1754 and move to smaller accommodation in nearby Aslacton, where he had been married, and where his wife was baptised and raised. This home was also sold. When their father died in 1761, he was heavily in debt, and the two boys, John and Richard, would have little or no inheritance with which to launch their adult lives. In many ways, this is a "riches to rags" story, quite the opposite of what had been achieved by the Mallom families of previous generations. John enlisted in the army almost certainly to escape from the challenges he would have encountered had he remained in Norfolk.

In Part 4, we examine the army career of John Mallom, beginning with his enlistment as Ensign in the 57th Regiment of Foot in 1761, a few months before the death of his father, sponsored by Charles Townshend, the brilliant, charismatic politician and MP, Chancellor of the Exchequer in William Pitt's government, and younger brother of George Townshend, the senior army officer, politician, and Lord Lieutenant of Ireland. Between 1761-1763, Mallom's Company was posted to Gibraltar, and later to Minorca when the island was still in British hands. John Mallom was promoted to Lieutenant in June 1769 after his regiment was posted to Dublin. The 57th Regiment of Foot which had been stationed in southern Ireland, sailed for America in February 1776, to support the British in their war against the American Patriots. Having arrived in Charleston, South Carolina, they led an unsuccessful attack on the town in June 1776.

In the spring of 1777, Lieutenant Mallom was given the task of supervising work to strengthen the defences of Paulus Hook Fort on the western side of the Hudson River, in what is now New Jersey, hoping to foil possible attacks by combined American and French forces. The British held the fort for over 2 years until it was captured by the Americans, led by Major Henry Lee (father of General Robert E Lee), on 19 August 1779, in the Battle of Paulus Hook. In the meantime, Mallom was steadily gaining the trust of his senior colleagues as shown by his service on five Court Martial Panels, the first in February 1777, while still a Lieutenant, to the last, in September 1779. Mallom was promoted to Captain in the 63rd Foot, in September 1777, not long after his successful work on of the Paulus Hook Fort defences. These promotions were not based solely on merit or length of service, but rather on the ability to pay for the commissions, which were costly, and so it appears that the young officer had gathered sufficient income in the intervening years to pay for his commissions.

By October 1779, Mallom's Company was stationed in Staten Island, New York, in the northern campaign of the war, and shortly afterwards, the 63rd Foot sailed south to Charles Town, (Charleston), South Carolina, where further military encounters took place in what became known as the southern campaign, led by Earl Charles Cornwallis. These battles included the Battle of Camden in August 1780, when Mallom's Company, having arrived on the scene shortly after the main event, was decimated by fever and sickness from what became known as "Revolutionary Fever." Many of his men died. During his career, Captain Mallom had the dubious privilege of serving under the notorious Colonel Banastre Tarleton ('Bloody Ban'), whose military exploits would today almost certainly be regarded as war crimes, and also under Major James Wemyss, who instituted a court martial in May 1780, against Mallom's colleague, Captain Hayes St Leger, for alleged disrespectful behaviour. These two British officers were the most hated by the Americans, and Mallom fought alongside them both. In November 1780, Mallom witnessed the death of his fellow officer, and friend, Norfolk-born Lieutenant John Money, who was mortally wounded during a skirmish at Blackstock's Farm, South Carolina.

In January 1781, Captain Mallom was honoured by being asked to carry a letter from Lieutenant Colonel Nisbet Balfour, Commandant of Charleston, on behalf of Earl Cornwallis, second in command to Sir Henry Clinton, to Lord George Germain, Secretary of State for the Colonies in Lord North's Government in London, summarising the current situation in the south. In the accompanying correspondence, to Germain, Mallom was described as "an Officer of Merit & who is Returning to Europe for the Recovery of his Health, has Lord Cornwallis's Directions to deliver this dispatch To Your Lordship." John Mallom's place of death and burial remains elusive, but on the balance of probabilities, it was most likely to have been in Charleston, South Carolina, having safely completed his voyage to and from England, although no documentary or gravestone evidence of this has been found.

In Part 5, we examine the connections by marriage of Captain John Mallom and his brother, Richard, and it is here that some completely unexpected discoveries were made. The grandmother of the two Wacton boys was Elizabeth (Suckling) Mallom, whose family had a distinguished ancestry of 12 generations, to Thomas Socling, of Woodton and Langhall, who was "admitted to certain estates in 1348." The earliest members of the family appear to have been known by the surname Socling, derived from the medieval term 'Socage,' one of many feudal duties required for tenure of land. Elizabeth was the great aunt of Admiral Lord Horatio

Nelson, who therefore became the 2nd cousin of John and Richard Mallom, although given the births of the boys in the early-mid 1740s, and Nelson's in 1758, it seems very unlikely that they met to play in the Rectory Garden in Burnham Thorpe. Elizabeth Suckling's mother, Sarah (Shelton) Suckling, came from another high-status Norfolk family, whose ancestry has been documented to a date even earlier than that of the Sucklings. The Sheltons reach back to at least John de Shelton, born in about 1140, and the first Lord of the Manor of Shelton, Norfolk. Sir Ralph Shelton, a member of the same family, was knighted by Edward III at the Battle of Crecy in 1346. Sir John Shelton married Lady Anne Boleyn in 1497, and her grandfather was Sir Geoffrey Boleyn, a member of the leading London Livery Company, the Mercers, having transferred from the Hatters. He was elected Lord Mayor of London in 1457. His grandson and Lady Anne's brother, was Sir Thomas Boleyn, father of Queen Anne Boleyn, wife of King Henry VIII, whose daughter became Queen Elizabeth I. Given the connections, it was confirmed that John Mallom and his brother were direct descendants of Sir Geoffrey Boleyn, and it follows, whether they were aware of it or not, that the Wacton boys were closely related to the Tudor Royal family: they were the 1st cousins seven times removed of Queen Anne Boleyn, and the 2nd cousins six times removed of her daughter, Queen Elizabeth I. Further work shows that, through Lady Margaret (Butler)Boleyn, their 7th great grandmother, the Mallom boys were descended from the Bigod Earls of Norfolk, two of whom acted as sureties to Magna Carta in 1215, and who were one of the most powerful, important, and wealthy families in 13th century England. The ancestry of Lady Margaret took us back through the Butler Earls of Ormond, to the marriage of James Butler, 1st Earl of Ormond, with Eleanor de Bohun, the daughter of Elizabeth Plantagenet and her second husband, Humphrey de Bohun, 4th Earl of Hereford. Elizabeth was the daughter of Edward I, and so the ancestry passed into the Norman and Plantagenet royal families of England. These discoveries are of considerable significance for the sons of an 18th century Norfolk family, and it propels them into a category of great interest.

Part 6 of the story looks at the descendants of Richard Mallom, younger brother of the army captain, and the hypothesis that my paternal ancestry in Norfolk is directly connected with the Malloms of Wacton Hall, and through them, to the other distinguished families mentioned above. Invaluable information in support of this hypothesis was found in the Sculthorpe Parish Burial Register entry of Ann Mary (Mallom) Large's father, John Mallom, who was buried in the village in 1810. The entry, in the unmistakable copper-plate handwriting of the Rector, Revd. Horatio Dowsing, reads "John Mallom, the son of Richard Mallom & Mary his Wife / late Mary Smith, Spinster / a married man, was buried July 25th 1810, aged 45 Years." Furthermore, the marriage entry of this John Mallom with Anne Hipkin in Sculthorpe in 1792, includes the name of Nathaniel Raven, the wealthy landowner and farmer of Brancaster and Sculthorpe, as the first witness, the only occasion he acted as a witness in Sculthorpe in 20 years. His presence and likely friendship with Richard Mallom, John's father, is considered a vital part of the supporting evidence. Was this Richard the younger brother of Captain John Mallom? The dates would certainly be appropriate.

The search for the marriage record of Richard Mallom and Mary Smith, was very protracted, since it involved checking every one of the more than 700 Norfolk Parish Registers, the Archdeacons and Bishop's Transcripts, Marriage Licence Bonds, and other records, in an attempt not only to find the marriage record, but to exclude alternative candidates. Ten years of research eventually clinched the family connections beyond all reasonable doubt, demonstrating how circumstantial evidence can be conclusive in detective work of this sort, when all other possibilities have been eliminated, and the principles of Ockham's Razor (in a complex question, the simplest explanation is likely to be correct) are fulfilled. The evidence shows that Richard Mallom was my 4th great grandfather, and his older brother, Captain John Mallom, my 5th great uncle, and what began as an unremarkable Family History project, transformed itself into something much more extensive, and extraordinary.

Pedigree 1: Ancestry of Captain John Mallom (A)

From the time his great grandfather, John Mallom, acquired Wacton Hall in 1672.

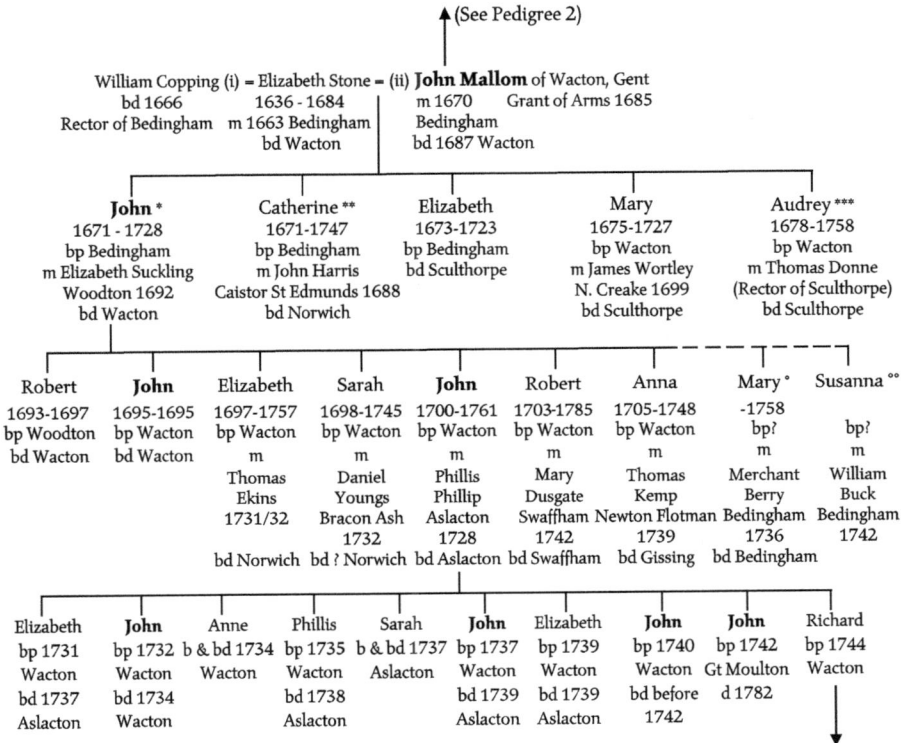

Notes

The wish to preserve the name John in each generation.

* John Mallom was bp 24 January 1671, and his sister, Catherine, on 28 December 1671, the same year.

** Catherine Mallom married John Harris, as Catherine Marlome. Both were living in Saxlingham, although the marriage took place in Caistor St Edmunds.

*** Audrey Mallom was baptised in the latinised name of Etheldreda.

° Mary Mallom's bp has not been found & so her birth relative to her siblings is unknown.

°° Susanna's origins are also unclear.

The children of Catherine (Mallom) Harris, Mary (Mallom) Wortley, Robert Mallom, Anna (Mallom) Kemp, and Susanna (Mallom) Buck have been omitted for the sake of clarity (see text).

Adapted and extended from "Mallom of Wacton, co. Norfolk" by Campling, A. East Anglian Pedigrees, Norfolk Record Society, vol. 13. 1940.

Pedigree 2: Ancestry of Captain John Mallom (B)

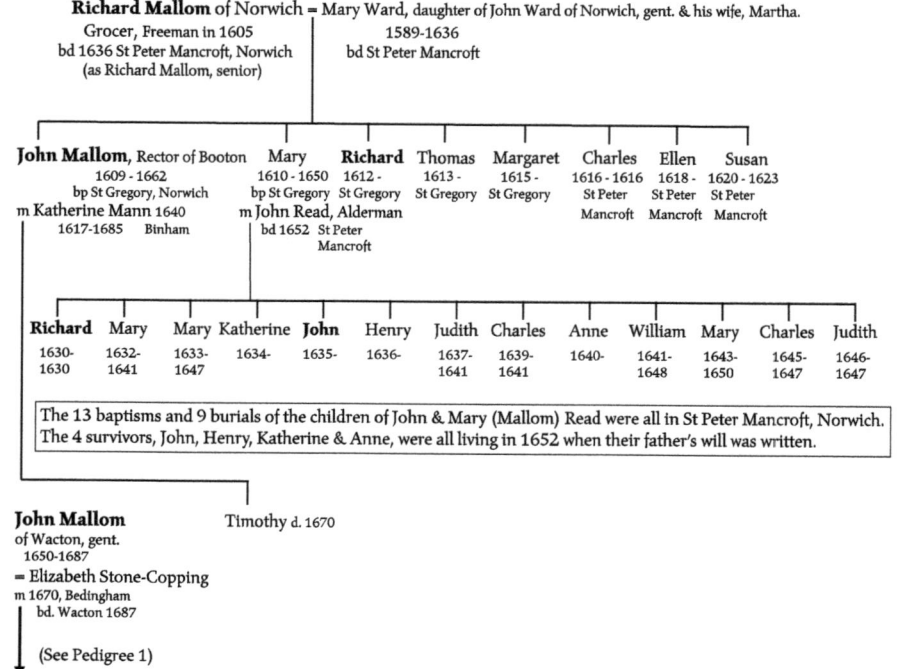

John Mallom
of Wacton, gent.
1650-1687
= Elizabeth Stone-Copping
m 1670, Bedingham
bd. Wacton 1687

(See Pedigree 1)

Timothy d. 1670

Note:

The names John and Richard among the sons and grandsons of Richard Mallom of Norwich, Grocer. *Adapted and extended from "Mallom of Wacton, co. Norfolk" by Campling, A. East Anglian Pedigrees, Norfolk Record Society, vol. 13. 1940.*

Pedigree 3: Tudor Royal Connections of Captain John Mallom

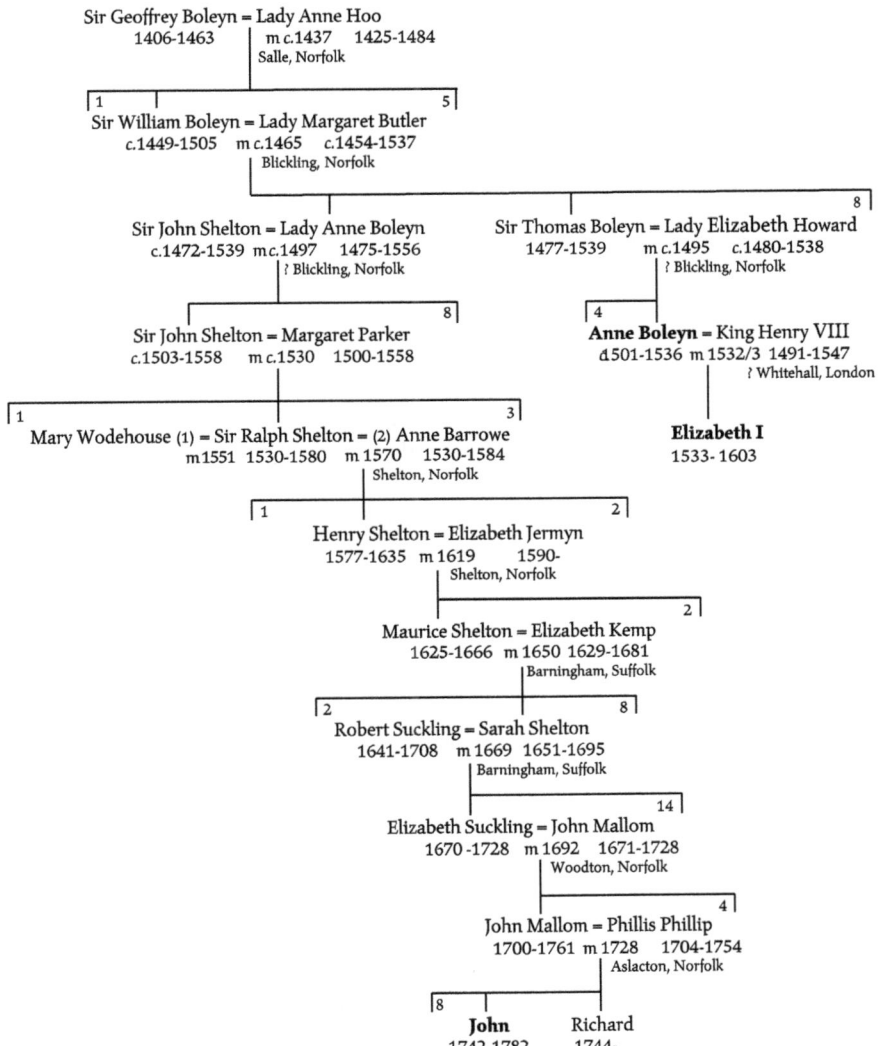

Note:

Through the Suckling and Shelton lines of the family, the Mallom boys were the 8th great grandsons of Sir Geoffrey Boleyn, and from him, the 1st cousins seven times removed of Queen Anne Boleyn, and the 2nd cousins six times removed of Queen Elizabeth I.

Small digits indicate numbers of siblings.

PEDIGREE 4: NORMAN ANCESTRY OF ELEANOR DE BOHUN, GRANDDAUGHTER OF EDWARD I

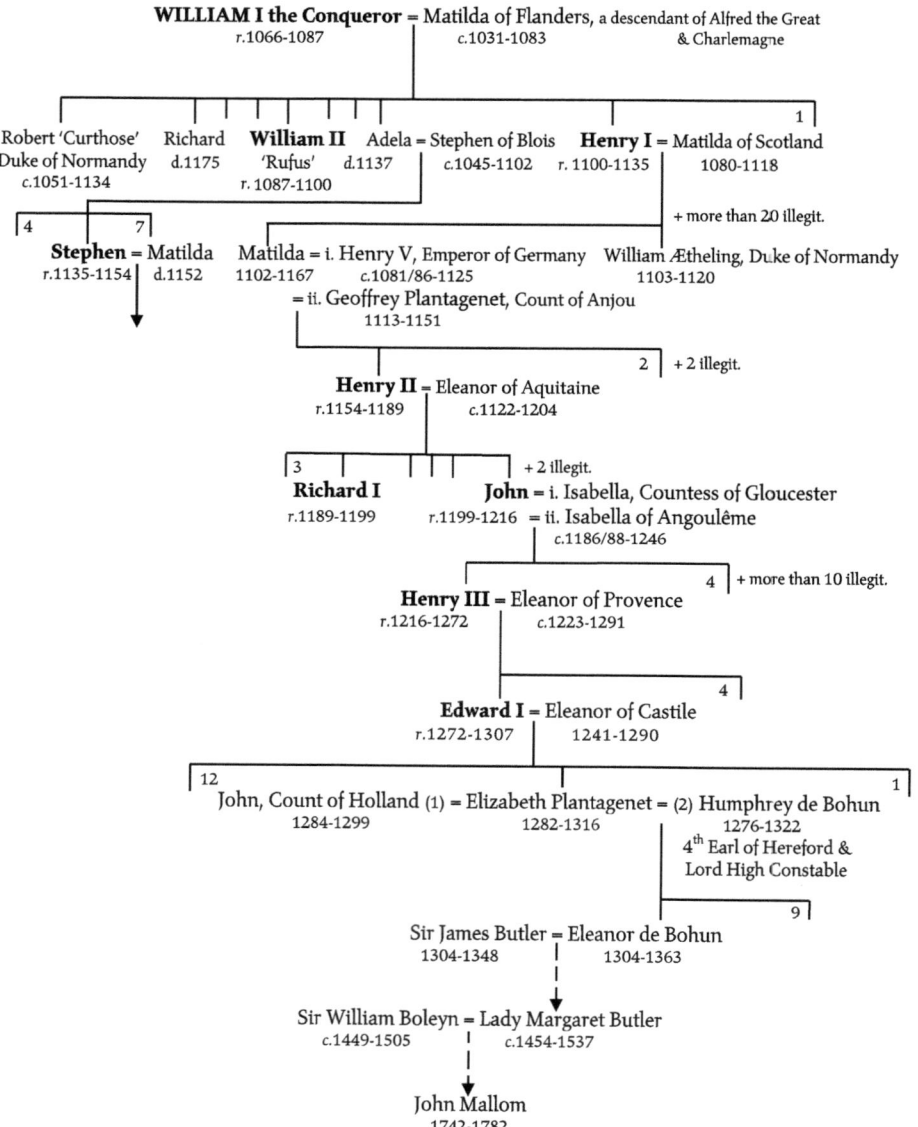

Notes:

Eleanor was the 6th great granddaughter of William the Conqueror, the 3rd great grandmother of Margaret (Butler) Boleyn & the 12th great grandmother of Captain John Mallom. See Pedigree 2 for later generations. Kings of England are shown in bold.

r. indicates years of the reign.

Small digits indicate numbers of siblings.

Pedigree 5: Bigod ancestry of Lady Margaret (Butler) Boleyn

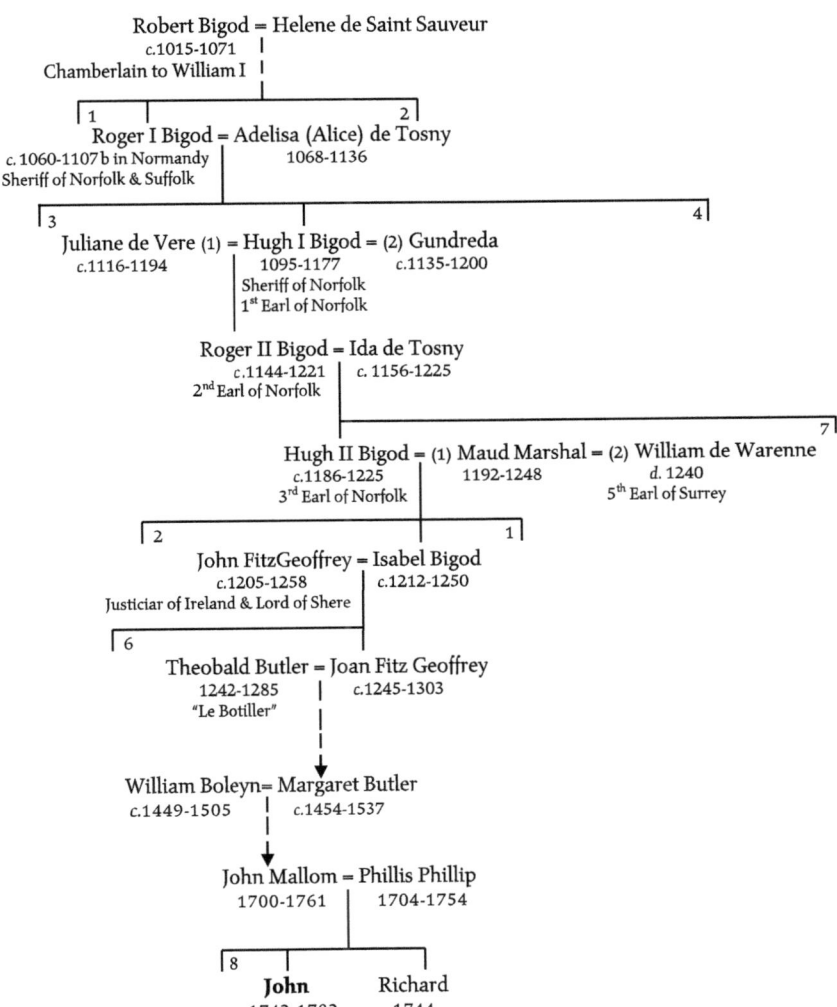

Notes:

Isabel Bigod was the 6th great grandmother of Margaret Butler & the 15th great grandmother of Captain John Mallom & his brother, Richard.

Small digits indicate numbers of siblings.

Part 1: The Family and Ancestry of Captain John Mallom

Our subject, John Mallom, was born at Wacton Hall, Norfolk, during the reign of King George II, a few months after Sir Robert Walpole, England's first Prime Minister, left office, into a family which had experienced almost unspeakable tragedy. His eight older brothers and sisters all died in infancy or early childhood, and his parents, John Mallom Esq. and his wife, Phillis, must surely have believed the chance of their producing a child who would survive to become an adult had all but vanished. However, things changed for the better when John was born. He was baptised on 24 August 1742 in St Michael's Church, Great Moulton, Norfolk (Fig. 01). Did his parents hope that taking him for baptism in a nearby church might somehow increase his chance of survival not enjoyed by his siblings who were baptised in their home church in Wacton? This must have been their fervent hope for their young son as they stood by the font that Friday morning.

Fig. 01. St Michael and All Angels Church, Great Moulton, and the font where John Mallom was baptised in August 1742.

John's father was the son of John and Elizabeth (Suckling) Mallom, baptised on 17 February 1700 in Wacton, and he was the fourth boy to be given the name, his three older namesakes having died in infancy. His parents were clearly desperate to have a son named John to maintain the family tradition. His mother, Phillis, was the daughter of Robert Phillips Esq. of Aslacton, and his wife, Elizabeth, baptised on 2 May 1704 in nearby Tibenham, within easy distance, either by foot or by horse-drawn carriage. John and Phillis were married by Licence on 3 September

1728 in Aslacton,[1] where Phillis was living, and our John was their oldest surviving son. Three younger sons named John were baptised and buried between 1732 and 1742, as follows:

John baptised 13 August 1732 in Wacton, buried 19 September 1734, in Wacton,

John baptised 2/12 March 1738 in Wacton, buried 21 May 1739, in Aslacton,

John baptised 25 August 1740 in Wacton, and buried before 1742, place unknown.

John's five sisters all died young several years before he was born.

Elizabeth baptised 13 July 1731 in Wacton, died 21 October 1737, buried 23 October 1737 in Aslacton, aged 6 years.

Anna baptised 25 January 1734 in Wacton, buried 12 October 1734 in Wacton.

Phillis baptised 8 February 1735 in Wacton, died 2 March 1738, buried 26 March 1738 in Aslacton, aged 3 years.

Sarah died 2 May, buried 5 May 1737 in Aslacton, aged 13 weeks.

Elizabeth baptised 9 August 1739 in Wacton, buried 23 August 1739, in Aslacton.

John's younger brother, Richard, was baptised on 6 April 1744, in Wacton.

The two boys, John and Richard Mallom, both survived the mid-eighteenth-century ravages of infancy and childhood, and were named in their father's will of 1761.[2] Elizabeth, Phillis, and Sarah were buried in Aslacton Church, where a black marble memorial slab in the floor of the chancel commemorates their short lives, recording their dates of death and ages (Fig. 03).

Fig. 02. St Michael's Church, Aslacton.

Detail of the armorial with Mallom impaling Phillips.

Fig. 03. Ledgerstone commemorating the children, Sarah, Elizabeth and Phillis Mallom (upper) and the memorial to their mother, Phillis (Phillips) Mallom (lower). See also Fig. 17, p. 90.

These memorial slabs are known as ledgerstones (from the German, legen, to lay, or to place). The names, dates of death and ages have been skilfully incised by the ledgercutter, using a fine chisel to produce the italic letters for the names, and the regular letters used for the dates and ages. The magnificent armorial carving at the head of the memorial, shows the Arms of Mallom and Phillips, impaled: the Arms of Mallom to the left and of Phillips, to the right. The Arms of Mallom were those granted by The College of Arms in 1685.[3] The Arms of Phillips are blazoned as follows: "Phillip, Azure, a chevron between three falcons close argent." The crest above the impaled arms, that of the Mallom family of Wacton, is also a fine piece of work, and a credit to the craftsmanship involved.[4] The three burial entries appear on the same page of the Aslacton parish records when Revd. John Phillips was the curate. He signed the Archdeacon's Transcripts (ATs) for the parish of Aslacton in 1725, and between 1735 and 1748, and given the surname, may have been a relative of Phillis. The tragic series of events, in which eight of their ten children died young, must have been absolutely devastating for the parents. Their obvious wish to have a son named John, as had been the case in the Mallom family for each of the previous four generations, is shown in Pedigree 1, p. 21. Elizabeth was the name of Phillis's mother, and so a daughter named after her would have been expected, but it is perhaps surprising that not one of the boys was named Robert after her father, who died in 1734, when his daughter and son-in-law were named in his Administration, bound in £200. Phillis was named the Administratrix.[5] However, a clue as to the possible reason for this decision may be found in the series of legal disputes between John Mallom and his brother, Robert, as will be discussed, later. In the light of these family conflicts, it is reasonable to assume that the baptismal name 'Robert' was not one which John and Phillis would have chosen for a son of theirs.

John and Richard would have been educated at school, possibly in Wymondham, which is less than 10 miles from their home, since their grandfather, John Mallom, of Wacton, attended here. The challenge in trying to find the boys' school is that no systematic record of Norfolk schools for the Georgian period seems to have been compiled. On the other hand, the education of the older John Mallom who went up to Gonville and Caius College, Cambridge, in 1689, is recorded as having taken place at Wymondham School under Mr Clarke.[6] In contrast, the boys' uncle, Robert Mallom, attended a school in Norwich under Mr Wingfield.[7] It is also possible that John and Richard were educated at one of the many Diocesan Schools established in East Anglia, with sixty-one in Norfolk, of which twenty were educating pupils by 1750, when the boys would have been eligible to attend. These included Wymondham Grammar School where Mr Will. Arderon was the Head from 1736 to 1758, and Thetford Grammar School, which although further from Wacton than Wymondham, might also have been considered appropriate for the boys' educational needs. In addition, in a Norwich Diocesan list of one hundred and eighty Parish Schools, one of these was in Wacton, where Mr Edward Aldis was the schoolmaster from 1740.[8] John's handwriting as a young army officer shows clear evidence of the education expected of the son of a gentleman, as illustrated in his correspondence with Sir Armine Wodehouse and, later, with Lord Cornwallis.

The small villages of Aslacton and Wacton are about 2 miles apart and Great Moulton lies almost between them as the crow flies. These three villages, where much of the activity in the following account took place, are approximately 13 miles south of Norwich, the county town of Norfolk (see map on p.xii). During the lifetimes of John and Phillis Mallom and their two surviving sons, the date of the beginning of the New Year in Great Britain was changed. Under the Calendar Act of 1750, the New Year was to begin on 1 January, and not 25 March (Lady Day). In addition, the Gregorian Calendar was introduced to replace the Julian. These changes were implemented in 1751–1752, and it follows that 1751 was a short year (25 March to 31 December). 1752 began on 1 January, and to align the country to continental Europe, a further adjustment was made, such that 2 September was followed by 14 September 1752, resulting in the loss of 11 days.[9] In the following account, the dates of baptisms, marriages and burials have been adjusted to reflect this new style. For example, the baptism of Phillis Mallom in Wacton, originally recorded as taking place on 8 February 1734/5 has been corrected to 8 February 1735.

Sometime after he and Phillis Phillips were married in Aslacton in 1728, a pastel portrait of John Mallom was drawn. He was the father of our subject and no doubt the portrait hung originally in the family home of Wacton Hall. A chance discovery of a black and white copy in New York Public Library[10] led to a reference to the original in a 1927 catalogue at the National Portrait Gallery of Norfolk and Suffolk portraits then held at the Guildhall, Thetford. A second reference to the portrait appeared in "The Connoisseur" magazine for September to December 1905, volume XIII, where it is illustrated in black and white. In the accompanying article, Prince Frederick Victor Duleep Singh (1868–1926) bemoaned the dispersal of portraits and contents of ancestral homes.[11] The portrait was donated by the Prince, the son of Duleep Singh, the last King of Punjab, who grew up near Thetford and studied at Eton and Cambridge University before serving with both the Suffolk and the Norfolk Yeomanry. He built up a collection of books, portraits and objects of antiquarian interest from the area, and subsequently presented the Ancient House in Thetford to the Corporation for use as a public museum, in 1921.[12] Although the catalogue at The National Portrait Gallery is not illustrated, it describes John Mallom as wearing a dove-coloured coat and white shoulder wig.

It also records that he was born about 1700 and married Phillis Phillips of Aslacton on 28 August 1728. The Ancient House Museum in Thetford, Norfolk holds the pastel portrait, which measures 41.5 cms x 32 cms. On the back of the portrait are written the words:

> *Head and shoulders pastel of John Mallom; in a dove-coloured coat; wearing a white shoulder wig; brass tag 49; THEHM : DS.49.*[13]

The artist is unknown, but the portrait is clearly not by one of the leading portraitists of the day, and it is in pastel, not oils. In particular, the face is poorly drawn and may be unfinished in comparison to the wig and the coat. The detail written on the back of the frame, however, correctly records Mallom's year of birth, the name of his wife, and the

Fig. 04. *Pastel Portrait of John Mallom (d. 1761).* On the back of the frame is written in Duleep Singh's hand: John Mallom of Wacton born about 1700; married on 28.8.1728 Phillis Phillips of Aslacton.

date and place of their marriage. The portrait was originally part of Duleep Singh's private collection at Blo Norton Hall, but how and when he took possession of it, and exactly when it was presented to The Ancient House Museum, is not known.[14] It is most likely that it was sold or put up for auction after Mallom's death in 1761 when the estate was sold to pay his debts. Its whereabouts and who took possession of it between then and the date it was acquired by Duleep Singh, more than 100 years later, is unknown. And so, although the portrait itself raises a number of questions, there is no need to doubt the fact that the sitter was indeed John Mallom of Wacton Hall, the father of our subject.

Mallom Families of Tudor Norwich

The name 'John' has been present in the Mallom family in every generation since the birth of John, son of Richard Mallom, grocer, and his wife, Mary, of Norwich, in 1609, until the birth of our subject in 1742 (see map on p.xii). Young John's mother was the daughter of John Ward of Norwich, gent, so the boy had a good start in life. Surname spelling variations were seen in the baptisms of Richard Mallom's children, as follows: John was baptised at St Gregory's Church, Norwich, on 10 January 1609, as the son of Richard Mallome (Fig. 05). Mary was baptised on 1 October 1610, at St Gregory's as the daughter of Richard Mallome; Richard was baptised at St Gregory's in March 1612, as the son of Richard Mallam; Thomas was baptised on 15 October 1613, at St Gregory's as the son of Richard Mallom. Margaret was baptised at St Gregory's on 9 July 1615, as the daughter of Richard Mallom; Charles, was baptised at St Peter Mancroft, Norwich, on 27 November 1616, the son of Richard Mallham, grocer, and Mary his wife, whereas he was buried the following day as the son of Richard Mallam, grocer; Ellen was baptised at St Peter Mancroft on 23 October 1618, as the daughter of Richard Malham, grocer, and Mary his wife; Susan was baptised at St Peter Mancroft on 7 November 1620, as the daughter of Richard Malham, grocer and Mary his wife, and buried

Fig. 05. St Gregory's Church, Norwich and its the font where the first John Mallom was baptised in 1609.

there on 19 November 1623, as the daughter of Richard Malham, grocer (Fig. 06). The entries in the Parish Register of St Peter Mancroft, the main civic church of Norwich, were all written in the same hand, and the formatting of the dates was similar in each case.

There are no surviving register bills for this parish for these dates, and so further comparisons of surname spelling could not be made.[15] It follows that the spelling variations were not because a different clergyman made the entries, but because he was unsure how to spell the name of his parishioners. The same applies to the entries in St Gregory's Parish Register, and although register bills do survive for 1608–9 and 1610–11, no Mallom or variant entries were included. Searches were also made for the marriage of Richard Mallom and Mary Ward in the Index of Norwich Marriages 1538–1585, and 1586–1620, compiled from all available sources by Patrick Palgrave-Moore, searched under the names Mallom and Ward, and variant spellings, but no record was found.[16] In contrast, when Richard senior was buried in September 1636, and his widow, Mary, in October 1636, both surnames were entered as Mallom in the register for St Peter Mancroft, Norwich. Variations in pronunciation and a lack of consistency was clearly a feature in the spelling of surnames, and to some extent, in baptismal names as well, particularly during a period when literacy was not widespread among adults, most of whom did not have the benefits of a formal education and could not write their own names. Fortunately, the father's name, and often, his trade, helped to confirm that the

Fig. 06. Church of St Peter Mancroft, Norwich and its font where many children of the Mallom family were baptised during the 1600s.

events described here were to members of the same family, particularly when they took place in the same church. Thomas, the third son of Richard Mallom, senior, gained his freedom in 1637 as a mercer, having been apprenticed to John Read of Norwich, mercer.[17] Through this arrangement, Thomas Mallom was received into what was regarded as the leading Livery Company of the age.

Teenage boys served an apprenticeship of 7 years with their Master, usually beginning at about the age of 14, before they could be made free. Richard's son, Richard, junior, was made free in 1633, and based on these figures, he was born in about 1612. His year of baptism in St Gregory's Church, Norwich, was in 1612, confirming this. Applying a similar argument to that of his father, Richard Mallom, senior, made free in 1605, would mean he was born in about 1584. On the other hand, Richard's son, Thomas, was made free in 1633, implying his birth was in 1616, whereas his baptism in St Gregory's Church was actually in 1613, three years earlier than predicted. Taking this into account, Richard, senior, was almost certainly born between 1581 and 1584, during the reign of Queen Elizabeth I. It is worth recalling that the six most popular boys' names in England during the Tudor period were John, Thomas, William, Robert, Richard and Henry,[18] and having established the naming tradition, the baptismal names John and Richard continued to appear in subsequent generations of the Mallom family. Whatever the origin of the naming tradition in this family, it continued until at least the birth of our subject in 1742. Richard Mallom's oldest daughter, Mary, married Mr John Read, citizen, mercer and Alderman of Norwich, another potential source of the name John. Read subsequently took his wife's younger brother, Thomas, as one of his apprentices

ORIGIN OF THE MALLOM FAMILY OF NORWICH

Having noted the presence of Richard Mallom of Norwich, grocer, searches were made in local parishes for the previous generations of the Mallom family, but without success. One possible candidate from outside Norwich was Richard Mallam, son of Arnold and Agnes Mallam of Great Yarmouth, baptised in February 1577. However, he was married in the same town in November 1600, and had five children baptised between 1602 and 1610. Richard Mallom of Norwich was made free in 1605, doubtless after serving a 7-year apprenticeship, and so the Yarmouth man was excluded. There were five more families named Mallom or a variant spelling living in Great Yarmouth between 1580 and 1610, and so this was a town where they were settled. Another Mallom family to whom Richard, the Norwich apprentice may have been related, lived in Cley-next-the-Sea, once a busy port with active trade to and from the Low Countries, 26 miles north west of Norwich.[19] It was here that a Richard Mallon married Margaret Cra[w]ford in February 1598, and where four individuals named Mallom were buried; John, in September 1592, Margaret, in February 1594, Thomas, in November 1597, and Mary, in January 1605, almost certainly members of the same family. The striking similarity in the baptismal names between the Malloms of Cley and those of Richard Mallom's first four children in Norwich, suggest that they may have been related in some way, bearing in mind that these were all popular baptismal names at the time. Margaret Mallom/Malham left an Administration, in 1594, so she died without leaving a will, although she had an estate to leave. The Latin document, in translation, reads as follows;

> Administration of all the goods of Margaret Malham late of Cley who died intestate was granted to Thomas Malham and Mary Malham, next of kin and assigns of the deceased, to administer her goods, pay her debts, exhibit an inventory and render their account. Thomas Malham is bound.[20]

It is quite likely that Margaret was the mother of Thomas Mallom, and Mary was his wife, although this cannot be proved from the few details available here. The evidence of an estate, of whatever size, does however mean that this family had assets at a time when very few individuals left a will. This might go some way to support the contention that the Malloms of Cley-next-the Sea, were the forebears of the Malloms of Norwich, who needed funds to place their sons in apprenticeships with merchants in the city in the early 1600s.

Tracing family names in the medieval period is complicated by the lack of consistency in surname spelling and the patchy survival of records. However, the names of individuals living in Norfolk at the time of the Lay Subsidy Rolls of 1327 and 1332 have been transcribed, and no examples of the name spelled as Mallom were found. Three examples of possible surname variants were included: in the village of Kerdestone (Kerdiston in Reepham): Galf′ Malyn (Galf[ridus] = Geoffrey) was assessed for taxation at ijs (2 shillings); in the village of Geyton (Gayton): Will′o Malyn (William), for ijs vjd (2 shillings 6 pence), and in the village of Brauncastere (Brancaster): Thm fil′ Marl′n (Thomas son of … Marlin,) for vjs (six shillings), in the Lay Subsidy of 1332.[21] However, these are sufficiently different from our surname to mean they were probably not part of a Norfolk Mallom family. A mid-14th century document recording a tax on Norwich households, to raise 100 marks, was also examined. About 148 'households' some recording a single name, and others with more than one are included, perhaps signifying owners and occupiers. Payments in marks, pounds and shillings, of between 5s and £8 10s are noted. However, no Mallom or variant surname is included. Could this tax have been levied to help fund the early period of the Hundred Years' War (1337–1453)?[22] The Poll Tax returns for Norfolk in 1377, 1379 and 1381 were searched for the surname Mallom and its variants in the lists of names which form part of the E 179 collection held at The National Archives, transcribed by Carolyn C. Fenwick. "The taxes were levied on householders, wives, dependants and servants individually," who were aged 16 years or above.[23] Nine examples of possible variants of our surname were identified in Norfolk, with the amount of tax paid, in pence (d) by each individual shown in brackets, Walterus Marham of Sturston (4d), Johannes de Marham of Swaffham (6d), Thomas de Marham of Sporle (4d), Johannes de Morham of Great Dunham (4d), Johannes de Marham of King's Lynn (6d) and Cecilia de Marham of the same place (4d). Ricardus Malyn of Wilton with Hockwold (4d), Johannes Malyn (4d) and Thomas Malyn of Cley-next the-Sea (4d). It could be argued that the Marhams originated in Marham, a few miles south east of Kings Lynn. The Malyns of Cley-next-the-Sea are of interest because of the village concerned, although the name is more likely to have been associated with a family who bore the later spelling, Mallon, than Mallom, where the terminal "m" appears to be a key distinguishing feature. This preliminary evidence shows that the surname Mallom was not found in Norfolk, inside or outside Norwich, during the early, mid and late 1300s. However, Poll Tax records for Depwade Hundred, which included the villages of Aslacton, Wacton, Gt Moulton and Shelton, for Loddon Hundred, which included Bedingham, and the record for Booton, which was in South Erpingham Hundred, have not survived. These were the villages where Mallom families lived some 300 years later, after leaving Norwich.

Malloms as Freemen of Norwich

Whatever his immediate ancestry, the apprenticeship which Richard Mallom took up in Norwich implies that his forebears either moved to the city from elsewhere, or that he left his family home as a young teenager and moved to Norwich to take up his apprenticeship in the mid-late-1590s; either option is possible. The example of Robert Large, mercer, later Sheriff, and Mayor of London, 1439–1440, and the first employer of William Caxton, serves as a useful reminder of the trend adopted by ambitious parents for their sons, who moved from their rural family origins to the cities of England to take up apprenticeships during the late Middle Ages. Large's father was buried in the village of Shackerstone in Leicestershire,[24] and Robert moved from his rural origins in the midlands to London, where he remained for the rest of his life. Taking up an apprenticeship such as this also implies that the families concerned had the financial means to meet the costs involved.[25] The members of the Mallom family of Norwich to which our John Mallom belonged, especially those who made their mark in one of the Livery Companies, achieved considerable distinction within the city, although not to the extent of that achieved by Robert Large in London. Furthermore, they entered into advantageous marriages with other members of the merchant class of Norwich. This is well-illustrated by the case of Mary, the oldest daughter of Richard Mallom, grocer, who married Mr John Read, citizen, mercer and Alderman of Norwich. His will of 1652 named his four surviving children, John, Henry, Katherine and Anne, to whom he bequeathed substantial sums amounting in total to £4,300, together with houses, grounds, lands, gardens and orchards, with the usual proviso of redistribution in the event of early death(s), or the girls wishing to marry without the approval of the Executors.[26] They were the grandchildren of Richard Mallom senior, and their father, John Read, had amassed an enormous estate by any calculation, and it is clear that Mary (Mallom) Read would have lived in Norwich in luxury. Calculating the present-day equivalent value of such a sum is fraught with challenges, and there is no single multiplier which will enable a simple conversion from 17th- and 18th-century amounts to today's value, although one method using a Purchasing Power Calculator for the Historic Standard of Living, converts the £4,300 to more than £630,000 today. "This calculation is obtained by multiplying the £500 by the percentage increase in Retail Price Increase (RPI) from 1552 to today." [27] However, other expressions of relative value give higher amounts than this, and so whatever the conversion procedure used, the purchasing power of Read's estate was very high, and would have placed him in an extremely advantageous position compared to the majority of his contemporaries in and around Norwich.

Mallom Families in Medieval Yorkshire

Part way through this piece of work, a four-generation Mallom pedigree came to light at the College of Arms in London, created in 1685 when John Mallom of Wacton Hall was in the process of being awarded a Grant of Arms. The pedigree is headed by the sentence:

> Richard Mallom of the City of Norwich descended from a family of that name in Com. Ebor

That is to say, in the County of York[shire].[28] Working on the basis that this ancestry was based on known family history, and not merely on supposition or hearsay, the question is when and why a branch of the Mallom family moved south from Yorkshire to Norfolk? The most likely reason was the growing attraction of the City of Norwich as a centre for commerce, trade and apprenticeships, outside London. Nevertheless, the College of Arms pedigree indicates, it is believed for the first time, that the Mallom family of Norfolk, came originally from Yorkshire. Furthermore, it includes years of death and ages in 1685, details which exactly match entries in Parish Registers. Preliminary searches for the name Mallom show that these were connected to the place name, Malham, in the Yorkshire Dales (Fig. 07). The following are examples: references in Early Yorkshire Charters for the Honour of Skipton, among other examples, record gifts of land in Malham, made to Bolton Priory and Fountains Abbey, between 1210–1243. Thus, Thomas, son of William de Malham, received 30 marks of silver from Bolton Priory, to fund a pilgrimage to Jerusalem.[29] The Malhamdale Poll Tax of 1379 includes the name of Johannes de Malghome, ffrankeleyn (a freeman) and his wife, who paid 6s. 8d. tax in Calton. All other individuals taxed in this vill paid either 2d or 4d, indicating that Malghome was a wealthy individual, holding both land and property.[30] Nine other men with the name Malghom/am/um were included in the 1379 Poll Tax lists for the Staincliffe Wapentake of Yorkshire West Riding, which has complete records. Willilmus Malghom paid 4d in Hebden, Stephanus de Malgham, a draper, paid 2s 0d in Skipton, Thomas de Malghom, a tailor (cissor), paid 6d in Skipton, Willelmus de Malghom paid 12d in Linton, where his servant also paid 4d, Johannes de Malghom paid 12d in Hawkswick, Thomas de Malghum paid 4d in Skibeden, Adam de Malghom paid 4d in Embsay, and Willelmus de Malghom paid 4d in the same vill, where he was one of the two PHs (probi homines, trustworthy men of good standing).[31] Each man's wife was included. These places are quite close together, within 10–12 miles of Malham, although no one called

Malgham (the Poll Tax name for Malham) lived in Malham in 1379. One other man, Willelmus de Mallom, paid 4d in 1379, in Bishop Thornton, 30 miles due east of Malham, so he moved further afield than the others. Furthermore, two men with the surname were registered for tax in York: Johanne Mallom paid 12d in the parish of St Martin, Coney Street, in 1377, and Johanne de Mallom, dyer, paid 12d in the parish of St Sampson, in 1381: neither had a wife or family.[32] Poll Taxes raised revenue mainly to fund the king's wars, and were a principal cause of the Peasant's Revolt of 1381.[33] In addition, a list of Mallom and variant surnames was extracted from a computerised database of individuals living in Yorkshire before 1550, held in York Minster Library.[34] 298 examples of the name and its variants were found, including: Malham[e]=129, Mallom=43, Mallum=10, Mallome=9, Malhome=7, Mallam=6 and Malhum=1. In particular, for Malham[e], the name is recorded in Charters before the year 1220. For Mallom[e], 7 individuals left a will between 1400 and 1544, and one was a reference to John Mallom of York, a member of the Mercer's Guild in 1423. Other examples were found in Feet of Fines for Yorkshire, in the 1400s, in Kirkby Malhamdale, near Skipton, and in transfers of land in 1451.[35] In 1478, Richard Mallom, transferred a piece of land in Clapham, Yorkshire, to Richard Chewe, for £30.[36] Further examples of the surname and its variants appear in a catalogue entitled "Skipton" held by Yorkshire Archaeological and Historical Society: in 1384 there was a grant from John de Malghom of Calton (noted in the 1379 Poll Tax returns), to Sir Robert del [F...] and Sir William de Rothwell, chaplains, of a toft and three oxgangs (or bovates, a measure of land equivalent to about 20 acres), held by Edmund son of Thomas de Kendal, in Stirton near Skipton. In 1386, Stephen de Malgham, was involved in a transaction of land in Skipton; in 1420, Richard Malhom took possession of a burgage - a property or strip of land rented in return for money or services rendered - in Skipton; in 1434 Thomas Wedyrherd received ten marks from Richard Mallom of Skipton as a final

Fig. 07. Towards Malham village, within the trees, from the rim of Malham Cove.

payment, probably the same man; and in 1449, William Malhom/Mallom had a grant of a messuage from Thomas, vicar of Skipton. Between 1501 and 1530, other men named Mallom or a variant spelling, sold or acquired property in and around Skipton,[37] indicating that they were relatively wealthy.

Finally, the Kirkby Malham Muster Roll of 1539 records that Rob't Malhom was enlisted in the militia in Scothorp, Malhamdale (modern Scosthrop), 10 miles north west of Skipton, with a bill, (a pole weapon with an axe blade shaped like a hook, often used to unseat horsemen).[38] He was one of 17 militiamen who carried a bill, 7 of whom were mounted, together with 2 archers from the same village.

In summary, the evidence from the College of Arms pedigree, taken with the findings of the toponymic* surname in medieval West Yorkshire, shows that members of the Mallom family left their rural home, keeping their place name of origin, to find new opportunities in York, and later in Norwich, sometime during the late medieval or the early Tudor periods to improve their financial and social outlook.[39] And in this ambition, they were very successful. The place-name Malham may be derived from the Old Norse "malg, maligr," a stony or gravelly place, and was recorded as "Malgun" in the Domesday Book in 1086, and "Malghum" in the Feet of Fines of Yorkshire in 1208.[40]

Thomas Mallom, Archer

Later in the quest for the origins of the ancestors of Richard Mallom of Norwich, the military service of a man from the Mallom families of Yorkshire who enlisted in King Henry IV's army against Scotland in 1400, during The Hundred Years' War, was found in the database of "The Soldier in Later Medieval England." [41] Thomas Mallom was an archer who served in the retinue captained by Sir Peter de Buckton, a leading Yorkshire supporter of King Henry IV, and steward of his household, commanded by the King in his Expedition to Scotland in the summer of 1400. He assisted Henry when he came back to England from exile, mainly in Paris, in 1399, landing at Ravenspur on the Yorkshire coast, and in return for royal favours: "Sir Peter remained in close proximity to his master, retaining a force of archers from the lordship of Knaresborough to serve on Henry IV's Scottish campaign of 1400."[42]

Thomas Mallom was one of 134 archers who enlisted on 24 June 1400, mustering at York.[43] None of the other Mallom surname variants discovered in Yorkshire was included in the database, although other research comparing names from the Poll Taxes (1379–1381) and the Soldiers' database, has shown that nobles, aristocrats and leading land-owners keen to support the Crown, enlisted men from their estates.[44] However, only a tiny number of places of origin appear within the Soldiers' database, presumably because the clerks who compiled the lists were not required

---

* a toponymic word, name, etc. is one that comes from the name of a place: toponymic surnames identify the places where people lived.

to enter the information, the names being used as the source for future payment by the Crown. None of Buckton's archers had their places of origin included in the retinue lists. Nevertheless, the origins of archers which can be clearly identified within the retinues of other Captains for the June 1400 muster, were mainly from Yorkshire: Clapham, Copley, Bilton (near Harrogate), Dewsbury, Swine (where Buckton was later to be buried), Ripon and York. It follows that although Thomas Mallom's place of origin was not recorded, we can have a high degree of confidence that he was indeed a Yorkshireman, and given the years involved, he may have been the man who paid tax, either in Skipton, or in Skibeden.

REVD. JOHN MALLOM OF BOOTON, NORFOLK

One of the two Executors of John Read's 1652 will was John Mallom[e] of Booton, clerk (in Holy Orders: clergyman). He was Read's brother-in-law, and he was given £30 for his work. As an educated member of the clergy, he might have reasonably expected to act as Executor to the wills of other wealthy individuals, and thereby supplement his stipend and the tithes due to him from his parish. This John Mallom, son of Richard Mallom of Norwich, grocer, went to school in Norwich under Mr Stonham, and then proceeded to [Gonville and] Caius College, Cambridge, where he was a scholar from 1624–1631, matriculating in 1624, graduating BA in 1627/28, and MA in 1631. He was ordained Deacon in Norwich Cathedral in December 1632, and Priest in September 1633, whereupon he was appointed Rector of Booton, a small village about 13 miles to the north west of Norwich, in February 1634[45] (see map on p.xii). Mallom was licensed as a Preacher in 1635 by William Laud, Archbishop of Canterbury.[46] In 1638, two years before his marriage, Revd. John Mallom acquired the deeds of Oak Farm, Booton from William Bacon: "a messuage with 31 acres of land, pasture and a meadow, near Eynsford Bridge, with other property in Booton and Great Witchingham with copyhold lands".

The farm thereby came into the possession of the Mallom family.[47] John Mallom married Katherine, daughter of Mr Timothy Mann, in Binham in February 1640. They had two sons, John, and Timothy, and although neither of the boys' baptisms has been found, each of them was named in the wills, both of their father, and their maternal grandfather. This detail was recorded on the 1685 pedigree held at the College of Arms, London.[48] The pedigree confirms that John and Timothy were the only two children of Revd. John Mallom (Pedigree 2, p. 22). The church of St Michael the Archangel in which the Rector carried-out his clerical duties no longer exists in its original medieval form. His church fell into disrepair and was rebuilt, partly enclosing some of the older walls, towards the end of the 19th century to an 'eccentric' design with twin west towers, by the then Rector, Revd. Whitwell Elwin. The building was later to be described by the architect, Sir Edwin Lutyens, as "very naughty but built in the right spirit." The church is no longer used for public worship.[49]

In addition to his church and parish responsibilities, Revd. John Mallom had business interests, so the family would have led a comfortable life in rural Norfolk, and although the Civil War raged in England between 1642 and 1651 during his period as Rector of Booton, it was only in the area around King's Lynn that was there any major conflict in the county. In 1647, the Rector was involved in the first of two cases heard at the Court of Chancery, concerning a property in the Parish of St Edmund's Norwich, with John Gleave.[50] In 1652, a second case involved the estate of William Overton of Cambridge, in which Mallom was a plaintiff.[51] John, Timothy and their mother, Katherine, were all named in Revd. John Mallom's 1662 will.[52] It seems possible that his final illness was acute and of a short duration, as the will includes only very brief details of his estate. Katherine was to receive the whole estate until their oldest son, John, came of age, out of which she was tasked with paying for the boys' education. The second son, Timothy, was to receive £500. Katherine was appointed Executrix and John Man[n] senior and John Man[n] junior were witnesses. In 1663, the year after Mallom's death, his widow, Katherine, continued the family property interests with a third case heard in the Court of Chancery, concerning property in Haverhill, Essex, formerly owned by John Hurst of Haverhill, deceased.[53] The bequest to Timothy of £500 may appear relatively modest today. However, it represents a considerable sum of money. Adopting the same methodology as was used for John Read's gifts, the £500 of 1662 converts to more than £65,000 today, or maybe more using other methods of calculating the comparison.[54] Whatever the precise value of the bequests, it represents great wealth in comparison to most of Revd. John Mallom's parishioners. Timothy Mann left a will written in February 1663, with a codicil added in February 1665, proved at Aylsham in April 1667. In addition to the bequests to his children and the grandchildren born to his sons, he left gifts to the two Mallom boys born to his daughter, Katherine, as follows:

> Item I give and bequeath unto my two grandchildren John Mallom and Timothy Mallum
>
> Ten pounds a peice to bee payd them within two yeares after my decease.[55]

These monetary gifts represent approximately £1,600 today, using the calculation described above. The bequests given to his other grandchildren varied between 40 shillings and £100. The acquisition of land and property and the involvement of Revd. John Mallom of Booton in legal cases heard in the Court of Chancery, is the earliest available evidence of the development of the Mallom family estates. These would later be considerably developed and extended by his descendants. It might be expected that the home occupied by Revd. John Mallom and his family in Booton would have been eligible for Hearth Tax payments, but there is no sign of this in 1664, and in 1666, there was no return for the Hundred of South Erpingham (includes Booton), nor incidentally for Loddon Hundred (includes Bedingham), nor Depwade Hundred (includes Wacton), where subsequent generations of the Mallom family were to live.[56]

The story of the Mallom family continues into the generation of the great grandfather of our subject, Captain Mallom, who was also named John Mallom. He was the oldest son of Revd. John Mallom of Booton and his wife, Katherine, and he was to become the first John Mallom of Wacton Hall, as shown in Pedigree 2, p. 22. In the spring of 1670, young John turned his attentions to Elizabeth, daughter of Thomas Stone of Bedingham, gent, and his wife, Audrey. Elizabeth, who was born in Bedingham in February 1633, had first married Revd. William Copping of Woodton, in December 1663 (see map on p.xii). He was the Rector of Bedingham,[57] and the couple had one child, a daughter named Audrey, baptised in December 1664, but who died 4 weeks later. On 2 December 1663, five days before his marriage, William Copping entered into an agreement with Thomas Stone of Bedingham, gent, and William Stone of Bedingham, his son, gent, his future father-in-law and brother-in-law. Extracts of the text, in which the original spelling, punctuation, names of individuals and properties have been retained for added interest, read as follows:

> **This Indenture** made the second day of December in the yeare of our Sovereigne Lord Charles the second by the grace of God Kinge of England, Scotland France and Ireland defender of the Faith, and the fifteenth. And in the year of our Lord one thousand six hundred and sixty-three. **Between** William Coppinge of Woodton in the County of Norfolk Clerke of the one part And Thomas Stone of Bedingham in the said County gent and William Stone of Bedingham aforesaid gent and sonne of the said Thomas Stone of the other part. **Witnesseth** … for and in Consideration of ffive shillings of Lawfull Englishe money unto him by the said Thomas Stone and Willm Stone in hand paid hath bargeyned, sold, demysed, granted and … **All that** Capitall Messuage situate in Woodton aforesaid wherein Symon Waters nowe dwelleth together with all and only the houses, edifices, buildings, barnes, stables yards gardens orchards …… Conteyninge together in the whole Two Hundred and Three score acres beinge in Woodton aforesaid … in the occupation of the said Symon Waters as fermor (undertenant) of the said Willm Coppinge att the yearly rent of One Hundred and Eighteen pounds of lawfull Englishe money. **And alsoe** all those groves thereunto adjoyninge Called by the name of Partridge Grove and Townishend Grove… **And alsoe** all the freehold and Charterhold lands, tenements and hereditaments whatsoever of him the said Willm Coppinge situate being in Woodton aforesaid now in the occupation of the said Symon Waters …. **To have and to hold** all such and soe much of the said Messuage lands tenements and premises as soe of free and Charterhold tenure with there and every of their Rights and Members and appurtements unto the said Thomas Stone and Willm Stone, their Executors and assignes from the Thirteenth day of November nowe last past before the date of the these presentes for the Terme of six months nowe next ensuenge fully to be complete and ended. **In Witness**

...

> Dorse — "Sealed and delivered in the p'sense of Tho: Stone Jnr, John Blankes and Will: Stone. 2º Dec 15º Carl 2 1663*, Will Copping, Clerk, his lease for 6 m[onths] to Mr Stone."[58]

Part of the original ribbon remains attached to the foot of the document, but the seal has not survived. This is an unusual form of Lease, there being no Release to accompany it, and the timing not the normal 12 months. The 5s rent paid to Copping was clearly a nominal sum, but no mention was made of any price or rent paid by Thomas Stone and his son, to William Copping.[59] Given the date, the parties must have had Copping's marriage with Elizabeth Stone in mind, but in view of the questions raised by the Lease, the opinion of an experienced Norwich Archivist was sought:

> From 1535, conveyances of freehold estates by bargains and sales were subject to the public scrutiny of enrolment in either a royal court at Westminster or in the local court of quarter sessions. The Statute of Uses of 1536 however, had the unintended effect of enabling secret conveyancing.[60] An owner of real estate wishing to transfer ownership secretly to another could then do so by leasing it to a tenant for a nominal sum of money, then before the expiry of the lease, releasing his future interest (the 'reversion') to the tenant. Normally such a lease would be dated the day before the date of the release, and the term would be a full year, though, of course, the intention was that the term would only be one day old before the release ended it forever. The payment of a nominal entry fine of 5s and, usually, a peppercorn rent, also indicated the nature of such a lease. Clearly, such a lease is present here, despite its slightly unusual six-monthly term and the fact that no rent is mentioned, indicating an intention to convey the estates from Copping to the Stones. Without the release and any associated records, we can only guess as to the circumstances surrounding this transaction. Copping, although a young man, was a member of a gentry family of means, so we cannot presume that the conveyance was an inducement for his bride's father to accept his suit. Although it may have been part of a dowry arrangement, we cannot tell from this lease what part of such an arrangement it actually was.[61]

William Copping died young in June 1666, aged 27 years, before he had prepared a will, leaving Elizabeth a widow, without any living children to be supported by a second husband.[62] Having land and property, a will would have been expected suggesting his final illness may have been acute. But he was unprepared, and died intestate. There was an outbreak of Bubonic Plague in Norwich in 1665—66 which killed hundreds of people, and it is possible that having regular contact

---

*   2 December in the 15th year of the reign of Charles II, was 1663.

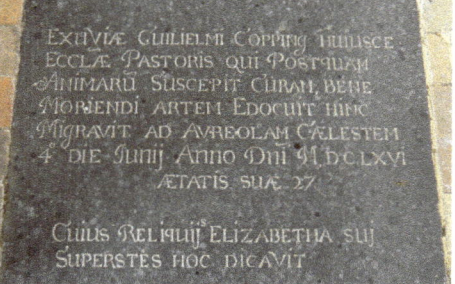

Fig. 08. St Andrew's Church, Bedingham with the memorial to Revd. William Copping, 1666, first husband of Elizabeth Stone, who later married John Mallom Esq.

with his parishioners, some of whom would have been in the habit of travelling to and from Norwich, this might have been the cause of his early death.[63] In August 1666, an Administration of all the goods, rights and credits of William Copping was granted to Susan Copping, widow, his mother. Today, the lack of reference to his widow, Elizabeth, might appear somewhat surprising and without any obvious explanation.[64] A memorial stone to Revd. William Copping was placed in the floor of the chancel of Bedingham Church (Fig. 08).

The Latin text reads as follows:

> EXUVIÆ GUILIELMI COPPING HUIUSCE
> ECCL[ESI]Æ PASTORIS QUI POSTQUAM
> ANIMARU[M] SUSCEPIT CURAM, BENE
> MORIENDI ARTEM EDOCUIT HINC
> MIGRAVIT AD AVREOLAM CÆLESTEM
> 4° DIE JUNIJ ANNO D[OMI]NI MDCLXVI
> ÆTATIS SUÆ 27
>
> CUIUS RELIQUIJS ELIZABETHA SUJ
> SUPERSTES HOC DICAVIT

That is to say,

"[Here lie] the mortal remains of William Copping, Pastor of this church, who after
he took up the care of souls, he taught the art of dying well, he departed from here to his heavenly reward (halo/crown)
on the 4th June 1666, at the age of 27

Whose surviving widow Elizabeth has said this"

References and Further Reading

1. Marriage Licence Bond for the marriage of John Mallom of Wacton, with Phillis Phillips of Aslacton, both of the County of Norfolk. 29 August 1728. "The said marriage to be openly solemnized in the Face of the Parish Church of Wacton, Aslacton aforesaid or Moulton in Norfolk, between the Hours of Eight and Twelve of the Clock in the Forenoon…" Sealed and Delivered in the Presence of John Mallom and John Francis. 29 August 1728. ANF 12/8/24. Norfolk Record Office (NRO), Norwich. From FamilySearch: Norfolk Marriage Licence Bonds: Archdeaconry of Norwich Court: 1727–1731: Image 33/417.
2. Details of baptisms, marriages and burials in this account are taken from Norfolk Parish Registers, Archdeacon's Transcripts (ATs), Bishop's Transcripts (BTs), and Marriage Licence Bonds, held at NRO, Norwich, many of which are available online at 'FamilySearch.org.uk' and through the "Indexes of Norfolk Marriages (NMI) by Hundred, 1558–1812, by Patrick Palgrave-Moore, also held at NRO, Norwich. Some preliminary searches were carried out using FreeREG.co.uk Ancestry.co.uk, FindmyPast.co.uk, and the services of the Norfolk Family History Society, avoiding the pitfalls of relying on transcriptions, which may include misleading errors.
3. Farrer, Revd. Edmund, The church heraldry of Norfolk: a description of all coats of arms on brasses, monuments, slabs, hatchments etc. now to be found in the county of Norfolk. Illustrated. With references to Blomefield's History of Norfolk and Burke's Armoury. Together with notes from the inscriptions attached. Farrer, Revd. Edmund, Norwich, A.H. Goose and co., 1887–93. p. 185.
4. Litten, Julian. Personal Communication, 24 September 2022.
5. Administration: Robert Phillips of Aslacton. NCC 1734, 34. NRO, Norwich.
6. Biographical History of Gonville and Caius College, Cambridge. Vol i: 1349–1713. http://venn.lib.cam.ac.uk/Documents/acad/2016/search-2016.html. Ref John Mallom, son of John Mallom, gent, of Wacton, Norfolk. School, Wymondham (Mr Clarke). Matric 1689: Hannah Verge, Archivist. NRO. Norwich. Personal Communication, 7 June 2018: Ellen Carr, Librarian, Norfolk Family History Society, Norwich. Personal Communication, 6 June 2018.
7. Mallom v Mallom. Plaintiff; John Mallom Esq. of Wacton, Norfolk, Defendant; Robert Mallom, gent. Bill and Answer. C 11/2258/12. TNA, London.
8. *The Clergy of the Church of England Database 1540–1835* (CCEd). Locations: Norwich, Schools.
9. https://en.wikipedia.org/wiki/Calendar_(New_Style)_Act_1750
10. https://digitalcollections.nypl.org/items/5e66b3e8-850a-d471-e040-e00a180654d7
11. Ingham, Erika. Assistant Curator (Archive and Library), National Portrait Gallery, London. Personal Communication, 8 January 2014.
12. Papworth, Andrew, 'Indian Prince Frederick Duleep Singh who devoted his life to preserving Norfolk and Suffolk's heritage to be commemorated.' Eastern Daily Press, Norwich, 18 January 2018. https://www.edp24.co.uk/news/prince-frederick-duleep-singh-norfolk-suffolk-history-150th-birthday-1-5361220
13. Bone, Oliver, Curator and Thorpe,Tim, Collections Officer, both of The Ancient House Museum, Thetford, Norfolk. Personal Communication, 9 January 2014.
14. Robinson, Keith and Morgan, Daniel, Collections Volunteers, The Ancient House Museum, Thetford, Norfolk. Personal Communication, 20 August 2019.
15. Spelman, Diana, Personal Communication, 26 September 2018.
16. ibid.
17. Millican, Percy, The Register of the Freemen of Norwich, 1548–1713. Norwich, 1934. NCR 17c/2.
18. Smith-Bannister, Scott, Names and Naming Patterns in England, 1538–1700. *Oxford Historical Monographs*, Oxford University Press, 1997. http://www.earlymodernengland.com/2014/10/the-most-popular-boys-names-in-tudor-england/

19. Cley next the Sea. https://en.wikipedia.org/wiki/Cley_next_the_Sea
20. Administration of Margaret Malham of Cley [ANW 22/2/58], NRO, Norwich.
21. Hawes, Timothy L., The Inhabitants of Norfolk in the Fourteenth Century. The Lay Subsidies 1327 and 1332: 42,000 names and payments. Preserved in the Public Record Office. [6 volumes], 2000–2002. NRO, Norwich.
22. Assessment to raise 100 marks [mid-14th century]. Listing households in Norwich and assessed totals. Headed, 'Le Payment de C. Marc'. Text on both sides of the parchment, size c.45 cms. x c.25 cms. In French. Text worn and faint with the parchment stained near its head. Norwich Corporation. NCR 7i/1. NRO, Norwich. I am grateful to Diana Spelman for examining this document.
23. Fenwick, Carolyn C. *The Poll Taxes of 1377, 1379 and 1381. Part 2 Lincolnshire – Westmorland.* Published for the British Academy by Oxford University Press, 2001, pp. 68–200 (Norfolk section), and also in Part 3, ibid, Wiltshire-Yorkshire, under Additional Documents, Norfolk, pp. 532–543.
24. Large, David M. *The Life and Family of Robert Large, Mercer, Mayor of London 1439–1440 and First Employer of William Caxton.* Foundation for Medieval Genealogy, 2008, pp. 1–5.
25. Large, ibid. p. 4.
26. PCC Will of John Reade or Read, Alderman of Norwich, Norfolk. PROB 11/221/615. TNA, London.
27. Purchasing Power of the Pound-Measuringworth, com/calculators/ukcompare/relativevalue.php
28. Dickinson, P., L., Clarenceux King of Arms. College of Arms, Queen Victoria Street, London EC4V 4BT. Personal Communication, 18 April 2019.
29. Clay, Charles Travis, Ed. *Early Yorkshire Charters Vol. VII: Honour of Skipton.* Printed for The Yorkshire Archaeological Society, Record Series, Extra Series Vol. V, 1947, pp. 151. Number 89 refers to Dodsworth cxliv, f. 13d. from the Bolton Chartulary, f. 25. Fountains Abbey Chartulary mentions gifts in Malham made by Thomas, son of William de Malham, to Fountains Abbey, before c.1235. https://archive.org/details/YASES5/page/n195/mode/2up?view=theater. : Clay, ibid. Number 90. refers to Dodsworth cxliv, f. 14, from the Bolton Chartulary, f. 28. p. 152, note, 2. https://archive.org/details/YASES5/page/152/mode/2up?view=theater
30. Kirkby Malhom.info. Subsidy Rolls – Malhamdale Poll Tax 1379 http://www.kirkbymalham.info/KMI/malhamdale/polltax.html (A list of names extracted from Fenwick, Part 3, ibid).
31. The probi homines—trustworthy men of good standing in the community had a supervisory role in the collection of the taxes. "For each vill (or, occasionally) group of vills, an indenture of acquittance was returned to the Exchequer witnessing that the representatives (probi homines) of the vill had paid to the Exchequer collectors a sum made up of as many fourpences as there were men and women over the age of fourteen, genuine mendicants excepted." See Beresford, M.A., The Poll Taxes of 1377, 1379 and 1381. *The Amateur Historian,* Vol. 3 No. 7, Spring 1958, p. 273.
32. Fenwick, Carolyn C. *The Poll Taxes of 1377, 1379 and 1381. Part 3, Wiltshire-Yorkshire.* Published for the British Academy by Oxford University Press, 2005, pp. 144, 145, 297, 440, 441, 442, 445, 449.
33. Schama, Simon, *A History of Britain at the Edge of the World, 3000BC-AD1603.* Published by BBC Worldwide Ltd. Woodlands, 80 Wood Lane, London W12 0TT, p. 247, and pp. 246–55.
34. Newman, Steven, York Minster Library Customer Services Co-ordinator, "York Biographical Database." Personal Communication, 21 May 2019.
35. Phillips, ibid. 25/1/279/151, number 28. http://www.medievalgenealogy.org.uk/fines/abstracts/CP_25_1_279_151.shtml
36. Phillips, C. G., Some Notes on Medieval Genealogy, CP 25/1/281/164, number 41. http://www.medievalgenealogy.org.uk/fines/abstracts, CP_25_1_281_164.shtml
37. Skipton, a Catalogue. A record held by the Yorkshire Archaeological and Historical Society, Skipton, 1384–1619. MD335/1/1/28. In Discovery, 207, The National Archives, Kew. https://discovery.nationalarchives.gov.uk/details/r/05f360f0-1cdb-4290-90c4-7f29aed1231c

38. Kirkby Malham info. Malhamdale Muster Roll 1539. http://www.kirkbymalham.info/KMI/malhamdale/muster1539.html
39. What's in a surname? https://blog.nationalarchives.gov.uk/whats-surname/ Blog by Jane Flood, Tuesday 19 July 2016: Wikipedia, Toponymic surname. https://en.wikipedia.org/wiki/Toponymic_surname : Guild of One-Name Studies, Toponyms. https://one-name.org/modern-british-surnames/taxonomy/toponyms/
40. Surname DB. The Internet Surname Database, Last Name: Malham. https://www.surnamedb.com/Surname/Malham : Pedes Finium Ebor. Regnante Johanne (Feet of Fines of Yorkshire for the reign of King John). The Publications of the Surtees Society by Andrews and Co. Durham. Whittaker and Co., 2 White Hart Street, Paternoster Square, Bernard Quaritch, 15, Piccadilly, Blackwood and Sons, Edinburgh, 1897. Vol. 94. p. 127, Number 330, refers to the sale of 3 roods of land with property in Malghum (Malham), Yorkshire, on 4 October 1208. https://archive.org/details/pedesfiniumeborr00grearich/page/126/mode/2up?view=theater : Hanks, Patricia, Coates, Richard and McClure, Peter (Eds), The Oxford Dictionary of Family Names in Britain and Ireland. Oxford University Press. Current Online Version: 2016. Malham Variants: Maleham, Mallam, Malam, Mallom, Maylam, Maugham : Smith, A. H. (1961–3), *The Place Names of the West Riding of Yorkshire*, 8 volumes, English Place-Name Society 30–7, Cambridge: Cambridge University Press. 6, pp. 133–5. https://www.oxfordreference.com/display/10.1093/acref/9780199677764.001.0001/acref-9780199677764-e-25578?rskey=5sb6K1&result=26996
41. Bell, Adrian, R., Curry, Anne, King, Andy and Simpkin, David, The Soldier in Later Medieval England. Oxford University Press, Great Clarendon Street, Oxford, OX2 6DP. 2013. The Preface describes the grant awarded by the Arts and Humanities Research Council, to digitise the records of every man known to have fought in the Hundred Years' war (1369–1453). 2,500 Muster Rolls from various sources were used to compile a searchable database of 250,000 entries; https://www.medievalsoldier.org/dbsearch/
42. Rawcliffe, Carol, Buckton, Sir Peter (c 1350–1414), of Buckton, Yorks. *History of Parliament Online*. Eds: J S Roskell, L Clark and C Rawcliffe.
43. Retinue TNA, E101/43/4, m21, and TNA, E101/43/4, m21d. Taken from The Medieval Soldiers' database.
44. Large, David M, "Using the Poll Tax to Identify Medieval Archers?" https://www.medievalsoldier.org/about/soldier-profiles/using-the-poll-tax-to-identify-medieval-archers/; Large, David M, "Men from Stamford, Lincolnshire, commanded by Edmund of Langley, Duke of York (1341–1402): comparison of Names in the Poll Tax and the Soldiers' database." https://www.medievalsoldier.org/men-from-stamford-lincolnshire-commanded-by-edmund-of-langley-duke-of-york-1341-1402-comparison-of-names-in-the-poll-tax-and-soldiers-databases/; Large, David M, "Soldiers named Large in the Protection and Attorney database." https://www.medievalsoldier.org/soldiers-named-large-in-the-protection-and-attorney-database/; Large, David M, "Soldiers named Large in the Garrisons of Lancastrian Normandy." https://www.medievalsoldier.org/soldiers-named-large-in-the-garrisons-of-lancastrian-normandy-1415-50/. These studies are included in the Soldiers' Profile section of the Reading and Southampton Universities website, "The Soldier in Later Medieval England."
45. http://venn.lib.cam.ac.uk/Documents/acad/2016/search-2016.html : Blomefield, Francis, An Essay towards a Topographical History of the County of Norfolk, Volume 6, Hundred of South Erpingham: Booton, pp. 352–359. https://www.british-history.ac.uk/topographical-hist-norfolk/vol6/pp352–359
46. CCeD Clergy of the Church of England database http://db.theclergydatabase.org.uk/jsp/search/index.jsp
47. Deeds of Oak Farm, Booton. MC 377/1-61, 715 x 4. NRO, Norwich: Diana Spelman, Personal Communication, 15 July 2013.

48. Dickinson, Patric L., Clarenceaux King of Arms, College of Arms, London, Personal Communication, 18 April 2019.
49. St Michael the Archangel Church, Booton, Norfolk. https://www.visitchurches.org.uk/visit/church-listing/st-michael-booton.html
50. Gleave v Mallome. Plaintiffs John Gleave. Defendants John Mallome and another. TNA, London. C5/606/8.
51. Mallome v Stonard. Plaintiffs John Mallome and Thomas Hurst. Defendants Clement Stonard and others. TNA, London. C7/402/94.
52. Will of [Revd] John Mallom. 9 February 1662. PROB/11/310/454. TNA, London.
53. Hurst v Mallom. Plaintiffs John Hurst. Defendants Katherine Mallom, widow. TNA, London. C5/613/75.
54. measuringworth.com, ibid.
55. Will of Timothy Mann. 3 February 1663. ANW will 1667/7, 213. NRO, Norwich.
56. Norfolk Hearth Tax Assessment Michaelmas 1664, Transcribed by M S Frankel and P J Seaman, Indexed by P T R Palgrave-Moore, Norfolk Genealogy Vol XV, Norfolk and Norwich Genealogical Society (now Norfolk Family History Society): Norfolk and Norwich Hearth Tax Assessment Lady Day 1666, Transcribed and Indexed by P Seaman, Norfolk Genealogy Vol XX, Norfolk and Norwich Genealogical Society (now Norfolk Family History Society): Norfolk Hearth Tax Exemption Certificates, 1670–1674, Norwich, Great Yarmouth, King's Lynn and Thetford, edited and introduced by Peter Seaman, with contributions by John Pound and Robert Smith, British Record Society in association with Norfolk Record Society. The name Mallom does not appear in any of these volumes. I am grateful to Paul White of Norfolk Family History Society for this information: Hearth Tax Digital, Tax exemption certificates for Norfolk towns, 1670–1671 (E179/338), 1671–1672 (E179/335), 1672–1674 (E179/337), and 1673–1674 (E179/336), includes no reference to Mallom. Online at https://gams.uni-graz.at/archive/objects/context:htx/methods/sdef:Context/get?mode=records
57. CCeD Clergy of the Church of England database. http://db.theclergydatabase.org.uk/jsp/persons/index.jsp
58. Indenture: Lease for 6 months. (1) William Copping of Woodton, clerk. (2) Thomas Stone of Bedingham, gent. 2 Dec 1663. Capital messuage in Woodton. NRS 26719, 149X5. NRO, Norfolk.
59. Spelman, Diana. Personal Communication, 24 August 2018.
60. Statute of Uses, 1536, https://en.wikipedia.org/wiki/Statute_of_Uses
61. Townsend, Tom, Archivist, NRO, Norwich. Personal Communication, 26 September 2018.
62. http://venn.lib.cam.ac.uk/Documents/acad/2016/search-2016.html
63. Blomefield, ibid: Volume 3. The History of the City of Norwich, chapter 31. Of the city in the time of King Charles II, pp. 403–421. https://www.british-history.ac.uk/topographical-hist-norfolk/vol3/pp403-421#highlight-first
64. William Copping of Woodton, NCC admon act book, 1666–68, fo. 5. NRO, Norwich.

Part 2: The Mallom Estates: Growth

Elizabeth Stone-Copping was a member of the high-status Stone family of Bedingham, Norfolk, which enjoyed considerable social advantages based on their land and property, and now single again, she would have been viewed as a very desirable marriage partner by an ambitious young man, keen to make progress and establish himself in the county. John Mallom, the son of the Rector of Booton and his wife, was such a man, and he clearly had no intention of following his father into the ministry of the Church of England.

MARRIAGE OF JOHN MALLOM WITH ELIZABETH COPPING (NÉE STONE)

Not very long after the death of her first husband, Elizabeth became romantically involved with John Mallom of Bedingham, and their marriage took place just under four years later in Bedingham on 7 April 1670, when he was described in the Archdeacon's Transcript as a gentleman, and she, correctly, as a widow. During the next 20 years, John and Elizabeth became increasingly prosperous, significantly developing the Mallom estates. With his marriage, John Mallom was now joined with the wealthy Stone family who lived in luxury compared with others in Bedingham: Thomas Stone, Elizabeth's father, for example, paid tax for 9 hearths in the family home of Bedingham Hall in 1664.[1] There are 3 carved memorials to members of the Stone family fixed to the north wall of the chancel in Bedingham church, and ledgerstones to other members of the family in the floor of the church. An item held at the Society of Genealogists in London proved to be a second Lease, between John Mallom and his wife, Elizabeth, of Bedingham (formerly Elizabeth Copping, née Stone), and George Copping of Woodton, Norfolk, probably William's brother, dated 17 January 1672.[2] Whereas the Release for the conveyance of the land and property from the Stones to William Copping in 1663 was not found for this transaction nine years later, the associated Release, dated 18 January 1672, has survived, although it is held in a different Archive.[3]

The 1672 Lease has a similar form and content to the Copping-Stone Lease of 1663, and it conveyed a similar estate with its land and property, together with some additions, from John and Elizabeth Mallom of Bedingham, to George Copping of Woodton (see map on p.xii). The following is a summary, in which the names of the meadows, groves and type of buildings within the estate provide invaluable information about the history of Woodton and the surrounding area, and they are included here for this reason:

dated 16 January 1672, during the reign of King Charles II, by the grace of God of England, Scotland, France and Ireland, King and Defender of the Faith. John Mallom of Bedingham, Norfolk, gent, and Elizabeth his wife, granted, bargained and sold to George Copping, of Woodton, gent, his Executors and Administrators, for the sum of 5 shillings, a capital Messuage or Mansion house with all its houses, edifices, buildings, barns, stables, yards, gardens and orchards, in Woodton. And also all the lands, meadows, pastures, feedings and hereditaments with all the passages, liberties and freedoms belonging to the same, that is to say, all the meadows called Shepcoate Meadow, Daynes Meadow, Blythes Meadow, Townsend Meadow, Partridge Close, Broad Close and Mallett Close in Woodton. And also all the parcels of land in the field called the Little Ffield in Woodton. And also one Enclosure called Elmeyard, one Enclosure called Midlewents, and several other Enclosures, including Winterpitt, Longsells, Upperbroad Close, Harwood, Townsend, Oat Townsend and Tower Townsend. The Lease also included all the other freehold Messuages, Lands, Tenements and Hereditaments of John and Elizabeth Mallom "in a certain Indenture or Deed dated the 3 December 1663" (see above). And all other the Freehold, Messuages, Lands, Tenements and Hereditaments of John Mallom and Elizabeth his wife in Woodton, or anywhere else in Norfolk. This estate contained a total area of thirteen score and two acres (262 acres), lately occupied by Symon Walters, at or under the yearly rent of one Hundred and Eighteen pounds (£118). And also the two groves or grovetts in Woodton called Partridge Grove and Townsend Grove.

This was conveyed to George Copping and to his Executors and Administrators from the 29 September 1672, for the term of one whole year. "In Witness whereof the parties first above named have set their hands and Seals the day and year first above written" (17 January 1672). Signed by John Mallom and Eliz[abeth] Mallom. The two ribbons attached to the document have both survived, but the wax seals have not.

The Release for the transaction was dated 18 January 1672, one day after the Lease, as expected, confirming the agreement between John Mallom of Bedingham and Elizabeth his wife, of the one part, and George Copping of Woodton, of the other part. John and Elizabeth sold the estate to George Copping and his heirs and assigns, for £700, and they Granted, Released and Confirmed to George Copping, all the lands and buildings listed in the Lease. After some legal comments, there followed the final sentence, "In Witness whereof the parties first above named have mutually set their hands and Seals the day and year first above written." Signed by John Mallom and Elizabeth Mallom. The two ribbons and wax seals at the foot of the document have all survived.

On the reverse side (Dorse) of the Release were written the names of the four witnesses to the transaction: Thom[as] Townsend, Henr[y] Reve, R[obert] Chet[t] leburgh and John Watts. And a note was included confirming that John Mallom had received £700 from George Copping, on 22 March 1672, in the presence of the witnesses. According to the method used previously to calculate present-day values, the estate conveyed by John and Elizabeth Mallom to George Copping was valued at £110,400, or a higher sum than this using other methodologies. This value is obtained by multiplying £700 by the 5-fold increase in the RPI from 1672 to 2017.[4] Whatever the precise value, the sale of this piece of real-estate raised a significant sum of money which greatly supplemented the Mallom's finances. In 1672, the estate was being rented by Symon Walters, who was occupying the property in 1663, and at the same annual rent of £118, despite the passage of nearly 10 years.

Malloms in the Court of Chancery

Two cases involving the Mallom family were heard in the Court of Chancery during this period. In 1675, property Mallom acquired from Henry Reve and Henry Ossant, in Wacton, was involved.[5] (It was from Henry Reve, that Mallom had purchased the Wacton Hall Estate in 1672). In 1686, a property in Moulton was acquired from Samuel Williams and John Grey.[6]

The legal ramifications following the early death of William Copping and the Administration of his assets which went to his mother, Susan Copping and her son, George, rather than his widow, Elizabeth Stone-Copping, came to a head in 1677, although discussions must have taken place between the parties from the time of Copping's death more than 9 years previously in 1666. During this period, as we have seen, other properties and estates were bought and sold, and Copping's widow, Elizabeth, married John Mallom of Bedingham and later of Wacton Hall. Now, in 1677, a case was lodged with the Court of Chancery, addressed to the Lord Chancellor, Heneage Finch, Baron of Daventry, dated 17 April 1676, the details of which are worth summarising since they raise some interesting legal concepts with respect to marriage covenants.[7] The complaint by John Mallom and his wife, Elizabeth, centred on the evidence that she had been given a gift of copyhold lands valued at £120 per annum, by Sir Robert Jermy, knight, and an even more generous gift by her father, Thomas Stone of Bedingham, worth £880. These gifts were to be her "Portion" (dowry). For his part, William Copping agreed to sell lands valued at £120 per annum as part of a Jointure, a device usually involving land or other income settled on a wife at her marriage, normally by her father, and held by the survivor should one of the couple die. However, when William Copping died in 1666, the assets were transferred to his mother, Susan Copping and her son, together with a John Blanks, a kinsman, who lived with Mrs Copping, and who was transacting her affairs on her behalf, "she being an ancient person". Not surprisingly, John and Elizabeth Mallom believed they were being badly treated, hoping that her dowry would fall to her and not to her in-laws. The challenge for the couple was that the complaint included the statement that the Jointure upon Elizabeth was entered into as a "Reversion." That is to say, a legal device whereby if "A" transferred estate or property to "B," then "A" retained some rights into the future. Thus, "B" had the use of the estate for the rest of his/her life. But if "B" should die, then the estate reverted to "A" and to his/her heirs, and not to "B's" heirs. Under this arrangement, although Elizabeth had been given a generous dowry, when her first husband, William Copping, died, the assets reverted to his family, and not to hers. During the nine years in which the claim and counterclaim ran, the parties failed to reach an agreement which satisfied them both, and the appeal to the High Court followed:

> ... your Orator and Oratrix in all the said premises be releeved according to right equity & conscience by the decree of this honourable Co[ur]t. May it please your good Lordshipp ... to grant unto your Orators his Ma[jes]ties high co[ur]t of chancery at a certain day & a certain paine therein ... & abide by such decreed order or direction as your Lordshipp shall seeme Agreeable ... And your Orator and Oratrix shall pray etc.

In their defence, Susan Copping, her son, George, and John Blanks, agreed that the gift to Elizabeth from Sir Robert Jermy of the mortgage and copyhold lands, and the money given by Thomas Stone, Elizabeth's father, she brought with her to the marriage, was worth £1000 (£120 + £880, worth more than £100,000 today). In the meantime, William Copping had sold a farm with two grovetts called Partridge Grove and Townshend Grove (which we have come across previously), valued in total at £120 per annum. This was clearly meant to off-set the value of Elizabeth's mortgage from Sir Robert Jermy. Blanks denied all the charges against him on behalf of the Coppings, stating that George Copping was the lawful heir of the estate under dispute. They insisted the claim be dismissed with costs being awarded to them. In the last few lines of the defendants' statement, the following phrase was included: "as of the Complaynant John Mallom these defendants understood was about [to] purchase of Mano[rs] & lands of considerable value and might have occasion for monies & was willing and desirous to raise some parte thereof from his then p[re]sent occasions by Sale of his sayd wives Jointure".

The Court subsequently issued a writ addressed to four lawyers, Richard Ireland, Andrew Brereton, William Chettleburgh and Henry Stone, ordering them to examine the defendants as to their response to the complaints and to send a written report to the Chancery by the Octave of Trinity* next. The document was dated 13 March in the 28th regnal year of King Charles II, which is 13 March 1677. (Abbreviated translation of the Latin original). It follows that the parties had 3 months to complete the report for the Court. Unfortunately, despite extensive searches, no evidence of a published judgement of this case has been found, and so how the matters were eventually settled, remains unknown.[8] It seems likely, however, that the inclusion in the written submissions to the court of the words "Jointure" and "Reversion" would mean that John and Elizabeth Mallom were

---

* The Octave of Trinity was a period of 8 days inclusive which ended on 13 June each year.

almost certainly going to be disappointed by the judgement.

John Mallom buys Wacton Hall

It is clear from what occurred before the case came to Court, that the Manor under consideration by John Mallom was Wacton Hall, an imposing Tudor longhouse surrounded by a moat which indicates the presence of a much earlier settlement believed to date from the 13th century, with stables, outhouses, barns, and a farm with 200 acres of fine arable meadow and pasture land, where he and his family would live from 1672 onwards.[9] Today, after extensive renovations, it is a fine Grade II listed building, described by Historic England as follows:

> long range mostly rendered timber frame. Brick faced north end. Two storeys and attic. Three storey gabled porch near centre with octagonal angled shafts with finials, round door archway with cornice over and semi-octagonal shafts above, original door and heavy moulded doorcase. Three widely spaced windows to left of porch and two to right of porch. 18th/19th century, 3 and 4 light casements with later dripmoulds. 18th century pilastered doorcase on right with entablature and semi-circular fanlight. Brick chimney stack on north end with 3 octagonal flues with moulded bases. External brick chimney stack at rear (west) with 2 octagonal flues.[10]

It may have been less grand and ostentatious than some other great houses of Norfolk, such as Kimberley Hall, home of Mallom's relative Armine Wodehouse, the Grade I listed, Neo-Palladian Houghton Hall, commissioned by Sir Robert Walpole, or the Jacobean Blickling Hall, with its 5000 acres of land, home of the Boleyn family. Nevertheless, John Mallom's new home, and his enviable social status represented a considerable achievement for his family, and no doubt he hoped his successors would add to it. Inevitably, he was keen to maximise the value of his assets so that he would be in a position to purchase the Manor of Wacton Hall, and develop it. Irrespective of the outcome of the case which concerned Elizabeth's dowry, Mallom had built up a considerable estate in his own right, having acquired much of this from his forebears, bearing in mind that his marriage with a wealthy widow who had a rich father and sponsor would contribute a great deal to his own financial security, if only he could convince the High Court to rule in his favour. However, the dates involved show that Mallom purchased the Wacton Hall estate several years before the case against the Coppings came to court, and so his ambition was not frustrated by the slow legal progress. Wacton Hall had previously been owned (but probably never occupied) by Henry Reve, of Brackendale, who had inherited it from his father, Augustine Reve (d. 1665).[11] He in turn had been left the estate by his brother, Sir Edmund Reve, Justice of the Common Pleas, who died without issue in 1647.[12] It is worth noting that Augustine Reve paid 18s Hearth Tax in Wacton in 1664, which, at a cost of 1s per hearth, payable 6-monthly, makes it appear that Wacton Hall was an extremely well-appointed property.[13] However, a detailed reconstruction of the house as it was in the period 1640–1660, allows for only 8 hearths, the remainder assumed to have been in outbuildings long-since demolished.[14] Wacton Hall was, nonetheless, a property much to be envied, which is why John Mallom was so keen to acquire it.

Coat of Arms of John Mallom of Wacton, 1685

Since 1672, John Mallom and his family had been living in the comfortable surroundings of Wacton Hall. He had married well, had become prosperous and well-established in the area a few miles south of Norwich. He was accustomed to being invited to social gatherings with his wealthy, extended family by marriage, who formed part of the gentility of this part of Norfolk, and who all had their own Coats of Arms. We can imagine that this was a point of discussion between the parties, and with this in mind, John Mallom began to believe that he had fulfilled the requirements of having his own Coat of Arms. After the necessary arrangements, on 4th May 1685 he was duly awarded a grant of Arms. The procedure required that John Mallom apply, in person, for Arms, using the following form of address to the Earl Marshal of England, through the College of Arms in London:

> That your Petitioner being desirous to have a Coat of Arms and Crest granted and assigned unto him as a Badge of Gentility and being (as he humbly hopes) fitly qualified for the same, as by the Certificate annexed is testified on his behalf, doth humbly pray your Grace to signify your consent to such of the Kings of Arms as to your Grace shall seem meet for their granting and assigning such Arms and Crest to your Pet[itione]r as he and his Descendants may lawfully bear.

An attached Certificate was supplied by two friends of his to attest to his eligibility. The full transcript of the Certificate, addressed to the Earl Marshal of England, was as follows:

> Wee Richard Marriot of the Inner Temple, London, and John Anguish of Great Melton in Com. Norf. Esqr. Do hereby humbly Certify your Grace that John Mallom of Woulton alias Walter-Acton in the County of Norfolk is a Person of good Reputation, Loyalty and Affection to the Government as now established by Law, and of a competent Estate to support the condition of a Gentleman, and whome we humbly conceive every way qualified and fit (yor. Grace being so pleased) to be admitted into the Rank of Gentility, and to have a Coat of Arms and Crest granted and assigned unto him as a Badge thereof, according to the tenure of his Petition hereunto annexed. In Witness whereof we have hereunto set our hands this 29th day of Aprill 1685.

The Earl Marshal duly issued a warrant to Garter and Clarenceux Kings of Arms on 1 May 1685 authorising them to grant arms to John Mallom. This they did on 4 May 1685; the Coat of Arms being blazoned as follows:

ARMS	Argent three Cheveronells braced in the Base of the Escocheon Gules on a Cheife of the Second a Lion passant between two Mullets of the first.
CREST	On a Wreath Argent and Gules A right Arme erected habited Vert the Cuffe turned up Ermine the hand proper holding a Lure feathered Argent garnished Gold String and Tassell Gules.

The arms and crest were "to be borne and used for ever hereafter by him the said John Mallom and the heirs and Descendants of his Body lawfully begotten."

A lure is an item used in the training of falcons and other hunting birds. Captain John and Richard Mallom, the grantee's great-grandsons would have been entitled to the arms.[15] The Earl Marshal at the time was Charles Howard, 10th Duke of Norfolk (1720–1786).

John Mallom was by now extremely well-connected by marriage, and he was now well-respected in his community thanks to his Coat of Arms and his new home. In the memorable words of Simon Schama describing Thomas Becket, Archbishop of Canterbury, although Mallom was obviously not in the same league "He was street smart and book smart. He was from the get-go, a Player."[16]

Extensive searches were made for an illustration in colour of the Arms and Crest of John Mallom. The College of Arms holds an uncoloured line drawing, but their rules prevent this from being reproduced.[17] A number of other Archives and Libraries were also approached, but without success.[18] Carvings showing the Arms have been noted on the marble burial slabs of John Mallom and his wife on the floor of the chancel in Wacton Church, Norfolk, where the family arms are impaling Mann, his mother's maiden name, and in Sculthorpe Church, where the memorial to Revd. Thomas Donne, Rector of the Parish, has the arms of Donne impaling Mallom. These representations of the Mallom family arms are carved in marble and show none of the vivid colours described in the Blazon of Arms of 1685.[19] In the absence of an illustration, The Heraldry Society recommended the Heraldic Artist, David Hopkinson, who created from the details supplied by the College of Arms, a painting of the Arms and Crest of John Mallom, using 'gouache' an opaque water-colour paint to give the dense matte finish ideal for the purpose (Fig. 09).[20]

The Arms of the Family of Mallom, of Wacton Hall, Wacton in the County of Norfolk

Fig. 09. *Arms granted to John Mallom Esq. of Wacton Hall in 1685.*

Before their move to Wacton Hall, John and Elizabeth Mallom had lived in Bedingham which is about 10 miles due east of Wacton, and where their first three children, John, Catherine and Elizabeth were baptised between 1671 and 1673. Their daughters, Mary, and Audrey whose name was entered in the Parish Register in the Latin form, as Etheldreda, were both baptised in Wacton, in 1675 and 1678, respectively, after the family moved to Wacton Hall. As a matter of interest, the four-generation Mallom pedigree at the College of Arms, includes the ages of the five children of John and Elizabeth at the time the grant of arms was awarded in May 1685, translated from the original Latin, as follows: John, son and heir aged 14 years in the year 1685; Catherine, aged 12 years in 1685; Elizabeth, aged 11 years in 1685; Mary, aged 9 years in 1685 and Etheldreda, aged 6 years in 1685.[21] These ages all correspond to those calculated from the baptismal entries, except in the case of Catherine, who is quoted as being 12 years old in May 1685, whereas the baptismal record shows she was actually baptised at the end of the year in which her brother, John, was baptised, namely, 1671, shown in Pedigree 1, p.

21. The reason for this discrepancy is not obvious, unless it was to make clear that John was unmistakably the oldest child and heir.

Life in Wacton

John Mallom the arms-bearer, his family, and his son, the younger John Mallom, and his family, were prominent members of the local community and the church in Wacton, and they would have expected special privileges believed to be appropriate at the time. On Sunday morning, the local people would trudge along the often-muddy paths through the village in all weathers, and gather in church, whereas John Mallom's family would ride in their carriage from Wacton Hall, down Sallow Lane and Hall Lane, and then turn into Bustards Green, to All Saints Church (Fig. 10). Here, the rich and the poor of the parish sat in the same building, sang the same hymns, and heard the same prayers, readings and sermons, but this is where the similarity ended, for rank and social status was very much in evidence. John Mallom's family would no doubt have been generous benefactors to the church, and they had pews allocated to them on this basis, towards the front of the nave, where they would have been easily visible to the rest of the congregation and the clergy. "People of rank needed to appear in public to maintain their status and influence. If they did not come to occupy the special places kept for them, they would be deemed remote and command less respect and loyalty," as had been the case since the Middle Ages.[22] With the passing years, local gentry families such as the Malloms were commemorated in memorials, as in Wacton and Aslacton, and families into which they married had memorial stones installed in Bedingham and Woodton. Some other churches featured elaborate statues in memory of high-status individuals, instead of memorials to the saints.[23]

John Mallom's wife, Elizabeth, died in September 1684, a few months before the grant of arms was awarded to her husband, and was buried at the entrance to the chancel of Wacton Church, where an inscribed black marble slab marks the site.

Fig. 10. All Saints Church, Wacton.

John Mallom, himself, died three years later, and was buried beneath the same slab on 12 August 1687.[24] (Fig. 11).

Fig. 11. Ledgerstone to Elizabeth (Stone) and John Mallom.

Hic jacet Corpus Elizabethæ
uxoris Johannis Mallom
Generosi, et Filiæ Thomæ
Stone Generosi, et Etheldredæ
uxoris ejus quæ obit duodecimo
die Septembris Anno d[omi]ni 1684.
Etiam predictus Johannes Mallom
obijt Augusto
Anno Dni 1687

That is to say "Here lies the body of Elizabeth wife of John Mallom, Gentleman, and daughter of Thomas Stone, Gentleman, and Etheldredae (Audrey) his wife who died 12 September 1684. And the above-mentioned John Mallom, died August 1687." Sometimes the exact date of death or burial was omitted, as in this example.

Unfortunately for the family, circumstances were such that Elizabeth Mallom did not live to see her husband's coat of arms, and John, himself, did not live very long to enjoy the fruits of his elevation into the gentry class of Norfolk. The family arms were also displayed as "Mallom impales Stone, per pal *erm.* and *gul.* an eagle displayed *az.*"[25]

The year after the death of Elizabeth Mallom, Katherine (Mann) Mallom, her mother-in-law, died, and she too was buried beneath the chancel of Wacton Church. She was the widow of Revd. John Mallom of Booton, who had died in 1662 (Fig. 12).

Fig. 12. Ledgerstone to Katherine (Mann) Mallom.

Hic jacet Corpus Katherine
uxoris Johannis Mallom
Cl[er]ici, et Filiæ Timo
thei Mann Generosi, et Elizabethæ
uxoris ejus quæ obit quinto
die Maij Anno d[omi]ni 1685
Aetatis Suæ 66

That is to say "Here lies the body of Katherine wife of John Mallom, Clerk (Clergyman), and daughter of Timothy Mann, Gentleman, and Elizabeth his wife, who died 5 May 1685. aged 66."

WILL OF JOHN MALLOM, 1686, AND THE CARE OF HIS CHILDREN

John Mallom's will, dated 1 May 1686, listed all the estates he held. Mallom gave to his son, John, and his heirs, all his "Manors, Messuages, Lands, Tenements and appurtenances in Wac[k]ton alias Woulton, Mowlton, Stratton, Taseburgh, Hempnall, Booton, Witchingham and Kerdiston in Repham and any other town within the County of Norfolk", on condition that he made the following payments when he became 21 years old; to his four daughters, Katherine, Elizabeth, Mary and Audrey, whoever was living at the time, £500, equally divided between them. His Executor was to receive all the rents and profits of the estate on behalf of young John during his minority, and ensure that the manors, messauges, lands, tenements and hereditaments (property held by the family which can be inherited) with their appurtenances, houses and edifices, be kept in a good state of repair, pay for his (John's) education at Cambridge and an Inn of Court, and also the education of his daughters. The money accruing from rents and profits during John's minority was to be divided amongst his daughters. All his stock and personal estate was to be sold and the proceeds used to meet the funeral expenses, debts and legacies, and the residue paid to his four daughters between them. When the girls were 21 years of age, they were to receive an equal share of the estate's profits, and if any of them married before they reached 21 years of age, then her share would be paid to her on her marriage or when she was 18 years old, whichever event occurred first. The poor of Wac[k]ton, Moulton, Stratton St Mary, Taseburgh, Booton, and Kerdiston in Repham (Reepham), were all well provided-for. His son, John, was left a gold ring with four stones, formerly belonging to his mother Mallome (Katherine, née Mann), together with all her linen. His wife's linen was to be equally divided between his four daughters when they reached the age of 18 years. Henry Stone of Wotton, near Bedingham, John's brother-in-law, was appointed Executor, for which he was paid £30. Signed by John Mallom and witnessed by John Mann junior, Frances Mann, Thomas Baleston and Roger Roote.[26]

Shortly after John and Elizabeth (Stone-Copping) died, her father, Thomas Stone of Bedingham, prepared his own will, dated 23 March 1688, "being aged and expecting a departure." One of the witnesses was the younger John Mallom from the next generation, born in 1671, who later married Elizabeth Suckling. Thomas Stone survived both his daughter and her husband, and amongst his bequests to his immediate family, were gifts to his Mallom grandchildren, as follows:

> Alsoe I give and bequeath unto every of the Children of my Sonne and Daughter Mallum deceased the Summe of Tenne pounds of lawfull money to be paid unto them att their severall Ages of one and Twenty yeares or their Severall Marriages with the Consent of the Executor of this my will &

the Executor of the will of their late Father.

Thomas Stone, who was born, according to his parents, on Good Friday, 1603, left to:

> William Stone my elder son to cause a sermon to be preached in Bedingham church every Good Friday, paying 15s for it & distributing 15s among the most industrious & well-living poor living in Bedingham … and the surrounding villages.[27]

The five Mallom children of this generation lost their mother in 1684 and their father in 1687, and when he died, John, junior, was 16, Catherine was 15, Elizabeth was 14, Mary was 11, and Audrey was 8 years old. It follows that they were not really in a position to look after themselves without assistance, and it is likely, therefore, that their care became the responsibility of Mallom's Executor, Henry Stone of Wotton, their uncle, until John and Catherine considered themselves mature enough to care for their younger siblings, and even then, they would have benefitted from his support and counsel.

THE SECOND JOHN MALLOM OF WACTON HALL GOES UP TO CAMBRIDGE UNIVERSITY

The family having recently been awarded a grant of arms, his father's 1686 will stipulated that his son and heir, John Mallom, should proceed to Cambridge University and from there to one of the Inns of Court in London, to be trained as a lawyer. In so doing, Mallom clearly appreciated the importance of a high-quality education for his son. The sons of high-status families would be expected to acquire a university education, and it was this as well as ownership of land and property that Mallom hoped would propel his family into the upper echelons of Norfolk society, a distinction which he undoubtedly craved. His baptismal record has not been found, but young John was educated at Wymondham School, Norfolk, under Mr Clarke, and he proceeded to Gonville and Caius College, Cambridge, his father's old college, in 1689, having been admitted as a pensioner, that is a student who paid for his studies, at the age of 18 years, matriculating in the same year.[28] An entry in the Matriculation Book confirmed his membership of the college and an entitlement to study there, as is the case, today. Surety for John Mallom was given by Mr Ellys, a former Bursar, and member of the college, who would have guaranteed the debt to the college.[29] College records show that there were twenty undergraduates in John Mallom's year (Michaelmas 1688–89), fourteen in the previous year (1687–88), and fourteen the following year (1689–90), so these year groups were relatively small in comparison with those of today.[30] Unfortunately, having gained admission to the college, there is no evidence that John Mallom ever graduated, because his name does not appear in the Biographical History of Gonville and Caius College Series (Vol. 1).[31] Without a written record in the Admissions Registers of any of the Inns of Court, it is also clear that he did not have any formal legal training, either, at least, not in London.[32] In the England of today, training for the intellectually demanding career as a barrister is undertaken by graduates, usually from Oxford or Cambridge or other leading Universities. However, until 1762, there was no prescribed educational requirement. In that year, the Inns of Court agreed that non-graduates should take a minimum of five years from their admission before being called to the Bar, whereas graduates need take only three years.[33] It follows that John Mallom could have been admitted to an Inn of Court without a degree, although his absence from all the Admissions Registers, excludes this possibility. It would have been a considerable advantage to the family to have a trained lawyer within its ranks, to deal with, or to assist with, the legal cases which were a regular feature of families with their social status. Buying and selling of property and land required lawyers, and the implementation of the 1715 will of George Bedell, Lord of the Manor of Woodrising, which would involve the family, would exercise legal minds in the High Court of Chancery for many years to come, as will be seen. Had he progressed in this way, John Mallom would have been following in the footsteps of some of his illustrious ancestors, including Sir John Shelton (Lincoln's Inn, 1517), and Philip Wodehouse (Lincoln's Inn, 1580).[34]

The four daughters of John and Elizabeth Mallom, Catherine, Elizabeth, Mary and Audrey, all survived into adult life and so it is reasonable to assume that they received the inheritances due to them when their older brother, John, was 21 years old. John's four sisters are all discussed in more detail in Part 6, because three of them, Elizabeth, Mary and Audrey, were to spend considerable parts of their lives in Sculthorpe, some 40 miles north west of Wacton, where they were all buried inside the church. The significance of this to the hypothesis which follows in Part 6 means that the sisters' stories merit special consideration.

JOHN MALLOM MARRIES ELIZABETH, DAUGHTER OF ROBERT SUCKLING OF WOODTON HALL

Soon after leaving Cambridge University, John Mallom of Wacton Hall married Elizabeth Suckling, daughter of Robert Suckling Esquire and his wife, Sarah, of Woodton, Norfolk, in August 1692 in All Saints Church, Woodton (Fig. 13). Sarah was the daughter of Maurice and Elizabeth Shelton of Wooton Hall, Norfolk, and so Elizabeth's parents both came from extremely prestigious families with very distinguished ancestries which have been the subject of independent research.[35] John de Shelton, born c. 1140, was the first Lord of the Manor, and Sir Ralph Shelton was knighted by Edward III at the Battle of Crecy in 1346.[36] The Suckling family, from which line Sarah was a direct descendent, was also a notable Norfolk gentry family with its documented origins in the medieval period, which featured Thomas Socling of Woodton and Langhall, "admitted to certain estates in 1348."[37] In 1664, Robert Suckling paid tax on 16 hearths in his Woodton mansion, far more than any other local inhabitant.[38] It was replaced in 1694 by 'new' Woodton Hall, demolished during the early Victorian era.[39]

John Mallom was to become the second John Mallom of Wacton Hall, and with his marriage, he was to move into the upper hierarchy of Norfolk society, the

Shelton and the Suckling families both being from this class. Part of the marriage settlement with Elizabeth Suckling was the advowson - the right to recommend an Anglican clergyman to a vacant benefice of Stratton St Mary - less than 2 miles north east of Wacton. It was believed that two of the five bells in the church steeple were owned by the village of Wacton where the benefice was held together with Stratton St Mary. That is, "until one John Mallom of Wacton Magna, in the reign of George the Second, sold the patronage of Stratton to Gonville and Caius College." He and his son John sold it to the college in 1725 for £600, with associated legal expenses amounting to £39 7s 4d.[40] Using the methodology applied for the value of the earlier inheritances, converts the £600 to approximately £85,000 today,[41] or more than this using another published conversion factor.[42] It follows that the sale of the advowson raised a relatively large sum of money which greatly increased the value of the Mallom estates.

John and Elizabeth (Suckling) Mallom had eight children, as shown in Pedigree 1, p. 21, and the details of their baptisms are as follows:

Their first child was a son, Robert, baptised on 6 July 1693 in Woodton the year after his parents were married, but buried later in 1697 in Wacton, where the family had moved after the death of young Robert's paternal grandparents in 1684 and 1687. Their second son, John, was baptised on 4 October 1695, and buried in Wacton 2 days later. Their third child was a daughter, Elizabeth, baptised in Wacton on 3 June 1697. The fourth child born in Wacton, was Sarah, baptised on 6 December 1698. The fifth child was another son, baptised John, in Wacton, on 17 February 1700, and this boy grew up to become the third John Mallom

Fig. 13. *All Saints' Church, Woodton, where John Mallom and Elizabeth Suckling were married in August 1692.*

of Wacton Hall the father of our subject Captain John Mallom. The sixth child was another son, baptised Robert, in Wacton, on 8 February 1703, his namesake having died young in 1697. The seventh child was a daughter, baptised Anna, in Wacton, on 30 July 1705. In addition, an eighth child was born to John and

Elizabeth (Suckling) Mallom, their fourth daughter, whose baptism has not been found. We know of her subsequent marriage and burial, but there is an interesting lack of clarity about her baptismal name, discussed below. Something of the later lives of the surviving children has been researched, but since the date of baptism of the fourth daughter, described as the eighth child, remains unknown, her details are included last in what follows.

Elizabeth married Thomas Ekins on 3 February 1731. No parish record of this has been found, but the event was documented in a case presented to the High Court of Chancery, on 20 January 1732, in which her brother, John Mallom, brought an action against Elizabeth and her husband, and Robert Suckling of Woodton, gent, his maternal grandfather, and Robert Bransby of Hapton, surgeon, concerning the legacy and portion (dowry) due to Elizabeth, and how this was managed. Mallom gave annuities to his three sisters, Elizabeth, Sarah and Anne, and he also gave Elizabeth £500. Promissory Notes for £60 were written to the three girls by John Amyas, attorney. In April 1732, Mallom paid Elizabeth a further £400 of her legacy, requesting the return of the Promissory Note. Ekins and Elizabeth were accused of "confederating" (conspiring together for an illicit purpose) with Thomas Donn[e], Daniel Sayer, Robert Suckling, Robert Bransby and others, in claiming that the deceased did not make and publish a will, that he was "non compos mentis" and that he died intestate. Mallom asked for a Writ of Subpoena against the defendants, most of whom were his close relatives, to appear in the Chancery Court to answer the charges.

In their answer, Ekins and his wife, Elizabeth, stated the Testator did die intestate, without making any bequests. She was entitled to the £60, but "purely in Affection to him the Complainant, and for the sake of ffamily Love and Union, Consented to Accept so small a sum for Her portion thereof." Amongst other details, Elizabeth agreed that she received £500 of her legacy of £900, and that in April 1731, her brother, with James Jermy[n], lawyer, came to their house in the Parish of St Andrew, Norwich, when Ekins was away, and where he paid her £400, the residue of her legacy. Ekins returned home to hear Mallom insist that the Debt and Demand papers be released. When this was refused, the Complainant "threw himself into a Violent Passion," and demanded the return of the £500 he had given to Elizabeth. Ekins stated that he had brought two Cases to the Court of Common Pleas, including one of them to sue Mallom for £60, and at the Assize Court in Norfolk, he had obtained a verdict in his favour. The defendants denied all the charges against them and asked the Court of Chancery to dismiss the case against them with costs. 9 October 1732. The document was signed by Thomas Ekins and Elizabeth Ekins on 19 October 1732.

In their answer, Suckling and Bransby agreed that the complainant's father, John Mallom Esq., died owning certain estates, which were unknown to them. They believed he was compos mentis when his will was prepared, denying that they had ever claimed the opposite, or that he died intestate. They stated that "they were strangers to" (had no knowledge of), the other matters of which they were charged, knowing nothing of any Articles between Ekins and Elizabeth concerning her fortune. They agreed that on the day of their marriage, an Indenture/Deed was issued on their behalf as Settlement of her inheritance. Robert Suckling held the Deed of Settlement until 22 May 1731, when Ekins and Elizabeth came to his house to ask for it to be destroyed or annulled. Elizabeth found the Deed in Suckling's study, and "burned it in the fire." They denied any "confederacy "towards the Plaintiff, and were ready to prove this in Court. They asked for the case to be dismissed with costs and charges to them. The document was signed by Rbtt Suckling and Robt: Bransby on 10 October 1732.[43]

Attached to the court papers was a paragraph in Latin, summarised in translation as follows: "This document is a writ from the king to various men to take the response of the defendants, following the complaint by John Mallom, and deliver a written record of it to the court."[44] It does not contain any information about the complainant, the defendants, or the case.

Despite extensive searches, no published summaries of the judgements of the Court of Chancery or the Court of Common Plea have been found, and so the outcomes are unknown. However, since Ekins had been successful in the lower court, it might be argued that the Defendants were able to mount a reasoned argument against the allegations. If, as seems likely, most, or perhaps all of Mallom's court cases were found against him, it is not surprising that the family had failed before 1761, because of his financial incompetence.

According to his will, proved in Norwich on 3 March 1742, Thomas Ekins (Elizabeth Mallom's husband) was a surgeon in the City of Norwich, and he left all his messuages, lands and tenements in Shottisham/Shotesham and elsewhere in Norfolk, with all his goods, chattels, and household stuff etc, "to my loving wife Elizabeth," who was the Executrix.[45] Ekins worked as Prison Surgeon at Norfolk County Gaol in Norwich where, between Easter 1733—34, for example, he was paid "for the cure of Mary Shepherdson a poor Prisoner." [46] In Georgian England, a surgeon was partly the forerunner of the modern general practitioner, who had a school education and served an apprenticeship, in contrast to a 'Physician', who would usually have been educated at Oxford or Cambridge University, and invariably claimed a higher status for himself in comparison to the 'Surgeon' or 'Apothecary'.[47] The name of Thomas Ekins, 'Surgeon', appeared in the Parish of St Andrews, Norwich, in the list of those entitled to vote in 1734—35, as a "Freeh[older]," and in the list of Freeholders in Shottisham/Shotesham in the same year.[48] Elizabeth (Mallom) Ekins was buried in November 1757, in the Parish of St George Colegate, Norwich, widow. No baptisms for children of Thomas and Elizabeth have been found, in line with Ekins will of 1742.

The fourth child and second daughter of John and Elizabeth (Suckling) Mallom, was Sarah, and she married Daniel Youngs by License, in St Nicholas' Church, Bracon Ash, approximately 7 miles north of Wacton, in January 1732. The Marriage License Bond recorded that Daniel was then living in the Parish of St Peter Hungate, Norwich, and in the Parish Register of Bracon Ash the details were entered as Mr Daniel Youngs and Mrs Sarah Marlum.[49] In other words, the groom and the bride were considered a high-status couple. In this context, the title Mrs implies a woman of status, and not that she was a married woman or a widow. A similar entry was found when Mrs Elizabeth Mallom was buried in Sculthorpe in 1723, when she was known to be a spinster. The church in Bracon Ash featured again a few years later, when Anne and Elizabeth, daughters of Revd. Thomas and Anne (Mallom) Kemp were baptised there in 1742 and 1744, respectively. The life events of members of the Mallom family often took place in villages which were quite close to each other. A Daniel Youngs was made a Freeman of the City of Norwich in June 1730, qualifying by serving an apprenticeship as a mercer to the Freeman, John Croshold Esq. a Sheriff of Norwich.[50] Given the social status of Daniel and Sarah Youngs, this is likely to be the same man, recognised and honoured by his home city.[51] His Master, had been not only Sheriff of Norwich, but also Mayor in 1724, and so Daniel Youngs, the son-in-law of John and Elizabeth (Suckling) Mallom was associated with influential company.[52] Sarah Youngs was buried in November 1745 in St Peter Hungate, Norwich, the parish where her husband was living at the time of their marriage. No evidence of children born to this couple has been found, but a few years after Wacton Hall was sold by John Mallom in 1760, it was occupied by a man named John Youngs, from 1767 to 1769, and after him, by his son, William, until 1776.[53] Despite the interval of time, the identical surnames of Youngs in families connected with Wacton Hall, is probably not a coincidence. It is also worth noting that Mr Youngs was the name of the Swaffham attorney with whom Robert Mallom had worked after completing his training to be an articled clerk.

Robert, brother of John Mallom of Wacton Hall

Robert was the fourth and last son to be born to his parents, in 1703, ten years after his namesake who had died in early childhood. The parents' wish to have a son named in memory of his maternal grandfather, Robert Suckling of Woodton, is a likely explanation for his baptismal name, and it was this Robert Mallom who became the subject of numerous legal challenges relating to an inheritance specified in the will of George Bedall Esq. Lord of the Manor of Woodrising in 1715.

Valuable biographical information has survived for Robert the younger brother of John Mallom, the heir to Wacton Hall and the family estates, through the legal entanglements which followed. Robert was to be the uncle of our subject, John Mallom, the Army Officer. The information was included in a case submitted to court in May 1743, in an attempt to resolve the dispute between the two brothers, Robert and John Mallom, concerning the Annuity left to Robert by George Bedell, and some of the details are worth recording.⁵⁴ In his "Bill of Complaint" as the Plaintiff, John Mallom stated that when their father died in 1728, his younger brother, Robert, was at boarding school with Mr Brett in Wymondham. He was there for about a year and then went to school in Norwich with Mr Wingfield, to learn to write so that he could train to be a [legal] clerk to Mr Sayer, an attorney in Harlestone, Norfolk, with whom he boarded. According to John Mallom, his brother, Robert, contracted smallpox, and he, John, paid for his medical and nursing care. Robert went to Norwich to convalesce, and later moved to Swaffham to become an articled clerk to Mr Youngs, a Swaffham attorney, "for several years." In his 'Answer' as the defendant, Robert Mallom acknowledged his schooling with Mr Brett, but reported that this did not continue after his father's death in 1728. Instead, Robert stated that he returned to the family home of Wacton Hall for a short time, and then went to stay with his sister Elizabeth Mallom. After this, he was sent to board with Mr Smears, and then he went to school with Mr Greenville, and not Mr Wingfield, as his brother, John alleged:

> to learn to write, in order to qualify him to be a Clerk to an Attorney, where he stayed for about a year and a half.

Robert agreed he had smallpox when he was with Mr Sayer, and that after he recovered, he went to Norwich:

> for some short time until he was quite recovered of the Smallpox, to the house of one Mr King.

From Norwich, he went to Mr Wychingham an attorney at Yoxford in Suffolk, to whom he was bound for 5 years by his sister Elizabeth Mallom. From Mr Wychingham, Robert returned to Norwich and:

> was by his sister Anne Mallom placed out to the said Mr Youngs … with whom [he] lived for the residue of the term he had to serve when he came from the said Mr Wychingham which was about three years.

Robert Mallom thereby qualified to be a legal clerk to an attorney, and in 1742, he married Mary Dusgate in Swaffham, when the Marriage Licence Bond stated that he was an "Attorney in Wacton". In 1743, Robert travelled the 20 miles to Norwich, to sign a document making a claim for payment from his brother, John, of part of an Annuity owed to him under the terms of the will of George Bedell Esq., as related below. Robert and Mary (Dusgate) Mallom set up home in Swaffham, where he worked as an attorney, and where their children were born and raised. Having successfully completed quite an arduous and prolonged period of training, it is perhaps unfortunate that Robert Mallom was not the son selected by his father to go to Cambridge instead of his older brother, John. Given his subsequent career, the evidence suggests that Robert would have completed a course of studies and graduated, and then gone on to train at one of the Inns of Court in London, something which his brother John had conspicuously failed to do. However, this was a period when the older son in a gentry family was invariably given all the opportunities, irrespective of ability or motivation.

THE THIRD JOHN MALLOM OF WACTON HALL GOES UP TO CAMBRIDGE UNIVERSITY

John went up to Corpus Christi College, Cambridge, in November 1719 in fulfilment of his father's wishes as recorded in his will, a few weeks after it was written on 9 August 1719. His father stated that he wanted his son to continue at Cambridge until he was 24 years old.[55] John's Tutor during his first year of studies was Mr [Thomas] Herring, Fellow of Corpus Christi College from 1716 to 1723, where he taught classics. Before the modern era, undergraduates at England's two universities, Oxford and Cambridge, were expected

> ...to read a little mathematics, mainly Euclid, a little classics, and a little religion.[56]

Herring was at the beginning of what was to become a distinguished career in the Church of England. He was ordained deacon in Ely Cathedral in 1716, and priest in 1719, and he graduated Doctor of Divinity in 1728. After parish duties in Cambridgeshire, Essex and Hertfordshire, he was appointed Chaplain to King George II, and later, Bishop of Bangor. He became Archbishop of York in 1743, and in 1747, he was consecrated Archbishop of Canterbury where he continued until his death in 1757. Unfortunately, the illustrious tutor was unable to assist his young student towards success in his studies, and John failed to progress, leaving the University before February 1722 without graduating, evidently because of lack of academic ability.[57] The entry concerning him was included in the College Chapter Book for 1709–1752, as follows:

> Whereas Mallom admitted formerly by proxy, upon examination was found by the College Officers unfit for admission, it was agreed that he be allowed to continue in the College upon condition that upon examination by the college officers this time twelve month he be found fit, otherwise to be sent out of the College.

In February 1722, his Caution Money (deposit) was returned, indicating that he had left the College.[58] There were only seven undergraduates in Mallom's year, so this was a very small group, and in addition to John Mallom, another of his class-mates, Charles Clarke, also left the University without a degree, so this was a very high rate of failure. It also suggests that Thomas Herring's work load was not particularly arduous, at least as far as his duties as tutor to first year undergraduates was concerned. John Mallom thus followed the disappointing example set by his father, although at a different Cambridge College, neither of them succeeding in completing their courses of studies, and both leaving University without graduating. Today, there would have been a sense of disappointment and concern in the family of a young student who returned home from university without the coveted degree, but John's father would have had to temper his response in the light of his own lack of success at Cambridge, although he would have hoped that his son would have made the grade which he had not achieved. However, there is another, rather more nuanced way of looking at this situation. It has been suggested that when both John Mallom and his father went up to Cambridge, completing a course of studies and graduating was not essential to advancing their status in society. Simply having spent a year or two at Cambridge to acquire the attitudes, airs and graces, and a circle of friends thought likely to be useful to them in later life, was considered valuable in itself.

> Plenty of time was left for other pursuits, frequently involving dogs, horses, and foxes. University was looked upon as a gentlemanly way of passing from schoolboy to adult… If one were not to be an independently wealthy landowner, one would most likely be destined for a profession such as law or medicine or for the clergy. Obviously, these demanded postgraduate training after university, for neither in practice nor in theory was English higher education expected to teach one anything that could be put to practical use. [59]

In other words, the arrangement functioned rather like a finishing school for young men. At Oxford University, similarly:

> the reluctance to graduate was scarcely surprising when only entrants to the church needed a degree, and a significant percentage of the intake gentleman's sons, for whom Oxford was a finishing school were.

And the same state of affairs was present at the Inns of Court, where:

> A significant proportion of the [Inns'] membership until the mid-nineteenth century had no intention of being called to the bar. [60]

It is worth bearing in mind, that the last of these young men called John Mallom of Wacton Hall, the father of our subject, developed an interest in horse-racing in later life, an interest which he inherited from his father, and which may well have continued at Cambridge, when no doubt his mind should have been on other things.

The seventh of the children of John and Elizabeth Mallom was Ann[a], born in July 1705. Ann married Revd. Mr Thomas Kemp, Rector of Flordon, in Newton Flotman in 1739, three years after her younger brother, Robert, had stayed with her. Thomas Kemp was the son of Sir Robert Kemp, 3rd Baronet of Ubbeston, Suffolk, formerly of Gissing, Norfolk, who left Thomas a total of £2,000 in his will of 1734. Ann predeceased her husband by 13 years, dying in 1748, and was buried at Gissing. Thomas and his daughter, Mary, by a second wife, were buried in the Kemp family vault in Gissing Church in 1761 and 1784, respectively.[61] Through his marriage with Ann Mallom, Revd. Thomas Kemp became the brother-in-law of John and Robert, and so Sir Robert Kemp, Baronet, was their uncle, although how this relationship was acknowledged within the aristocratic circles in which the Kemp family moved, or at family gatherings, is unknown. It follows that Thomas and Ann (Mallom) Kemp were the uncle and aunt of Captain John Mallom and his brother, Richard.

The Mallom's daughter named Mary, married Merchant Berry in January 1736, in Bedingham, although her baptism has not been found. Bedingham was the village where the girl's grandparents, John and Elizabeth (Stone-Copping) had lived and where her father was born in 1671. There was some apparent confusion in the mind of the Vicar of Bedingham, Revd. Joseph Parsons, who made the entries in both the Bedingham Parish Register and the Archdeacon's Transcript, because the bride's name was entered as 'Mary' in the Parish Register, but as 'Eliz[abeth]' in the Transcript. Mary, wife of Merch[an]t Berry was buried in Hempnall in January 1758, where, incidentally, Revd. Joseph Parsons was also the vicar. The handwriting of the entries in Bedingham and Hempnall is identical, and we know that Joseph Parsons was the vicar of both parishes from 1725–1774.[62] There is no burial for an Elizabeth Berry, and no children have been found for Merchant with Mary or Elizabeth Berry. However, the matter is further complicated by the fact that Merchant Berry was married twice, his first wife being Mary Pope, whom he married in Hempnall in October 1717. The Hempnall Register includes a burial for Mary Berry in January 1729, "an aged woman," but in the absence of any other contenders, we can be confident that this was Merchant Berry's first wife. His second marriage in January 1736 was with Mary Mallom, by Banns. When Merchant Berry died, the burial entry in September 1766 recorded that he was 96 years old, and the term "widower" was included. Had he been even approximately this age, a birth year in about 1670 would have meant that he was middle aged (aged 47) when he married Mary Pope, and older still (aged 66) when he married Mary (or Elizabeth) Mallom. It is not surprising therefore, that no children have been found for Merchant Berry with either wife. It is difficult to believe that the baptism of a daughter of a high-status family would have been omitted from the Baptism Register, but Mr Parsons' lack of precision when recording her name when she was married, might mean that he simply forgot to make the entry. Taking everything into account, it is likely that she was the daughter of John and Elizabeth (Suckling) Mallom. Exactly when she was born and baptised will probably never be known, although her subsequent marriage and burial means that she should be included in the discussion. In other words, a missing baptismal entry clearly does not mean she never lived. Later searches unearthed the marriage by Banns between William Buck and Susanna Mallom in Bedingham, in 1742, both single and of the parish. They baptised 8 children between 1743–1762 in nearby Hempnall, implying that Susanna was born no earlier than 1715–1720. The identity of her parents is unknown because no baptismal record has been found, but is it possible that she was the youngest daughter of John and Elizabeth (Suckling) Mallom? Could the lack of Susanna's baptismal entry be another of Revd. Joseph Parsons' omissions when he was Vicar of Bedingham, as appears to have been the case for Mary Mallom? A teenage affair involving John or Robert Mallom of Wacton is considered very unlikely indeed, and the most plausible explanation is that Susanna and Mary were both daughters of John and Elizabeth (Suckling) Mallom. The exact sequence in their births and baptisms relative to their siblings is unclear, and so their names have been included in the broken line in Pedigree 1, p. 21.

The surviving brother and the three sisters of the John Mallom who was baptised in February 1700, were the uncle and the aunts of Captain John and his brother, Richard Mallom, as shown in Pedigree 1, p. 21. Elizabeth's father, Robert Suckling of Woodton, was fortunate to live to see all his daughter's children born and baptised, including the youngest child, Anna, but soon after this, he prepared his will, dated 29 September 1707, proved in Norwich in April 1709.[63] His extensive estate and wealth was distributed amongst his surviving nine children, and included £1,000 left to his daughter, Sarah, "for her portion;" in effect, the dowry for her marriage. However, in contrast to the Mallom fathers-in-law, Robert Suckling made no bequests to his married daughters, namely Elizabeth (Suckling) Mallom, who was his first child, or Anna (Suckling) Berney.[64] In this deliberate omission, he must have taken the view, that despite his wealth, he regarded the care of his married daughters as the responsibility of their husbands, rather than his.

As if his family responsibilities, the bringing-up and education of his children, and the management of his estates, together with the associated legal challenges were not enough to fill his life, the Lord of the Manor of Wacton had other civic duties to perform. John Mallom's name appears in the Voting Registers for Norfolk, the 1714 Poll. This was for the election of two Knights of the Shire for the County of Norfolk, who were, in effect, MPs for Norfolk.[65] The Election took place on 18 February 1715, at Norwich, and was supervised by the High Sheriff. Elections at this time were very different from those which followed the introduction of universal suffrage, and very few individuals were able to cast their vote. County Freeholders, such as John Mallom Esq. of Wacton, was one of four Freeholders in the parish who were eligible to vote, and it is clear from the record, that Mallom duly discharged his duties, and voted for one of the four candidates who stood for election, Thomas de Grey, who received 3183 votes.[66] The other three candidates were Sir Ralph Hare (2840 votes), Erasmus Earle Esq. (2635 votes), and Sir Jacob Astley (3059 votes). Astley and de Grey were elected, both with convincing majorities.[67]

WILL OF JOHN MALLOM OF WACTON HALL, 1719, GOES TO PROBATE, 1728

Having watched his six surviving children grow up to become teenagers in Wacton, John Mallom prepared his will, on 9 August 1719, and the following is a summary: after revoking all his previous wills, he charged his Executors and administrators to take the rents, issues and profits of all his Messuages, Lands, Tenements and Hereditaments, except those in Jointure to Elizabeth his wife (property given to

Elizabeth on their marriage for her use after his death), until his eldest son John Mallom (then aged 19 years), attained the age of maturity of 24 years. This, on condition that his daughters, Elizabeth, Sarah and Ann Mallom, were maintained, educated and brought-up, well. When John reached his maturity, he and his heirs would inherit all the family estate, on condition that he pay Elizabeth, his daughter £30 annually, free of tax, during the lifetime of his mother, Elizabeth (the testator's widow), and these payments were to be made quarterly. Daughter, Sara[h], was given £25 annually every year during the lifetime of his wife, Elizabeth, from the date of John's 24th birthday. A similar arrangement was stipulated for Ann[a], in the sum of £12 annually. Within one month after Elizabeth's death, son John was instructed to pay daughter Elizabeth, £600, to Sarah, £500, and to Ann[a], £200. Mallom wished his son, John, to:

> be kept at Cambridge till he shall attain his said age of four and twenty years.

He appointed his Brother [in-law], Thomas Dun (Donne), Clerk, the Rector of Sculthorpe and husband of Mallom's sister, Audrey, and Daniel Sayer of Pulham, gent, as his Executors, to whom he gave £10 each "for their Care and pains." Signed and sealed 9 August 1719, by John Mallom. Witnessed by William Cole, William Blome and Margrat Blome.

On the same day, a codicil was annexed to the will in the same hand: in addition to the gifts to his daughters noted in the will, Mallom gave his daughter Elizabeth, an additional £300, daughter Sarah, an additional £200, and his daughter, Ann[a], an additional £400, these legacies to be paid within one month of the death of his wife, Elizabeth, by his son, John, his heirs or assigns. In addition, an annual sum of £20 free of tax, was to be given, paid half-yearly to Robert Mallom, his (the testator's) son:

> until he shall be in possession of some part of the rents and profits of the real Estate devised (left) to him in and by the last Will and testament of George Bedell Esquire, deceased.

Signed, sealed published and delivered and annexed to the will, on 15 October 1724.

Witnessed by John Sayer, Offley Smith and John Hammant. Proved at Wacton 31 July 1728. Thomas Donne, clerk, and Daniel Sayer, who was sworn at Harleston, 1 August 1728.[68] Sayer, was the name of one of the attorneys with whom Robert Mallom trained, in Harlestone, and the name of Daniel Sayer appeared in the Court of Chancery Case as one of the Defendants, brought by John Mallom against his sister, Elizabeth, and her husband, Thomas Ekins, in 1731.

John Mallom appears in the Letters of John Buxton, Norfolk Gentleman and Architect 1719–1729

John Buxton, a landowner in south Norfolk at Channonz Hall, Tibenham,[69] wrote a series of letters to his son, Robert, while the boy was at school and at Cambridge University, which shed a fascinating light on the life of a country gentleman who was in a similar social class to that of John Mallom.[70] The letters, "from an educated sensitive man reveal a picture of rural landownership far from that of the stereotypical crude, ill-mannered, sporting squire and are an important addition to our knowledge of early eighteenth-century society." [71] They follow in the tradition of the Paston Letters, written between 1422–1509 and which are a rich source of information about the life of a family of gentry folk in Norfolk during the Wars of the Roses and the early Tudor period.[72] Channonz Hall, Tibenham, is 3 miles south west of Wacton Hall where John Mallom and his family lived, and is the village where Phillis Phillips, Mallom's daughter-in-law was baptised. Buxton's bailiff was Robert Phillips,[73] and in view of the geography, it is quite likely that he was a member of the same Phillips family. Buxton and Mallom were clearly acquainted, and the letters record that they met several times during the 1720s: they were friends. The following are the entries which include reference to John Mallom of Wacton Hall, with the dates the letters were written to Robert Buxton, retaining the original spelling:

10 May 1725:	If Mr Mallom continues his resolution of going this day to the horserace you will receive this letter by his servant which is to thank you for yours received last Friday when you were particularly remembered.
17 May 1725:	We have received two letters from you since I writ. I also heard of you by Mr Mallom and Mr Layman [a surgeon of Diss].
5 June 1726:	Mr Mallom gives himself the trouble of this letter & has promised to send it in due time. The enclosed is from Mr Jermy. I was with him when he wrot it & we both agreed in our opinion that it would not be proper for our children to go to Ipswich horserace.
14 June 1726:	Your letter by Mr Mallom to your mother gave us great satisfaction. I saw his yesterday & never with so much pleasure heard him talk while he gave me so good an account of your health, how well you looked, how cheerful, &c. till he was interrupted by some new incident, & you know how very apt he is to digress.

25 October 1726:	Mrs Mallom has borrowed the poem [?]. I will send it next week.
17 December 1727:	You will receive with this a hare & a pheasant, a brace of partridges & some small foul, which you are obliged to Jack Mallom for, who brought them himself this morning.
18 March 1728:	Your letter of the 14th found us well though the sickness is pretty much in our neibourhood. Mr Mallim's family is at last fallen ill, the two youngest ladies are very much so, as your mother says who saw them yesterday. You may compound for a little cold which I hope be all you will feel now, having already had your share of this general disorder.
7 July 1728:	Your grandmother Buxton went with me in the coach on the election day to Norwich. I got out in Swardeston field to head my party, & to joyn S[i] Edm[un]d Bacon at Harford Bridges, where we were met by Mr Branthwayt, Mr Mallom, Mr Sayer & abundant of other gentlemen & freeholders who came in compliment to Sir Edm[un]d to wait on him into the town, & he entered with upwards of 1200 men.
24 November 1728	I neither hear of nor see my neibour Mallom; his mother is dead & I suppose he taken up with the settling his affairs.[74]

These entries in the letters from father to son, give details about Buxton's neighbour and friend, John Mallom, which are not available elsewhere. They moved in similar social circles, and met from time to time, when Mallom acted as postman to Robert Buxton when he was staying at Mr D'Oyly's house in Playford (Ipswich, Suffolk). Mallom's interest in horseracing was continued by his son, and a certain difficulty concentrating on the matter in hand is noted in the letter of 14 June 1726. The gift of game mentioned in December 1727 implies that John Mallom took part in hunting and shooting, a common pastime amongst country gentlemen.[75] The death of Mallom's mother, in the letter of 24 November 1728, refers to Elizabeth (Suckling) Mallom, who was buried in Wacton Church on 17 November 1728 (Fig. 14). Sir Edmund Bacon (1693–1738) was the Whig MP for Thetford,[76] and in the election which features in the letter of 7 July 1728, Mallom was present at the hustings to show his support, and, arguably more importantly, to be seen. John Buxton died in 1731, three years after the death of his friend, John Mallom, Captain Mallom's grandfather.

BURIAL OF JOHN AND ELIZABETH (SUCKLING) MALLOM, IN WACTON CHURCH, 1728–1729

John Mallom of Wacton Hall, died on 24 July 1728, aged 58 years, and was buried in Wacton Church. His widow, Elizabeth (Suckling) Mallom lived for only a further four months after the death of her husband, and she died, intestate, on 14 November 1728, aged 53 years, and was also buried in Wacton Church, beside him, on 17 November that year. For reasons which are unrecorded, but which may have been due to increasing ill-health requiring the care of a family member or a close friend, Mallom's widow, Elizabeth, moved from Wacton to Hethersett, about 4 miles to the north, presumably not long before her death. Her Administration, on its printed sheet, with handwritten entries of names, place of death and the signatures of the administrator and the witness, was as follows: John Mallom of Wacton Esquire and Christopher Smeare of Norwich, apothecary, were bound in £50. John Mallom, lawful son and administrator of Elizabeth Mallom late of Hethersett, widow deceased, intestate, [was] to exhibit an inventory by 21 May next and render account by 21 November 1729. Signed: John Mallom and Christo[pher] Smear. The witness was Joh[n] Francis.[77]

John and Elizabeth Mallom were both buried beneath the chancel of Wacton Church, as befitted the man who was effectively Lord of the Manor, and his wife. Two black marble slabs (ledgerstones) mark the burial sites, with the chiselled inscriptions beneath the carved family coats of arms:

Fig. 14. Ledgerstones to John Mallom (L), and Elizabeth (Suckling) Mallom (R).

Sub hoc Marmore Corpus
JOHANNIS MALLOM, Armigeri
Jacet.
Qui vicesimo quarto diem Mensis Julij,
Anno Salutis 1728.
Ætatis 58.
Diem clausit Extremum

That is to say, Beneath this marble lies the body of John Mallom Arms-bearer/ Esquire, who died on the 24 day of July in the year of our Lord 1728, aged 58 years (Fig. 14).

The coat of arms shows Mallom impaling Suckling, and "*Mallom's* crest, *viz.* an arm in pale cooped at the shoulder, sleeved proper, holding a cord with a tassel at each end, bent in form of a bow." In other words, a Lure. Next to the memorial to John Mallom, lies the body of his wife, Elizabeth, with the inscription as follows:

>Depositum *ELIZABETHÆ* uxoris
>*JOHANNIS MALLOM* Armigeri
>Filiæque *ROBERTI SUCKLING*
>de *Woodton* Armigeri
>Natu maximæ
>Decimo quarto die mensis
>Novembris Anno Salutis 1728 Obijt
>Ætatis 53

That is to say, "Here lies Elizabeth, wife of John Mallom, daughter of Robert Suckling of Woodton, Arms-bearer/Esquire, his first-born; [who died] 14 day of November in the year of our Lord 1728, aged 53 years."

John Mallom of Wacton Hall marries Phillis Phillips of Aslacton

In whatever way the Mallom family responded to the young man's lack of academic success, sometime after returning to the family home at Wacton Hall, John's fortunes were to change for the better, when he met Phillis Phillips who was living in the neighbouring village of Aslacton. Less than two months after the death of his father, John and Phillis were married in St Michael's Church, Aslacton, on 3 September 1728. John's mother lived just long enough to witness her son's marriage, although she died soon afterwards in November that year. At least his mother knew that her son, who had inherited the Mallom estates, had the potential to make something of his life, and hopefully to follow in the footsteps of his forebears, and build on their success in the county. How disappointed she would have been had she been able to see into the future.

Mallom involvement in the Legal Cases from the Estate of George Bedell Esq

During the next few years, the children of John and Elizabeth Mallom grew up in their privileged circumstances of Wacton Hall, oblivious to the legal drama which was beginning to unfold around them. Aspiring gentry folk such as the Malloms, eager to extend and enlarge their estates, were often involved in legal cases to secure the deals they struck, and the first half of the 18th century was a particularly busy period for them in this respect. Between 1715 and 1743, a series of cases was heard before the High Court of Chancery, contesting aspects of the will of George Bedell, Lord of the Manor of Woodrising, Norfolk, and in which members of the Mallom family were named. John Mallom senior was involved in six cases, Elizabeth, his wife, was named in nine, John Mallom junior, the father of our subject, was named in six cases, and a further 16 involved his younger brother, Robert. The cases challenged the legal basis on which bequests were made by Bedell to the extent that, in 1724, a codicil was added to the will of John Mallom of Wacton, stating that his son Robert's older brother, John, was to pay him and his assigns £20 annually, in half-yearly instalments, until Robert received at least some of the legacy due to him under the terms of George Bedell's 1715 will. This involves so much of the Mallom family, and tells us a lot about them, that it is worth examining closely:

George Bedell died, unmarried and childless in 1715, aged 31 years, leaving a will dated 9 August 1715, which went to probate in London, on 29 August 1715.[78] Bedell bequeathed his estate to John Marsh of Haberdasher's Hall, London, and John Amyas of Hingham, Norfolk, gents, who were appointed his Executors and given £500 each for their duties. Under the terms of the will, Marsh and Amyas were to pay Elizabeth Mallom, £150 annually in four quarterly instalments for the rest of her life, free of tax. The rents and profits of any part of the Bedell estate which remained unsold were to pass to her son, Robert, until he reached the age of twenty-one years, and then to his heirs and assigns, forever. Furthermore, John Mallom was not to "intermeddle" (interfere) with this during Robert's minority. If Robert died before the age of twenty-one, his bequest was to go to Isabella Bedell, Mary Burgess and Elizabeth Bedell "my sisters." The bequests bestowed on Elizabeth Mallom and her son, Robert, were very generous, but the will does not make clear why Elizabeth would receive almost £2,000 before she died in 1728, or why her son, Robert, was so well provided-for. No family connections have been discovered between Bedell, and the Mallom and Suckling families, and nothing in the will suggests that Robert was George Bedell's godson, although this is a possibility. Using the same calculation for Purchasing Power as was applied in the case of Timothy Mallom, above, shows that Elizabeth Mallom's legacy converts to almost £300,000, today.[79]

The report of the final judgement in what was, at the time, the most significant case involving the Wacton family, was entitled "Robert MALLOM on the Demise of John Marsh and John Amyas against John Bringloe and Elizabeth his Wife and Mary Apolonia Burgess." In other words, what would happen to Robert's bequest after Marsh and Amyas died? The jury found that George Bedell inherited the estate on the death of his brother, John, in 1707, when George was 24 years old. To complicate matters, in November 1700, when he was 17, Parliament passed an "Act for the further preventing the growth of popery" [80] which was relevant because George Bedell was a Roman Catholic who did not sign the Act of Settlement designed to secure the Protestant Succession in Great Britain.[81] All the others named in the will were Protestant. The defendants, Elizabeth Bringloe and her husband, occupied the mansion in Woodrising four days before Bedell died, ejecting him, and thereby laid claim to the estate. The court decided that it was lawful for George Bedell to leave his estate to Marsh and Amyas, since he was under age when the Act of Settlement became law. Judgement was awarded to Robert Mallom, the plaintiff, by Lord Chief Justice Raymond at the Norwich Assizes in 1738, that is, twenty-five years after the Bedell's will was written.[82] Blomefield commented that Mrs Bringloe and Mrs Burgess, Bedell's "sisters" were to be his co-heirs.[83] However, it is clear from the will that John Marsh and John Amyas were to inherit the estate, the sisters being given much smaller bequests, worth £25 and £20, respectively. John Marsh, who inherited half of Bedell's estate, was Clerk to the Haberdasher's Livery Company of London from 1708–1729, and Master of Apprentices. John Amyas of Hingham, who also inherited half the Bedell estate, left a will dated in August 1763, the year he was buried in Hingham.[84] He is likely to be the man who featured in George Bedell's will because among his many bequests, Amyas left "£154 to Mr Robert Mallom, who lives with me." His will does not name a wife or children, but his servants and the poor people of Hingham received small bequests. John and Elizabeth (Suckling) Mallom both died in 1728, ten years before the dispute was resolved in their son Robert's favour. It follows that Robert's older brother, John Mallom, must inevitably have borne some of the later legal costs, and as such, he was continuing the business activities of his father, grandfather and great grandfather.

John Mallom, now of Wacton Hall, the father of our subject, was also involved in two cases concerning the purchase and subsequent sale of property in the Parish of St Martin at Oak, Norwich, in 1734.[85] Nineteen years later, on 28 September 1753, this property was sold by John Mallom, to John Crome of Norwich, patten maker.[86] Pattens were under-shoes worn to keep the wearer's free of mud and dirt in the streets.[87] 1754 was the year before John and Phillis Mallom and their two sons moved from Wacton Hall into smaller accommodation, in Aslacton, and the sale of the Norwich property may have been to raise extra income to assist the family in what was becoming a time of significant financial challenges, as we will see. In May 1734, the month after the first property deal in Norwich, John Mallom's name appeared in the Norfolk Voting Register in the Poll for Knights of the Shire for Norfolk, and his was one of the seven names of Resident Freeholders registered for the parish of Wacton that year.[88] Despite the settlement of 1738 in Robert's favour, the legal controversies surrounding George Bedell's will, dragged on.

A few years later, two more cases went to the High Court of Chancery, the first in 1742 and the second in 1743, both involving the two Mallom brothers, alone. These were both "Bill and Answer" cases, in which the "Bill of Complaint" set out the case for the Plaintiff, and the "Answer" was the case for the Defendant. In 1742, Robert was the Plaintiff and John the Defendant, and in 1743, John was the Plaintiff and Robert the Defendant. This sorry state of affairs indicated that a serious dispute had arisen between the two brothers which was not resolved through amicable discussions, and they had to resort to the courts to try and settle the matters at issue between them.

On 12 January 1742, Robert Mallom submitted his Bill of Complaint "To the Right Honourable Philip Lord Hardwicke…Lord Chancellor of Great Britain," alleging that his brother, John, had refused to pay him the £20 Annuity promised in the codicil to his father's 1724 will, pending receipt of income from George Bedell's property, leaving him "unprovided for." He claimed that his brother refused to pay "the same but sometimes pretending one thing and sometimes another…" It was alleged that John had declared that their father did not add a codicil to his will, and that "if he did, he was not of Sound Mind and Memory at the time…" or that the codicil was not properly witnessed, and that he had already paid the Annuity with Interest. In short, Robert claimed that his brother had cheated him, and he asked the Court to adjudicate in his favour.[89]

The Answer by John Mallom came sixteen months later, on 30 May 1743. It was acknowledged that their father made a will and added the codicil on the 15 October 1724, and that a £20 Annuity was due to Robert from John's inheritance, until his brother received some of the income from George Bedell's estate. In his defence, John stated that he had paid for Robert's education for two years following their father's death, so his brother could become a clerk to an attorney. He claimed that he had paid "the Sum of One hundred and ninety-five Pounds and upwards …" but could not recall exactly how much, although this exceeded what he was due under the terms of the codicil. John stated that he had asked his brother to settle the account and to tell him exactly how much money he had received from him. He denied all the charges, was ready to prove his innocence, and he asked for the case to be dismissed with costs and charges.[90]

Two weeks before the 30 May 1743 Answer, John Mallom had submitted a Bill of Complaint to the High Court of Chancery, dated 16 May 1743, in which he acknowledged that Robert was due the £20 Annuity from their late father's codicil. In addition to paying for Robert's maintenance, education, medical and nursing care, John claimed he had paid for his brother's clothes and "other necessarys." At the same time, John was involved with Robert in a Bond of £60 to John Howes, for the capital sum and interest (for what was a £60 loan). He paid £40 costs as part of the claim on the estate of George Bedell, prosecuted by Mr Youngs, allegedly on the direction of Robert Mallom, and these expenses exceeded the £20 Annuity Robert was due. John also claimed that his brother attempted to sell both the Annuity and also his income from the estate of George Bedell, to John Amyas, thereby excluding him from any future income from the Estate. John stated therefore that he was no longer required to pay the £20 Annuity to his brother, claiming that he could not prove exactly how much he had spent on his brother, but that this exceeded the £20 a year due to him, and Robert should provide this information to the Court, "on oath." Finally, John Mallom asked the court to issue a subpoena to Robert

Mallom, to appear in court to answer the charges.

On 30 June 1743, Robert Mallom submitted his Answer to his brother's new charges, and there were disagreements on many points of fact. He denied that after their father's death he returned to school in Wymondham, stating that any costs were incurred before their father died. He went to school with Mr Greenville where he remained for no more than 6 months, and not as his brother had stated. The total expense for his education was unknown, but what was recalled was submitted in a Schedule annexed to the Answer. Robert moved to his sister, Elizabeth Mallom's house, until he went to Mr Sayers (the Attorney). He knew nothing of payments for medical and nursing care during his smallpox, but Mr Sayer asked for £8 3s. 6d. in 1738 while he was recovering at his home, and Robert could prove that this bill was paid. He convalesced in Norwich with Mr King, stating that his brother paid nothing for this. His next move was "to one Mr Wychingham an Attorney at Yoxford in Suffolk (and not to Mr Youngs...) to whom he was bound for 5 years by his said sister Elizabeth Mallom, and from Mr Wychingham this Defendant came to Norwich and was by his sister Anne Mallom placed out to the said Mr Youngs mentioned in the Complainants Bill" and he lived with him for the next three years. He agreed that Mr Youngs prosecuted the case concerning their mother's Annuity of £150 from George Bedell, but this was directed by John, not Robert Mallom and Robert claimed that John paid the £40 costs for this case. Robert also suggested that their disagreements should be referred to "Thomas Wackhouse Esq, a gentleman at the Bar of a fair character, and that the Complainant would agree thereto, which this Defendant likewise offered to agree with for quiet sake..." Robert said he travelled from Swaffham to Norwich to sign a legal document, but John's representative, Mr Neve, refused to sign this. Robert alleged that the only part of the Annuity he had received amounted to £24 18s 0d. It was also claimed that his brother had received £625 as the Executor of their late mother's estate, part of which could have used to pay his Annuity. In addition, Robert stated that in about 1733, he made an agreement with John Bringloe and his wife, to sell them his rights to the Bedell Estate, but his brother had refused to sign the agreement, so that Robert received no payment. In November 1736, Robert made another agreement with Mrs Bringloe for the sale of his rights for £1375, of which he had so far received £687 10s. 0d, the residue coming to him in July 1739. All Robert's rights were conveyed to Mrs Bringloe and Mrs Burgess, and not to Mr Amyas, as his brother had stated. Furthermore, Robert said that his Annuity of £20 should not cease just because he had sold his rights to Bedell's Estate. Robert stated that he had stayed at the home of his brother, John Mallom, at Wacton Hall, for 5–6 months, free of charge, during 1735 after his clerkship with Mr Youngs. Robert reported that during this time he had undertaken a great deal of business for his brother, for which he received no payment. Robert also claimed that he had offered to set aside from the Annuity due to him, any money received from his brother, and he included all this in a letter to his brother in about October 1741, suggesting that they should reach an agreement ("come to a fair account"), but for John to pay him the arrears of his Annuity. In addition, Robert admitted he was involved with his brother in the matter of the Bond of £60, but with Thomas Howes (clerk = clergyman), rather than John Howes, probably dating from January 1741. He asked the court to dismiss the case with costs and charges awarded to him. The Schedule attached to the "Answer" of Robert Mallom detailed payments he had received amounting in total to £24 18s. 0d, including £10 for school expenses and pocket money, and £14 18s. 0d. from his brother through intermediaries.[91]

Many of the details in the two cases have been included to demonstrate the effort to which individuals within the gentry classes went to secure what they believed was rightfully theirs, and in these examples, how much the brothers disagreed on simple matters of fact. It is evident that Robert believed he had a genuine grievance against his brother for non-payment of his Annuity, and that, as would be expected of a legal clerk to an attorney, he had kept written records which would have helped his case. John's recollection of details appears sketchy and considerably less reliable, and, apparently, he had kept no record to assist him. Unfortunately, in contrast to the 1738 case in favour of Robert Mallom, no published record has been found of the judgements in the cases between the Mallom brothers in 1742 and 1743, despite extensive searches.[92] Whatever the outcome, the disagreements between the brothers would have led to a souring of their relationship for years to come, perhaps indefinitely.

From the point of view of the family of John Mallom of Wacton Hall, the legal disagreements of 1742 and 1743 were part of a much bigger picture. In the previous eleven years, while other court cases were in progress, John and Phillis Mallom lost eight of their children in infancy or early childhood. 1742 was the year in which their son, John, our subject, was born, and the legal entanglements between his father John, and his uncle Robert, were the last thing the family would have wanted. John's younger brother, Richard, was born in 1744, the year after the second of two court cases was heard and his birth would at least have brought some comfort to his parents, because coping with the loss of their other eight children would have been more than enough for one couple to bear.

The cases of 1742 and 1743 inevitably introduced a serious note of family disharmony which would have reached the public arena. But nevertheless, the achievements of their ancestors, meant that the two Wacton Hall boys came from a line of increasingly prosperous Norfolk merchants and gentry folk, through which extensive estates had been acquired. These were first achieved by Revd. John Mallom Rector of Booton (d. 1662), building on the foundations left by the Malloms of Tudor Norwich, followed by his son, the first John Mallom of Wacton (d. 1687), by his grandson, the second John Mallom of Wacton (d. 1728), and finally, by the Rector's great grandson, the third John Mallom of Wacton, (d. 1761), the father of our subject. It is worth noting that the third John Mallom died almost exactly 100 years after his grandfather and namesake, the Rector of Booton, so the three Mallom generations spanned precisely one century. Wacton Hall had been purchased by John Mallom from Henry Reve on 21 December 1672, and the Hall remained in the Mallom family until 1760, when our subject's father sold it to John Ramey Esq. of Great Yarmouth.[93] The family estates were in Wacton, Moulton, Stratton, Taseburgh, Hempnall, Booton, Witchingham and Kerdiston in Reepham.[94] And in 1734, the year John and Phillis Mallom buried two of their infant children, the couple acquired the Bunwell Brick Works, previously owned by Phillis's father, Robert Phillips, who died that year.[95]

References and Further Reading

1. Norfolk Hearth Tax Assessment, Michaelmas 1664. Transcribed by M. S. Frankel and P. J. Seaman, Indexed by P.T.R. Palgrave-Moore. Norfolk Genealogy XV. Norfolk and Norwich Genealogical Society, 2005. p. 63. Online version at https://www.familysearch.org/library/books/viewer/204870/?offset=&return=1#page=82&viewer=picture&o=info&n=0&q=
2. Indenture:Lease between John Mallom and his wife Elizabeth Mallom, of Bedingham and George Copping of Woodton, Norfolk, for the sale of some land and associated property. 17 January 1672. 'Munumenta Antiqua: Crisp's Norfolk Folio Series. Volume 1, Folio 44. Society of Genealogists, London.
3. Indenture:Release of (1) John Mallom of Bedingham, gent, and Elizabeth, his wife, and (2) George Copping of Woodton gent. 18 January 1672. NRS 26560.148X1. NRO, Norwich.
4. measuringworth.com, ibid.
5. Mallom v Reve. Plaintiff John Mallom, defendants Henry Reve and Henry Ossant. Property in Wacton, Norfolk. Court of Chancery, C 10/493/159. TNA, London.
6. Mallom v Williams. Plaintiff John Mallom, Defendants Samuel Williams and John Grey, property in Moulton, Norfolk. Court of Chancery, C 10/271/35. TNA, London.
7. C10/182/45. Plaintiffs John Mallom and Elizabeth his wife versus Susan Copping, widow, George Copping and John Blanks. Marriage Contract. Bill of Complaint and Answer, 1676/77.
8. Bryan, Sam. Royal Courts of Justice Assistant Librarian, The Strand, London. Searches for the judgement in the case of Mallom v Copping, were made in English Reports, Nominate Reports, the Digest and general books on Probate/Wills and online legal databases, JustisOne, ICLR, Westlaw and the Lexis Library. Personal Communication, 6 August 2019.
9. Kelly, Geoffrey I. WACTON HALL, A History. NRO Typescript, Norfolk. pp. 24–31. Copy courtesy of Geoffrey Kelly, November 2017. p. 4: Ipswich Journal, Saturday 12 June 1756. British Newspapers Archive, online.
10. British Listed Buildings, Wacton Hall. A Grade II Listed Building in Wacton, Norfolk. Historic England, listed 11 September 1951. Extensive external and internal renovations have been undertaken recently. https://britishlistedbuildings.co.uk/101050822-wacton-hall-wacton: Architectural Notes included in Savill's Sales Brochure, used the same description. A fine and well restored Grade II* 16th century house set in extensive moated grounds with far reaching views. https://media.onthemarket.com/properties/1002049/doc_1_0.pdf
11. Kelly, ibid. p. 23: Will of Augustine Reve of Norwich (Brackendale), 1666. PROB-11-322-433, TNA, London.
12. Blomefield, Francis, Hundred of Depwade: Stratton, in *An Essay Towards A Topographical History of the County of Norfolk: Volume 5* (London, 1806), pp. 187–204. British History Online http://www.british-history.ac.uk/topographical-hist-norfolk/vol5/pp. 187–204. Blomefield refers to Edmund Reve as Chief Justice of the Common Pleas, whereas his appointment as Justice of the Common Pleas is mentioned in, Reve, Sir Edmund (c.1589–1647), by D.A.Orr, *Oxford Dictionary of National Biography*, Published in print: 23 September 2004. Published online: 23 September 2004. This version: 03 January 2008. https://www.oxforddnb.com/display/10.1093/ref:odnb/9780198614128.001.0001/odnb-9780198614128-e-23293?rskey=Wd5Y9a&result=1
13. Norfolk Hearth Tax Assessment, Michaelmas 1664, ibid. p. 12. The return for Wacton in 1664 records that 28 properties were subject to Hearth Tax, of which Augustine Reve paid for 18 hearths. John Frost, gent paid for 9, and the rest, paid for 4 or less. See text for further details.
14. Carter, Alan, WACTON, Wacton Hall, TM 180 902. A detailed description with a series of drawings of the history of Wacton Hall (no. 9), on behalf of Garran Patterson and Frances Henry of Long Stratton, Norfolk. Centre of East Anglian Studies, University of East Anglia, Norwich, 16 April 1988.

15. Dickinson, P.L., Clarenceux King of Arms, College of Arms, London, UK. Personal Communication, 18 April 2019.
16. Schama, Simon, A History of Britain: At the Edge of the World? 3000BC-AD1603. BBC Worldwide Ltd. Woodlands, 80 Wood Lane, London W12 0TT. 2001, p. 128
17. Dickinson, P. L., ibid. Personal Communication, 19 February 2019.
18. Kattenhorn, Jeff, British Library Manuscripts, London, including Harley MSS, and the Foster Collections MS 37147-49: Bowles, Frank, Archivist, Department of Archives and Modern Manuscripts, Cambridge University Library, Cambridge: Mouron, Anne, Senior Library Assistant, Bodleian Library, Oxford: Saville, Amanda, Librarian, The Queen's College, Oxford, including MSS 90 and 115, copies of earlier C17th Visitations: Carr, Ellen, Librarian, Norfolk Family History Society, Norwich: Palfrey, Ian, Senior Archivist, Norfolk Record Office, Norwich: Rix, Janice, Library and Information Assistant, Norfolk and Norwich Millennium Library, Norwich: Smith, Anthony, Honorary Archivist, Raynham Hall, Norfolk: Sims, Tony, Norfolk Heraldry Society.
19. Farrer, Revd. Edmund, FSA, "The Church Heraldry of Norfolk. A description of all coats of arms on brasses, monuments, slabs, hatchments etc, now to be found in the County." Vol II, Norwich, Agas H Goose, Rampant Horse Street. 1889, pp. 296—297.
20. Tunesi, John J., Secretary, The Heraldry Society, Baldock, Hertfordshire.
21. Dickinson, P., L., ibid. Note: the name of the female infant baptised in Wacton as "Etheldreda" in 1678 was rendered as "Ethelreda" on a 4 generation Mallom pedigree held by The College of Arms.
22. Orme, Nicholas. Going to Church in Medieval England. Yale University Press, New Haven and London, 2022. p. 145.
23. Strong, Roy. A Little History of the English Church. Jonathan Cape, London, 2007, pp. 110, 112, 174, 188—189.
24. Adapted from Kelly, ibid. pp. 24—31.
25. Blomefield, Francis. Wacton Church Memorials. 'Hundred of Depwade: Wacton-Magna', in *An Essay Towards A Topographical History of the County of Norfolk: Volume 5* (London, 1806), pp. 298—303. British History Online http://www.british-history.ac.uk/topographical-hist-norfolk/vol5/
26. Will of John Mallom of Wackton gentleman. ANF will 1687—89, no 101. NRO, Norfolk.
27. Will of Thomas Stone of Bedingham. NCC Original Will, 1690, no 49. NRO, Norwich.
28. http://venn.lib.cam.ac.uk/Documents/acad/2016/search-2016.html
29. *Biographical History of Gonville and Caius College, 1349—1897*: 1349—1713. John Venn, Cambridge at the University Press, 1897. Vol I. 1349—1713. Talmage, Sarah, Assistant to the Archivist. Personal Communication, 19 September 2013. James Cox, College Archivist, Gonville and Caius College, Cambridge. Personal Communication, 15 January 2019.
30. Venn, John. *Biographical History of Gonville and Caius College, 1349—1897*. Volume I, 1349 - 1713. pp. 484—490. Cambridge at the University Press, 1897, from Jessica Paterson, Trainee Archivist, Gonville and Caius College, Cambridge. Personal Communication, 11 March 2019.
31. Paterson, Jessica, ibid. Personal Communication, 7 May 2019. Liber Matriculationis 1679—1833, The Gesta 1669—1716, and The Exit and Redit Book 1678—1747, have not been checked.
32. Speight, Dunstan. Librarian, Lincoln's Inn, London WC2A 3TN, on behalf of the Admissions Registers of Lincoln's Inn, Middle Temple and Gray's Inn. Personal Communication, 25 October 2018: Celia Pilkington, Archivist, Inner Temple, London EC4Y 7HL. Personal Communication, 23 November 2018.
33. Baker, J.H., An Inner Temple Miscellany, p. 12 and Foot Note 33. (Inner Temple, 2004). Courtesy of Ben Taylor, Archives Assistant, Inner Temple, London. Personal Communication, 18 March 2019.

34. Virgoe, Roger, Woodhouse, Philip (d. 1623), of Kimberley, Norfolk, admitted to Lincoln's Inn, 1580, and Shelton, Sir John, admitted to Lincoln's Inn, 1517. Biographies in The History of Parliament, British Political, Local and Social History, http://www.historyofparliamentonline.org/research/members.
35. The Shelton Family: descendants of John de Shelton, 1150. http://www.tudorplace.com.ar/SHELTON.htm
36. https://en.wikipedia.org/wiki/Shelton_family
37. Alfred Suckling, 'Barsham', in *The History and Antiquities of the County of Suffolk: Volume 1* (Ipswich, 1846), pp. 35—46. British History Online. http://www.british-history.ac.uk/no-series/suffolk-history-antiquities/vol1/pp35—46.
38. Norfolk Hearth Tax Assessment Michaelmas, 1664, ibid. p. 64.
39. The Sucklings, in Woodton Parish Council. https://woodtonpc.wixsite.com/woodtonpc/woodton-in-history
40. The Caian, The Annual Record of Gonville and Caius College, Cambridge. Vol. XI. 'The College Livings.' p. 137—138. Sarah Talmage, ibid. Personal Communication, 26 September 2013.
41. Measuringworth.com/calculators/ukcompare/relativevalue.php
42. Hume, Robert D. The Value of Money in Eighteenth-Century England: Incomes, Prices, Buying Power— and Some Problems in Cultural Economics. Huntington Library Quarterly. Vol. 77, no. 4. pp. 373—416. (p. 381). Read online, at https://hlq.pennpress.org/media/34098/hlq-774_p373_hume.pdf
43. C11/2710/22. Mallom v Suckling. Document type: Bill and three answers. Plaintiffs: John Mallom, gent (eldest son and heir of John Mallom, esq deceased) both of Wacton, Norfolk. Defendants: Robert Suckling, esq, Robert Bransby, gent, Thomas Ekins and Elizabeth Ekins his wife, Thomas Donne and Daniel Sayer. Date of bill (or first document): 1732.
44. Diana Spelman. Personal Communication, 14 October 2019.
45. Will of Thomas Ekins of the City of Norwich surgeon [ANW 1740—41, no 183]. Abstract courtesy of Diana Spelman.
46. Records of Norfolk County Gaol at Norwich Castle Museum. Norfolk Record Office, MF/RO 581/7. See also Higgins, P.M. Medical Care in English Prisons, 1770—1850. PhD Thesis, Open University, April 2004, pp.52, 81, 99, 107, 129—130, 132.
47. Irvine Loudon, *Medical Care and the General Practitioner 1750—1850*. Clarendon Press, Oxford, 1986. pp. 2—6, 11—13, 19—21, 25, 26. Online edition: Sally Irvine, Surgeons and Apothecaries in Suffolk: 1750—1830 City Slickers and Country Bumpkins—Exploring Medical Myths. PhD Thesis, University of East Anglia, April 2011. pp. 126—142: Doctors: Physicians, Surgeons, Dentists and Apothecaries in England. https://www.familysearch.org/wiki/en/Doctors:_Physicians,_Surgeons,_Dentists_and_Apothecaries_in_England :
48. Norfolk: Norwich, Voting Registers - Polls 1734—35. Transcribed by Mike Bristow, March 2014
49. Howell, Shirley, Norwich Archives Researcher. Microfilm MR/RO 254/5. NRO, Norwich. Personal Communication, 3 February 2015.
50. Norfolk Public Houses. Curat's House, Norwich. http://www.norfolkpubs.co.uk/norwich/cnorwich/nccuh.htm
51. Millican, Percy. The Freemen of Norwich 1714—1752: A Transcript of the Third Register, (ed.) P. Millican, (Norfolk Record Society, 1952). http://nfro.norwichfreemen.org.uk/detail/5662/
52. Blomefield, Francis, ibid. The city of Norwich, chapter 36: Of the city in the time of King George I. https://www.british- history.ac.uk. /topographical-hist-norfolk/vol3/pp4 36-443#h3-0002
53. Kelly. ibid. p. 31.
54. C11/2258/12, Bill of Complaint and Answer. John Mallom Esq. of Wacton, Norfolk v. Robert

Mallom, gent. 1743. TNA, London.
55. Will of John Mallom of Wacton Esquire [NCC will 1728, 176 Thacker]. NRO. Norwich
56. Ruse, Michael. The Darwinian Revolution. The University of Chicago Press, Ltd., London, 1979. p. 20. Courtesy of Meghanne Flynn, Reference Department, Cambridge University Library, Cambridge, UK. Personal Communication, 23 March 2019.
57. Leedham-Green, Elizabeth. Formerly Archivist, Corpus Christi College, Cambridge. Personal Communication, 9 December 2013.
58. Venn's Alumni Register 1698–1795, p. 347: Lucy Hughes, Archivist, Corpus Christi College, Cambridge. Personal Communication, 15 March 2019: Corpus Christi College Book, 1709–1752, shelf mark CCCC01/C/3, p. 73: Herring, Thomas (1693–1757) by Robert Holtby, *Oxford Dictionary of National Biography*. Published online 23 September 2004.
59. Ruse, ibid. pp. 19–20.
60. Brockliss, L.W.B., *The University of Oxford: A History*. Oxford University Press, 2016, p. 238: Holborn, Guy, Sources of Biographical Information on Past Lawyers, British and Irish Association of Law Librarians: 1999, p. 25: Prest, W.R., The Inns of Court, Longman, 1972, p. 23. Courtesy of Ben Taylor, ibid. Personal Communication, 19 March 2019.
61. ACAD, A Cambridge University Alumni Database: CCEd, Clergy of the Church of England: Ubbeston Parish Council website, Will of Sir Robert Kemp 3rd Baronet of Ubbeston Hall, Suffolk, 1734: Image of the Kemp Vault in Gissing Church, Norfolk, on the same website.
62. CCED. The Church of England Database. http://db.theclergydatabase.org.uk/jsp/search/index.jsp
63. Will of Robert Suckling of Woodton Esquire. NCC will 1709, 58 Famm. NRO, Norwich
64. The Slatter Family History Pages, http://www.slatters.org.uk/index.htm: http://www.slatters.org.uk/history/bowdens/bk/f4612.htm
65. Knights of the shire. https://www.parliament.uk/about/living-heritage/evolutionofparliament/originsofparliament/birthofparliament/overview/knights/ UK Parliament 2020.
66. De Grey, Thomas (1680–1765), of Merton, Norfolk. MP for Thetford 1708–1710; MP for Norfolk 1715–1727. Sedgwick, Romney R., The History of Parliament, Volumes 1715–1754. http://www.histparl.ac.uk/volume/1715-1754/member/de-grey-thomas-1680-1765
67. Bristow, Mike, Norfolk Voting Registers – Poll 1714. https://www.genuki.org.uk/big/eng/NFK/Voting/Poll1714. Transcription by Mike Bristow, April 2012. Last updated 2 October 2020, by Mike Bristow and Pat Newby.
68. Will of John Mallom of Wacton Esquire. NCC Will 1728, 176 Thacker. NRO, Norwich.
69. Cannonz or Chanons Hall, Plantation Road, Tibenham, home of the Buxton family. Norfolk Heritage Explorer, NHER Number 10937. https://www.heritage.norfolk.gov.uk/record-details?MNF10937-Channonz-or-Chanons-Hall-Plantation-Road-Tibenham
70. Mackley, Alan, Editor, John Buxton, *Norfolk Gentleman and Architect: Letters to his Son 1719–1729*. Norfolk Record Society, 2005. I am grateful to Patrick Palgrave-Moore for drawing my attention to this work.
71. Mackley, ibid, cover note.
72. Schama, ibid. pp. 269, 272.
73. Mackley, ibid, pp. 29, 63, note 84, and Appendix C, p. 181.
74. Mackley, ibid, pp. 62–3 and n. 81, 87–8, 122, 130, 141, 147, reference to Mrs Mallom, p. 95.
75. Huggins, Mike, Animals, Humans and Sport in Eighteenth-century England. Archival Research, British Society of Sports History [BSSH], Canine Sport, Equestrian, Leisure, The Great Outdoors. May 17, 2021. https://www.playingpasts.co.uk/articles/the-great-outdoors/animals-humans-and-sport-in-eighteenth-century-england/
76. Sedgewick, Romney R., BACON, Sir Edmund, 5th Bt. (1693–1738), of Gillingham, Norf. The

History of Parliament: the House of Commons 1715—1754, ed. R. Sedgewick, 1970. https://www.historyofparliamentonline.org/volume/1715-1754/member/bacon-sir-edmund-1693-1738
77. Administration of Elizabeth Mallom of Hethersett. ANF admin. 1728—35, no. 38 on MF 281. NRO, Norwich.
78. George Bedell of Woodrising, Esq. PCC Will. PROB 11/5477. TNA, London.
79. measuringworth.com, ibid.
80. Parliamentary Papers, Volume 14. H.M. Stationery Office, 1845. Appendix to Report on Penalties and Disabilities, Act for Preventing the Growth of Popery. pp. 86—88. https://books.google.co.uk/books?id=fG4SAAAAYAAJ
81. The Act of Settlement 1701. https://en.wikipedia.org/wiki/Act_of_Settlement_1701
82. Mallom on the Demise of John Marsh and John Amyas, against John Bringloe and Elizabeth, his wife and Mary Apollonia Burgess. Reports of Adjudged Cases in the Court of Common Pleas during the Time Lord Chief Justice Willes. Charles Durnford, Middle Temple Inn. Printed by John Exshaw. London, 1800. Easter Term 11 George II (15 May 1738). pp. 75—82. Google Books online.
83. Blomefield, Francis. Mitford Hundred and Half: Wood Rysing. An Essay Towards A Topographical History of the County of Norfolk. Volume 10. Originally published by W Miller, London, 1809. pp. 273—281. http://www.british-history.ac.uk/topographical-hist- norfolk/vol10/pp273-281#highlight-first
84. PCC Will of John Amyas, Gentleman of Hingham, Norfolk. PROB 11/890/422. 11 August 1763: Burial in Hingham, 21 June 1763. https://www.familysearch.org/ark:/61903/3:1:S3HT-D4D3-3HC?i=93&wc=4JDN-Z2S%3A29727201%2C29358102%2C29945701&cc=1416598
85. MS 19534. NRO, Norwich.
86. MS 19535. NRO, Norwich.
87. The Worshipful Company of Pattenmakers, City of London Livery Company. http://www.pattenmakers.co.uk/
88. Norfolk Voting Registers-1734 Poll. GENUKI UK and Ireland Genealogy. Transcriptions by Mike Bristow. 2010. http://www.genuki.org.uk/big/eng/NFK/Voting/Poll1734/W#wacton
89. C11/2476/14. ibid. Bill of Complaint by Robert Mallom. 12 January 1742. TNA, London.
90. C11/2476/14. ibid. Answer by John Mallom. 30 May 1743. TNA, London.
91. C11/2258/12, John Mallom Esq. of Wacton, Norfolk v Robert Mallom gent. TNA, London.
92. TNA, London: NRO, Norwich: Timothy Large, Berryman Lace Mawer, Solicitors. 42 King Street West, Manchester: Tayo Ajibade, Information Services Enquiries, ibid: Jane Riley, Librarian, Manchester Law Library, 207 Deansgate, Manchester: Barnaby Bryan, Archives and Library of Middle Temple, Ashley Building, Middle Temple Lane, London; Sam Bryan, RCJ Assistant Librarian, Judicial Office, Royal Courts of Justice, London.
93. Kelly, ibid. p 30: Wacton Parkes Manor Court Book, 1746—1862. [Pomeroy and Sons 25/11/1993], 30th April 1673. NRO, Norwich: Geoffrey I Kelly. Personal Communication, 17 November 2017.
94. Will of John Mallom of Wac[k]ton gentleman. ANF will 1687—89, no 101. NRO, Norwich.
95. Manor of Bunwell, Carleton, Tibenham with the Members Court Book, 1734—1760, MC 1807/25. NRO. Norwich.

Part 3: The Mallom Estates: Decline

Wacton Hall had been a home fit for a family on quite a steep upward trajectory, socially speaking, and was well-suited to the earlier generations of the family who had occupied it since the early 1670s (Figs. 15 and 16). No doubt it contained furniture and fittings entirely suited to the taste of its former occupants, but now things were changing again, and this time, not for the better.

John and Phillis Mallom leave Wacton Hall for Aslacton

The Malloms had risen to local prominence, but now financial and social decline, loss of the family estates, and expenses which could no longer be sustained, meant that Wacton Hall and its farm had to be put on the market. The family of John and Phillis moved from Wacton to a smaller property in nearby Aslacton in 1754, where the burials of their children show they already had some association, and where Phillis had lived before her marriage. In modern terminology, the family was compelled to downsize. The following Notice "To be Lett" appeared in the *Ipswich Journal* in June 1756:

> A very good farm, known by the name of Wacton Hall Farm, with a convenient farm-house, barns, stables, and other outhouses, and upwards of 200 acres of fine arable meadow, and pasture land, which have been occupied by the owners (the Mallom family) for 70 years past, except for the last 2 years. NB there is a good Right of Commonage for 14 beasts on Wacton Common, which lets at 14s. each beast, or upwards, and a Right of Commonage on three other large Commons, for young cattle and sheep, without limitation. For further particulars enquire of John Mallom Esq. at Aslacton. Wacton Hall is distant from Norwich ten miles, from Harleston six.[1]

Fig. 15. Wacton Hall with the Farm, part of the original 200-acre estate of the Mallom families, 1672–1761.

Between 1754 and 1760, Wacton Hall was let to tenants, Thomas Barritt, a Mr Keen and finally, to John Ward.[2] Shortly before his death, John Mallom surrendered all his messuages, lands and tenements to Eleanor Collin of Brancaster, spinster, who took up her tenancy.[3] In May 1762, John Ramey Esq. came to the court and produced a lease and release by John Mallom, deceased, dated 4 and 5 February 1760, in which he released to Ramey all his freehold and copyhold properties in Aslacton and Moulton and other land called Herring Meadow, which Mallom had acquired on the death of his father, as reported at the court held on 3 October 1729, and also 2 acres 1 rood called Moulton Field, which John Mallom the son took up on the surrender of Samuel Cock and his wife Mary, at the court held in December 1734.[9] John Ramey of Great Yarmouth was a barrister who was the town's mayor in 1760 and in 1773.[4] He was an absentee landlord of Wacton Hall, and John Ward occupied the Hall as the tenant.

Fig. 16. Wacton Hall, today.

John and Phillis moved from Wacton to nearby Aslacton in 1754, and there can be no doubt that their new home was smaller than the former, and the associated lands significantly less in acreage, as the subsequent announcement of the Sale by Auction of the home in Aslacton, in 1761, by William Chase of Norwich, displays. The expenditure required to maintain it would have been less, and this was the main driver of the move. A detailed description of the home and surroundings was accordingly quite brief:

A Capital Messuage" (a dwelling house), "with a new built Stable, Barn, other Outhouses, a Garden and Orchard well planted, together with about thirty Acres of Arable and Pasture Land, in Aslacton in the said County, about ten Miles from Norwich, and within an easy Ride of Five Market Towns, now in the Occupation of John Mallom Esq…The said Premises are convenient for a Gentleman's Family as a Country-House, and are of a Yearly Value of £40 at least."[5]

It appears that the family home had been quite extensively rebuilt or modernised by John Mallom, making it a less painful move for them, and the outbuildings and land, which were included in the sale, made it an attractive proposition for a new owner. Phillis Mallom, John's wife, died in 1754, the year of the relocation, and was buried in Aslacton on 21 May that year, as "the wife of John Mallom Esq. of Wacton" leaving her husband a widower and his younger son not yet a teenager. Indeed, Phillis's death or her impending death, may have precipitated the move, although other financial considerations were by now playing an increasingly important role.

A second black marble slab in the chancel of Aslacton Church, abutting the lower edge of the memorial to the three children, marks Phillis's interment, but why the lettering was in classical Latin, and that to her children, 16 years earlier, in English, is unknown. The letter-cutter used a different chisel from that on her children's stone, which was by far the finest. Did this suggest that John's dwindling finances had affected the work for his wife's ledgerstone?[6] Space was left beneath the memorial to Phillis to add the death of her husband on the same stone (Fig. 17).

Fig. 17. St Michael's Church, Aslacton: Memorial to Phillis Phillips.

Hic jacet PHILLIS Uxor
JOHAN MALLOM de Wacton Arm^ri.
Quæ Obijt XVII Maij MDCCLIV.
Etat LIV.
Qualis erat si quæras,
non ex hoc leges Marmore
Sed Conjugis, Filiorum, Pauperumq.
Vultu

That is to say, "Here lies PHILLIS wife of John Mallom of Wacton Gentleman who died on the 17 May 1754, aged 54. If you ask what kind of person she was, you will not read it from this marble, but in the faces of [her] spouse, her children and the poor."

Two years later, in 1756, the guardianship of John Mallom gent (junior), was committed to his father, John Mallom Esq. The younger John was 14 years old, but he was already being styled as a gentleman in his own right, and this was the first occasion his name was included in a public record.[7] A few years after the loss of their mother and their Wacton home, the lives of the two Mallom boys, John and Richard were disrupted again, this time by the death of their father, and his burial in Aslacton on 31 October 1761. Deteriorating finances contributed to the decision to move from Wacton Hall to Aslacton a few years earlier, and some of the debts may well have been related to Mallom's interest in horse racing, since an item published in the Ipswich Journal "Country News" 20 years earlier, in June 1739, mentions his horse "Foxhunter" together with others in the racing fraternity.[8]

The Bunwell Heritage Group has reported that the Bunwell Brickworks was subsequently inherited by John Mallom junior in 1761 when he was still under the age of 21 years, but it was sold soon afterwards by auction in May 1761, a few months before his father died.[9] The details of this transfer to John junior, were recorded in the Bunwell Carleton Court Book in October 1756, and are worth reviewing here, verbatim:

> Now comes John gent, eldest son and heir of Phillis Mallom deceased, a minor under the age of 21 years, that is to say aged [blank] years, by the said John Mallom Esq. his father and guardian, acting as his attorney, seeks to be admitted as tenant to the property of which his mother was seized*, ie to 2 acres and a half of copyhold soiled land lying in Haughfield in Bunwell, which premises Phillis had taken up at this court held 11 April 1735, as only daughter and heiress of Robert Phillips her father deceased. John Mallom the son is admitted as tenant.

Although John Mallom senior was described in this Court entry as an attorney, he had no formal legal training, and the term was used here to mean that he represented

---

* owned.

his son as a litigant in person. Regulation of attorneys was unsatisfactory at this time, and the title was abolished with the Supreme Court of Judicature Act in 1873, and the creation of the Supreme Court.[10] Before this, attorneys practised in Common Law Courts, and solicitors in the Court of Chancery, and after 1873, the term "Attorney" was replaced by "Solicitor." However, the term attorney may still be used in English law to refer to someone legally appointed or empowered, who may be, but need not be, legally qualified, to act for another person.[11] It was in this sense that John Mallom was acting for his son.

The Bunwell Carleton Court Book includes a marginal note stating that the:

> Guardianship [of John junior] was committed to John Mallom Esqr. And because John Mallom the son is still a minor under the age of 21 years, the custody of his body and occupation of his lands and tenements is granted to his father until he reached the age of 21.[12]

WACTON HALL AFTER THE MALLOMS

The transfer of the Bunwell part of the Mallom family estate to John, junior, is intriguing, and it raises the possibility that it may have been a device to exclude it from the estate, and avoid it being part of what was sold five years later to pay his father's debts. If John Mallom Esq. knew of the extent of his debt, the question is why no other parts of the family estate were transferred to his sons, in a similar way? On the other hand, the family had recently moved from Wacton Hall to a smaller home in Aslacton, and in 1756, the year in which Bunwell Carleton Court met, John Mallom was already in the process of selling the Hall.

During the last few months of John Mallom's life, he had to endure the embarrassment of arranging for the sale of the family home in Aslacton, while watching as the Wacton Hall Estate was passed from one tenant to another. He was a widower with two young sons, and he had a great deal to cope with. The estate in Aslacton, of which the home was just a part, came onto the market five months before John Mallom died, and the details of the estate were listed in the sale particulars in May 1761, as follows:

> Also a Farm consisting of a Dwelling House, Barn, and proper Outbuildings, with about sixty Acres of Arable and Pasture Land, lying together next Tibenham Long-Row, in the Occupation of William Fisher, a good Tenant, under Lease (at least £50 per Annum) for three Years from Michaelmas next.

> Also a Cottage and Orchard near the said Farm, of the Yearly Rent of £2 15s. in occupation of Snelling.

> Also a Messuage in Moulton (next the Common) and Farm consisting of about 25 Acres of Arable and Pasture Land included, and a new built convenient Cottage, to which are five Acres of said Land adjoining,

which may be conveniently occupied therewith, which Premises are, and for many Years have been in the Occupation of Samuel Rayner, a good Tenant, without Lease at the Yearly Rent of £26 5s.

Also two Cottages, and two Acres of Land next the said Common, and adjoining to the said last mentioned Premises in the Occupation of Threadgell and Riches, at £9 6s. per Annum.

Also a well-accustomed Publick House, known by the Sign of the Fox and Hounds, next Moulton Green, with two Orchards, and about Four Acres of Pasture Ground adjoining, in Occupation of John Church, at £15 15s. per Ann. On lease about three Years to come.

Also a well-accustomed Public House, known by the Sign of the Duke's Head near Wacton Green, now in the Occupation of Henry Lease, at £16 5s. per Ann. Under Lease for 20 Years.

Also a House and well-accustomed Blacksmith's Shop, with two good Gardens, in Aslacton, in Occupation of John Coleman, at £6 10s. per Ann.

Also a Brick-kiln, and about two acres of Land in Bunwell, in the Occupation of Peter Roberts, under Lease for seven Years to come, at a Yearly rent of Five Guineas.

Also two Inclosures of Pasture in Bunwell, containing about six Acres in the Occupation of the said Mr Mallom, of the yearly Value of Five Guineas.

Also two Cottages in Aslacton, in good Repair, with an Orchard and Hampland* adjoining, at the Yearly Rent of £7 5s.

NB The several Tenants will shew the Premises to any enquiring Person. The greatest Part of the said Estates are freehold, and are not far distant from each other. For Particulars enquire of John Ramey, Esq. in Yarmouth, or of Mr Robert Hopkins, Attorney at Law, at New Buckenham.[13]

It was John Ramey who acquired Wacton Hall and the Mallom property in Moulton and Herring Meadow, in 1760/1762, so he benefitted considerably from the sales. Including the family home with the eleven individual premises with their land listed as part of the Aslacton Estate would yield an annual income at the prices quoted, of £99 11s.0d. Including the Capital Messuage, the house in which John Mallom lived, which was valued in the Auction Sale particulars as worth at least £40 per annum, gives a total annual rental yield of at least £140 in 1761 values. Using the Purchasing Power Calculator adopted in the earlier examples, converts this amount to a sum between £20,500 (real value) and £296,400.00 (income value), today. The first of these amounts is produced by multiplying £140.00 by

---

*   Hampland, otherwise Hempland, was a small enclosure for growing hemp or flax, usually for family use. (Townsend, Tom, Archivist, NRO, Norwich. Personal Communication, 30 July 2018.)

the percentage increase in the Retail Price Index (RPI) from 1761 to 2017, the last year for which figures are available. The second amount is an assessment of how much the estate would raise today, and may be the more realistic.[14] It was this sum, or whatever was realised at the sale, together with the amount raised by the sale or rent of Wacton Hall and Wacton Hall Farm which were used to pay Mallom's debts after his death, debts which must have amounted to a very considerable sum. In addition, the rental values of the properties listed, give some idea of the size of the Mallom home in Aslacton. Admittedly, this included a stable, a barn, other outhouses, a garden and orchard, with about thirty acres of arable and pasture land. In short, this was a valuable piece of real-estate. The family may have downsized, but John Mallom was certainly not living in a cottage or a small farm building with few amenities; far from it. Unfortunately, there is no direct comparison of the estimated values of Wacton Hall and the Aslacton home, because the value of Wacton Hall was not published. However, abstracting the description of the home from a later announcement in 1780, when the Aslacton house and out-buildings became available for rent again, gives much more information about the amenities the family enjoyed after they left Wacton, as follows:

> A Capital Messuage of Brick and Tile with sash windows, a kitchen, two parlours, and a hall, with convenient chambers and mattress over the frame, brew house, wash house, coach house, barn, stables, and a large garden and orchard well planted with fruit, and about 3 acres of good land adjoining to the same. The above premises are situate[d] in Aslacton, in this county of Norfolk, distant about 12 miles from Norwich, 7 from Diss and 4 from Long Stratton…formerly in the occupation of John Mallom Esq, deceased, and now of Mrs Collins. N.B. About 24 acres of very good land adjoining to the above may be hired with the same, if desires.[15]

John Mallom's last High Court Case, 1759–1761

On 24 April 1759, John Mallom "Esq. of Aslacton" submitted a Bill of Complaint to the High Court of Chancery, alleging that since 1744, rents and interest were owed by John Howes on property including Welhams, Reezes, Kirks and Stratton Hall, where Mallom was Lord of the Manor. This was to be John Mallom's last court case, and it was the culmination of a dispute which had been going on for nearly 20 years. The Complainant was now unmistakably describing himself as "of Aslacton" rather than "of Wacton." In addition, Mallom's brother, Robert, owed Howes £60, and in 1740, John Mallom had entered into a Bond with Howes for £60 to cover the debt and interest, with Thomas Howes named as Trustee. In 1746, Mallom paid Howes the interest to date, and £9 of the Bond, claiming that Howes was liable for £4 5s 1½d for rent, suggesting he deduct this from what he owed Howes. Furthermore, Mallom stated that Howes had cut down "Timber and Trees" on his land without permission or payment. Mallom tried to settle their differences, but in 1748, Howes successfully brought an action against Mallom for debt, with costs. Mallom claimed he had been wrongfully charged and appealed to the Court to remedy this. Incidentally, we came across the names of John and Thomas Howes in the case between John Mallom and his brother, Robert, in 1743, when the matter of the Bond of £60 was first noted. John Howes entered Gray's Inn in 1715, and was trained as a barrister, and he was the brother of Revd. Thomas Howes, Rector of Morningthorpe, Norfolk.[16] They must have been a formidable pair of adversaries, both of them Cambridge graduates, one a barrister and the other, a Clergyman, in comparison to John Mallom, himself, who gave every impression of finding difficulty mounting a cogent and convincing legal argument.

In his reply, John Howes stated that rent was paid to the end of 1747, acknowledging that more was due until 1759. Two or three trees valued at 40s, and 10–12 'pollen trees' also worth 40s had been felled in 1754, apparently without realising that they were on Mallom's land. Howes stated that Robert Mallom had not repaid any of the Capital (Principal), although he had received interest from John Mallom up to 24 April 1746, as shown in a Receipt he gave to Mallom. Howes claimed that Mallom would not settle this in a "Fair and Just Manner." The Defendants denied wrongdoing, asking for the case against them to be dismissed with costs.

In April 1761, Mallom submitted a "Supplemental Bill," claiming that Howes still owed him money. A meeting had been held in May 1759 at Stratton Hall, when Howes insisted that Mallom still owed £60 of the Bond, agreeing that interest had been paid until April 1746. Rents were due to Mallom from Howes, with interest, and the value of the trees was agreed at £5. Mallom paid Howes £30, including £18 interest, producing a signed receipt from Howes, dated 5 September 1746. Howes claimed that this was payment to a widow named Mary Tawell of Norwich, for the £150 she had loaned Mallom and his wife, in July 1744, as Mortgage on the Estate of Old Buckenham, Norfolk, and she now requested repayment. Mallom stated that he had given Howes two Bank Bills for £150, with instructions that £100 should be paid to Tawell, alleging that in September 1746, John Howes paid Thomas Howes £50, and £15 7s 6d as part of what was due on the Mortgage, leaving the sum of £34 12s 6d in John Howes' hands. Mallom claimed that this was concealed from him, thereby defrauding him. Mallom's problems were compounded by the Howes case against him in August 1760, when the Sheriff made a charge (a writ of fieri facias)* on his "Goods and Chattels" in payment of £56 6s 0d on the Capital and interest of the Bond. The Sheriff's poundage (commission) was £5 16s 0d and the Bailiff's fees were £3 3s 0d. In their second Reply dated 3 August 1761, a few short weeks before Mallom's death, John and Thomas Howes included a detailed summary of amounts paid and owed to them by John Mallom showing a debt of £56 6s 3d. This equates today to £8,500, using the RPI methodology, or higher sums using other formulae for conversion.[17]

---

* A writ of Fieri facias (fi.fa. that is to say "what you cause to be made") was a writ of execution after judgment in the High Court from an action for debt or damages, levied by the sheriff on goods belonging to the debtor.

Although no published record of the final judgement of this very protracted case has been found, it looks as if John Mallom's challenges had finally come to a head. He had been compelled to sell the estate of Wacton Hall, and now even more financial stringencies were being imposed upon him. Perhaps these new circumstances may have contributed to his death a few weeks later. He had, in effect, lost the estates and all the associated property which had been accumulated by his family over the preceding centuries, and was left with debts and a much-diminished reputation among the gentry families of Norfolk.

WILL OF JOHN MALLOM OF WACTON/ASLACTON, 1761

John Mallom, our subject, was named in his father's will, dated 12 September 1761, written six weeks before his death, and soon after the conclusion of the court case summarised above. The will began without any preliminary comments, "I, John Mallom of Aslacton Esq. ..." As soon as convenient after his death, the Executors were to bargain, sell and dispose of all Mallom's Messuages, Lands, Tenements and Hereditaments in Aslacton, Moulton/Great Moulton, and Bunwell, and wherever else in the County of Norfolk. His Freehold and Copyhold [lands and/or property] was to be offered for sale for the best possible price. The money from the sales, with the rents and profits of all the premises, together with all his personal estate, and after deducting reasonable expenses for his Executors, was to be used to pay his debts "as shall be justly due and owing from me at the time of my Decease to any person or persons whomsoever." And after payment and satisfaction of the same, and after paying his funeral expenses, the remainder was to pass to his two sons. John Mallom was to receive two thirds, and Richard Mallom, one third, to be paid one month after the sale of the estate. Mallom also stated that his Executors should not be held responsible for "any loss or losses in the management of the Trust other than that occasioned by their wilful neglect." The Executors were James Lincoln of Tibenham, gentleman, and Robert Haskins of New Buckenham, gentleman, but no remuneration was offered to them for their services. Signed and sealed by J[ohn] Mallom, 12 September 1761. The Witness were James Sewell, Robert Haskins, the lawyer who represented him in the case against John Howes, in the final court case summarised above, and James Crow. Proved by the Executors on the 3 October 1761.[18]

It is clear from this that virtually all of the proceeds of the sale of the Mallom estates went to pay his creditors, otherwise the house and the estates in Aslacton and elsewhere, and their father's personal possessions, would have passed to Mallom's two sons, taking into account Richard's minority. As it was, the boys were to be disappointed, because their inheritances were almost certainly very meagre, or non-existent. There is no mention of even a small personal gift to either of his sons, such as had been the case in the will of the boys' great grandfather, John Mallom, in his 1686 will. It has been suggested that John Mallom's will was written mainly to save face at a time of very different social customs compared to today, when a country gentleman would be expected to make a will, partly as a public statement of his worldly wealth.[19] In addition, his sons were not appointed Executors, despite John having reached an age when he could reasonably have expected to be involved. However, he was in the process of enlisting in the army, so he had already left Aslacton to join his regiment. The will confirms that of the ten children, only John junior and Richard survived into adult life. No further entries for Mallom have been found in parish registers, ATs or BTs, in this part of Norfolk after 1761. In addition, Wacton was one of eight Norfolk villages where a census containing names of inhabitants was taken in 1811, 30 years before the first national census in 1841. The name Mallom and its possible variants does not appear.[20] Glebe Terriers for Aslacton, inventories of church goods and ornaments, for the period 1760 to 1785, were checked, but no reference was made to Mallom.[21] Finally, in this section, deeds for Aslacton for the period 1760 to 1785, did not include any references to Mallom either.[22]

Following the death of John Mallom in 1761, notices appeared in July 1764 and July 1765 in *The Ipswich Journal* advertising Creditors' Meetings at the Saracen's Head, Diss, to receive "a Dividend of the Estate and Effects of the said Mr Mallom, and such Creditors as have not sent an Account of their Demands … are desired to send the same immediately to Mr Meadows at Diss aforesaid, or otherwise they will be excluded the Benefit of the said Dividend." [23] The Aslacton home was also the subject of several notices in local newspapers when it was advertised to be let, or for sale, including, for example, in *The Ipswich Journal* of September 1780, when it was "To be Lett." The property was described as follows,

> A Capital Messuage of Brick and Tile with sash windows, a kitchen, two parlours, and a hall, with convenient chambers and mattress over the frame, brew house, wash house, coach house, barn, stables, and a large garden and orchard well planted with fruit, and about 3 acres of good land adjoining to the same. The above premises are situate[d] in Aslacton, in this county of Norfolk, distant about 12 miles from Norwich, 7 from Diss and 4 from Long Stratton…formerly in the occupation of John Mallom Esq, deceased, and now of Mrs Collins. N.B. About 24 acres of very good land adjoining to the above may be hired with the same, if desired. Enquiries for further particulars of Mrs Collins (who had acquired the property in 1761), at Mrs Roope's at Pelham, or of Mr Wright, at Aslacton, who will show the premises. In the same item, A Farm at Aslacton was to be sold, then in the occupation of Mr Zach. Browne. Further particulars of this estate may be had of Mrs Collin, and of Messrs Meadows and Browne at Diss in the same county.[24]

Many years later, in *The Norfolk Chronicle and Norwich Gazette* in December 1821, the former Mallom residence in Aslacton came onto the market again, this time, for sale. The description was similar to that published earlier, but not identical, because additional out-buildings appear to have been added or converted from their previous use:

A brick and tiled Dwelling House, with sash windows, including parlours, hall, kitchen, wash house, dairy, brew house, chaise house, six-stalled stable, barn, with orchard, garden planted with fruit trees, and about 20 acres of excellent land. The house stood in the centre of the village of Aslacton, and was formerly the residence of John Mallom Esq... [25]

These accounts nicely supplement the details of the Aslacton home which were included in the Auction Sale particulars of May 1761, and it is clear that the area of the Aslacton estate had been reduced: land was a valuable asset, and more of it was sold-off in the intervening years to raise much-needed finances. The announcement of further creditors' meetings in 1764 and 1765 created even more difficulty for the Mallom boys, because four years after his death, some of their father's debts were apparently still to be paid. It follows that unless special arrangements had been put in place for them, and for which there is no record, they probably received nothing of what little inheritance remained. Nevertheless, the name of John Mallom lived on for 60 years after his death, at least in the bill of sale of his former home in Aslacton.

REFLECTIONS ON THE LIFE OF THE LAST JOHN MALLOM OF WACTON HALL, DIED 1761

In contrast to these undoubtedly very serious challenges, newspaper announcements of his death included the fact that for many years John Mallom had served as Commission[er] of the Peace, a position which today would be referred to as Justice of the Peace (JP). He was fulfilling this role as early as 1738, since the term "pacis conservatoris" (preserver of the peace) was included in the baptism entry of his second son to be baptised John, in Wacton, in March that year. An example of a case in which John Mallom adjudicated was reported in the *Ipswich Journal* on 13 March 1756, less than 2 years after the death of his wife, when he sat with William Leech and John Foster in court at Banham, 20 miles south west of Norwich, to hear an allegation concerning Benjamin Chapman of Banham, "Cyder-Maker" who "took into his house and premises" the bed and clothes of a person who had recently died of smallpox, through which it was alleged, Chapman's apples became infected, "to the detriment of his trade and reputation." Having had his premises examined, and hearing the allegation, Mallom and his colleagues decided that the case against Chapman was "groundless and without any Foundation whatsoever" and the Calumny (false allegation) was removed: case dismissed.[26] It had long been a requirement that a man selected to be "Commission[er] of the Peace, should be of good character and law-abiding, able to display good judgement and temperament. However, in the absence of a salary, such appointments inevitably went to members of the gentry, although the family move from Wacton Hall to Aslacton, seems to have had no impact on Mallom's perceived ability to fulfil his social responsibilities to the community.

Despite all this, it is not difficult to imagine the likely consequences of these financial challenges to John Mallom, especially after the death of his wife. Some members of the social class to which he aspired may have been sympathetic, but others would have kept him at a distance, and the contrast with his grandfather's undoubted success in 1685 could not have been more marked. Fewer invitations to gatherings and dinner parties would have followed. Mallom may have tried to borrow money from his family and his wealthy friends to help him manage the situation, but his ability to repay them would have been questioned. All in all, these were extremely difficult times for the former Lord of the Manor of Wacton and his two teenage sons, whose opportunities in life would have also been diminished. He and the boys moved to a smaller home in nearby Aslacton, his friends kept away and there is no evidence that his estranged brother, Robert, in Swaffham, came to his aid, although he had the means to do so. The final indignity was the absence of a memorial to him in the space left for his name below his wife's inscription on the ledgerstone in the chancel of Aslacton Church. There were no funds to pay for this, and no one willing to make the arrangements, either. This is almost the exact opposite of the "rags to riches" story so favoured by the script-writers of popular Christmas Pantomimes: the disappointments were his responsibility, alone.

On the other hand, it would be all too easy to focus on the personal setbacks experienced by John Mallom, the father of our subject; his lack of academic ability as shown by his failure to graduate from Cambridge University, and the loss of the family homes both of Wacton Hall, which had been held by the family for nearly 100 years, and in Aslacton (Fig.17). The evidence suggests that his interest in horse racing, which may have begun while he was an undergraduate in Cambridge, and the likely gambling associated with this, may have played a part in the deteriorating circumstances experienced by the family. The phrase used by Sir Armine Wodehouse in his May 1770 letter to General George Townshend on behalf of Mallom's son, Lt John Mallom, "the Circumstances of his Family are well known to you," mentioned later, might partly refer to this. However, despite not having records of the final judgements, the High Court cases referred to earlier give the impression that Mallom was not particularly adept at negotiating court procedures, and there is precious little evidence that he had taken the trouble to keep detailed financial records and accounts of his transactions, apart from a few notes of alleged debts due to him or paid by him. This is in marked contrast to the skill of his final adversary, John Howes, Barrister at Law, who had done so with apparently good effect in the eyes of the court. However, John and Phillis Mallom had witnessed the most appalling series of family tragedies in the loss of eight of their ten children during infancy and childhood. It is true that infant mortality in mid-Georgian England was high and many parents suffered the anguish of watching their children die of what would today be regarded as preventable diseases. The Parish Registers of Norfolk for this period include the burials of infants and young children on virtually every page, and studies show an infant mortality rate for mid-eighteenth-century London, of 250 per 1000 births, and of childhood mortality of 150 per 10,000 live births, based on Bills of Mortality,[27] but for one family to lose so many children must have been absolutely heartbreaking. Against this background, John Mallom's interest in horse racing is easier to understand as a distraction, and his community activities appear all the more commendable. Furthermore, the sale of Wacton Hall and the move to smaller accommodation in Aslacton can be seen as quite sensible, because only two sons survived to become teenagers. Sadly, maintaining a spacious family home for ten children was no longer required despite the undoubted achievements of John Mallom's predecessors. In any case, it could no longer be afforded.

The unfortunate state of affairs which befell their father was inevitably to become the backdrop to the early lives of John Mallom junior and his brother, Richard. This was a distinguished Norfolk family which had fallen on hard times, but in which the two sons who survived their father were entitled to the arms, and to style themselves "Gent[leman]" or "Esq[uire], if they chose to."[28] It is evident that our subject, John Mallom, used his courtesy title when he enlisted in the army, but whether Richard did or not, is unknown. John and Richard Mallom were left to their own devices to manage the situation in which they now found themselves in the best way they could. John resolved the dilemma on his part by enlisting in a regiment of the British Army, but what happened to his younger brother, Richard, remains to be seen. The following comment summarises a considered approach to the past, when fortunate and unfortunate experiences jostle together for our attention:

> I'll say it again: history is not there to make us feel good, proud or comforted. It's simply there to be fully understood, in all its wonder, pain and, yes, its cruelties and injustices.[29]

What is known of the extended family of which the two Mallom boys were a part?

Uncles, Aunts and Cousins of John and Richard Mallom

As part of a family which included several siblings in each of the preceding generations, it might be anticipated that John and Richard Mallom would have had a number of cousins, most of whom would have lived close enough to them to make family gatherings a real possibility. Their father, John Mallom, had four siblings who survived infancy and childhood to become adults and marry, and any children they produced would have been the boys' 1st cousins. Their aunt, Mary Mallom, married Merchant Berry in 1736, but no children have been found for them. Aunt Sarah Mallom married Daniel Youngs in 1732, and no children have been found for them, either. Aunt Anna Mallom married Revd. Thomas Kemp, Rector of Flordon, in Newton Flotman, 5 miles north of Wacton, in 1739. This couple had two daughters, Anne born in 1742, and Elizabeth in 1744, by coincidence, exactly the same years in which John and Richard Mallom were born. Anne, daughter of Revd. Thomas Kemp, was buried in 1745 in Gissing, where her father was the Rector, and an Elizabeth Kemp was buried in the same parish in 1762, plausibly Anne's younger sister. On the other hand, Uncle Robert and Aunt Mary (Dusgate) Mallom of Swaffham, produced children who survived, and they were apparently the only 1st cousins John and Richard had on the Mallom side of their family. There was a period in their early lives, as children and teenagers, given the appropriate circumstances, when John and Richard might have spent time with their 1st cousins in Swaffham or Wacton, but whether this ever happened, given the legal entanglements between the fathers, remains a matter for speculation. The opportunities for John, who enlisted in the British Army in 1761, would have been restricted to periods of leave after this date, but for Richard, no such limitations have been discovered. The Wacton boys' Swaffham 1st cousins were as follows: Robert was baptised on 18 April 1743, John on 5 November 1744, Frances on 9 January 1752, and William on 3 October 1753. A burial for their cousin, Thomas, was recorded in August 1748, but his baptism was not entered in the Swaffham records. One other proposed son of Robert and Mary Mallom, James, will be discussed later. The Swaffham cousins grew up in the town, where John was apprenticed to James Raven, Baker, of Swaffham, in September 1766; Robert, junior, became a master butcher, and had his own apprentices in December 1772 (Isaac Balls), in May 1779 (Robert Colvin), and in November 1785 (James Boyce).[30]

William Mallom, became a butcher and a member of the crew of the East India Ship "Nassau," on which he prepared a will dated 23 December 1775, and which went to Administration on 28 August 1777, soon after his death. The printed document which included some hand-written personal details, reads as follows:

> I Willm Mallom, Butcher on Board the Ship Nassau, Capt Arthur Gore Esq, Com[mander], being in bodily Health, and of sound and disposing Mind and Memory, and considering the Perils and Dangers of the Sea and other Uncertainties of this transitory Life (do for avoiding uncertainties after my decease) make, publish and declare this my last Will and Testament in manner following... I give, bequeath, and dispose hereof as followeth: That is to say Unto my Beloved Friend Robt. Mallom Butcher in Swaffham in the County of Norfolk, Wages, Sum and Sums of Money, Lands, Tenements, Goods, Chattels and Estate whatsoever...I do give, devise and bequeath the same unto the above Mentioned Robt Mallom. And do hereby nominate and appoint the same Robt Mallom, Butcher of Swaffham... my Executor of this my last Will and Testament...of Willm Mallom. In Witness whereof to this my said Will, I have set my Hand and Seal the 23 Day of December in the Year of our Lord One Thousand Seven Hundred and 75 ...And in the Sixteen[th] Year of the Reign of His Majesty King George the Third over Great Britain &c. Signed by Willm Mallom in the presence of Witness[es] John Griffiths and Henry Johnston.

Administration was granted to John Berry, Robert Mallom's attorney, who was also the executor named in the will at Swaffham in the County of Norfolk.[31]

The East India Company ship "Nassau" of 723 tons sailed between 1771 and

1785, taking goods and produce to and from India and South East Asia, but exactly when William Mallom joined the crew and how many voyages he sailed with her, is unknown. During the season 1775 to 1776, the ship sailed from Portsmouth on 9 January 1776, and after a return voyage to the East of almost 18 months, returned to the Downs on 23 July 1777.[32] Is it possible that William Mallom was a member of the crew on this voyage? If so, he must have died while "Nassau" was sailing for home waters, or soon after she reached the Downs, the sea-lane in the southern part of the North Sea between the mouth of the Thames and Dover where merchant ships would wait for favourable winds after sailing out of the Thames.[33] William was born in October 1753, so he was a young man of 23 years when he died. Before enlisting with the East India Company, he would have served an apprenticeship as a butcher, arguably with his older brother, Robert, who became a master butcher in Swaffham, and to whom William left everything he owned in his will. William was the nephew of John and Phillis Mallom of Wacton, and the 1st cousin of Captain John Mallom and his brother, Richard.

The final Swaffham cousin of the Mallom boys was James, whose baptism was omitted from the Swaffham Register, as was also the case for his brother, Thomas. He was married in Swaffham and buried as an old man in North Creake aged 85 years, in May 1831, and the calculated birth year of 1746 falls exactly within the period when Robert and Mary Mallom were baptising their children. James was not a baptismal name seen in the Mallom family, but it did occur in Mary Dusgate's family, in her nephew, James. James Mallom married Eleanor Ollet, in Swaffham, in November 1787. She had been baptised 'Ellen' in December 1770, so she was a minor on her wedding day. Their eight children were all baptised in Swaffham between 1788 and 1813, with examples of spelling variations in both surname and baptismal names. The surname of the couple was written as 'Marham' in all eight baptism entries. Their daughters, Sophia, Ann and Eleanor, were baptised to James and Eleanor, Mary and Thomas were baptised to James and Ellen, Thomas to James and Ellen, formerly Ollet, spinster, and Susan was baptised to James and Ellen Marham, formerly Ollet. This additional information confirms the identity of the parents who were married as James Mallom and Eleanor Ollet, so precisely which version of her first name she used is debatable. In each case, the handwriting in the register entries was that of Revd. William Yonge, the Vicar of Swaffham, who had a large parish with a great many baptisms, marriages and burials every year in comparison to the small villages where other members of the Mallom family lived. Is it possible that James Mallom pronounced his surname with a long initial 'a' vowel, and it was this which gave rise to the Marham favoured by Mr Yonge in his Parish Registers and Transcripts? On the other hand, the Banns of Marriage clearly named him as James Mallom when they were read out in Swaffham Church on 21 and 28 October, and 4 November 1787, implying that Mr Yonge had not formed a settled opinion about his parishioner's surname. Of their children, who were all the 1st cousins once removed of John and Richard Mallom, Hellen was buried 2 days after birth, Thomas, when he was 22 months old, and the two sisters,

Sophia and Ann, both had children while unmarried. James Mallom was named in the will of his father-in-law, Edward Ollet, labourer of Swaffham, in November 1795, which went to probate in October 1797.[34] Referred to as James Marham, he was appointed guardian and trustee of Ollet's son, Richard "an ideot," to whom all the household furniture, clothes and other assets were left. Richard was to live with James, who was given discretion how best to use the bequeathed items. James's wife, Eleanor, Ollet's daughter, was not named in the will, although it is unlikely that a young man with a severe mental handicap would live in a household which lacked a woman's care.

As a final note in this part of the story, a woman called Elizabeth Mallom was married to John Smith in November 1803, in Swaffham, by Banns. Both parties were single, and of the parish, implying that Elizabeth was not a minor, and therefore born before 1782, otherwise parental consent would have been required, and be noted in the register entry. Bride and groom both signed their names in a fluent hand, indicating education and literacy. Given the surname, Elizabeth may well have been a member of the family of Robert and Mary Mallom, but the question is, how? She can't possibly have been Robert and Mary's daughter, but, in the absence of register entries, we don't know whether Robert or John had children baptised in Swaffham, or nearby. As a butcher in the town, it might be anticipated that Robert would have produced a family, of which Elizabeth could have been a member. Her grandmother was Elizabeth (Suckling) Mallom, and so selecting this baptismal name would have been perfectly understandable. Even less is known about John Mallom, Robert's brother, after his baptism in 1744. James and Eleanor were married too late to have produced a daughter who was not a minor when she was married in 1803. And Thomas Mallom was buried in 1748. This lack of evidence means that Elizabeth Mallom cannot be confidently assigned to any of the sons of Robert and Mary Mallom of Swaffham, and all we can say is that she was almost certainly their granddaughter.

Announcements of the deaths of Mr Robert Mallom, junior, and Mrs Frances Mallom, appeared in *The Norfolk Chronicle* on [Saturday] 1 April 1815, and [Saturday] 1 July 1815, respectively. For Robert, the entry was as follows:

> Mr Robt. Mallom, son of Robt. Mallom, Gent. dec[eased] and nephew of John Mallom Esq. late of Wacton Hall in this county.

He was 72 years old, but despite his evident trading and apparent economic success, no entries for a marriage or baptisms of children have been found. For Robert's sister, Frances Mallom, the entry was as follows:

> "Mrs Frances Mallom, of this city, Aged 64."[35]

Frances was the daughter of Robert and Mary (Dusgate) Mallom, and recalling that *The Norfolk Chronicle* was published in Norwich,[36] it looks as if she was living in Norwich at the time of her death. However, her remains were taken to Swaffham for burial, on 25 June 1815. We should again note that the title Mrs indicates that she was a woman of status, rather than implying that she was a married woman.

Were there any 1st cousins of John and Richard Mallom on their mother's side of the family, children of the siblings of Phillis Phillips? The short answer is, no; there were none. The sad story of the brother and sisters of Phillis (Phillips) Mallom, who would have been John and Richard's maternal uncle and aunts, is that they all died young, well before they could have had children of their own. Hannah, Jonas, Maria, Joanna and Elizabeth, all died in infancy or early childhood. Phillis, herself was baptised in May 1704, and she was the only child who survived to adulthood. All these events took place in Tibenham, 2 miles south west of Aslacton, where Phillis and her husband lived after the move from Wacton Hall. These tragic early deaths were equivalent to the eight deaths of the children of John and Phillis Mallom, between 1732 and 1742, but whether the children died of infectious diseases or from congenital abnormalities which may have run in Phillis's family, is unknown, because no relevant entries were included in the Burial Registers. In any case, the causes of death may not have been recognised.

The ancestors of our subject, John Mallom, had made enviable progress in developing their estate during the 200 years before his birth, and with this, they had acquired a certain standing and social status in their community south of Norwich. However, his future life and well-being was to face significant challenges because there would be no useful inheritance from his father, whose estate had to be sold to pay the debts which had accumulated over several years while young John was a boy. How he chose to deal with these difficulties is the subject of the next section of the story.

References and Further Reading

1. *Ipswich Journal*, Saturday 12 June 1756. British Newspapers Archive, Online.
2. Kelly, Geoffrey I. ibid p 30–31. NRO, Norwich.
3. Parkes Manor Court Book, 1740–67 [MC 1804/5 - MF/X/63]. NRO. Norwich.
4. Blomefield, Francis, *East Flegg Hundred: Great Yarmouth, bailiffs and mayors. An Essay Towards a Topographical History of the County of Norfolk*. Volume 11, pp. 322–345. Originally published by W. Miller, London, 1810.
5. *Norwich Mercury*, 9 May 1761. NRO, Norwich.
6. Litten, ibid.
7. Manor of Bunwell, Carleton, Tibenham with the Members Court Book, 1734–1760, MC 1807/25, p. 141. NRO. Norwich.
8. *Ipswich Journal*, 23 June 1739. British Newspapers Archive, Online.
9. Herne, John, (copyright). Brickmaking in Bunwell: Bunwell Heritage Group, 2011, p. 7.
10. Speight, Dunstan ibid. Personal Communication, 25 October 2018: Pilkington, Celia, ibid. Personal Communication, 23 November 2018. See Part 2, Ref 32.
11. Solicitor. https://en.wikipedia.org/wiki/Solicitor.
12. Manor of Bunwell, Carleton, Tibenham with the Members Court Book, 1734–1760, MC 1807/25. NRO, Norwich.
13. *Norwich Mercury*, ibid.
14. Measuringworth.com/calculators/ukcompare/relativevalue.php ibid.
15. *Ipswich Journal*, 9 September 1780. British Newspapers Archive, online. Enquiries for further particulars of Mrs Collins (who had acquired the property in 1761), at Mrs Roope's at Pelham, or of Mr Wright, at Aslacton, who will show the premises. In the same item, "A Farm at Aslacton was to be sold, then in the occupation of Mr Zach. Browne. Further particulars of this estate may be had of Mrs Collin, and of Messrs Meadows and Browne at Diss in the same county".
16. ACAD, A Cambridge Alumni Database http://venn.lib.cam.ac.uk/cgi-bin/search-2018.pl?sur=Howes&suro=w&fir=Thomas&firo=c&cit=&cito=c&c=all&z=all&tex=&sye=&eye=&col=all&maxcount=50
17. C12/1284/11. Mallom v Howes. TNA, London. Note the section included here summarises 15,000 words in the original documents.
18. John Mallom of Aslacton Esq. ANF Will 1760/61, No. 119. NRO, Norwich.
19. Maidstone, Robert. Local Historian, Great Moulton and Aslacton, Norfolk. Personal Communication, 9 December 2013.
20. Pre 1841 Norfolk Censuses and other Name Lists. GENUKI UK and Ireland Genealogy. Transcription by Mike Bristow, March 2002.
21. DN/TER 5/2. NRO, Norwich.
22. ETN 1/4/27. NRO, Norwich.
23. *Ipswich Journal*, Saturday 7 July 1764; Ipswich Journal, Saturday 27 July 1765. British Newspapers Archive, Online.
24. *Ipswich Journal*, 9 September 1780. British Newspapers Archive, online.
25. *The Norfolk Chronicle and Norwich Gazette*, Saturday, 1 December 1821. British Newspapers Archive, Online.
26. *Ipswich Journal*, Saturday 13 March 1756. British Newspapers Archive, Online.
27. Woods, Robert, Mortality in eighteenth-century London: A new look at the Bills, Local Population Studies, 77 (2006), 12–23, Fig 3.
28. Churchill, Else, Genealogist, Society of Genealogists, London. Personal Communication, 28

February 2017: Dickinson, Patric, Clarenceux King of Arms, College of Arms, London. Personal Communication, 18 April 2019.
29. Olusoga, David A., "Imperialism lasted centuries — we're just a few years into righting injustices." Saturday Interview with Michael Odell. *The Times*, Saturday, April 6, 2024, pp. 30–31.
30. UK Register of Duties Paid for Apprentices Indentures, 1710–1811. Originals in IR 1 Series: 58f 113, 61f 67, 63f 201, TNA, London. From Findmypast.co.uk.
31. Will of William Mallom, Butcher. PROB 10/2728. TNA, London.
32. Hardy, Charles. *A Register of Ships, Employed in the Service of the Honourable the United East India Company, From the Year 1760 to 1819*. T. Bensley, London, 1820. p. 67, online.
33. India Office Library. Logs of East India Company Ships, 1759–1827. India Office Records, The British Library, London. National Library of Australia, State Library of New South Wales. Filmed 1983–84. Historical Note.
34. Will of Edward Ollet of Swaffham, Labourer. ANF will 1797, no 77 on MF 236, NRO, Norwich: Administration of Edward Ollett of Swaffham. ANF administrations 1794–97, no 106 on MF 293. NRO, Norwich.
35. Death entry of Robert Mallom, *Norfolk Chronicle*, 1 April 1815, page 3, column 1.: Death entry for Mrs Frances Mallom, *Norfolk Chronicle*, 1 July 1815, page 2, column 5. Both entries courtesy of The Norfolk Heritage Centre, from The British Newspaper Archive.
36. Penny, Janelle, *A Snapshot in Time, the Norfolk Chronicle* from 1780 – 1783. The Foxearth and District Local History Society. https://www.foxearth.org.uk/searchNorfolkChronicle.php : Extracts of the *Norfolk Chronicle* may be seen online at The British Newspaper Archive, https://www.britishnewspaperarchive.co.uk/

Part 4: The Army Career of John Mallom of Wacton

This section of our account looks at the army career of John Mallom, of Wacton Hall, who chose this career path as a way out of the family challenges he would otherwise have faced had he remained in Norfolk. John enlisted in the 57th Regiment of Foot on 4 May 1761 five months before the death of his father, by which time, the young man would have known that there would be virtually no inheritance for him in Wacton or Aslacton:

— Mallom, Gent; to be Ensign in our 57th Regt of Foot commanded by Major General David Cunnyngham, Bart.

Six of the seven entrants into commissions whose names were entered on this page were styled "Gent" and the other was "Clerk" (Clerk in Holy Orders, or Chaplain).[1] Having no useful inheritance with which to pay for his commission, John was extremely fortunate in being sponsored by Charles Townshend MP, a politician of exceptional ability and flair, who was the younger brother of George Townshend, Lord Lieutenant of Ireland, the politician and senior army officer. A salary and the prospects of promotion would have been very attractive to Ensign Mallom, and in any case, the oldest son of a gentleman, frequently entered the army. The cost of purchasing an ensigncy in an Infantry Regiment of the British Army was £360–£450.[2] The 57th Regiment of Foot was an Infantry Regiment of the Line, originally raised as the 59th Foot in 1755, but preparation for service during the Seven Years War meant expanding the number of British regiments, whereupon the 57th Foot was reformed as a permanent feature within the British Army.[3] In 1881, the Regiment was amalgamated with the 77th Regiment, the East Middlesex Regiment of Foot, to form the Middlesex Regiment (The Duke of Cambridge's Own).[4] The Seven Years' War, an almost global conflict from 1756–1763, began with a British attack on French colonies in North America and Canada, and later involved many European nations. Anglo-French hostilities came to an end in 1763 with The Treaty of Paris, but the implications for other national interests, were enormous.[5] In 1755, the regiment formed part of the British Squadron in the Mediterranean, initially at Gibraltar from 1757–1763, and later, at Menorca from 1763–1767.

Ensign Mallom in Gibraltar, Menorca and Dublin: Promotion to Lieutenant

Ensign Mallom served with the 57th Foot in Gibraltar, from 1761–1763, in part of the Seven Years' War fought mainly between Great Britain and the Bourbon dynasty of France and Spain. During this period, the Commanding Officer of the

57th Foot was Colonel Sir David Cunynghame/Cunningham, as shown on the Printed Annual Army Lists. Between 1761 and 1782, the Lists were supplemented by handwritten notes, deletion of names of officers by virtue of promotion or death, with the names of replacements with the relevant dates.[6] The 57th Foot was also based in Menorca whilst the island was in British hands, and during which time Mallom was promoted Lieutenant on 3 June 1767.[7] The cost of purchasing this rank was £700, although an officer in this position would pay only the difference between this and the cost he had incurred in the purchase of an ensigncy, that is £250.

Shortly afterwards, his regiment was posted to Dublin, Ireland, from 1768–1776, under the command of Colonel Sir John Irwin. The regiment included 1 Major, 6 Captains, 1 Captain Lieutenant, 10 Lieutenants, including John Mallom, and 8 Ensigns. In addition, there was a Chaplain, an Adjutant, a Quarter-Master and a Surgeon. Between the years in Dublin, from 1768–1776, John Mallom's name rose in the list of Lieutenants from 9th of 10 in 1768, to 2nd of 13 by 1776, an indication of his length of service, and by implication, that he was being seen as a competent and reliable officer.[8]

LIEUTENANT MALLOM APPEALS TO SIR ARMINE WODEHOUSE AND LIEUTENANT GENERAL GEORGE TOWNSHEND

British Regiments stationed in Ireland moved their base every summer, and, no doubt keen to show his connections, to make his mark in the army, and to secure additional income following his father's financial difficulties, John Mallom wrote to Sir Armine Wodehouse of Kimberley, Norfolk (Fig. 18), asking for a recommendation from George Townshend, the Lord Lieutenant of Ireland, in Dublin. Both men were MPs for Norfolk and members of the Norfolk Aristocracy, and Mallom was related to Wodehouse by marriage, so his Norfolk credentials appear impeccable. Without showing all the details of the relationships, Mallom was the 3rd cousin once removed of Sir Armine Wodehouse, although the social courtesies of the period prevent this relationship from being declared in the letter. Armine Wodehouse was, in any case, well above John Mallom in the social order of the time. Their common ancestors were Sir Thomas Wodehouse 2nd Baronet, and his wife, Blanche.[9] It is worth noting note that P. G. Wodehouse, author of the Jeeves and Blandings Castle novels, was the great grandson of Sir Armine Wodehouse through his second son, Revd. Philip Wodehouse, and so he too was a cousin of John Mallom.

The letter from Mallom to Sir Armine Wodehouse, from Ireland, in April 1770, reads as follows: [10]

Wexford April 26th 1770

Dear Sir Armine,

You will not I hope think me
Too impertinent in once more begging leave
to trouble you to apply to my Lord Townshend in
my behalf. When I had the honour of seeing his
Excellency last year, he signified to me that
nothing would give him greater pleasure
than to be able to oblige his Norfolk friends.
I know Sir Armine that you are one of the
First of that number, which makes me flatter myself
If you will be so kind as to make an application
To His Lordship at this time, will be of infinite
Service to the person who is now writing,
There are a number of employments which are
generally given to military men, entirely at
my Lord Townshend's disposal, who is at
present Invested with as much power, as any
Lord Lieutenant has had for many years.
Consequently, it is as much in his power to serve
His Friends. I should not have taken the liberty
of addressing myself to you, but in consequence of an
order we have received to march from hence to
Dublin, where we are to be Quartered for a year,
during which time I shall have frequent opportunities
of being seen, by His Excellency, and my being made
known to him, through you, will be
I flatter myself of great advantage, believe me,
Sir Armine, I think myself much indebted for the many
Civilities, I have formerly received from you, which I shall
always with gratitude acknowledge.

> I am, Sir Armine
> Y[ou]r most obed[ien]t and obliged
> Humble Servant. J Mallom.
> 57th Regiment at the Barracks, Dublin.

The letter from Sir Armine Wodehouse to Townshend, who was then the 4th Viscount Townshend, was addressed, appropriately, to Lord Townshend. It was dated 7 May 1770, and it reveals more of the kind of social interactions of the period to which John Mallom was appealing:

Kimberley May 7th 1770

My Lord,

    The letter which I have the Honour
to present to your Lordship comes from a
Gentleman who rec[eive]d his first Commission in
the army from Mr Charles Townshend, your
late Brother, the Circumstances of his
Family are well known to you, he is a very
Deserving young man in all Respects, which
will be a sufficient Apology for my
Presuming to mention his name to you.
your Lordships Situation gives you an
opportunity of rewarding merit either in
Church or army and of the Greatest
Pleasure[s] a man can have is Conferring
Favours on your Particular Connections.
I have the honour to assess your
Lordship that I am with much Respect
my Lord,

                    Your Lordships most
                      Obedient & Obliged
                      Humble Servant.
                      A Wodehouse
                      I beg my Particular
            Comp[liment]s to Lady Townshend. [11]

Charles Townshend's sponsorship of John Mallom, through his family connections with Sir Armine Wodehouse would have been very useful to him, and the correspondence gives the impression that Mallom would have taken full advantage of this. His ambition was borne out to some extent as his career progressed, and he was promoted from Ensign to Lieutenant, and to Captain.

The correspondence between Mallom and Wodehouse, and between Wodehouse and George Townshend raises some intriguing points of interest. Mallom's letter to Wodehouse shows that this was not the first time the young officer had asked Sir Armine to appeal to Townshend on his behalf, and it may well have been the latest in a series of requests. Furthermore, Mallom deliberately uses the term "His Friends" with reference to His Lordship, and their meeting the previous year. It would be easy to overstate the significance of this, but it would be consistent with the idea that young Mallom had been introduced to Townshend, and his brother, Charles, his sponsor, in person. Where else might this have occurred but at Cranmer Hall, Sculthorpe, the imposing red-brick mansion, where Townshend was the tenant between 1752–1763, and where Mallom's great aunt Audrey

(Mallom) Donne had lived with her husband, the Rector?

During this period, Townshend was known as Colonel, the Honourable George Townshend, before he succeeded his father, and returned to the family seat of Raynham Hall, where he was known as 4th Viscount, and from 1787, as 1st Marquess Townshend. Audrey Donne continued to live in Sculthorpe after her husband's death, where she would undoubtedly have been part of the social circle of the village, as was the custom for the families of clergymen of the period. As will be shown in Part 6, it is almost inevitable, after their mother's death in 1754, that the two Mallom boys, John, a young teenager, and his brother, Richard, still a child, were packed-off to live with their great aunt Audrey in Sculthorpe. She lived in much better circumstances than their widowed father, whose financial difficulties were steadily worsening, and she would have had the accommodation and the staff to look-after them. It is more than likely that the Mallom boys were introduced to Townshend, and his brother, Charles, at Cranmer Hall, and the suggestion

Fig. 18. Sir Armine Wodehouse, 5th Baronet, in 1773. *This portrait was painted three years after the correspond-ence between John Mallom—Wodehouse—Townshend, and so it is an almost contemporary representation of the man.*

Fig. 19. Cranmer Hall, Sculthorpe.

that John join the British Army, with Townshend's sponsorship, emerges here (Fig. 19). The arrangement was almost certainly brokered by his Aunt Audrey and his father, who would have been keen to see young John's future be as secure as possible. Given the challenges at home, the army was an obvious career choice for young John Mallom. This would give him a purpose in life, the comradeship of fellow officers, the possibility of promotion to a more senior rank, especially with such impressive backing, and equally important, a steady source of income to make up for the lack of a useful inheritance.

As it was, Mallom's finances were almost certainly less than that of his contemporaries, and a successful appeal to George Townshend would have helped him in many ways, although it may not have improved his popularity amongst his colleagues in the regiment. On the other hand, many of them were probably involved in similar strategies with their own wealthy and influential relatives: if there were strings to pull, they would have been pulled. From John Mallom's point of view, as a teenager in rural Norfolk wishing to launch himself into adult life as an army officer without family finances, it would be difficult to image a more prestigious trio of aristocratic supporters than Sir Armine Wodehouse, George Townshend, the 1st Marquess, and his brother, the Rt Hon Charles Townshend MP. They were influential, well-known both in Norfolk and nationally, and they were rich: they were exactly what the young man needed.

Sir Armine Wodehouse (1714–1777), 5th Baronet, of Kimberley Hall, Norfolk, was MP for Norfolk, a politician, friend of George Townshend, and a near neighbour of George Walpole, 3rd Earl of Orford who was Lord Lieutenant of Norfolk. Although he did not hold a regular commission in the British Army, he was Colonel of the 2nd or Eastern Militia, dividing the Norfolk men with George Townshend, who was Colonel of the 1st or Western Regiment of Norfolk Militia. Paintings of leading aristocrats and army commanders reviewing their troops, were favourite subjects at the time, since they display their power and authority, even if the main subjects of the paintings had not passed through officer training, somewhat akin to the roles by some members of the royal family of today. The painting by David Morier illustrated here (Fig. 20), is an outstanding example of this genre. Townshend is seen presenting his militia.

George Townshend (1724–1807) (Figs. 20 and 21), and his younger brother, Rt Hon Charles Townshend MP (Fig. 23), were major figures both within Norfolk and nationally. George Townshend was a military leader, politician and caricaturist, and George I was a sponsor at his baptism at St Martin-in-the-Fields, London.

Realising the importance of political propaganda and satire, Townshend became known as a caricaturist and cartoonist, in pen and ink, often lampooning his parliamentary colleagues and others. The National Portrait Gallery in London holds a collection of his drawings, including the image of George II (Fig 22).

Townsend produced caricatures of bare-knuckle boxers, native Indians drawn in colour, and several individuals described as "unknown" but probably identifiable by their contemporaries, to their dismay. After his reinstatement in the army, Townshend saw action in Quebec, as brigadier under Major General James Wolfe, leading his troops in part of the battle on the Heights of Abraham, when Wolfe was killed. He was appointed Lieutenant General in 1772. Perhaps the half-length portrait in armour by James Northcote, was to mark his promotion. His subsequent political career was in part thanks to his brother Charles's outstanding abilities, under whose influence, Townshend became Lord Lieutenant of Ireland

Part 4: The Army Career of John Mallom of Wacton

Fig. 20. *George, 1st Marquess Townshend, with The Norfolk Militia.*

Fig. 21. *George Townshend, 4th Viscount, later 1st Marquess Townshend (1724–1807).*

Fig. 22. *King George II by George Townshend, later 4th Viscount and 1st Marquess, ink, 1751–1758.*

Fig. 23. *The Rt Hon Charles Townshend, PC (1725–1767) by Sir Joshua Reynolds PRA and studio.*

Townshend was the Chancellor of the Exchequer in the Earl of Chatham's government from 2 August 1766–4 September 1767.

in Dublin, in 1767, and it was here that John Mallom was serving as an officer with the 57th Foot when he approached Wodehouse, asking him to appeal to Townshend for his support. Part of Townshend's role in Dublin was to enlarge the Irish armies to be similar in size and fighting ability to their British equivalents. This was opposed by Irish politicians, eventually leading to Townshend's loss of influence and authority, although seen later as helping to promote union between Great Britain and Ireland. Spending his later years as a country squire, including as a tenant at Cranmer Hall, Sculthorpe, and later, at the family seat of Raynham Hall, Townshend never again held a public office, and he died at Raynham in September 1807.[12]

The Rt Hon Charles Townshend (1725–1767), younger brother of George Townshend, was destined for the law, and after training in London, Cambridge and Leiden, he was called to the bar in 1747, aged 22 years. The same year, he was elected MP for Great Yarmouth, and the attraction of a career in politics beckoned. After serving in, amongst other ministries, the Board of Trade and Plantations, the Admiralty, the War Office, and as Paymaster General, he was appointed Chancellor of the Exchequer by William Pitt, from 1766 until his early death. His particular speciality was the ability to give brilliant, dazzling speeches in parliament, so much so that he was described by Pitt in the following terms: "no one person near Townshend. He is the orator; the rest are speakers." In 1767, not long before his death, he proposed a series of Acts (The Townshend Acts), which included plans to increase London's revenue from the American Colonies and impose trade regulations, all of them designed to boost taxation yields from America, but without the Colonies having any direct representation in the British Parliament.[13] Inevitably, this played a major part in the aggravation which led to the American War of Independence.

THE 57TH REGIMENT OF FOOT IN DUBLIN

John Mallom's 57th Regiment of Foot was stationed in Dublin in 1774 at the time of General Drogheda's Review in July that year.[14] They were commanded by Lieutenant General John Irvine, and the Officers' Lists included 1 Major, 7 Captains, 1 Captain Lieutenant, 11 Lieutenants, 8 Ensigns, together with a Chaplain, an Adjutant, a Quartermaster, a Surgeon and a [Surgeon's] Mate. In the table indicating the Country of Origin of the Officers, 10 were English, 12 were Scotch and 7 were Irish, including the Commanding Officer. Against the name of Lieutenant John Mallom was the date he enlisted as an Ensign, 4 May [17]61, and the date he was promoted to Lieutenant, 3 June 1767. Their last move was to Kilkenny in 1775, in preparation for the voyage to America to assist the British forces in the American War of Independence.[15] The uniform of a Grenadier in the 57th Regiment of Foot is shown in Fig. 24, and a pen and ink sketch of a militia man, by George Townsend is shown in Fig 25.

THE BRITISH ARMY AND THE AMERICAN WAR OF INDEPENDENCE

Part 4: The Army Career of John Mallom of Wacton

Fig. 24. Uniform of a Grenadier in the 57th Regiment of Foot during the American War of Independence.

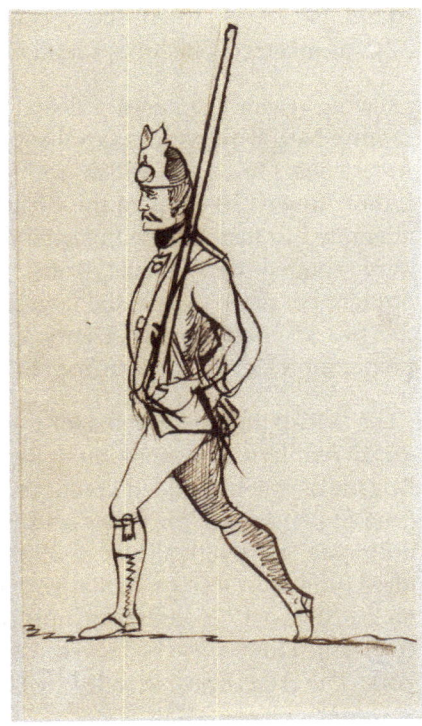

Fig. 25. Militia Soldier by George Townshend 1st Marquess Townshend. Pen and ink 1751–1758.

As has been fully described elsewhere, the American War had its origins in the dispute between 13 American Colonies in the east of the continent, and the government in London: they refused English rule and subsequently declared Independence.[16] British troops in southern Ireland, ordered to cross the Atlantic to quell the uprising, were held up for 4 months awaiting vessels to begin their voyage. The 57th Foot, with its 400 troops, were part of the 6th Brigade of the army, and they eventually sailed for America in three vessels: "Ann and Isabella," "Earl of Orford" and "Manuel," on 12 February 1776. They reached Cape Fear, North Carolina, after storms, on 18 April 1776. They marched to attack Charleston, South Carolina in June 1776, under Lieutenant General Henry Clinton (Fig. 26), Howe's second in command, but failed, and on 1 August 1776, the 57th Foot sailed to Staten

Fig. 26. General Sir Henry Clinton.

Island, New York, where the Commander-in-Chief, General William Howe (Fig. 27) was mustering his troops ready for an attack on New York itself.

Having recently suffered a defeat in the siege of Boston, Howe's plan was to capture New York, with its Loyalist population, and inflict a crushing defeat on the Americans. On 2 July, British troops began to land on Staten Island, and, within a short time, 130 ships of the British Navy were stationed off the Island. Howe attempted to negotiate with General Washington in July 1776, but his overtures were rebuffed. By 1 August, British ships, eventually numbering more than 400, brought yet more troops, the largest force ever to sail for America, together with the two senior Generals, Henry Clinton and Charles Cornwallis (Fig. 28), in preparation for the advance from Staten Island to Long Island, New York.

The British units assembled for the assault included troops of the Light Infantry, Royal Artillery, Dragoons, and Regiments of Foot within 7 Brigades, the 6th Brigade of which included Mallom's 57th Regiment of Foot. The troops embarked, from Staten Island, for Gravesend Bay, Long Island, on 21 August 1776, in flat-bottomed boats with a force of 25,000 men from British and Hessian Regiments, hired from several German States, in preparation for the Battle of Brooklyn, fought on 26 August 1776, and which proved to be a significant victory for the British[17] (Fig. 29). Howe's forces moved east of Brooklyn and captured the city of New York. The Americans were led by General George Washington, whose army was

Fig. 27. General Sir William Howe.

Fig. 28. Charles Cornwallis, 1st Marquess Cornwallis.

Fig. 29. Disembarkation of Troops at Gravesend Bay under the command of General Sir George Collier RN.

eventually surrounded on Brooklyn Heights, although they were evacuated and withdrawn. The British held the important port of New York for the duration of the war, providing an invaluable base for the navy. The local population, with their royalist sympathies, welcomed the victors, and raised the Union Flag in support.

After the Battle of Brooklyn, the 57th Foot stormed Redbank, whereupon the American forces retreated to New York itself. The 57th, under Colonel Campbell, embarked again to take New York Island, and later they attacked Paulus Hook (sometimes referred to as Powell's Hook), once more embarking in flat boats.[18] A number of paintings and engravings record aspects of the scene, highlighting the role played by the celebrated flat-bottomed boats which carried the British troops from ships to their destinations in preparation for further engagements on land (Fig. 30).[19]

Paulus Hook Fort, New Jersey

Following the successful attack on New York during August–September 1776, the 57th Foot was detached to capture and hold the American post at Paulus Hook on the opposite (western) side of the Hudson River, in what is now part of Jersey City. The fort was originally designed to block the passage of British ships in the Hudson River. The word "Hook" derives from the Dutch "Hoeck" "a point of land" and Paulus Hook was one of a series of fortifications which had been constructed on a piece of high ground to defend the west bank of the Hudson River, opposite New York.

Under its new masters, it was strengthened and reinforced to become a major

Fig. 30. The British landing at Kip's Bay, New York Island, 15 September 1776 by Robert Cleveley, 1777.*
Inset right: the flatboats used to land troops.

part of the defence by the British of New York and New Jersey. During the next few months, from 11 October to 10 November 1776, and early the following year, between 21 to 30 January 1777, a unit led by Lieutenant John Mallom was given the task of repairing and strengthening the existing redoubts (temporary fortifications) and erecting Log-Breast Works (Fig. 31). These were additional forms of defence, sometimes built with earth, but here and elsewhere, from logs of wood, erected as the name suggests, to breast or chest height, to provide protection for the infantry men standing behind them, who would be firing on an advancing enemy approaching the fort.[20] Nine men under Mallom's supervision took almost two months to complete the work, which increased the defences on the north and

---

* Note that the Robert Cleveley painting illustrates the successful landing on 15 September 1776, of 4,000 and later that day, a further 9,000 British and German Grenadiers, British Light Infantry, Brigade of Guards, and others, from five warships, at Kip's Bay on the eastern shore of Manhattan Island. The scene was viewed from Long Island, where the British were encamped. General Sir Henry Clinton was tasked with ordering the assault, and the British flatboats were the key to the amphibious landings on the American beaches, because their shallow draft allowed them to approach much closer to the shore before disembarking than would have been the case with standard longboats (Fig. 30). Landings were preceded by heavy bombardment of the shore by British warships, since the troops on board the flatboats would not have been able to fight their way onto the beaches. This was the Georgian equivalent of the D-Day landings in Normandy in June 1944.

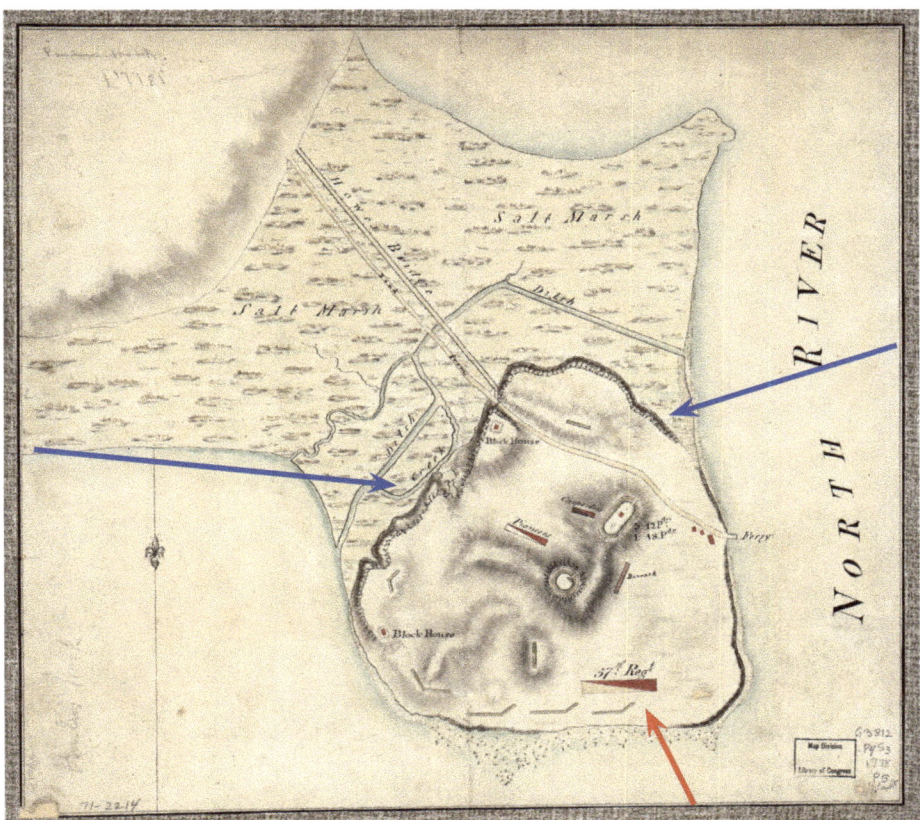

Fig. 31. Paulus Hook Fort, at the mouth of the North River (Hudson River), in 1778.
Shows the position of reinforcements to the west and the north (➤), the construction of which was supervised by Lt John Mallom in early 1777. The 57th Regiment building appears in the lower part of the fort (➤). Salt marshes, ditches and creeks lay between the fort and the mainland

west sides of the fort, as illustrated diagrammatically, in the contemporary map, shown above.[21] Beyond the new defences, to the north, lay salt marshes which were difficult for armed troops to cross. In addition to the improved wooden fortifications, the British dug a deep ditch about 20 feet wide through the marsh, from shore to shore, north of the fort, shown in light green on the map. This was defended by a drawbridge and a barred gate, blocking access to Paulus Hook Fort by land.[22] To the south, south-west and east of the fort lay the river waters. In other words, this was an ideal site for the British to construct a strong defensive position. The map also shows the approximate positions of the Block Houses, the barracks and the building occupied by the carpenters, who were responsible for building the improved fortifications, under Mallom's supervision.

Lieutenant Mallom submitted a written claim for costs of £16 4s 2d together with a personal allowance of £10, signed in his own hand, and countersigned by

Lieutenant Colonel John Campbell on 13 April 1777 (Fig. 32).

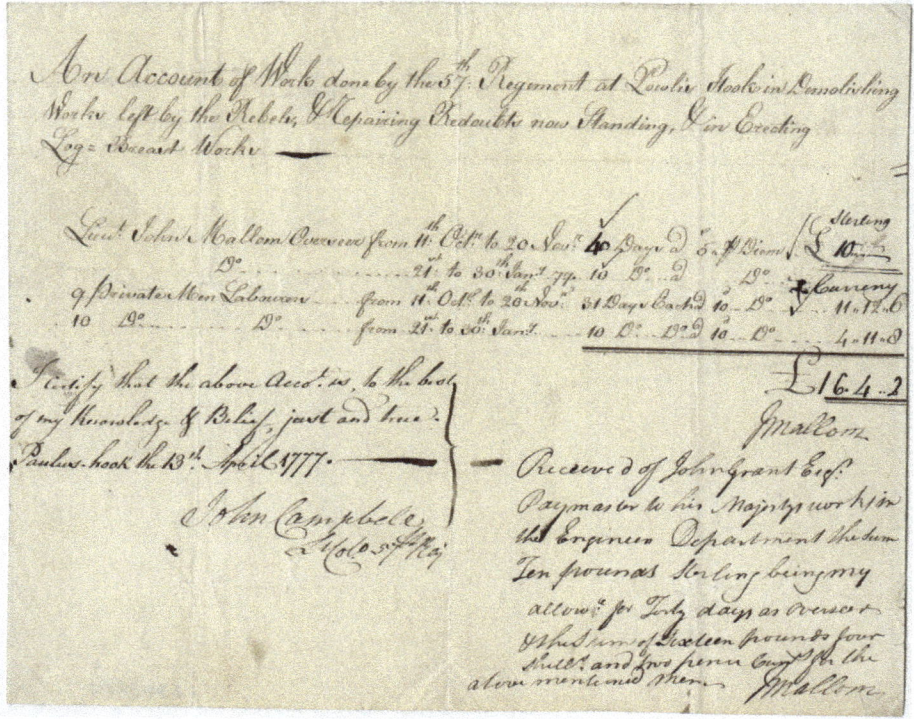

Fig. 32. Work carried-out at Paulus Hook Fort in 1777, under the supervision of Lieut. John Mallom of the 57th Regiment of Foot "Repairing Redoubts now Standing, & in Erecting Log Breast Work" Certified by Lt Col John Campbell and signed by J Mallom.

Using the methodology described earlier with a Purchasing Power Calculator for the Historic Standard of Living, and multiplying £10 by the percentage increase in the Retail Price Index from 1777 to 2020, converts the £10 to a value in 2020 of £1,315.00. Other calculations produce higher sums. Whatever the precise modern equivalent sum, the work at Paulus Hook Fort illustrates how John Mallom continued to supplement his Army income as he had attempted to do through his appeal to Lord Townshend in 1770, when his regiment was based in Dublin. The Paulus Hook claim form survived and was sold at auction in New York, in October 2012,[23] and again shortly afterwards, when it was acquired on behalf of "The Society of the Cincinnati" of Washington DC, the oldest patriotic organisation in the United States of America. The document appears to be a rare item within the history of the American War of Independence, and an experienced military historian of the conflict commented:

It is widely recognized that the standard rate of pay for a British soldier was barely enough to live on, but at least it was secure in an age where labouring and even trade jobs were not. [However], what is seldom mentioned in the literature is that soldiers had a great many opportunities to earn money over and above their base pay. Men with trades such as tailoring, carpentry, or working as a gunsmith, could do work for their regiments or for the army in general, drawing extra pay; men without trades, or with trades like weaving that had no military value, earned money doing things like building and maintaining fortifications, mending military roads, and similar activities.[24]

This is exactly what John Mallom and his men did at Paulus Hook Fort, and no doubt it was a mark of the calibre of the man, that he was selected to supervise the work.

The British held the fort until 19 August 1779, when it was recaptured by the Americans led by Major Henry Lee (Major Light Horse Harry Lee), the father of General Robert E Lee.[25] Paulus Hook Fort has long since disappeared, and nothing now remains of it. In the early 1800s, a ferry service connected the site with New York, about 15 minutes away.[26] With the passing years, the growth and development of Jersey City, New Jersey, has completely covered the site. The salt marshes were drained, and now the entire area, west of the Hudson River, has become part of a modern American city. In 1903, a 25-foot granite obelisk, the Paulus Hook Monument, was erected to mark the struggle of the 'Daughters of the American Revolution' fought on the ground where the fort once stood (Fig. 33). The obelisk stands at the junction of Washington Street and Grand Street, Jersey City, having been moved and reconstructed following previous damage.

LIEUTENANT MALLOM SERVES ON COURT MARTIAL PANELS

First Court Martial Panel: having been in charge of a party of men tasked with strengthening the defences at Paulus Hook Fort whilst he was a Lieutenant, it appears that John Mallom was becoming a trusted junior officer. At the same time as this work was being completed, Mallom was appointed to serve on the Panel of a General Court Martial which took place between 1 February and 4 March 1777 in New York. This was to be the first of five such Panels on which he would serve, between February 1777 and June 1779, and extracts of a few of the cases have been included to give a sense of the types of misdemeanours brought to trial by Court Martial at this time, and who took part. The names of other Panel members have been included for the benefit of historians of the period, and for general interest. The Panels on which John Mallom

PAULUS HOOK
WASHINGTON'S "FLYING CAMP" HERE IN 1776. LATER FORT HELD BY THE BRITISH DURING ENTIRE WAR DESPITE AMERICAN ATTACKS.

Fig. 33. Paulus Hook Monument, Jersey City, New Jersey, USA

served were held at New York, Head of Elk in Maryland, Philadelphia, Mount Holly in New Jersey, and Stoney Point in New York.

The President at the New York Courts Martial was Lieutenant Colonel John Maxwell, of the 27th Regiment of Foot and Stephen Payne Adye Esquire was the Deputy Judge Advocate. The other Panel Members were Captain John Webster, 4th Foot, Captain John Lemoine, Royal Artillery, Captain Gerard Lawrence, 57th Foot, Captain Edward Hubbard, 45th Foot, Lieutenant Alex[ande]r. Shand, Royal Artillery, Captain William Cotton, 27th Foot, Captain Francis Needham, 17th Dragoons, Captain Charles Brownlow, 57th Foot, Captain George Gillman, 27th Foot, Lieutenant David Hay, 57th Foot and Lieutenant James Hussey, 17th Dragoons.

The first case before the Court was that of Patrick Snow, a private soldier in His Majesty's Regiment of Royal Highland Emigrants, charged with desertion. It was claimed that the Prisoner had confessed to desertion, but in his defence, Snow claimed he was a member of a ship's crew based at the Newfoundland Station, and that he came across a group of soldiers of the Royal Highland Emigrant Regiment on shore, and that in a drunken state, he was told he had enlisted in the regiment. He claimed to have been at sea since the age of 14 years, and had no knowledge of the duties of a soldier. After considering the evidence, Patrick Snow was found "guilty of the Crime laid to his Charge in breach of the 1st Article of War of the 6th Section." He was sentenced to 300 lashes on his bare back with a cat of nine tails (the cat). The punishment was approved by Sir William Howe, Commander in Chief of His Majesty's Forces.[27]

It is worth noting that of the Panel Members, four of them were from the 57th Foot, including Lieutenant John Mallom, no doubt because of easy availability, the regiment being stationed at the time in New York. This Panel met for more than four weeks, although not necessarily every day, during which time it heard a total of 15 cases, including that of Private Snow. Three prisoners were privates, one was a corporal, two were mariners, one was a 'Gentleman Ensign', and three were civilian inhabitants of the Garrison of New York, one of whom was described as a negro, such was the terminology of the period.[28] The charges included desertion, desertion and bearing arms in the Rebel Army, desertion and theft, including of both crown and private property, forgery of a Bill of Exchange leading to gain of $452, and the murder of a fellow private. Those found guilty of desertion and murder were sentenced to death by hanging.

Confusion might be claimed as an excuse for a serious offence: Private John Ingram of His Majesty's 6th Regiment of Foot was charged with desertion, but the Prisoner claimed he was intoxicated when he enlisted on 29 April 1776, and that he did not realise what he had done. The Court found him guilty, and he was sentenced to 1000 lashes on his bare back with the cat of nine tails.[29]

Corporal John Stewart of the 7th Regiment of Foot (Royal Fusiliers) was accused of having deserted, corresponded with the rebels, and borne arms in the Rebel Army. Evidence was given in support, but Ingham stated that he had been taken prisoner by the rebels, and that he was "over-persuaded" to go with them, although he surrendered himself to a party of the 42nd Regiment at Newark, New Jersey, in early December (1776). Captain Kineer gave testimony of the Prisoner's previous good character, but the Court found him guilty and sentenced Private Ingham to death.[30]

Other prisoners tried at the same Court Martial were Thomas Randal, a Mariner on board the *"Stevenson,"* a transport ship, accused of theft from Thomas Brown, a carpenter of the same ship; William Johnstone, a mariner accused of theft from a Mrs Reade's house, in New York; William Walsh, Catherine Walsh and Joseph Van Black, of New York, accused of stealing Crown Property; Michael Newman, a 'Gentleman Ensign' of the 35th Foot, accused of forging the name of a fellow officer intending to defraud him; Joseph Smith, a private in the 45th Foot, accused of the murder of William Smith a private in the same regiment; William Hays, a private in the 40th Foot, accused of theft from the house of an inhabitant of Staten Island, and of murdering a Cornelius Symondson; John Garretson, and finally of Jacob Van Tassel and Thomas Gibson, retainers of the Army, employed in recruiting to His Majesty's Service, accused of theft from the house of William Seton of Collas Barrack in the Province of West Chester.

Second Court Martial Panel: Lieutenant Mallom served on a second General Court Martial Panel held at Head of Elk, Maryland, on 1 September 1777. The President was Lieutenant Colonel William Meadows of the 55th Regiment of Foot, and the other Panel Members were Major Peter Craig, 57th Foot (same regiment as Mallom), Hon. Major John Maitland, 71st Foot, Captain Michael Cuffe, 27th Foot, Captain George Harris, 5th Foot, Captain John Hatfield, 43rd Foot, Captain Archibald McAlister, 35th Foot, Hon. Captain Charles Cochrane, 4th Foot, Captain George Hamilton, 52nd Foot, Lieutenant Arthur French, 22nd Foot, Lieutenant Samuel Ruxton, 45th Foot and Lieutenant Joshua Paul Minchin, 5th Foot. The Deputy Judge Advocate was Captain Alexander Ross, 45th Foot. The Prisoner was Private Daniel Holwell, 33rd Light Infantry Company who was charged with desertion, and after the evidence of nine witnesses was heard, Holwell was found not guilty and acquitted.[31] No other cases were heard at Head of Elk.

JOHN MALLOM'S PROMOTION TO CAPTAIN IN THE 63RD REGIMENT OF FOOT

Ten days after the completion of the Head of Elk Court Martial hearings, on 12 September 1777, Lt. John Mallom was promoted to Captain in the 63rd Regiment of Foot as shown in the Promotions Listing.[32] This would have involved his purchasing the vacant office, since promotion in the British Army of the 18th century was not solely on merit or length of service, but by the ability to pay. The cost of purchasing his new position had increased by £450 in 1772. In 1854, when the price of an ensigncy was still £450, that of a captaincy was £1800, although as already seen, the officer paid the difference in costs between his lieutenancy and the captaincy.[33] In contrast, a contemporary American publication quotes the cost of purchasing a captaincy in a British Army Regiment of Foot in 1776, as £1500, representing a difference of £950 from the rank of Lieutenant.[34] It is no surprise therefore, that officers within this rank and higher were mainly the sons of the wealthy and privileged. The 63rd Foot had been raised as a new Regiment in 1758 out of the 2nd Battalion of the English or The King's Regiment of 1756. In 1783, it was renamed The 63rd West Sussex Regiment of Foot, and it was amalgamated with the 96th Regiment of Foot, under the Childers Reforms of 1881, to become The 1st Battalion The Manchester Regiment.[35] From 1768–1781, the 63rd Foot was under the command of Lieutenant General Francis Grant, whose name appears at the head of each of the Muster Rolls of the Regiment which includes the name of Captain Mallom, and which are noted below. At this time, the regiment included 11 Captains, including Mallom, 1 Captain Lieutenant, 13 Lieutenants, including Mallom's friend, John Money, who features later in the account, and 11 Ensigns.[36] Each Company within a Regiment was usually commanded by a Captain, in this case, John Mallom, by whose name the Company was identified in its Musters.[37] Regiments of the British Army normally comprised 10 Companies, made up of 2 Flank Companies (1 Grenadier Company and 1 Light Infantry Company) and 8 Companies of Foot (or Infantry), the term 'Flank' referring to the right and left side of an attacking line of battle, the most vulnerable positions.[38] As already implied, promotion to a more senior rank in a regiment of the British Army would inevitably involve more than merely an assessment of competence and suitability. "Who you know" appears to have been crucial as well. Competition and ambition inevitably played a part when junior officers vied for promotion, as shown in an entry recorded in the diary of Lieutenant John Peebles of the 42nd Regiment of Foot, 1776–1782, as follows:

> Monday 19 May [1777] a good deal of rain these two nights past-yesterday a Lieut. [John? Mallon came to join the 57th Compy Grrs. who is senior to me, advised to speak to Colo[nel [Henry] Monckton about it—instead of which I wrote him a letter setting forth my services & the hardship it would be to lose my chance of promotion in the flank Corps by an elder L[ieutenant]t popping in now who declined serving in them before...

The "Compy Grrs" was the Grenadier Company of the 57th Foot, and it is clear that Peebles was concerned that Mallom would be appointed Captain in preference to him. In fact, four months later, Mallom was indeed appointed Captain in the 63rd Foot and Peebles became a Captain in the 42nd Foot, so any form of competition or animosity between the two officers was short-lived. On the other hand, the illustration shows how complex and involved the process of officer promotion could be, and how much was at stake at a personal level between contenders for a new position. Some British Army Officers kept diaries of their activities, regimental responsibilities, battles, and personal details, and some of the diaries written during the American War of Independence have survived. They shed a unique light on the conflict from the perspective of an individual officer, which adds greatly to the historical record.[39] No sign of a War Diary kept by John Mallom has been found, and so his own personal views on the War in America, are unknown.

Third Court Martial Panel: after his promotion, Captain Mallom served on a third Court Martial Panel, which took place at the Army Headquarters in Philadelphia, between Tuesday 24 February and Wednesday 11 March 1778, under the Presidency of Lt. Col. Thomas Musgrave of the 40th Foot. A total of nine cases were heard. The other Panel Members were Major Henry Fox, 49th Foot, Major George Harris 5th Foot, Captain Peter Traille, Royal Artillery, Captain John Stewart, 37th Foot, Captain Frederick Cornwallis, 33rd Foot, Captain Peregrine Thorne, 4th Foot, Captain George Thwaites, 10th Foot, Captain Baldwin Leighton, 46th Foot, Captain William Norton, 44th Foot, Captain Hildebrand Oakes, 33rd Foot and Captain John Birch, 27th Foot. The Deputy Judge Advocate was Captain Stephen Payne Adye, Royal Artillery. The first prisoner was James Duncan, Master of the ship *"Rose"* who was charged with enlisting three mariners from His Majesty's Ship *"Zebra"*. He pleaded guilty and no witnesses were called.[40] Duncan was: "sentenced to pay £20 Sterling for each of the Three men he enlisted, knowing them to belong to ... Zebra."[41]

Corporal John Fisher was charged with having committed rape on Maria Nicholls a "Woman Child of Nine Years of Age." Seven witnesses were called, including Maria Nicholls herself, George Kitson, a Surgeon's Mate, and four Officers from Fisher's regiment. Graphic detail of the assault was included in the Court's report. Fisher was found guilty and "Sentenced to suffer Death by hanged by the neck until he is dead."[42] The Commander-in-Chief approved the sentence.

Private John Walker of His Majesty's 10th Foot was accused of robbing Christina Hudson, an inhabitant of Philadelphia, and deserting from his regiment. Witnesses, including Ms Hudson, were called, and Walker was found guilty of both Robbery and Desertion. He was sentenced "to suffer Death by hanging until he is dead." Confirmed by W[illiam] Howe.[43]

Private John Mills of the 64th Foot was charged with Desertion and bearing Arms in the Rebel Army. He was found guilty and "sentenced to death by being hanged until he is dead." The Commander in Chief confirmed the Sentence.[44]

On 17 March 1778, the Prisoners, Corporal John Fisher, John Walker and John Mills, were executed "on Monday 23rd Instant, on the Common, between the hours of Ten and Twelve in the forenoon."[45]

Captain Alexander Campbell of the 2nd Battalion, 84th Foot, Aide to General Sir William Erskine, was accused of Treachery based on the testimony of a young woman named Mary Figis/Fygis. He was accused of corresponding with and giving intelligence to General Washington. More than 20 witnesses were called, mainly private citizens, and

> the Court having Duly Considered the Evidence for and against the Prisoner, together with what we [he] had to offer in his defence is of the Opinion that there is not a sufficiency of evidence on the part of the Prosecutor to Convict him of the crime laid to his charge, and doth therefore acquit him. The Commander in Chief confirms the above Sentence, and orders the Prisoner Capt. Campbell to be released from his Confinement.[46]

The other prisoners tried at this Court Martial were Thomas Beck, a boatswain on the ship *"Rose"* accused of enticing a mariner to desert from the *"Zebra"* and Silver Crispin, a carpenter on the transport ship, *"America"* with Mary O'Hara, accused of assault upon a Lieutenant White.

Fourth Court Martial Panel: John Mallom served his fourth Court Martial Panel, at Mount Holly in New Jersey Province, on Sunday 21 June 1778, to hear the case of John Fisher, a Drummer in His Majesty's 28th Regiment of Foot, while he (Mallom) was conveniently based at Mount Holly. The other Panel Members were, Lieutenant Colonel Duncan McPherson, 42nd Foot, Major Will[ia]m Gardiner, 10th Foot, Captain Mathew Johnson, 46th Foot, Captain Primrose Kennedy, 44th Foot, Captain Walter Home, 7th Foot, Captain Charles Broconion, 57th Foot, Captain John Nixon, 49th Foot, Captain Sam[ue]l. Waring, 27th Foot, Captain William Gore, 33rd Foot, Captain John Peebles, 42nd Foot, and Captain Dennis Kelley, 64th Foot. As was the case during the trial of Captain Campbell at Philadelphia, no officer lower in rank than Captain served on this Panel. The President was Lieutenant Colonel William Grant, 42nd Foot and Stephen Payne Adye Esquire was the Deputy Judge Advocate.

John Fisher was accused of desertion and of bearing arms in the Rebel Service, a capital offence. Six witnesses testified and it was stated that Fisher had deserted from his regiment on 11 April 1777. In his defence, the Prisoner claimed he had been separated from his comrades by opposition forces, and had escaped to Morris Town, some 15 miles to the north, in the territory held by the Americans. He claimed he worked there as a labourer and was married, but had subsequently attempted to return to his regiment. The Court reviewed the evidence and concluded that he was "Guilty of the Crimes laid to his Charge," and "of a Breach of the 1st Article of War of the 6th Section, and the 19th Article of the 14th Section." John Fisher was sentenced to death, the execution by hanging being carried-out on 22 June 1778, "on a tree by the road on the army's route of march, where any soldiers contemplating desertion could ponder his fate."[47] The Court Martial was led by

William Grant, President, and Stephen Payne Adye, Deputy Judge Advocate.[48]

Private Joseph Reade of the 63rd Foot (Mallom's Regiment), was charged with desertion, but after hearing evidence from four witnesses, including Serjeant Daniel Gantley of the 63rd Foot, the prisoner was found not guilty and acquitted.[49]

The other prisoners tried at this Court Martial were Primus Cuffey, a negro and Follower of the Army, accused of Plundering, and James Power and Samuel Martin, both negros and also Followers of the Army, accused of Plundering.

Fifth Court Martial Panel: the final panel in which Captain Mallom took part was at Stoney Point Camp, New York, on 7 June 1779, under the Presidency of Lieut. Col. Henry Johnson of the 17th Regiment of Foot. The other Panel Members were Major Robert McLeroth, 64th Foot, Major Thomas Barclay, Loyal American Regiment, Captain Robert Clayton, 17th Foot, Captain Christopher Hatch, Loyal American Regiment, Captain Hayes St Leger, 63rd Foot, Captain John Kennedy Strong, 64th Foot, Captain Morris Robinson, Loyal American regiment, Lieutenant John Birmingham, 63rd Foot, Lieutenant William John Mawhood 17th Foot, Lieutenant David Bolswell, 64th Foot and Lieutenant Duncan Fletcher, Loyal American regiment. The Deputy Judge Advocate was Lieutenant John Thomas Layard, 54th Foot.

Five Prisoners were brought before the Court, including Private Benjamin Reynard of the 37th Regiment Grenadier Company charged with "being two miles from Camp without leave, and for plundering in the Country." Mary Baker, a local inhabitant, stated that the Prisoner, with others, entered her house and plundered it of valuable articles including clothing, and that he killed a pig and stole it. Other witnesses gave evidence in the prisoner's support, but he was found guilty and sentenced to 1000 lashes on his bare back with a cat of nine tails.[50]

The other prisoners tried at this Court Martial were all soldiers: John Boswell, a Serjeant Drummer in the Volunteers of Ireland, accused of rape, George Watkins and Richard Sharpe, both Privates in the 38th Grenadier Guards, accused of desertion and robbery, and George Burns, Private in the 71st Grenadier Company, accused of desertion.

Details of the discussions by the Panel members which took place after hearing the evidence and before the Court reached its conclusions, have not survived, but it is likely that John Mallom's contributions in the first Court Martial Panel satisfied the authorities that he was able to handle the requirements of military law and offer a sound and balanced opinion. In other words, he was seen as a safe pair of hands. On the other hand, officers were usually selected for Court Martial Panel service if they were based near-by, for convenience and timing, although personal suitability and good standing would have been taken into account. Mallom was a member of a Court Martial Panel which heard the cases of 35 prisoners between

February 1777 and June 1779. Some other officers heard as many cases as this or more.[51] The penalties for those found guilty were very harsh. The "cat" might inflict fatal injuries, but the army had to try and ensure discipline in difficult circumstances.

THE 63RD FOOT IN THE NORTHERN CAMPAIGN

The role of the 63rd Regiment of Foot in the campaigns of the American War is clearly documented in the *History of the Manchester Regiment, Volume I, 1758–1883*.[52] In October 1777, Sir William Howe, Commander-in-Chief of British forces in America, having successfully captured and occupied Philadelphia the previous month, asked to be relieved of his duties, citing inadequate resources. He was succeeded by Sir Henry Clinton, who took up the post in March 1778, and commanded the British forces until the Yorktown surrender, four years later.[53] By the time of Clinton's appointment, the 63rd Foot appears to have withdrawn from New York, where Mallom's Company was based from June to December 1778, to Philadelphia. According to Wylly, the strength of the 63rd Foot on 24 March 1778, was 1 Major, 4 Captains (including John Mallom), 7 Lieutenants, 3 Ensigns, 1 Adjutant, 1 Quartermaster, 1 Surgeon, 1 Surgeon's Mate, 15 Sergeants, 12 Drummers, 271 Rank and File. There were almost 100 men who were absent; sick.[54] By late 1778, Mallom's Company had moved back to Staten Island, New York, and to Paulus Hook, where Lieutenant Mallom, as he then was, had supervised work to strengthen the Fort. However, during the last few months of 1778, the 63rd Foot saw little action in and around New York.[55] In January 1779, the 63rd Foot had 1 Major, 6 Captains, 6 Lieutenants, 1 Ensign, 1 Adjutant, 1 Quartermaster, 1 Surgeon, 21 Sergeants, 14 Drummers, and 282 Rank and File. 25 were sick and 10 were prisoners, and the regiment was stationed on New York Island. By October 1779, Mallom's Company was on Staten Island, as recorded on the relevant Muster. By December 1779, the total British force of men at New York was 19,153 of all ranks, with the strength of the 63rd Foot given as 407 of all ranks. Although the British held New York, its harbour and Long Island for the rest of the war, they failed to subdue the Patriots or recapture the northern states, and in the light of this, the British turned their attention to the south, concentrating on the states of Georgia and South Carolina, and it was here that Mallom's Company was to be based, in Charleston.

THE 63RD FOOT IN THE SOUTHERN CAMPAIGN

The 63rd Foot sailed from New York to Charles Town (Charleston), South Carolina (Fig. 34), where they were to form part of the garrison.[56] The Southern Campaign of the American War was now under way, commanded by Earl Charles Cornwallis. Much has been written about the role of Cornwallis during the American War of Independence, including his conduct of the Charleston campaign, and the recent editing and publication of the "Cornwallis Papers" has greatly improved the overall assessment of the war in the south.[57]

Clinton took Charleston with a force of 14,000 men, in what was a serious defeat for the rebels, and provided the British with a sea port in which to bring in men and supplies. Clinton oversaw the campaign in the south from New York, and on 13 May 1780, he wrote to the Right Hon. Lord George Germain (later 1st Viscount Sackville PC), Secretary of State for the Colonies, in London, summarising the situation in Charleston, mentioning the defeat of General Lincoln on 12 May.

Fig. 34. Siege of Charleston (1780).

63rd Foot   **96th Foot**

Private, battalion company, holding musket

Officer, wearing sash and sword

Officer, battalion company

Private, grenadier company wearing mitre cap, with musket

Private, battalion company with musket

Fig. 35. Uniforms of the 63rd Foot (L), and the 96th Foot (R), by Gerald C. Hudson.
The 63rd and the 96th Regiments of Foot were amalgamated in 1881 under the Childers Reforms, to form The Manchester Regiment.

The commander of the troops in George Town was Brigadier-General James Paterson, who was Lieutenant Colonel in the 63rd Regiment of Foot, and it follows that John Mallom's Company was part of a body of troops occupying Charleston, South Carolina.[58] During the war, part of the 63rd Foot served as cavalry, in effect, mounted infantrymen and took an active part in several brilliant affairs under the celebrated light cavalry leader, [Lieutenant] Colonel [Banastre] Tarleton (Bloody Ban).[59] The uniforms worn by officers and men of the 63rd Regiment of Foot, are illustrated in Fig 35.

Musters which include the name of Captain John Mallom as Company Commander

It is inevitable that more has been written about the military commanders and high-ranking army officers in the conduct of the war, than about the junior and middle-grade officers, such as the Lieutenants and Captains, like John Mallom. The commanders had both the oversight of the military situation and the staff to help them compile diaries, keep correspondence and written records which would later be published. Mallom and his fellow officers of equivalent rank did not have these advantages; that was not their role, and few of them kept diaries. Nevertheless, there is value in examining their activities and responsibilities, using whatever surviving records include their names. Records of the 63rd Foot which hold the names of its officers and others during the period 1777–1782 when John Mallom was included in the list of Captains, are to be found in the Annual Printed Army Lists prepared during the American War.[60] Considerably more information was kept in hand-written documents in the series of Musters for the 1st Battalion, 63rd Regiment of Foot, in the name of "Captain John Mallom's Company." The first Muster was entitled "Major Kinneer's Company." And he was Mallom's immediate superior at the time of his promotion into the 63rd Foot as Captain.[61] The administrative cost to the British Army of documenting all the changes which occurred in a regiment in the field, both in the Musters and also in supplementing the Annual Printed Army Lists with hand-written notes, must have been considerable, but they illustrate the position during the American War in both the northern and the southern campaigns. Each Muster, compiled six-monthly, is entitled "His Majesty's 63rd Regiment commanded by Lieut[enan]t General Francis Grant," in which the names of its officers and numbers of individual ranks have been included for the benefit of those interested in the details. The first 8 Musters follow here, and the remainder after the intervening events, later, so as to maintain the chronological order of the actions.

> Muster 1. Major Francis William Kinneer's Company for 183 days commencing 25 June 1777 ending 24 December 1777, both days inclusive. The Establishment (Proof Table) included Captain Mallom, promoted to the regiment, and taking up his duties on 7 October 1777, 2 Lieutenants, 1 Adjutant (John Money), 1 Quarter Master, 1 Surgeon and 1 [Surgeon's] Mate, 2 Ensigns, 5 Sergeants, 5 Corporals, 2 Drummers,

1 Chaplain; Edward Philips, 15 men Sick, and 19 Casuals from 25 June 1777, of whom 6 had died, and 1 of whom was promoted to Captain Mallom's Company (Thomas Buffey). Signed by Fr[ancis] W[ilia]m Kinneer, Major, Matt[hew] La[w]lor, Ens[ig]n and J. Money Adj[utant] in Philadelphia on 22 April 1778. Captain John Mallom was promoted into Major Kinneer's Company of the 63rd Foot, but soon assumed command of his own Company, as we see next:

Muster 2. Captain Mallom's Company for 183 Days from 25 June 1777 to 24 December following, both days inclusive. The Establishment included: 1 Captain (Mallom) and Captain Francis Jones (died, 13 Oct 1777), 2 Lieutenants (including 1 dead), 1 Ensign, 3 Sergeants, including 1 promoted to be Captain in Lord Rawdon's Company, 5 Corporals, including 1 appointed Sergeant in Captain St Leger's Company, and 1 in Captain McKinnon's Company, 2 Drummers, 12 men Sick, and 12 Casuals, including 3 transferred to other Companies, and 7 now dead. Signed: J Mallom Capt[ain] and J Money Lieut[ant], in Philadelphia on 22 April 1778.

Muster 3. The next Muster in the series for Captain Mallom's Company, by inference taken between December 1777 and June 1778, seems not to have survived.[62] During the period of this Muster, Captain Mallom's Company of the 63rd Foot was apparently in Philadelphia where the previous Muster was signed in April 1778, and they may have continued here until the order was received for them to move to South Carolina. In support of this assessment, Wylly commented that "… the 63rd Regiment appears to have moved from New York to Philadelphia, there joining the main army under General Howe …"[63]

Muster 4. Captain John Mallom's Company for 183 Days from 25 June 1778, to 24 December following, both days inclusive. The Establishment included: 1 Captain (Mallom-Absent), 1 Lieutenant, 3 Sergeants, 3 Corporals, 2 Drummers and 27 Privates (and 8 absent). The post of Ensign was vacant. The names of 3 'Prisoners with the Rebels' were also included. In addition, were the names of 19 'Casuals,' 9 of whom had been discharged, 5 of whom had died, and 1 of whom had deserted. The initial period of absence of Captain Mallom may have been due to his presence at the second Court Martial Panel in New Jersey. And at the end of the Muster, the following: "This Muster is taken for 183 Days commencing the 25 June 1778 and ending the 24 December following both Days inclusive." Signed: J Mallom Capt[ain], Tho[mas] Gibson L[ieutenan]t, at New York Island Greenwich, 24 Dec[ember] 1778. Similar statements were written on each of the Musters summarised here.

Muster 5. Captain John Mallom's Company for 182 Days from 25 December 1778, to 24 June following (1779), both days inclusive. The

Establishment included: 1 Captain (Mallom), 1 Lieutenant, 1 Ensign (Absent), 2 Sergeants (and 1 Absent), 1 Corporal (and 3 Absent), 1 Drummer (and 1 Absent), and 36 Privates (and 17 Absent), total 53 men, of which a note is added that one man was absent after the 24 June. Total 52 men. Signed: J Mallom, Capt[ain], Thomas Gibson L[ieutenen]t. Staten Island [New York], 5 October 1779.

Muster 6. Captain John Mallom's Company for 183 Days from 25 June 1779 to 24 December 1779, both days inclusive. The Establishment included: 1 Captain (Mallom), 1 Lieutenant, 1 Ensign, 3 Sergeants, 3 Corporals, 2 Drummers and 57 Privates with No Casuals. All present. Signed by J Impett, Lieut[enant] and Will[ia]m Watson, Ensign, both of the 63rd Reg[imen]t, [New] York Harbour, 24 December 1779.

Muster 7. Captain John Mallom's Company for 182 Days from 25 December 1779 to 24 June following (1780), both days inclusive. The Establishment included: 1 Captain (Mallom-Present), 1 Lieutenant, 1 Ensign, 3 Sergeants, 3 Corporals, 2 Drummers and 57 Privates, together with 1 Casuals since 24 June. Total 58 men. Signed by J Impett, Lieut[enant] 63rd Reg[imen]t, Charles Town, 24 June 1780. Within a few days following the onset date of this Muster, the main British force left New York for the southern states of America. The 63rd Foot was assessed in total as 407 men of all ranks on the day they embarked on 26 December 1779 for what was to be a very stormy sea voyage. Some ships were lost and others captured by privateers before the fleet arrived off the coast of [South] Carolina in early February 1780.[64]

Muster 8. Captain John Mallom's Company for 183 Days from 25 June 1780 to 24 December 1780, both days inclusive. The Establishment included 1 Captain (Mallom-Present), 1 Lieutenant, 1 Ensign, 3 Sergeants, 3 Corporals, 2 Drummers and 46 Privates, together with 16 Casuals since 24 June, total 62 men. Signed J. Impett, Lieut[enant], and Will[ia]m Watson, Ensign, 63rd Reg[imen]t, Charles Town, 24 December 1780. A note was added beneath the heading of the Muster stating that Lieutenant Gibson died on 20 November 1780. The Muster also included the names of 20 Prisoners of War.

The movement of the 63rd Foot to Charleston, South Carolina, was to form part of the garrison in the city after the siege which lasted from 28 March to 12 May 1780. British troops under Sir Henry Clinton, numbered almost 13,000 according to some accounts, supported by a fleet of Royal Naval vessels commanded by Vice Admiral Mariot Arbuthnot. The fleet included warships, armed galleys, and a large number of transports. The American Patriots were led by Major General Benjamin Lincoln, who were outnumbered and forced to surrender.[65]

Musters 9 to 11 of Captain Mallom's Company follow after the Battle of Camden, and the death of Lieutenant John Money.

COURT MARTIAL OF CAPTAIN HAYES ST LEGER IN CHARLESTON, SOUTH CAROLINA

On 6 May 1780, while the 63rd Foot was stationed in Charleston, John Mallom's name appeared in another Court Martial report, not as a member of the Panel, but as a witness. There had been a serious altercation between two officers of his regiment, Captain Hayes St. Leger and Major James Wemyss.

> St Leger [was] accused of mutinous and Disrespectful behaviour to Major Wemyss as his Commanding Officer.

The President of the Court was Lieutenant Colonel Alured Clarke of the Royal Fusiliers, and Lieutenant John Blucke of the Royal Welch Fusiliers was the Deputy Judge Advocate. Of the 12 Panel Members, one was a Major and the others, Captains, including Captain Croker of the 63rd Foot. Hayes St. Leger was also Captain in the 63rd Foot, so they were both Mallom's colleagues. Major Wemyss introduced the prosecution by stating that he had sent Lieutenant John Money, (Mallom's friend), with a message to St. Leger and fellow officers, on 20 April 1780, that they should not use any room in Perrinvou's House, Charleston, without his permission. Half an hour later Wemyss saw Captain St. Leger and Captain Roberts coming out of the house, whereupon

> St. Leger said to him that he had received an order which he looked upon to be a very extraordinary one, such (as he believed) no Commanding Officer ever gave out before, and added that he should not obey it till he had consulted his friends.

That evening, after the regimental parade, a further conversation took place between the prisoner and Wemyss,

> that the order should be laid before the Commander in Chief, or cleared up at Head Quarters, or words to that effect.

Major Wemyss believed that this constituted a serious breach of orders, leading to the Court Martial. Asked if Money had heard anything which might constitute a mutinous or disrespectful attitude to Major Wemyss, Money replied

> No, I did not." However, Money "was in your Room at the time, when the Band was playing and therefore [I] could not hear what passed." Major Wemyss claimed the prosecution was brought "with the utmost reluctance" stating that regimental discipline was at stake

His order applied equally to the other officers, but only St. Leger had queried it, and in his opinion, this amounted to mutiny. Wemyss added that

> this is the first time I ever appeared before a General Court Martial either as Prosecutor [or] Prisoner and have to lament the occasion that has now

compelled me to trouble this Court. I beg leave to say that I am particularly sorry this affair should have come before a General Court Martial, as Captain St. Leger, had he not been reported to the Commander in Chief, has expressed a desire of making me such an apology as I should have been perfectly satisfied with.

In his defence, Captain St. Leger stated that he and some fellow officers had found a large room in Major General Huyne's Quarters (Perrinvou's House), which was unoccupied. He and Captain Roberts applied for permission to use it as an Officers' Mess, and the General's permission was given. On the morning of 20 April, he was surprised when Lieutenant Money brought the order from Major Wemyss that the room should be vacated, particularly as the General had not withdrawn his agreement for it to be used. St. Leger argued that he had no intention of disputing authority, but he regarded Wemyss's Order "as having the appearance of Illegality" By this he meant that:

> had the order been given with a view to promote the discipline and good order of the Regiment no one would with more pleasure have tacitly complied with it than myself, but in this Case the order proceeded from views of a private nature, and discipline seemed totally out of question, for I cannot suppose that our dining in a Room within our Quarter Guard with the Major Generals permission could by any means affect the discipline of the Regiment.

St. Leger cross-examined Major Wemyss concerning General Huyne's permission for the officers to use the Room, and how this affected his order. Wemyss called Lieutenant Cope of the 63rd Foot, who agreed that he had conveyed the Major's disapproval of the actions of Captain St. Leger and his fellow officers. He told the Court that St. Leger had said that the Major Wemyss's orders should be issued in writing, and not just verbally. St Leger called Captain Roberts, of the 63rd Foot, who stated that St. Leger had apologised to Major Wemyss, and he named Captain Mallom as the officer who brought Major Wemyss's response that he would accept this if it were offered in the presence of the Captains of the Flank Companies of the regiment. Although he was named on four occasions in this section of the trial, Mallom was not called to give evidence in person. The implication, however, is that he was in Court that day, on 6 May 1780, in Charleston, where his regiment was based. The concluding statement to the Court by Captain Roberts in reply to Major Wemyss, was as follows:

> Capt. St. Leger told me immediately after he had left Major Wemyss that he had told Major Wemyss he was determined to obey his Order: and that Major Wemyss replied, 'you have done very right, for if you had not, by G-d I would have broke you.' Capt. St. Leger also told me I suppose in Confidence that he said to Major Wemyss had the affair happened between two Gentlemen independent of the Commanding Officer, it would

or should have been settled here.

The Court acquitted St. Leger of mutinous behaviour, but he was found guilty of disrespectful behaviour towards Major Wemyss as his Commanding Officer. Captain Hayes St. Leger was sentenced to be reprimanded at the Head of the 63rd Regt. of Foot by Major Andre, the Deputy Adjutant General.[66] To the modern reader, this case bears the hallmarks of a disagreement between two officers which blew-up out of all proportion. However, the Army had a responsibility to maintain discipline, particularly when a regiment was preparing for action in the field. On the other hand, Major Wemyss had an extremely bad reputation in the eyes of the rebel army, being described as "the second most hated British Officer in the South."[67] Even his British contemporaries referred to the "wanton cruelties committed on Peedee by Major Wemyss ... unleashing his own brand of barbarism on the inhabitants of South Carolina..."[68]

John Mallom, therefore, had the dubious honour of serving both with Colonel Banastre Tarleton, and also with Major James Wemyss, the two British officers most hated by the Americans, although there is nothing to suggest that their activities tainted the life and career of Captain Mallom. On the other hand, the way a senior officer conducted himself in the heat of battle may well have been reflected in the way he dealt with his junior colleagues, as was undoubtedly the case for Wemyss with St Leger.

As for the two contenders in Court that day, Major Wemyss was seriously injured and taken prisoner by the Americans under General Sumter at the skirmish at Fishdam Ford in November 1780.[69] Wemyss returned to England in late spring 1781, carrying letters to the government in London, and to recover more fully from his injuries. A brief visit to join his wife, Rachel, in Scotland followed, but after her death, Wemyss returned to America, where he helped to negotiate the exchange of prisoners. He retired to his native Scotland with the rank of Lieutenant Colonel, and a few years later, returned to America, settling on a farm on Long Island with his second wife, where he died in 1833.[70] Captain St. Leger was fatally wounded during the Battle of Eutaw Springs on 8 September 1781, dying of his wounds four weeks later.[71]

BATTLE OF CAMDEN, 16 AUGUST 1780, AND SUBSEQUENT EVENTS

Immediately before the Battle of Camden on 16 August 1780, the "State" of the 63rd Foot was 2 Captains, one of whom was John Mallom, 1 Lieutenant, 1 Ensign, 1 Adjutant, 1 Surgeon's Mate, 10 Sergeants, 11 Drummers and 125 rank and file. 12 Sergeants, 4 Drummers and 195 rank and file were absent (away from the headquarters) and a further 2 Sergeants and 89 rank and file were sick. According to a despatch on the encounter at Camden by Cornwallis, who led the British troops, the 63rd Foot remained in Charleston, and they took no part at the Battle of Camden, apart from a detachment of mounted men of the 63rd. Nevertheless, this was a significant victory over the American forces [72] (Fig. 36).

Fig. 36. The Battle of Camden. Death of [American General] Kalb, 16 August 1780.

However, battles were associated not only with death from injuries, but in some cases by fever and sickness, as illustrated in the following extract reported soon after the Battle of Camden. Major James Wemyss sent a letter to Cornwallis from the nearby High Hills of Santee, dated 3 September 1780, in which he noted that: "half of Mallom's detachment from Camden has died, or nearly."[73] "The 63rd Regiment arrived in Camden a few days after the battle in a very sickly state. In one unit, nearly half the men had died." And the 63rd was "totally demolished by sickness that it will not be fit for actual service for some months." "As fall approached, many men suffered relapses of their fevers, and the new cases of fever were more severe than before."

Wemyss's letter provides a valuable independent comment on the circumstances immediately after Camden, which corroborates the despatch from Cornwallis, because Wemyss does not state that Mallom's Company fought in the battle. On the contrary, they arrived in a dreadful state soon afterwards from what became known as "Revolutionary Fever." This included yellow fever, typhus and malaria, and was responsible for countless days of sickness, and frequently, death of the troops.[74]

DEATH OF CAPTAIN MALLOM'S FRIEND, LIEUTENANT JOHN MONEY

On 18 November 1780, a further skirmish occurred at Shirar's Ferry (also known as Brierley's Ferry), in which elements of the 63rd Foot was involved, in which the American General Sumter and the cavalry leader, Lieutenant Colonel Banastre Tarleton, with the 63rd Foot, were engaged (Fig. 37). Tarleton's British Legion Cavalry (The Green Dragoons) joined the 71st Foot and a mounted detachment of the 63rd Foot, led by Captain Mallom's friend, Lieutenant John Money. A British soldier is said to have deserted and informed Sumter of the plan of action, whereupon the Americans moved to Blackstock's Farm where fighting continued and intensified.[75] During the ensuing encounters, from the 63rd Foot, Lieutenants Gibson and Cope were killed and Lieutenant Money was mortally wounded.[76] According to the Muster, Captain Mallom was present with his Company during this period, and so it is likely that he fought in this action, and he may have witnessed the wounding of his friend, Lieutenant John Money. In his letter of 3 December 1780 to Clinton, Cornwallis wrote of the loss of 50 men killed or wounded, or taken prisoner from the 63rd Foot. There would have also been understandable dismay at the deaths of his three officers, Gibson, Cope and his aide-de-camp, John Money, "who was a most promising officer, and who died of his wounds a few days later." [77] The loss of these officers and men left the 63rd Foot very much weakened, and by 1 December 1780, its complement was: 1 Captain (Mallom), 2 Lieutenants, 1 Ensign, 1 Adjutant, 1 Surgeon, 1 Mate, 14 Sergeants, 11 Drummers and 160 rank and file. 26 men had been taken prisoner and 41 had been wounded.[78] These losses were very serious, and John Mallom was now the only Captain to survive in the 63rd Foot, a Regiment which had been badly depleted. The war was not going well for the British.

Fig. 37. Colonel Tarleton, 1782.

> Muster 9. Captain John Mallom's Company for 182 Days from 25 December 1780 to 24th following, both days inclusive (24 June 1781). The Establishment (Proof Table) included 1 Captain (Mallom-present), 1 Lieutenant, 1 Ensign, 3 Sergeants, 3 Corporals, 2 Drummers and 50 Privates, all present and 5 Casuals since 25th December. Total 55 men. Signed J. Imprett, Lieut[enant] and Will[ia]m Watson, Ensign 63rd Reg[iment]. Charles Town, 24 June 1781. In particular, the Captain (John Mallom) was marked as "Present" in the Proof Table, so he was

with his Company on 24 June 1781, when the document was signed. The implication is that he returned to his regiment in South Carolina after the voyage to London with his Commander's Letter, the details of which follow here.

Captain Mallom carries his Commanding Officer's Letter to London, January 1781

Captain Mallom was sent to London in January 1781, carrying a letter from Lieutenant Colonel Nisbet Balfour, Commandant of Charleston, on behalf of Earl Charles Cornwallis, to Lord George Germain, Secretary of State for the Colonies in Lord North's Government, dated 16 January 1781, summarising the situation in the south.[79] The letter followed a dispatch from Cornwallis, dated 11 January 1781, which included a note that the Army was marching towards North Carolina, to Bullock Creek, between the Catawba and Broad Rivers, by 16 January. The full text of the letter is included here since it includes the reference to Mallom, who was given the responsibility of carrying the dispatch to London:

Charlestown Jan[uary] 16th 1781

My Lord

I am honoured with Lord
Cornwallis's Directions to Address myself to
your Lordship during his Absence from
this Province, to have the Honour of informing
your Lordship from time to time, of the State
of the Army, and Situation of Affairs here.
By the last Dispatches from
Lord Cornwallis, which were dated the 11th Instant
the Army was then in Motion and Advancing
towards North Carolina so that His Lordship
would reach Bullock Creek between Catawbaw
and Broad Rivers, by the 16th; to which I am
happy to add, that the Troops under his
Command were, at that Time, in the highest
Health.
The latest Accounts of the Enemy
inform us, that General Green, with his Army
is at Hayly's Ferry, on the Eastern Bank
of the Pedee.
In order to cooperate with
Lord Cornwallis's Views on Cape Fear River,
& to afford Provisions and other Supplies for
his Army, a small Force of about 300 Men
under Major Craig of the 82nd Regiment,

will sail from hence with the Paquet.
Capt. Barclay in the Blonde, with the delight
and Otter Sloops of War, convey this Corps,
and will Cooperate with the Troops upon
this Expedition, which I trust, will be
successful & give us Possession of Wilmington
and of this very essential Communication.
It is with pleasure I inform
Your Lordship that many of the principal
Inhabitants of the Province, & some who
held the Chief Office under the late Rebel
Powers, have reverted to their Loyalty, &
Declared their Allegiance to His Majesty's
Government.
I have also the Satisfaction
to acquaint Your Lordship that Major Ross
and Captain Broderick are arrived with
the dispatches; & as the former Gentleman
has Mentioned to me Your Lordships great
anxiety to receive frequent Information
from [him] & as there has of late been no
eligible Conveyance, I have from these
Motives taken it upon me to change the
Course of the Packet, by sending her directly
Home, to which have been rather induced,
as a Ship of War shortly is to sail for N. York,
& will take with her the Commander in Chief's
dispatches & the Mail for that Place.
Capt[ain] Mallom of the 63rd Reg[imen]t,
an Officer of merit & who Returning
to Europe For the Recovery of his Health, has Lord
Cornwallis's Directions to deliver this dispatch
to Your Lordship.

I have the Honour to be
My Lord
Your Lordship's
Most Obedient Servant
Lord George Germain N B
& & &   (Nisbet Balfour)

General Nathaniel Greene was the Commander of a Rebel Army at Hayly's Ferry, on the eastern bank of the Pedee (Pee Dee) River, and Major Craig's task was to support the troops in the assault on Wilmington, the largest port in North Carolina. The information that some of the leading figures in South Carolina had reverted to the Loyalist cause would have been very welcome in London, where good news about the war was always well-received.

Mallom wrote to Cornwallis acknowledging the honour which was being bestowed on him, on 14 January 1781, in Charleston, South Carolina, where the 63th Foot was based.[80] This was two days before the letter from Balfour to Germain was prepared, so he must have been alerted to his forthcoming task before Balfour put pen to paper. The 10-line handwritten letter is laid out as follows:

> Charles town 14th Jan[ua]ry 1781
>
> My Lord,
>
> I take the liberty of
> forwarding to your Lordship, the inclosed,
> which came directed to my late poor
> friend Money. I am infinitely obliged
> to you My Lord for your Goodness,
> in permitting me to go to Europe, and
> particularly so, for the Honor you have
> done me, by intrusting me with the
> charge of your Lordship's Dispatches
> Home.
>
> I have the Honor to be,
> My Lord, with the greatest
> Respect, Your Lordship's Most
> Obed[ien]t Humble Servant.
> J Mallom.

On the reverse of the letter is written, in Mallom's hand:

> Captain Mallom
> to
> Earl Cornwallis
> 14 Jan[uar]y 1781.

The honour of carrying His Lordship's dispatches may have been partly an indication of Mallom's reputation, and although it is not exactly the equivalent of being mentioned in despatches, the phrase would not have done Mallom's cause any harm. By implication, therefore, had he lived longer, it is possible that he might have progressed further in his army career and been promoted to a higher rank. As it was, Mallom's ill health may have been due either to battle injury or to fever contracted during the southern campaign, although the phrase "... recovery of his health" could be interpreted in either way. However, a few weeks later, Major Wemyss was sent to London with another letter, this time from General Clinton to Lord George Germain, in which he wrote:

Major Wemyss of the 63rd Regiment, who will have the honour of delivering this letter to your Lordship, having received several very severe wounds in South Carolina which obliges him to return to Europe for the recovery of his health, I cannot suffer an officer of so much merit and long service in this country to depart from hence without taking the liberty of introducing him to your Lordship ...[81]

The first part of the phrase is identical to that used in the letter taken to London by Captain Mallom in January 1781, suggesting that he, too, might have been returning to England to recuperate following battle injuries, although no mention was made in the covering letter of Mallom having been wounded. Both men were described in quite glowing terms, as appropriate for a trusted officer carrying a dispatch from a field commander to the British Government in London, although, unfortunately for the 63rd Foot, there were few other middle ranking officers who could have fulfilled the responsibility.

Given the depleted state of the regiments, it is significant that both letters to Lord North's Government were carried by officers who were recovering from injuries or sickness, and who were not fit for active service. The British Army could ill afford to send officers on long voyages to and from England who were fit and well and who were needed in the field, and the selection of both John Mallom and James Wemyss needs to be seen in this light. It was to Lord Germain that Captain Mallom was instructed to deliver the letter from his Commander-in-Chief. George Germain, later 1st Viscount Sackville, was Secretary of State for the Colonies between 1775–1782, and Lord North, later 2nd Earl of Guilford, was Prime Minister of Great Britain between 1770–1782. Both these periods coincided with the American War of Independence, and both were blamed for the loss of the American Colonies.

The content of Mallom's letter with its ten lines of handwriting to Cornwallis is also interesting, in that he refers to his friend Lieutenant John Money, aide-de-camp to Lord Cornwallis until he was fatally wounded whilst leading a mounted detachment of 80 men of the 63rd Foot at the Battle of Blackstocks Farm in South Carolina on 9 November 1780. Lieutenant Colonel Banastre Tarleton and his British Legion Dragoons was in command at this encounter. Lieutenant Money died of his wounds a few days later on 15 November 1780, aged 24 years. Earl Cornwallis made honourable mention of him in his official dispatches to the Secretary of State, and seemed to lament the loss with a concern almost equal to that of his nearest friends and family connections.[82]

The quotation with the details of the death of Lieutenant Money is taken from the writings of Richard Gardiner (alias Dick Merry-Fellow), who was the older brother of Money's mother, Margaret (Gardiner) Money. Gardiner also composed the Memorial Poem to John Money which was published in the Norfolk Chronicle on 17 March 1781, mentioned below.[83] Money was not only an officer in the same regiment as Mallom, he had served in John Mallom's Company, as Adjutant in 1777, and later, as Lieutenant in 1778, while they were based in Philadelphia. It is feasible that the two officers knew each other in Ireland before they found themselves in the same Company in America when Mallom was promoted to Captain in the 63rd Foot, because the two officers both came from Norfolk families. Mallom was a son of Wacton, and Money a son of the Revd. Thomas Money, late of St Giles's Parish, and Rector of St Michael at the Pleas, Norwich.[84] It is very likely that John Money, given his position of trust as aide-de-camp to Lord Cornwallis, would have been sent to England with his Commander's letter had he not been killed in action. This is because on 9 November 1780, Cornwallis had received a dispatch from Lord Germain which was carried by his then aide-de-camp, Major Ross, confirming that an officer in this position within His Lordship's personal staff would be expected to carry important dispatches to and fro across the Atlantic.[85]

The death of Mallom's friend John Money was marked, not only by a statement of the fact, but also by the publication of a poem in *The Norfolk Chronicle* on 17 March 1781, celebrating his gallantry in the face of the enemy led by General Thomas Sumter,[86] who was described by Tarleton, as having "fought like a gamecock."[87] In the memorial poem, Tarleton was named as the officer who stopped to tend Lieutenant Money's wounds in the field, from which he later died. Incidentally, Banastre Tarleton (1754–1833), was 12 years younger than John Mallom (1742–1782), and only 2 years older than John Money (1756–1780), and it follows that he was promoted extremely rapidly in comparison to them, and especially to Mallom. Tarleton was a Lieutenant Colonel when he was 23 years old, and was celebrated as a brilliant, tactical cavalry leader by the British, but hated as a brutal, vicious opponent by the rebels.[88] Indeed, in the modern era, some of his actions, as at the Battle of Waxhaws, for example, may be regarded as war crimes.[89] Whatever the final assessment of his military activities, he produced one of the most authoritative accounts of the war in the southern states of America, which is noted for its detail, copies of correspondence and its maps, in particular, of the siege of Charleston.[90]

An approximate idea of the time taken for a Commander's dispatches to reach London can be shown by comparing the dates of the hand-written letters with the date the transcriptions appeared in *The London Gazette*, one of the official British Government journals, and which carried notes of events happening in America. In the case of letters/dispatches written in 1781 by Lieutenant Colonel Nisbet Balfour, the Commandant of Charleston, South Carolina, the following is of interest: the letter carried by Captain Mallom to Lord Germain, dated 16 January, was published in *The London Gazette* in the issue which covered the dates 13 to 17 February 1781, 32 days later. The notification to the *Gazette* from Whitehall was dated 17 February 1781, which was a Saturday; Nisbet's letter dated 18 February, was published in London on 27 March, 37 days later;[91] a letter dated 1 May was published on 2 June, 32 days later, [92] and a letter dated 27 June was published 41 days later, on 7 August,[93] all dates in 1781. It follows that Mallom's journey appears to have been, together with that of the May–June voyage, the fastest in this small selection, no doubt reflecting a prompt departure and favourable winds from west to east across the Atlantic. No evidence has been found in Lord Germain's papers as to how receipt of letters and dispatches addressed to him from Army Commanders in America was recorded, although his office must have had a method of noting receipt and taking action, as appropriate. Germain's papers for the months of February and March 1781 have been searched for the names "Cornwallis," "Balfour" and "Mallom," but without success, suggesting that any notes on the receipt of dispatches from the field are held elsewhere, or have not survived.[94] General Leslie's Letter Book includes a total of 45 letters/dispatches written by Balfour in 1781. Eleven of these were sent to Lord Germain in London, and seventeen to Sir Henry Clinton in New York. Clinton had succeeded Sir William Howe as Commander-in-Chief of the British forces on the latter's retirement in 1778, and Clinton led the main body of the British attack on the Carolinas in 1780.

Captain Mallom was clearly not with his Company during his voyage to England, but his absence was not recorded on the Muster taken on 25 December 1780, because he was still with his Company in Charleston at the time. Mallom's name and rank appeared at the head of this Muster, and he was marked "Present" in the Proof Table which showed the Establishment of his Company. The implication is that the forthcoming voyage to England had not then been notified to him.[95] In addition to the announcement of Mallom's return to England in *The London Gazette* in February 1781,[96] news of his arrival appeared in at least ten provincial and regional newspapers of the day, from as far afield as the *Stamford Mercury*, Lincolnshire (weekly), the *Newcastle Chronicle* (weekly), the *Cumberland Pacquet and Ware's Whitehaven Advertiser* (weekly), *The Scots Magazine*, Edinburgh (monthly), and *The Norfolk Chronicle*, Norwich, his home county (weekly), amongst others. These newspapers were nearly all published between 21 and 27 February 1781, in other words between one and two weeks after the report which appeared in *The London Gazette*,[97] no doubt because news of this type travelled slowly, relying on horses to transport the mail. As a matter of interest, *The London Gazette* was published twice a week at this time, on Tuesday and Saturday. The issue in which Balfour's letter to Lord Germain was published was subtitled, "From Tuesday February 13, to Saturday February 17, 1781," and it contained news and information gathered between these dates. Furthermore, the same edition includes the name of the vessel which carried three dispatches from Charleston, South Carolina to Lord Germain, from Earl Cornwallis, from Major General Leslie, and from Lieutenant Colonel Balfour. Cornwallis wrote a brief covering letter to Germain on 18 December 1780 to accompany a copy of his letter to Sir Henry Clinton, dated 3 December 1780. Leslie wrote his letter on 19 December 1780 and Balfour, his, on 16 January 1781. This represents an interval of 29 days between the writing of the first and the last dispatch taken to London on this journey, a delay which was probably partly due to bad weather, since Leslie's letter was written at sea, on board a vessel which had been buffeted by gales, greatly delaying his arrival on land with a force to join Lord Cornwallis "up the country." The vessel involved was the Packet, "*Antelope*" which sailed from Charleston on 18 January 1781, and since no other army officer was named as having been given the responsibility of carrying them, it is arguable that Mallom had personal charge of all three dispatches during the voyage, although, admittedly, he was named only in the one from Balfour to Germain. Packets were medium-sized vessels designed to carry domestic mail, passengers, and freight to and from European countries and their colonies, including North America. Numerous ships have sailed under the name "Antelope" but ours was almost certainly the West Indian vessel launched in 1780, and subsequently captured by the French. She was 190 tons, with a crew of 27 and armed with six 3-pounder guns.[98]

It is also worth noting that Balfour referred to his letter to Germain of 16 January 1781, carried by Captain Mallom, in a subsequent letter written on 18 February 1781, which began,

> By the letter in which I had the hono[u]r to Address your Lordship the 16th Jan[uar]y last you will have been informed of the situation of affairs here to that Period and by Lord Cornwallis's Dispatch dated the 18th of the same Month, of Lieut. Colonel Tarleton's unfortunate action on the preceding day ... [99]

The assumption is that Balfour believed that Germain had received the dispatch carried by Captain Mallom the previous month, and that his voyage to England had been successful. There was no reason for him to think otherwise; he had not received any news to the contrary and no evidence of a duplicate letter has been found as might have been the case if Mallom's voyage had failed. The circumstantial evidence strongly supports the opinion that Captain Mallom sailed to England and later returned to Charleston, although no document has been found which unequivocally records this. Sometimes, circumstantial evidence is all there is.

63RD FOOT IN CHARLESTON, 1780–1781

The 63rd Foot, based in Charleston, was not engaged in action during the winter of 1780–81, and so they were not involved at Cowpens on 17 January 1781, when Tarleton and his troops suffered a heavy defeat at the hands of the American General, Daniel Morgan. More than 700 Loyalist and British prisoners were taken, including 200 wounded, in addition to the more than 100 British killed. These losses included many of Cornwallis' finest troops, and Tarleton's men in particular suffered an extremely high casualty rate, a great reversal after Camden, and one which re-energised the American forces.[100] In any case, Captain Mallom had left on his voyage to London three days before the Cowpens debacle. The 63rd Foot was not involved in the action at Guildford in March that year, either. In April

1781, Cornwallis planned to march into Virginia no doubt to try and consolidate his hold on the southern states, but this movement ended badly at York Town, in which the Light Infantry Battalion of the 63rd Foot was involved.[101] However, his absence from active duties in England, meant that Captain Mallom was not involved in any actions during the early spring of 1781, including at Hobkirk's Hill near Camden, on 25 April 1781.[102] However, the information within the Muster for the period December 1780–June 1781, suggests that Captain Mallom had returned to Charleston and was, once again, with his Company. Captain Mallom's name appeared in the Printed Annual Army List for the 63rd Foot in America for 1781, and was not deleted, indicating that he was still on active service.[103] His whereabouts at the time however, remain unclear.

Muster 10. We return to the penultimate Muster which features Captain John Mallom's Company, this time for 183 Days from 25 June 1781 to 24 Dec[em]ber [1781]. Mallom's name and rank appeared at the head of this Muster, countersigned by Charles Stuart (Stewart), Major Command[ing] the 63rd Reg[imen]t. But in front of Mallom's name appeared the words "Absent by Leave from the Command[e]r in Chief" The Establishment (Proof Table) included: 2 Sergeants, 3 Corporals, 2 Drummers and 19 Privates, 1 Lieut[enant] Absent, 1 Ensign Absent, and 22 Privates Absent, 1 Casual since 24 December 1781. The boxes for Captain (Present and Absent) were both empty, suggesting that Mallom was not with his regiment, although why the "Absent" box was not marked is unclear. The Muster included the names of Prisoners of War, and the names of a further 20 Casuals from 25 June 1781, who were either dead, discharged, or deserted. Signed J. Impett, Lieut[enant] and W[illia]m Watson, Ensign, Charles Town, 22 May 1782. This date is puzzling because the Muster covered the dates from 23 June 1781 to 24 December 1781. The previous four Musters for Captain Mallom's Company of the 63rd Foot had been signed by the Lieutenant and the Ensign on the date on which the period of the Muster ended, and so the 6-month interval in this last Muster appears irregular. However, in the second Muster, from December 1778 to June 1779, the document was signed on 5 October 1779, that is, more than 3 months later. Evidently, the preparation of the Muster with its end-date, and the signing-off were not always perfectly synchronised, and it looks as if regimental duties and the pressures of the war, interfered with the documentation processes. The additional interest, in the wording at the head of the Muster for late 1781, is that the Company was still being described as "Captain John Mallom's Company," even though he was clearly absent. In other words, Mallom's name on this Muster should not be taken to imply that he was present with his Company in the field, in person. Until he sold his captaincy on promotion, was transferred, injured, or died, the Company was still "his" even if he were absent 4000 miles away in England, and the Muster would still be described as such.[104] The value of the Proof Table within the Muster, which lists the Establishment of the Company and acts as a check on the presence or absence of individual Officers, is made clear by this simple administrative device.

BATTLE OF EUTAW SPRINGS, 8 SEPTEMBER 1781

This period of service for the 63rd Foot included the Battle of Eutaw Springs on 8 September 1781, in which Captain Hayes St Leger, John Mallom's colleague in the 63rd Foot, was fatally wounded, dying about 4 weeks later, and Lieutenants David Campbell and Owen Lloyd, and Ensign Murray were injured. [105] The Muster recorded a significantly smaller Company than previous Musters, with the names of the men who had died, some by virtue of injury and others possibly from fever and sickness:

> The enemy attacked us with great impetuosity ... and the veteran troops of the 63rd and 64th Regiments, who had served the whole of the war, lost none of their fame in this action."[106] According to reports, "The Americans lost more than 700 men, including 60 Commissioned Officers. British losses were also very heavy and among the 63rd Foot, 2 Sergeants were lost, and 6 rank and file were killed. 3 Officers, 1 Sergeant and 33 rank and file were wounded, with 2 officers and 20 rank and file reported missing. This was the sharpest action of the whole war; the American artillery was taken and retaken several times. It was our farewell greeting to the Americans, for no other contest of any moment took place..."[107] (Fig. 38).

However, Mallom's "Absent by Leave of..." at the time may mean that he did not see active service at the Battle of Eutaw Springs. Or did he? He was not mentioned in reports of the battle in which his Company colleagues were killed or injured, although this would not necessarily have been the case unless there was good

Fig. 38. Battle of Eutaw Springs, 8 September 1781.

reason to name him. But if the term: "Absent by Leave…" meant that he had been sent out on a mission or was perhaps in hospital on the day the Muster detail was collected, or there was an administrative error of some sort, then it is arguable that Captain Mallom might well have been involved at Eutaw Springs. Unfortunately, it is impossible to be certain, either way.[108]

Muster 11. This would be the final Muster involving Captain John Mallom's Company for 183 Days from 24 December 1781 to June 1782, but which has not been found despite searches at The National Archives in London, and in relevant American Archives and Libraries.[see 62] It would have been of considerable interest because Captain Mallom was still living when the period of the Muster began. However, his whereabouts during the 3-month period which immediately follows this remain unknown, although it is likely that he had returned to his regiment attached to the British Garrison in Charleston, South Carolina.

WHEREABOUTS OF CAPTAIN MALLOM AFTER THE VOYAGE TO ENGLAND IN JANUARY 1781

The relevant Muster of the 63rd Regiment of Foot for the previous 6 months, including the Proof Table of the Establishment, confirmed that the Captain of the Company, John Mallom, was present when the document was signed on 24 June 1781 in Charleston, South Carolina. In addition, the Printed Annual Army List for the 63rd Foot for 1781, includes Mallom's name in the list of Captains, and his name was not crossed-out as was the case for four other Captains, two of whom had been promoted to more senior posts in other regiments, and two who had died. The Annual Lists were normally published at the end of April each year, and these pieces of information, taken together, strongly suggest that John Mallom returned to his regiment in Charleston after his voyage to England, by late spring-early summer 1781. As we have seen, the next Muster in the series for the 63rd Foot, for the period from June 1781 to December 1781, shows that although Mallom's name appeared on the front of the document "Captain John Mallom's Company …," the following words were added to the head of the Muster, "Absent by Leave from the Commander in Chief," as recorded in Muster 10, above. Captain Mallom's whereabouts during the last six months of 1781, are unknown, despite searches having been made in every one of the Annual Printed Army Lists for the period in America, England and Europe, in the lists of Half Pay and in the lists of Garrison Staff, where British troops were also based.[109] Based on this assessment, at least, it follows that he probably did not leave his position with the 63rd Foot.

On the other hand, is it possible that Captain Mallom was transferred to the staff of Earl Cornwallis in place of his friend, Lieutenant John Money who had been killed, or to the staff of another senior British Army Commander, or was he sent away for a prolonged period of "Sick-Leave"? In respect of the personal staff of Cornwallis, no evidence has been found that Mallom was ever appointed as his aide-de-camp, and his name does not appear in a Charles Cornwallis 'British

Orderly Book' for the period December 1780 to January 1781.[110] Furthermore, by the time Mallom was on the way to England, Cornwallis had left Charleston and moved north, towards North Carolina.[111] It is therefore very unlikely that Captain Mallom joined Cornwallis in the place of his friend, John Money. However, his "Absent by Leave of..." has another possible explanation: he might have been chronically unwell, and though able to return to Charleston from London, he was still unfit for active service, especially in the position of company commander. He might have been in hospital, since the term "Revolutionary Fever" included severe recurrent illnesses such as malaria, yellow fever, and other infections caused by mosquitos and tics, 'putrid fever,' dysentery, smallpox, typhus and typhoid fever.[112] A modern review of the infectious diseases which contributed to "Revolutionary Fever" and which assesses the impact on the conduct of the war comments that very heavy casualties were caused to both sides by them, especially in the south, where Captain Mallom was stationed:

> Reading the evidence in contemporary accounts, it is hard to escape the conclusion that the microbes may have done more than the patriots to ensure an American victory.[113]

The reality of this is well-illustrated by the effects of sickness on Mallom's Company after Camden, as reported by Major Wemyss, and the dreadful impact it had on the 71st (Highland) Regiment, which appeared healthy when Cornwallis posted them to Cheraw Hill east of Camden, South Carolina, and yet during July 1780, more than two-thirds of them were seized with "fevers and agues and rendered unfit for service".[114]

An additional and more personal connection between Captain Mallom and his late friend and colleague, Lieutenant John Money, appears, not in an official Army document, but in a letter to Cornwallis from Money's mother, Margaret, on 5 March 1781. Written from East Bergholt, a village close to the parish of Stratford St Mary, Suffolk, where her husband, Revd. Thomas Money, was serving as Rector, this is a letter which displays not only her emotions, but also an appreciation of the manner in which she had been informed of the death of her son. Margaret Money, who was grieving for the loss of her son four months earlier, mentioned that in his last letter home, on 5 October 1780, he had made a will, and that she wished his papers to be sent on to her. She was concerned for her husband's chronic ill health, which was evidently the reason she wrote the letter rather than he, the phraseology suggesting that he may have been suffering from a form of dementia:

> If I have offended in the requests I have made, it will add one affliction more to the many ones I am sinking under, my husband deprived of his faculties, my only child having embark'd with his regiment last November, but his destination is not yet known...

This older son of Revd. Thomas and Margaret Money, was Thomas, born and baptised in October 1752 at St Giles Church, Norwich, became a Captain in the

69th Regiment of Foot, serving in the West Indies.[115] Mrs Money paid tribute to Lord Cornwallis, with whom her younger son, John, had served as aide-de-camp, and she described her efforts to make contact with his regiment, the 63rd Foot, which was commanded by his friend, Captain John Mallom:

> I am much surprised that I have received no account from any officer of the 63rd, nor do I know to whom to apply… I have made all the enquiry I can in hopes of finding Captain Mallom, but in vain. Had he arrived in England, I should have returned your Lordship thanks. [116]

Her letter is interesting not only because of the inclusion of Captain Mallom's name, but of what it may reveal about his whereabouts in early 1781. Had Mallom remained with his men in the British Garrison in Charleston, rather than leaving for England, why was Mrs Money unable to make contact with him? Was this because he was already on the voyage to or from England when her letter reached Charleston? Perhaps Mallom's health had deteriorated and he was in hospital, or possibly away from Charleston on other duties, hence the reference to "Absent by Leave from the Command[e]r in Chief" on the Muster of Mallom's Company. Evidently, by early March 1781, for whatever reason, Captain Mallom had not made contact with Lieutenant Money's parents, either by letter, or in person. It is also worth bearing in mind, that assuming Cornwallis wrote to Lieutenant Money's parents immediately after his death, they would probably have received his letter 4–6 weeks later, that is, just before or just after Christmas 1780. Her letter to Cornwallis in response, some 3 months later, on 5 March 1781, was written after her failed attempt to contact Captain Mallom or his Company, correspondence which has not been found and may not have survived.

During the last few months of 1781 and the first two months of 1782 when Captain Mallom's whereabouts remain unknown, great changes were taking place in the fortunes of the opposing sides in the conflict, and on 19 October 1781, with the loss of Yorktown, Virginia, and the capture by the American separatists of 8000 British troops, Cornwallis surrendered to the inevitable. And so ended the major operations by the British and their allies in the American War of Independence. A painting (5.5m x 3.7m) which hangs in the Rotunda of the United States Capitol in Washington DC, records the surrender, by artist John Trumbull, who served as an aide to George Washington. This event was the prelude to the British Parliament voting to end the struggles in North America, and in February 1782, the month of John Mallom's death, peace was actively being sought, and a resolution was brought before the House of Commons "praying His Majesty to no longer pursue the war in America."[117] Preliminary articles of peace were signed on 30 November 1782, and the Treaty of Paris, signed on 3 September 1783, finally brought the American War of Independence, to a conclusion.

Death of Captain John Mallom

John Mallom, the man from Wacton Hall, Norfolk, was succeeded as Captain in the 63rd Foot, by William Marshall on 1 March 1782, so he must have died shortly before this date, although the place and circumstances of his death remain uncertain. On the other hand, a note of his replacement by Captain-Lieutenant Marshall was not published in *The London Gazette* until 13 July 1782, a delay from the presumed date of death of over 4 months.[118]

By 30 April 1782, the Annual Printed Army List showed that Mallom's name had been deleted as "dd," (discharged dead), and his replacement's name substituted. One modern American publication suggests that Captain Mallom died on 28 February 1782, the day before his successor was appointed to the 63rd Foot, on 1 March 1782, although this appears not to be based on firm documentary evidence.[119] It is curious that no announcement of the death of Captain Mallom, wherever it occurred, appeared in *The Norfolk Chronicle* or any other East Anglian journal, and the entries for his friend, Lieutenant John Money, are in marked contrast to this. It is difficult to imagine, had Mallom died in England, that there was no published announcement of his death in his home county, especially considering his high-status origin, and the widespread announcements of his voyage to England, in comparison to Lieutenant Money. However, Mallom's parents were both dead by the date of his enlistment into the 57th Foot, although his brother Richard, and the family of his uncle Robert Mallom of Swaffham, could have submitted the details of his death for publication had they been informed. On the other hand, his death must have been notified to the Army authorities, since the hand-written note about his successor was added to the Printed Army List for that year. It follows that Captain John Mallom must have died in late February 1782, probably a few days before the end of the month.

The circumstantial evidence could reasonably be interpreted as suggesting that Mallom returned to America after his voyage to London with Colonel Balfour's letter. The interval between his arrival in England and his death at the end of February 1782 was approximately 12 months, which should have been time for an otherwise fit young army officer to recover from battle injuries. He was clearly not so seriously unwell as to have made his voyage to England in January 1781, hazardous, and it is unlikely that he would have been given the responsibility had this been the case. Whereas a long period of illness following "Revolutionary Fever" would arguably have left him in a state of chronic ill-health, although not such as to prevent his return to South Carolina to re-join his Company in Charleston. Assuming, for the sake of argument, that his health recovered sufficiently, as appears to have been anticipated before he left America, but that he died, unpredictably, either during the voyage, or in England, a published notice of his death would have been expected. However, no such notice appeared in *The Gentleman's Magazine* during 1781–1782, the most likely periodical to announce the death of an officer with gentry connections. This would have been the more likely had Mallom remained in England, providing his death was notified to the Editor.[120] *The London Gazette* did not include his name either, although this periodical dealt mainly with living officers and promotions. Furthermore, detailed searches have found no evidence of a burial, a surviving wife and family, or a will, anywhere in England or Ireland. Major Wemyss, who also carried a dispatch to London, with his "…very severe wounds in South Carolina which obliges him to return to Europe for the recovery of his health…" did return to his regiment after a period in England, and was active in New York in April 1782.

On the basis that Captain Mallom survived his voyages to and from London, having successfully delivered his Commander's dispatch, and then returned to his regiment in Charleston, taking into account his period "Absent by Leave of the Commander in Chief," then, without any evidence to the contrary, is it not most likely that he died in or near Charleston, South Carolina? If so, then he would have been buried, with many other British troops, in an unmarked grave with no record in any surviving documents. The British Army left almost no papers behind them when they left Charleston, and the only local burial records to survive from 1782 are from St Philips Anglican Church (later Episcopal). John Mallom's name does not appear in them. Microfilm copies of the Charlestown Board of Police records (1780–1782), are held in the South Carolina State Archives, but preliminary searches by an experienced local historian do not suggest that the name of John Mallom is included in them, either. A "public burying ground" to the west of Charleston, where "strangers" and others were buried, has no grave markers or other records for it. Newspaper notices during and immediately after the period of the British occupation of Charleston, indicate that several hundred soldiers died of disease, probably the equivalent of the "Revolutionary Fever" noted earlier. Whatever the precise causes of death, the large numbers of corpses led the British military authorities to bury their dead in unmarked graves in pasture land to the northwest of the public cemetery, land which was later given over to urban development in the late 1780s and 1790s.[121] As if to confirm this opinion, an independent but preliminary search by an academic historian, with a special interest in the Revolutionary War, has not found a record of Captain Mallom's death in America nor his place of burial.[122]

The events in the UK to mark the centenary of the end of The Great War in 1918 served as a useful reminder that the battles of any era result in the loss of huge numbers of men whose remains are never recovered. The names of these men were at least inscribed on war memorials, whereas in 1782, no such dignity was afforded. Based on current circumstantial evidence, the sad reality is that John Mallom's remains were probably buried somewhere in Charleston, in a grave for which there is now no record, and no Georgian War Graves Commission to tend the place. He enlisted in the British Army in 1761 with high hopes, keen to leave his Norfolk home behind, and he achieved a good deal during his career with the 57th, and later with the 63rd Regiments of Foot. As to the sort of a man he was, we have little or no idea. There is no evidence that he kept a diary as did a few of his contemporary officers, in which he might have conveyed some of his personal likes and dislikes. He formed close friendships with John Money and others, but witnessed many of them dying on the battlefield or from "Revolutionary Fever." He served under distinguished Commanding Officers, and under others whose reputations were seriously problematic, but there is now no grave stone to mark his life. His parents both died before he left England, and only his younger brother, Richard, assuming he was still alive, his nephew, John, who was a teenager in 1782, his uncle Robert, and the family in Swaffham, were left to mourn his loss. There is a pastel portrait of his father, John Mallom, senior (d. 1761), but there is no likeness of the officer, himself: no sketch, drawing, engraving or statue.

There is no evidence of a marriage, a family, a burial or a will for Captain John Mallom in England or Ireland, despite extensive searches, and there is no documentary evidence that he ever returned to his native Norfolk, and, in fact, the earlier family difficulties from which he had emerged with great credit, may have dissuaded him, had the opportunity ever arisen. The evidence will show that he was survived by his younger brother, Richard, but since his whereabouts in the early 1780s are not known, it is unclear how or if he was notified of his brother John's death, or how any personal items or savings would have been sent to him. Having been a Lieutenant and later a Captain in the British Army, he should have been able to accrue at least some savings, particularly if he had supplemented his income as suggested earlier in his career, and in the absence of any other family, Richard would have inherited his brother's assets. The surname "Mallom" in this spelling is rare in Norfolk, and detailed searches in the parish records for Norfolk, Suffolk and further afield for the relevant period, show no other plausible candidate with this surname and gentry background. It is also worth recording that John and Richard Mallom were entitled to bear the arms awarded to their great-grandfather, John Mallom of Wacton Hall, had they chosen to do so.[123] In any case, John Mallom's connections with Sir Armine Wodehouse and Lord Townshend shown in the correspondence from Ireland in 1770, serve to confirm his impeccable Norfolk credentials and origins.

However, just over 10 years later, in 1792, in Sculthorpe, Norfolk, a young man, also called John Mallom, confidently believed to be the captain's nephew, married a girl called Anne Hipkin, and eight of their grandsons were baptised John, no doubt partly in memory of their great uncle. As they grew up, the children would have heard the story of "Uncle John, who fought in America," from their father, the captain's nephew. And so, the name of John Mallom, the British Army Captain who wore the scarlet coat uniform with white facings, lived on, and his memory was preserved in the lives of these little boys in north-west Norfolk.

References and Further Reading

1. WO 25/28. Commission Books [Series I]; 1761–62: p. 17 of the handwritten book. The National Archives (TNA), London.
2. Bruce, A.P.C., *The Purchase System in the British Army, 1660–1871*. London, Royal Historical Society, 1980, quoted by Alastair Massie. National Army Museum, London. Personal Communication, 1 February 2017.
3. *Historical records of the Fifty-Seventh or West Middlesex Regiment of Foot, compiled from Official and Private Sources from the date of its formation in 1755 to the present time, 1878*. Edited by Lieut-Gen. H. J. Warre, C.B. London, W. Mitchell and Co. 39 Charing Cross, S.W. 1878. https://archive.org/details/historicalrecor00regigoog/page/n8
4. 57th (West Middlesex) Regiment of Foot. https://en.wikipedia.org/wiki/57th_(West_Middlesex)_Regiment_of_Foot
5. Seven Years' War. https://en.wikipedia.org/wiki/Seven_Years%27_War#Summary
6. Printed Annual Army Lists. WO 65/11-12. The National Archives (TNA), London.
7. Printed Annual Army Lists. WO 65/14-16. TNA. London.
8. Printed Annual Army Lists. WO 65/18-26. TNA. London. These Lists record the names and ranks of Officers of the 57th Regiment of Foot between 1768 and 1776, inclusive.
9. The Pedigree was compiled using information from www.thepeerage.com: www.historyofparliamentonline.org: https://en.wikipedia.org
10. Bradfer-Lawrence Collection: BL/T 8/6/132-151. 1767–1770. NRO. Norwich. Letter from John Mallom to Sir Armine Wodehouse, 26 April 1770.
11. Bradfer-Lawrence Collection: BL/T 8/6/132-151. 1767–1770. NRO. Norwich. Letter from Sir Armine Wodehouse to Lord Townshend, 7 May 1770.
12. Powell, Martyn J., Townshend, George, first Marquess Townshend (1724–1807). *Oxford Dictionary of National Biography*. Published in print and online: 23 September 2004. This version 3 October 2013. https://doi.org/10.1093/ref:odnb/27624 : Namier, Sir Lewis, TOWNSHEND, Hon. George [1724–1807], of Raynham, Norf[olk]. Published in *The History of Parliament: The House of Commons 1754–1790*. Ed. L. Namier, J. Brooke, 1964. https://www.historyofparliamentonline.org/volume/1754-1790/member/townshend-hon-george-1724-1807
13. Charles Townshend, British Statesman. *Encyclopaedia Britannica*, online: Peter D.G. Thomas, Townshend, Charles (1725–1767). Oxford Dictionary of National Biography. Published online 23 September 2004.
14. General Return of the Names, Country, Age and Service of the Officers of The Fifty Seventh Regiment of Foot. Commanded by Lieutenant General John Irwin…Courtesy of Don N. Hagist, Military Historian, USA, 17 November 2012.
15. Printed Annual Army Lists. WO 65/24. TNA. London.
16. *Journal of the American Revolution*. Established 2013. Managing Editor: Don N. Hagist. https://allthingsliberty.com/about/
17. The Story of the Duke of Cambridge's Own Middlesex Regiment (formerly the 57th Foot [West Middx.] and the 77th Foot [East Middx.] combined). Kingsford, C L., *Country Life*, London. 1916: Historical Records of the 57th (West Middx) Regiment. Lieut General H J Warre. London, W Mitchell and Co. 1878: For a more detailed account of the Battle of Long Island, with tactics and maps, see Gibbs, Ronald S., Spikes, Courtney, and Paper, Thomas, Terrain and Tactics: Detailed perspectives from William Howe's war plan of 1776. *Journal of the American Revolution*, Edited by Don Hagist. https://allthingsliberty.com/2021/10/terrain-and-tactics-detailed-perspectives-from-william-howes-war-plan-of-1776/
18. Warre, Lieut.-Gen H. J., Late Lieut.-Col. Commanding 57th Regiment. Editor. *Historical Records of the*

Fifty-Seventh, or West Middlesex regiment of Foot, compiled from Official and Private Sources, from the date of its formation in 1755, to the present time, 1878. London: W. Mitchell and Co., 39 charing Cross, S.W. 1878. This edition held at Harvard College Library, read online: file:///C:/Users/david/Downloads/ HistoricalRecordsoftheFiftySeventhorWestMiddlesexRegimentofFoot_10906960.pdf : Battle of Long Island. https://en.wikipedia.org/wiki/Battle_of_Long_Island : Order of battle of the Battle of Long Island, https://en.wikipedia.org/wiki/Order_of_battle_of_the_Battle_of_Long_Island#British_units

19. Hagist, Don N., Independent Researcher of the American Revolution, and Editor, Journal of the American Revolution. Personal Communication, 25 November 2022: Hagist, ibid, A New Interpretation of a Robert Cleverley Painting. *The Marriner's Mirror* (The Journal of the Society of Nautical Research), 2008, vol. 94, no. 3. pp. 326–30: Harrington, Hugh T., Invading America: The Flatboats that landed thousands of British troops on American beaches. *Journal of the American Revolution*, March 16, 2015.

20. Breastwork (fortification). https://en.wikipedia.org/wiki/Breastwork_(fortification): A more detailed account of Breastworks and Redoubts constructed by the American troops can be found in *The Sites of Forbes' Last Three Breastworks*. Thomas, Harold A. 1964. PDF, https://journals.psu.edu/wph/article/download/2006/1854: Pete Payette, American Forts Network. American Forts East: Paulus Hook. https://www.northamericanforts.com/East/nj.html#paulus

21. Stoner, Julie, Reference Librarian, Geography and Maps Division, Library of Congress, Washington DC. Plan of Paulus's Hook and fortifications. Paulus Hook, No. 46, Call Number G3812. P4S3 1778. P5. Library of Congress Control Number gm71002214. Image used with kind permission.

22. Farrier, George H., Editor. *Memorial of the Centennial Celebration of the Battle of Paulus Hook, August 19th 1879; with a History of the Early Settlement and present Condition of Jersey City, N.J.* Reynolds Historical Genealogy Collection. Digitised by the Internet Archive in 2016. https://archive.org/details/memorialofcenten00farr_0.

23. Details of the Auction Lot as follows: AMERICAN REVOLUTION-NEW JERSEY. Mallom, John. An Account of Work done by the 57th Regiment at Powlus Hook in Demolishing Works left by the Rebels. Document signed as Lieutenant in the 57th Regiment of Foot in the Royal Army, and countersigned by Lieutenant Colonel John Campbell. One page, 7½ x 9¼ inches. (JMR). Paulus Hook, NJ, 13 April 1777. Provenance: John Gray Bell 1857 catalogue, item 226. Swann Auction Galleries, 104 East 25th Street, New York, Auction Date, 2 October 2012, Lot 65. Sold for $798: Felcone, Joseph J., Princeton, New Jersey, USA. Personal Communication, 21 December 2021: Clark, Ellen M., The Society of the Cincinnati, Washington DC. USA. Personal Communication, 18 January 2022. Beekman, John, The New Jersey Room, Jersey City Free Public Library, New Jersey, USA. Personal Communication, 11 February 2022.

24. Hagist, Don N. Military Historian. Personal Communication, 14 July 2013.

25. *The Battle of Paulus Hook*. Historic Paulus Hook Association. Adapted from an account by Craig Mitchell, Bergen Historical Society, 1979. https://www.paulushook.org/battle

26. *Paulus Hook—Library Guides* at New Jersey City University. https://njcu.com > paulushook

27. Online Institute for Advanced Loyalist Studies. Courtesy of Todd Braisted. http://royalprovincial.com/military/courts/cmsnow.htm: WO 71-83, pp. 157–160.

28. WO 71-83, pp. 157–227.

29. WO 71/83, pp. 171–172.

30. WO 71/83, pp. 160–164.

31. Kemble, Stephen, *Journal of Lieut. Col. Stephen Kemble 1773–1789: British Army Orders, Gen. Sir William Howe, 1775–1778, Gen. Sir Henry Clinton, 1778 and Gen. Daniel Jones, 1778.* Prepared by the New York Historical Society. Gregg Press, Boston, 1972, p. 484. Online edition: WO 71-84, pp. 209–214.

32. 63rd Regiment Promotions: Lt. John Mallom from 57th Regt to be Capt. v. Lt. V McKinnon. 12th

Sept 1777, 4/8. WO 25/33 "Commission Books [Series I:] 1776–78; p. 229 of the handwritten book. TNA. London: Promoted Captain v. Jones died of wounds, 7 October 1777. Journals of Lt. Col. Stephen Kemble 1773–89, and British Army Orders. *Collections of the New-York Historical Society*, Vol XVI, 1884. Reprinted by First Gregg Press edition, 1972, p. 545.

33. Bruce, A.P.C., *The Purchase System in the British Army, 1660–1871*. London, Royal Historical Society, 1980, quoted by Alastair Massie. National Army Museum, London. Personal Communication, 1 February 2017.
34. Simes, Thomas, Prices of Commissions in Regiments of Foot; The Organisation of the British Army in the American Revolution. In *The Military Guide for Young Officers*, Humphreys, J., Bell, R., and Aitken, R., London and Philadelphia, 1776. Quoted in www.AmericanRevolution.org.—Your Gateway to the American Revolution. Created by Edward St. German (1945–2009). The JDN Group. LLC.
35. Wylly, H.C. *History of the Manchester Regiment (late 63rd and 96th Foot)* Volume I, 1758–1883. London, Forster Groom and Co. Ltd. 15 Charing Cross Road, S.W. 1. 1923: 63rd (West Suffolk) Regiment of Foot. https://en.wikipedia.org/wiki/63rd_(West_Suffolk)_Regiment_of_Foot: 96th Regiment of Foot. https://en.wikipedia.org/wiki/96th_Regiment_of_Foot#96th_Regiment_of_Foot_-_(1824): The Manchester Regiment. https://en.wikipedia.org/wiki/Manchester_Regiment: Childers Reforms. https://en.wikipedia.org/wiki/Childers_Reforms Museum of the Manchester Regiment: History. 63rd Regiment of Foot. Later the 1st Battalion The Manchester Regiment. https://www.tameside.gov.uk/MuseumsandGalleries/63rd-Regiment Includes details of the Childers Reforms (after Hugh C.E.Childers, Secretary of State for War in Mr Gladstone's government). On 1 May 1881 he passed General Order 41, which outlined a series of improvements known as the Childers reforms.
36. Printed Annual Army Lists, 1778. WO 65/28. TNA, London.
37. For a detailed review, see Hagist, Don, N., Untangling British Army Ranks. *Journal of the American Revolution*, 19 May 2016. https://allthingsliberty.com/2016/05/untangling-british-army-ranks/
38. Schenawolf, Harry, British Army Command and Structure in the American Revolution – Grenadier and Light Infantry Battalions. *Revolutionary War Journal*, 31 January 2017. http://www.revolutionarywarjournal.com/british-army-command-structure-in-the-american-revolution-grenadier-light-infantry-battalions/
39. Gruber, Ira D., editor. *John Peebles' American War: The Diary of a Scottish Grenadier*. Army Records Society, vol. 13, Stackpole Books, Mechanicsburg, PA., 1998, pp. 1-18.
40. WO 71-85, pp. 284–285.
41. Kemble ibid, p 555.
42. Kemble ibid, p. 554. WO 71-85, pp. 290–307: Court Report transcribed (1995) and made available by Don N. Hagist, April 2019.
43. WO 71-85, pp. 302–305.
44. WO 71-85, pp. 365–366: Kemble ibid, pp. 555–556.
45. Kemble ibid, p. 556.
46. WO 71-85, pp. 305–365: Kemble ibid, p. 553.
47. Drummer Fisher Hung from a Tree. Don N. Hagist. *Journal of the American Revolution*, The War Years (1775–1783), June 8, 2016. https://allthingsliberty.com/2016/06/drummer-fisher-hung-from-a-tree/#_ednref9
48. Trial of Drummer John Fisher, WO 71/87 p. 202–208. TNA. London, Transcribed by Don N. Hagist, 1995.
49. WO 71-85, pp. 370–373: Kemble ibid, p. 555.
50. WO 71-88, pp. 536–537: Court Report transcribed (1995) and made available by Don N. Hagist, April 2019.

51. Hagist, Don N., Personal Communication, 18 March 2019.
52. Wylly, ibid
53. Wylly, ibid. pp. 66–67.
54. Wylly, ibid. p. 67.
55. Wylly, ibid. p. 68.
56. Wylly, ibid. pp. 73, 75, 76.
57. Saberton, Ian, *The Cornwallis Papers: The Campaigns of 1780 and 1781 in the Southern Theatre of the American Revolutionary War*. Uckfield: The Naval and Military Press Ltd, 2010. Volume I deals the Charleston campaign and the occupation of South Carolina and Georgia; volume II with the Battle of Camden; volume III with Cornwallis's refitment at Winnsborough, volume IV with the winter campaign in North Carolina and the march to Virginia; volume V with the Virginia campaign; and volume VI with the occupation; siege and capitulation of Yorktown and Gloucester. As discussed in Ian Saberton's essay in support of the degree of PhD in history by publication. University of Warwick, September 2015. University ID Number: 1390417. http://wrap.warwick.ac.uk/80231/1/WRAP_THESIS_Saberton_2015.pdf
58. Slack, Major James. *The History of the late 63rd (West Suffolk) Regiment*. The Army and Navy Cooperative Society, Ltd. London, 1884, pp. 22–24.
59. Slack, ibid, pp. 26–27.
60. Printed Annual Army Lists, 1778–1782, WO 65/28 – 32. TNA, London.
61. 63rd Foot 1st Battalion, 1778–1788. Note: all these Muster documents come under the general title, "Subseries within WO 12, 63rd Foot."
62. Searches for the "Missing Muster" of the 63rd Regiment of Foot (December 1777–June 1778) have been made by staff at the following American Institutions: Tom Ruller at New York State Archives; Erin Scrimger at Philadelphia Archives; John P. Deeben at the National Archives in Washington DC; Jayne Ptolemy at William L Clements Library, University of Michigan; Joanie Gonzalez at Staten Island Museum, New York; Bette M. Epstein at New Jersey State Archives, Trenton, New Jersey; Wade Dorsey at South Carolina Department of Archives and History; Nic Butler, Resident Historian at Charleston County Public Library, South Carolina; Karen Stokes at South Carolina Historical Society, Charleston, S.C.; Katherine Ludwig at the David Library of the American Revolution, Washington Crossing, Pennsylvania: Brittany Mayo at Georgia Historical Society, Savannah, Georgia; Aaron McWilliams, Pennsylvania State Archives, Harrisburg, Pennsylvania; Will Elsbury at The Library of Congress, Washington, D.C.; Erin Weinman at New York Historical Society, New York; New York State Library, New York; Meredith Mann at The New York Public Library; Matthew Guillen at Virginia Historical Society, Richmond, Virginia; Research Staff at Harvard University Archives, Cambridge, Massachusetts; All December 2018–February 2019. Replies were not received from The Museum of the American Revolution and New Jersey Historical Society.
63. Wylly, ibid. p. 67.
64. Wylly, ibid. p. 73.
65. Siege of Charleston. https://en.wikipedia.org/wiki/Siege_of_Charleston.
66. WO 71, Volume 91, pp. 395–411. Courtesy of Don N. Hagist.
67. Purvis, Randy A., Major James Wemyss: Second most hated British Officer in the South. *Journal of the American Revolution*, November 27, 2018.
68. Saberton, Ian, Editor, Harrington to Turnbull, 12th November 1780, In *The Cornwallis Papers: The Campaigns of 1780 and 1781 in The Southern Theatre of the American Revolutionary War. Volume III*. East Sussex. Naval and Military Press, 2010, p. 162.
69. Tarleton, Lieutenant Colonel, Commandant of the Late British Legion. A History of the Campaigns of 1780 and 1781, in the Southern Provinces of North America. London: Printed for T. Cadell, in the Strand. 1787. p. 201. read online at https://archive.org/details/historyofcampaig00tarl/page/n9/

mode/2up.
70. Purvis, ibid, quoting General Alexander Leslie to General Nathanael Greene, 18 September 1782, Dennis M. Conrad, editor,*The Papers of General Nathanael Greene. Volume XI, 7 April—30 September 1782* (Chapel Hill, NC and London: University of North Carolina Press, 2000) 672.
71. Slack, ibid, p. 31.
72. Wylly, ibid. p. 76: Battle of Camden. https://en.wikipedia.org/wiki/Battle_of_Camden.
73. PRO 30/11/64/11-12). TNA, London.
74. McCardless, Peter, Revolutionary Fever in *Slavery, Disease, and Suffering in the Southern Lowcountry*. Cambridge University Press, 2011.
75. Slack, ibid. pp. 28—29.
76. Slack, ibid, pp. 29—30: Wylly, ibid. p. 82.
77. Wylly, ibid. p. 82.
78. Wylly, ibid. p. 82.
79. Letter from Balfour/Cornwallis to Lord George Germain. Charleston 16 January 1781. From 'General Leslie's Letter Book' in the 'Thomas Addis Emmet Collection,' ref. EM 15489. Courtesy of Cara Delatte, Reference Archivist, The Brooke Russell Astor Reading Room for Rare Books and Manuscripts, The New York Public Library, USA: *The London Gazette*, 13 February 1781. Issue 12162, p. 4.
80. Letter from Captain J Mallom to Earl Cornwallis, Charleston, 14 January 1781. PRO 30/11/67/18-19. TNA, London.
81. Wylly, ibid. p.82, quoting CO 5/1102.
82. Gardiner, Richard, ibid, p. 8.
83. Gardiner, ibid, p. 10.
84. Norfolk Chronicle Newspaper Selections, The Foxearth and District Local History Society. Announcement of the death of Lieutenant John Money. 24 February 1781. p.2, col. 4.
85. Letter from General Earl Charles Cornwallis to Lord George Germain, 17 March 1781. Volume 17, Page 995. https://docsouth.unc.edu/csr/index.php/document/csr17-0306
86. Norfolk Chronicle Newspaper Selections, The Foxearth and District Local History Society. Poet's Corner for the Norfolk Chronicle. To the memory of Lieutenant John Money, Aid-de-Camp to Lord Cornwallis. 24 February 1781. p.4, col. 4.
87. Thomas Sumter. https://en.wikipedia.org/wiki/Thomas_Sumter#cite_note-14
88. Conway, Stephen. Tarleton, Sir Banastre, baronet (1754—1833). *Oxford Dictionary of National Biography*. 5 Jan 2012, online: Robert D. Bass, *The Green Dragoon: The Lives of Banastre Tarleton and Mary Robinson*. Sandlapper Press. 8 Jan 2003, online.
89. https://en.wikipedia.org/wiki/Battle_of_Waxhaws
90. Tarleton, ibid.
91. The Thomas Addis Emmet Collection, 'General Leslie's Letter Book,' ref EM 15502 and *The London Gazette*, Issue 12174, p. 2.
92. Leslie's Letter Book ibid, EM 15513 and *The London Gazette*, Issue 12195, p. 5.
93. Ibid., EM 15521 and *The London Gazette*, Issue 12214, p. 3. Note: Electronic access to Colonel Balfour's original letters to Lord Germain, in 'General Leslie's Letter Book,' held within 'The Thomas Addis Emmet Collection,' was given by Cara Delatte, Reference Archivist, on behalf of 'The Brooke Russell Astor Reading Room for Rare Books and Manuscripts,' at The New York Public Library.
94. Ptolemy, Jayne. William L Clements Reference Library, University of Michigan, 909 S. University Avenue, Ann Arbour, Michigan, USA. Personal Communications, 1 April 2019, 11 July 2019.
95. WO 65/30. TNA, London.

96. Recorded in *The London Gazette*, issue 12162, p. 4. 13–17 February 1781.
97. From The British Newspaper Archive online. https://www.britishnewspaperarchive.co.uk/search/results/1750-01-01/1799-12-31?basicsearch=mallom
98. "*Antelope*", 1780 Packet ship. https://wikivisually.com/wiki/Antelope_(1780_packet_ship)
99. Leslie's Letter Book, ibid, EM 15502.
100. Battle of Cowpens. https://en.wikipedia.org/wiki/Battle_of_Cowpens#cite_ref-18
101. Wylly, ibid. p. 83.
102. Battle of Hobkirk's Hill. https://en.wikipedia.org/wiki/Battle_of_Hobkirk%27s_Hill
103. WO 65/31. TNA, London.
104. Massie, Alastair, ibid. Personal Communication, 2 August 2013.
105. Slack, ibid. p. 31: Wylly, ibid. p. 87.
106. Slack, ibid. p. 30.
107. Slack, ibid. p. 31: Wylly, ibid. pp. 86–87.
108. Carpenter, Professor Stanley, D.M. Professor of Strategy and Command Historian, Chair, Strategy and Policy Department, US Naval War College, Newport, Rhode Island, USA, Personal Communication, 4 February 2019.
109. WO 65-31. TNA, London.
110. Ross, Charles. Correspondence of Charles, First Marquis Cornwallis. London: John Murray: Albemarle Street, 1859: Charles Cornwallis Orderly Book 1780–1781. Courtesy of Jayne Ptolemy, Assistant Curator of Manuscripts, William L. Clements Library, Michigan: Stanley D.M. Carpenter, ibid. Personal Communication, 4 February 2019, quoting Charles Stedman, in *The history of the origin, progress and termination of the American War, 1794*.
111. Carpenter, ibid.
112. Burdick, Kim, Fever. *Journal of the American Revolution*, 12 November 2015.
113. McCandless, Peter. Revolutionary Fever: Disease and War in the Lower South, 1776–1783. *Transactions of the American Clinical and Climatological Association*. 2007, 118: 225–249. Courtesy of American Clinical and Climatological Association. https://www.ncbi.nlm.nih.gov/pmc/articles/PMC1863584/
114. McCandless, ibid. quoting the following: Cornwallis to Clinton. 1780. Aug 20, PRO 30/11/76; Cornwallis to Clinton, Aug. 10, 1780, Carleton Papers, PRO 30/55/25; Rawdon to Cornwallis, Aug. 1, 1780, PRO 30/11/63/3–4.
115. Gardiner, ibid. p. 8.
116. *The Cornwallis Papers: The Campaigns of 1780 and 1781 in the Southern Theatre of the American Revolutionary War*. Ian Saberton, ed. East Sussex, England. The Naval and Military Press Ltd., 2010, 5: 268–269. Courtesy of Don Hagist. Personal Communication, 16 April 2019.
117. Wylly, ibid. p. 90.
118. *The London Gazette*, 13 July 1782, Issue 12313, p. 4.
119. Baule, Steven M and Gilbert, Stephen, *British Officers who served in the American Revolution 1775–1783*. Heritage Books. Michigan, 2004. This work is based on an earlier version by Worthington Chauncy Ford (1858–1941) entitled *British Officers serving in the American Revolution 1774–1783*, Brooklyn N.Y., 1897, although Ford's work does not include dates of death.
120. Massie, Alastair, National Army Museum. Personal Communication, 12 December 2012.
121. Butler, Nic. Charleston County Public Library Resident Historian. Personal Communication, 10 December 2018: Nic Butler, Charleston's Victory Day, Part 1, 14 December 2017, and Part 2, 21 December 2017. https://www.ccpl.org/charleston-time-machine/
122. Piecuch, Professor James, Kennesaw State University, Georgia, USA. Personal Communications, 10 October 2013, 11 April 2014, 14 June 2014, 18 June 2014 and 4 August 2014.
123. Dickinson, P. L. ibid. Personal Communication, 18 April 2019.

Part 5: Connections by Marriage of Captain John Mallom

The next part of our story looks at the connections of Captain Mallom with some very illustrious families in Norfolk, and then further afield, by virtue of the marriage of his grandfather, the second John Mallom (1671–1728), of Wacton Hall, who married Elizabeth Suckling (1670–1728), the oldest daughter of Robert and Sarah (Shelton) Suckling of Woodton, Norfolk, in August 1692. Given the social and financial considerations of gentry families of the day, both branches must have agreed to the match, and although, at first sight, the Malloms may appear to have been the main beneficiaries, the fact remains that John Mallom's extensive estates and his grant of arms in 1685, would have placed him in a favourable light amongst the higher echelons of Norfolk society of the period, and an appropriate marriage partner for the daughter of Robert Suckling. The ancestry of Elizabeth Suckling's mother, Sarah Shelton, was traced to the family of Sir Geoffrey Boleyn, eight generations earlier, as shown in Pedigree 3, p. 23. Boleyn was the great grandfather of Anne, who became Queen Anne Boleyn, Henry VIII's second wife, and the mother of Elizabeth I. In the light of this, the Mallom-Suckling marriage could quite reasonably be described as a 'gateway' event. It led also, through the forebears of Margaret (Butler) Boleyn, to the Bigod earls of Norfolk, two of whom stood surety at Magna Carta in 1215, and the Plantagenet, Angevin and Norman kings of England. As a result, Captain Mallom was a direct descendant of the medieval families which stood at the very pinnacle of nobility, aristocracy and royalty, something of which he was probably completely unaware.

SUCKLING, WODEHOUSE AND SHELTON FAMILIES

Elizabeth's Suckling ancestry has been documented elsewhere through 12 generations, to Thomas Socling, who was born before 1338.[1] This part of the work is partly reliant on the studies of Revd. Alfred Inigo Suckling (1796–1856), the clergyman and antiquary, whose surname was originally Fox, but whose mother was the daughter of Robert Suckling of Woodton, Norfolk. Alfred subsequently took the surname Suckling, and inherited the family estates in Suffolk.[2] The earliest recorded members of the family had the surname 'Socling'—a man who held his lands by socage—a note of which appears in a detailed biography of Sir John Suckling (1609–c.1641), the 'Cavalier Poet', inventor of cribbage, and gambler.[3] Socage was one of the many feudal duties required for tenure of land. A farmer, for example, held the land in exchange for a fixed payment to be made at specified intervals to his feudal lord. It could also involve the supply of other non-military service to a superior.[4] A pedigree of the Suckling family (not illustrated), shows that Revd. Alfred Inigo Suckling was the 2nd cousin twice removed of Captain Mallom, with Robert Suckling and Sarah (Shelton) having been their common ancestors.

Elizabeth Suckling's grandmother, Anne (Wodehouse) Suckling, was the daughter of Sir Thomas Wodehouse, 1st Baronet of Kimberley, and his wife, Blanche Hunsdon. Sir Thomas succeeded to the title in 1623 and became MP for Thetford, Norfolk, in 1640, two years before the start of the English Civil War, a period of "the most turbulent events in the whole course of British history."[5] In an earlier generation, John Wodehouse was the Constable of Castle Rising in 1402, and amongst his other achievements, he held the office of Esquire of Body to King Henry V between 1413 and 1422, Steward of the Duchy of Lancaster in 1414, and Chamberlain of the Exchequer in 1415.[6] John Wodehouse represented Norfolk as MP in 1410, 1416, 1417 and 1421.[7] A second marriage connection between the Wodehouse and the Shelton families appears in the ancestry of Captain Mallom, when their paternal great grandfather, Robert Suckling, married Sarah Shelton. Elizabeth's younger brother was Maurice (1676–1730), later to become Revd. Dr Maurice Suckling, Rector of Barsham and Woodton, and a Prebendary of Westminster Abbey.[8]

FAMILY OF ADMIRAL HORATIO NELSON

Horatio's mother, Catherine Suckling, was born in 1725 in Barsham, Suffolk, close to the border with Norfolk, and it was here that she met Revd. Edmund Nelson, when he was the Rector of nearby Beccles.[9] They were married in May 1749, and moved to Swaffham, to Sporle, and, finally, to Burnham Thorpe, near the coast of north Norfolk. Through his marriage, Edmund Nelson acquired very influential relatives, since Catherine's father was related to the 'Cavalier Poet', Sir John Suckling, and her mother to the powerful Walpole family: she was the great-niece of Prime Minister, Sir Robert Walpole.

Elizabeth Suckling, the grandmother of Captain Mallom, was the first of the fifteen children born to Robert and Sarah Suckling. Elizabeth was the aunt of Catherine (Suckling) Nelson, although she died when her niece was only 3 years old. The children born to Edmund and Catherine Nelson in Burnham Thorpe included William, Ann, Edmund, Suckling, Catherine, George, and Horatio, named after his godfather, Horace Walpole, who was born on 29 September 1758. Young Horatio entered the Navy with the help of his uncle, Maurice Suckling, who was later to distinguish himself as Comptroller of the Navy.[10] Nelson's subsequent exploits and naval victories are well known, but in the light of these family connections, Captain Mallom was the 2nd cousin of Admiral Lord Nelson (Fig. 39). John Mallom and Horatio Nelson had Robert and Sarah Suckling as their common ancestors. The Malloms may have been aware of their connection by marriage with the Nelson family of Burnham Thorpe, but young Horatio was only 3 years old when his cousin John left home to join his regiment in 1761, and this age difference means that the boys would never have met to play in the garden of the Rectory.

As expected, Sarah (Shelton) Suckling, Elizabeth's mother, also came from a distinguished Norfolk family whose lineage can be traced back even further than the Sucklings, to John de Shelton, 1st Lord of the Manor of Shelton, who was born in c.1140.[11] Nicholas, the 3rd Lord of Shelton and Peter, the 5th Lord, are said to have been among the group of knights who confronted King John before Magna Carta in 1215. Sir Ralph Shelton, 14th Lord of Shelton (1315–1378), fought with King Edward III at Crecy in August 1346, when he was knighted for helping to save the life of the king's son, Edward the Black Prince.[12] Ralph Shelton (1348–1414), son of Sir Ralph and Anne (de Burgillion) Shelton, followed his father and became a soldier, serving at sea, before 1373, with Humphrey de Bohun, earl of Hereford, and with John of Gaunt, duke of Lancaster, in the siege of St Malo in 1378. He later found favour at the court of Henry IV, and he attended the great council in August 1401. He was elected to parliament in 1393 and 1402.[13] Sir John Shelton (1476/7–1539), was elected Sheriff of Norfolk and Suffolk in 1504, and at the coronation of Henry VIII in June 1509, he was made a knight of the Bath. It was this Shelton who married Lady Anne Boleyn of Blickling, the daughter of Sir William Boleyn, and the sister of Sir Thomas Boleyn, father of Queen Anne Boleyn, as shown in Pedigree 3, p. 23. In a later generation, Sarah Shelton (1651–1695), married Robert Suckling (1641–1708), in 1669, and their eldest daughter, Elizabeth, married John Mallom of Wacton Hall, as we have seen.

Fig. 39. Admiral Horatio Nelson

The Shelton family took its name from the village of Shelton, which is about fourteen miles due south of Norwich, and they became prosperous and influential, holding properties in both Norfolk and Suffolk. And through the Sheltons, we discover the connections of the Mallom family with some of the great families of England, culminating in the Plantagenet and Norman royal lines, which were completely unexpected.

Sir John Shelton marries Lady Anne Boleyn

In c.1497 Sir John Shelton the 21st Lord of Shelton, married Lady Anne Boleyn (1475—1556), the daughter of Sir William and Lady Margaret Boleyn, of Blickling, Norfolk. A stained-glass window in St Mary's Church, Shelton, commemorates their lives[14] (Fig. 40). Lady Anne's brother was Sir Thomas Boleyn, who married Elizabeth Howard, daughter of the 2nd Duke of Norfolk, and Anne Boleyn (c.1501—1536) was their second daughter. There is debate about the precise year of her birth, but she was the sister of Mary 'The Other Boleyn Girl', and her brother, George Boleyn. Her other two brothers, Thomas and Henry, both died young.[15] The Boleyn family of Norfolk descended from John Boleyn of Salle, Norfolk, who was living in the late 13th century,[16] and Geoffrey Boleyn was the father of William Boleyn, as shown in Pedigree 3, p. 23. The family owned the Tudor manor house at Blickling in Norfolk, later rebuilt as the present Jacobean Hall, and Hever Castle in Kent, where the future Queen Anne spent much of her youth. Blickling and its estate, a few miles north of Norwich, was purchased from his friend, Sir John Fastolf of Caister Castle, by Geoffrey Boleyn, Queen Anne's great grandfather.

Fig. 40. *St Mary's Church, Shelton, with the stained-glass window commemorating Sir John Shelton and his wife, Lady Anne Boleyn.*

Anne and her siblings were probably all born at Blickling.[17] Sir Geoffrey Boleyn (1406—1463) was a distinguished citizen and Freeman of the City of London, an Alderman, and eventually, Lord Mayor of London in 1457—58. He was also a leading Mercer, having previously been apprenticed as a Hatter, transferring from the Hatters to the more prestigious Mercers Company in 1435.[18] John Fastolf also came from an ancient Norfolk family, and fought in the Hundred Years' War. His name became well-known after William Shakespeare adapted it for his character, Sir John Falstaff, in his plays 'Henry IV' parts 1 and 2, 'The Merry Wives of Windsor' and with a eulogy to the name in 'Henry V.' [19] Captain Mallom and his brother, Richard, were the 6th great grandsons of Sir John and Lady Anne (Boleyn) Shelton. Lady Anne was the aunt of Queen Anne Boleyn, the second wife of King Henry VIII.[20] They, in turn, were the parents of the Princess Elizabeth, their only surviving child, who would later be crowned Queen Elizabeth I.

Of the Mallom boys' Tudor connections, the Boleyns may be the best known today following the popular films and TV series in which they feature, but the life of Sir John Shelton was also very distinguished as noted above. He became an influential courtier and servant of the crown, and by 1536, the year of Queen Anne's execution, he had been appointed comptroller of the household of the Princesses Mary and Elizabeth. In the meantime, in 1533, his wife, Lady Anne, was given the responsibility of the care of the young Princess Mary while she was living at Hatfield House in Hertfordshire.[21] It was the wealth and influence of Geoffrey Boleyn that established the financial security of the family into which the future consort of Henry VIII would be born.[22] It follows from this ancestry that the two surviving Mallom boys, John and Richard, whether they appreciated this or not, were the 1st cousins seven times removed of Queen Anne Boleyn, and the 2nd cousins six times removed, of her daughter, Queen Elizabeth I. Even so, it is unlikely that the two brothers knew anything of their connections with Tudor royalty, although the possibility cannot be completely ruled-out. By an intriguing coincidence, Geoffrey Boleyn was a contemporary within the Mercers' Company of London, of Robert Large, the author's namesake, who rose to prominence in the Company, becoming Warden and later, Master, and he supported the application of Geoffrey Boleyn to be admitted to the freedom of the city, "in the Art of Mercery." One of the apprentices of Robert Large was William Caxton, to whom he left 20 marks in his will. [23] In view of its significance both to the ancestral story, and the descendants of the Malloms of Wacton Hall, research on the Suckling, Shelton and Boleyn families was carried-out at Norfolk Record Office by a professional genealogist.[24]

Ancestry of Lady Margaret Butler, 7th great grandmother of Captain John Mallom

Lady Margaret married William Boleyn, son of Sir Geoffrey Boleyn, of Blickling Hall, Norfolk, and Hever Castle, Kent, Lord Mayor of London in 1457. Among their ten children, their first son, Thomas Boleyn, 1st Earl of Wiltshire and Earl of Ormond, married Lady Elizabeth Howard, daughter of Thomas Howard, 2nd Duke of Norfolk. The second daughter of Thomas and Elizabeth was Anne, later Queen Anne Boleyn (Fig. 41), second wife of Henry VIII,[25] and so Margaret was

Queen Anne's grandmother. The daughter of Queen Anne and King Henry VIII was Elizabeth, who became Queen Elizabeth I (Fig. 42).

Much has been written about the Boleyn family, but for present purposes, the following paragraph summarises work on their ancestry:

> Most historians seem to agree that a branch of the Boleyn family came from northern France, possibly Boulogne and settled in England at the time of the Conquest. Lauren Mackay, in her book *Amongst the Wolves at Court*, a biography of Thomas Boleyn (father of Queen Anne Boleyn), specifically mentions Eustace de Boulogne, who is said to have commissioned the Bayeux Tapestry, as being the founder of the English Boleyn dynasty. This branch of the family eventually settled in Norfolk—and it is from here that Anne is descended.[26]

Others agree that the Boleyn family came originally from France:

> an upwardly mobile family originating from the English-held territories in France, recalling that "Baldwin de Bolon came from Boulogne, which in the Chronicles of Calais is spelt Boleyn."[27]

A provisional pedigree of Queen Anne Boleyn (not included), shows the descent from Eustace I, Count of Boulogne.[28] And it has been proposed that the Counts of Boulogne were themselves descended from Charlemagne, King of the Franks and Holy Roman Emperor (747–814), and the Carolingian dynasty which dates from

Fig. 41. Queen Anne Boleyn, circa 1533–1536   Fig. 42. Queen Elizabeth I, circa 1575.

Queen Anne Boleyn was Captain Mallom's 1st cousin seven times removed, and Queen Elizabeth I, his 2nd cousin six times removed.

the early-mid 600s AD.[29]

The sections which follow include summaries of the lives and times of some very distinguished men and women who lived during the medieval period, and who form part of the ancestry of both Margaret Butler, and the two Mallom boys, Captain John and his brother, Richard, of Wacton Hall. The aim of this section is to point interested readers to historians who have written extensively about the individuals concerned, rather than to present original research.

The lives of many women who lived in the distant past have often been ignored, and moves to correct this are welcome.[30] Even so, the challenge is that they often came to attention because of what was recorded about their fathers, husbands and sons, rather than of them in their own rights. Each of the wives of the seven generations of Butler males leading to Margaret came from distinguished families, and they are relevant to the Mallom family of Wacton Hall. Margaret Butler was the daughter of Thomas, 7th Earl of Ormond, and his first wife, Anne Hankford, the daughter of Sir Richard Hankford, and Lady Anne de Montague. Thomas and Anne had two daughters, Lady Anne and Lady Margaret, co-heiresses of the Ormond estates in Ireland, through which the Boleyn family prospered after Margaret married William Boleyn.

The origin of the Butler family, Earls of Ormond, is not straight-forward because the family originally bore the surname 'Walter' from Hervey Walter of West Dereham, Norfolk, owner of estates in East Anglia.[31] In 1185, during the reign of Henry II, Hervey's son, Theobald, accompanied the king's son, John, to Ireland where the prince assumed the title Lord of Ireland, and where Theobald was given extensive lands, including in northern Tipperary; hence the title, in the Gaelic, "Oir Mhumhan," or, Ormond.[32] Theobald was made "botellier" or "Chief Butler of England," and was the first to adopt the surname 'Butler' which became the hereditary office of Butler, owing fealty (sworn loyalty) to the English crown. Theobald and his successors attended the Kings of England at their coronation, to present them with a cup of wine.[33] He died in 1205, and was probably buried in Limerick.[34] There followed a sequence of generations in which the heirs were named Theobald Butler, Chief Butlers of Ireland, and on 2 November 1328, James Butler was created 1st Earl of Ormond.[35] The previous year, Butler had married Eleanor, the daughter of Humphrey de Bohun, 4th Earl of Hereford, and Lady Elizabeth Plantagenet, Edward I's daughter, a union which enlarged the English estates of the Butlers.[36] Eleanor de Bohun was 3rd great grandmother of Margaret Butler.

Hubert Walter (c.1160–1205), was arguably Theobald's more famous brother, and he retained his family surname. He and his brother were brought-up in the household of their uncle, Ranulf de Glanville, chief justiciar of Henry II, who introduced Hubert to the court circle. He went on crusade with Richard I, and later helped raise funds for, and negotiate, the king's release from captivity in 1193.

By Christmas 1193, Hubert was appointed justiciar, a role somewhat similar to that of the modern Prime Minister. The king made him in turn, Dean of York, Bishop of Salisbury, and Archbishop of Canterbury (1193–1205). His later years involved the promotion of reforms to the financial and tax systems, and ruling England as the king's viceregent. Following the death of King Richard, Archbishop Hubert Walter crowned King John on 27 May 1199, and on the same day, the new king made Walter his Chancellor. He died at the manor of Teynham, Kent, in July 1205, and was buried the next day in Trinity Chapel, Canterbury Cathedral.[37] Archbishop Hubert was the 9th great uncle of Lady Margaret Butler, and the 18th great uncle of Captain John Mallom.

Each of the Butlers, Earls of Ormond, married brides who had their own fascinating ancestry, and as expected, they all came from the high-status families of English aristocracy. They were the ancestors of Margaret Butler, and Captain Mallom, and to illustrate some of the points of interest, brief biographies on the following have been included, concentrating wherever possible, on family connections and relationships:

> Joan de Beauchamp, 1396–1430, wife of James Butler, 4th Earl of Ormond
>
> Eleanor de Bohun, 1304–1363, wife of James Butler, 1st Earl of Ormond
>
> Isabel Bigod, c.1212–1250, wife of John Fitz Geoffrey, mother of Joan, who married Theobald Butler, 'le Botillier'
>
> Ida de Tosny, c.1156–1225, wife of Roger Bigod, 2nd Earl of Norfolk

Joan de Beauchamp (1396–1430) was Margaret Butler's grandmother, and she married James Butler, 4th Earl of Ormond ("The White Earl"). Joan was the daughter of Sir William de Beauchamp, KG, 1st Baron of Bergavenny, and his wife, Lady Joan FitzAlan, daughter of Richard, Earl of Arundel and Lady Elizabeth de Bohun.[38] Joan's father, William, was the fourth son of Thomas de Beauchamp, 11th Earl of Warwick, and his wife, Katherine, daughter of Roger Mortimer, 1st Earl of March, and so Joan had a very distinguished ancestry. Her father was created Knight of the Garter in 1375 after military service in the Castilian campaign led by Edward the Black Prince, and he acquired extensive lands in Warwickshire, and in South Wales, where he became Justiciar in 1399. He was Councillor to the Black Prince, and Chamberlain to Richard II. Joan's great grandfather, Roger Mortimer, (1287–1330), 1st Earl of March and Baron of Wigmore in Herefordshire, owned estates in the borderlands between England and Wales (The Marches), and in Ireland, where he was appointed Lord Lieutenant in 1316. Always keen for personal power, he led a revolt against Edward II for which he was imprisoned in the Tower of London, from which he escaped, and, later, was romantically involved with Isabella, Edward's queen.[39] Mortimer's rebellion led to the king's imprisonment in Berkeley Castle, Gloucestershire, where rumours that the king was murdered in a particularly gruesome way with a red-hot iron, have since been called into question.[40] Mortimer's quest for power inevitably attracted opposition, and when he summoned a parliament to meet in Nottingham in October 1330, he and his supporters were overcome. He was arrested and imprisoned in the Tower of London, again, and executed at Tyburn on 29 November 1330.

Joan de Beauchamp's ancestry places her in the upper echelon of English nobility, and her descendants followed in her train. She was the grandmother of Margaret (Butler) Boleyn, and the 2nd great grandmother of Queen Anne Boleyn. In addition, she was the 9th great grandmother of Captain Mallom, and Joan's great grandfather, Roger Mortimer, 1st Earl of March, was Mallom's 12th great grandfather.

Fig. 43. *Presumed portrait of Edward I, possibly from the Sedilia* in Westminster Abbey.*

King Edward I was the 14th great grandfather of Captain Mallom.

Eleanor de Bohun (1304–1363) was a member of a family of English noblemen of Norman origin,[41] and the dynasty of which she was a part lasted for almost 350 years, during which time they became one of the preeminent families of the period.[42] Eleanor, named after her grandmother, Eleanor of Castile, was the daughter of Humphrey de Bohun, 4th Earl of Hereford and 9th Earl of Essex,

---

*   Sedilia: the seats in the Chancel for the officiating priests.

Hereditary Constable of England, and his wife, Elizabeth Plantagenet, daughter of Edward I (Fig. 43), and Eleanor of Castile.[43] Elizabeth was also known as Elizabeth of Rhuddlan, the castle in Denbighshire where she was born, and royal blood flowed in her veins. She was raised at Amesbury Priory, Wiltshire, in the care of her aunt, Mary of Woodstock, the king's sister, who was a Benedictine nun. Nun she may have been, but her brother provided for her very generously, if not extravagantly.[44] Elizabeth Plantagenet, Eleanor's mother, was married twice; her first marriage with John, Count of Holland, was childless, and he died as a teenager. Her second husband, Humphrey de Bohun, was Eleanor's father, and the couple had ten children as shown in Pedigree 4, p. 24.[45]

Shortly before his marriage with Elizabeth, Humphrey granted to the king all his lands and estates, together with his earldoms, and at the time of his marriage these were all returned, jointly to him and his bride. In the same year, Humphrey was granted Loch Maben Castle and the lands of Robert the Bruce, in Annandale, Scotland. There followed service with Edward II in the wars with Scotland, during which he led part of the assault on the Scots at the Battle of Bannockburn fought near Stirling in June 1314, during which he was taken prisoner, but later exchanged for the wife of Robert the Bruce, who had been held in England. However, his increasing opposition to the king and his favourite, Piers Gaveston, led to a realignment with barons opposing the king. Humphrey de Bohun, was killed in action fighting against the king's forces, in March 1322, at the Battle of Boroughbridge, after which his body was buried at the Dominican Friary in York.[46]

Humphrey de Bohun, Eleanor's father, is the first of his family for whom a will has survived.[47] Written on 13 August 1319 in Old French, it describes almost untold wealth and opulence, leaving 1000 marks to pay for his funeral alone. His family, servants and friends, all benefitted, and his daughter, Eleanor, was left £200 "for her apparel for her marriage."[48] At a conservative estimate, this converts to over £100,000 today.[49]

Sir Henry de Bohun, Humphrey's 1st cousin once removed, was also one of Edward II's knights at Bannockburn, and he was Eleanor's 1st cousin twice removed.[50] On the first day of the battle, 23 June 1314, de Bohun saw the Bruce, and without warning, charged with his lance at the ready towards the Scottish king, As the two came side by side, Robert the Bruce skilfully manoeuvred his pony and avoided the English knight's lance. He brought his battle-axe crashing down on de Bohun's head, splitting his helmet and skull, killing him instantly (Fig. 44). As a result, the morale of the Scots increased dramatically and may have contributed to the outcome of the battle. Bruce was admonished by some of his men for recklessness, but replied saying, simply, "I have broken the haft of my good battle-axe." [51] The battle on that June day in the area which now lies to the south of the city of Stirling, saw the English army suffer a humiliating defeat against a considerably smaller Scottish force.[52] Captain Mallom was Henry de Bohun's 1st cousin sixteen times removed.

Fig. 44. The encounter between Robert the Bruce and Henry de Bohun, at Bannockburn, 23 June 1314.

Eleanor de Bohun married James Butler, 1st Earl of Ormond, and their children included a son, James, who became 2nd Earl of Ormond, and a daughter, Petronella, later to become Baroness Talbot. Eleanor's husband died in 1338 when she was still only 27 years old, leaving her a widow and free to remarry. Her second husband was Thomas, Lord Dagworth, a baron and soldier, who is believed to have fought at Crécy in August 1346. He was killed in Brittany in 1350, thereby predeceasing his wife, who was made a widow for the second time.[53] Eleanor also outlived her brothers and sisters, dying in October 1363, aged 58 years. Her descendants included the dukes of Beaufort, Newcastle, and Norfolk, the earls of Ormond, Shrewsbury, Rochester, Arundel and Stafford, an impressive legacy as befits the granddaughter of a king.[54] Eleanor was the 12th great grandmother of Captain John Mallom.

As the granddaughter of Edward I, Eleanor was descended from the royal line of English kings stretching back through the Plantagenet and Angevin periods.[55] She was the niece of Edward II, and the 1st cousin of Edward III, and so her husband had married into the most prestigious family in the land, shown in Pedigree 4, p. 24. In addition, Eleanor was the 6th great granddaughter of William the Conqueror, through his son, Henry I, whose daughter, Matilda, married Geoffrey Plantagenet, Count of Anjou, the founder of the Angevin dynasty. Their son was Henry II, whose son in turn, King John, was the father of Henry III, the father of Edward I, on whose tomb in Westminster Abbey are inscribed the words "Hic est Edwardus Primus Scottorum Malleus": that is to say, "Here lies Edward I, Hammer of the Scots." The Norman and Plantagenet royal ancestry of Captain Mallom is fascinating, but it is probably safe to assume that he was completely unaware of it.

A great deal has been written about the lives and times of the Angevin and Plantagenet kings of England, and apart from including notes relevant to the ancestry of Eleanor de Bohun, little would be served by attempting to summarise this huge body of work here.[56] The official website of the British Monarchy, describes the Angevin and the Plantagenet dynasties as follows:

> Henry II, the son of Geoffrey Plantagenet and Henry I's daughter Matilda, was the first in a long line of 14 Plantagenet kings, stretching from Henry II's accession [in 1154] through to Richard III's death in 1485. Within that line, however, four distinct Royal Houses can be identified: Angevin, Plantagenet, Lancaster and York... [57]

The first eight Plantagenet kings of England ruled from Henry II to Richard II, and the last six, from Henry III to Richard III. This group comprised the House of Lancaster and the House of York, who fought the 'Wars of the Roses.' The Lancastrian kings were Henry III, Henry IV, Henry V and Henry VI, and the Yorkist kings who followed them, Edward IV, Edward V, and Richard III.

Henry II ruled lands from the Scottish borders to the Pyrenees, together with Ireland. He was the son of Matilda, daughter of Henry I, and her second husband, Geoffrey of Anjou: he was William the Conqueror's great grandson. The duchy of Anjou was a province around the river Loire with its capital at Angers, hence the name of the Angevin dynasty of kings who ruled England and huge areas of what was later to become France, including Normandy, Maine, Aquitaine, and Anjou itself. Brittany was under Angevin control during the reigns of Henry II and Richard I, but not otherwise. In addition, the Channel Islands, once part of the Duchy of Normandy at the time of William the Conqueror, came under English control after 1066, although they are now Crown Dependencies rather than an integral part of the United Kingdom. During Henry's reign, a new system of government and justice was introduced, despite major disagreements with the Church, whose influence increased after the murder of Archbishop Thomas à Becket in Canterbury Cathedral on 29 December 1170. Henry II and his son, Richard, spent more time abroad in conflicts and the crusades than they did at home, and Richard's reign of ten years included a period of only ten months in England after succeeding his father in 1189. Modern readers know him as 'Richard Coeur de Lion' or 'Richard the Lionheart,' because of his skill as a military leader, and his appearance in films which feature Robin Hood increased his reputation in the popular imagination. The last Angevin king was John (r.1199–1216), who lost virtually all the Angevin empire, but retained the Channel Islands. Henry II was Eleanor de Bohun's 3rd great grandfather, and John, her 2nd great grandfather, and it is tempting to imagine that she may have been aware of her royal ancestors through stories recounted during her childhood, by her mother, Elizabeth Plantagenet, who died when Eleanor was 12 years old, as shown in Pedigree 4, p. 24. The loss of Anjou and Normandy between 1202–1205, followed by challenges at home in which John's wish to raise taxes at the expense of the population, inevitably led to serious unrest. Resistance to John's rule led to the meeting with the barons and churchmen on the meadow at Runneymede, between Staines and Windsor, on 15 June 1215, where the king set his seal to what became known as 'Magna Carta,' or the 'Great Charter.' The sixty-three clauses proposed political reform, rights of freemen, protection of church rights, levels of taxation, and access to justice denied in the past, but with no commitment to democratic government as we now understand it. Nevertheless, arbitrary rule by one individual, however exalted, was to cease.[58] A council of twenty-five barons was to oversee the implementation, no doubt looking to their own interests as members of the landed class, in the face of a king in retreat. Magna Carta has become one of the most important documents in our nation's history, but needless to say, John had no intention of keeping his side of the agreement, claiming, with the Pope, that it was illegal, and launching war against those who opposed him, both English and French.[59]

The council of barons did not sign the document, although their names were recorded by Matthew Paris, the chronicler of St Alban's Abbey. Clause 61 and the security clause, designed to hold the king to his agreement, included the following sentence: "the barons shall choose any twenty-five barons of the realm as they wish, who with all their might are to observe, maintain and cause to be observed the peace and liberties which we have granted".[60] The twenty-five names include Henry de Bohun, 1st Earl of Hereford, born c.1176, son of Humphrey de Bohun and Margaret of Scotland, ancestors of Eleanor, together with Roger II and Hugh II Bigod, Earls of Norfolk and Suffolk, who were also her ancestors, and who we will meet in the next section.[61]

Isabel Bigod (c.1212–1250) was the daughter of Hugh II Bigod, 3rd Earl of Norfolk, and his wife, Maud (also known as Matilda) Marshal, the eldest daughter and co-heir of William Marshal, 1st Earl of Pembroke, who was called 'the Marshal' (c.1146–1219), and his wife, Isabel de Clare, 4th Countess of Pembroke, heiress of vast estates in the south of England and Wales.[62] On her father's side of the family, Isabel was descended from the Bigod Earls of Norfolk, whose lineage dates from before the Conquest, probably to Robert Bigod (c.1015–1071), a poor Norman knight who uncovered the threat of rebellion against Duke William, and was given land in Normandy by the duke, as a reward. Robert later became Chamberlain to William the Conqueror.[63] The connection with the Butler family came about through the marriage of Theobald Butler "le Botiller" (1242–1285), with Joan FitzGeoffrey, daughter of John FitzGeoffrey and his wife, Isabel Bigod, as shown in Pedigree 5, p. 25.

Before the Conquest, Isabel's ancestors in Normandy, were called Bigot, although this changed to Bigod or le Bigod, after the family moved to England. To help distinguish the individuals with the same baptismal name in different generations, the device adopted by others of using Roman numerals, has also been used here.[64] The first Bigod to cross the Channel was Roger I Bigod, based in Suffolk in about 1070, and later also in Norfolk, on lands given to him by William the Conqueror, in return for the promise of loyalty, financial dues and military service.[65] In the late 1070s, he was appointed a King's baron, witnessed royal charters, and became a royal councillor. Amongst the many documents in which his name appears is the following:

> This Roger Bigot was with Robert Earle of Mellent & others a Witnesse to a Charter of King William the First of Confirmation of the Gift of gilbert [Crispin] Abbot & the monks of Westminster to Hugh de Coleham to be steward to the Abbey & Proctor under the Abbot.[66]

Roger I Bigod married Adelisa (Alice) de Tosny, daughter and heiress of Robert de Tosny, of Belvoir in Leicestershire.[67] In those days, land meant power, and the Bigod estates were the greatest in East Anglia, rivalled only by William de Warenne, 1st Earl of Surrey.[68] Roger's loyalty to the king continued under William II (Rufus), and Henry I, whose coronation he attended in August 1100. However, later disagreements with the king led to an alignment with his brother, Robert Curthose, as the following reveals:

> In the year 1088, Roger bigot revolting from King William Rufus & siding with his brother Robert Curthos seized the Castle of Norwich & made a great Spoil in the adjacent country.[69]

Roger I Bigod was responsible for the construction of part of the keep of Norwich Castle, one of the largest in England (Fig. 45). The entrance to the living spaces was through Bigod's Tower (Fig. 46), with a stone staircase leading to the first-floor rooms through the Bigod Arch [70] (Fig. 47). Ashlar blocks of stone with carvings of lions passant, described in Tudor accounts of the keep, are believed to signify the involvement of the Bigods, who used lions on their seals, although the carvings have not survived.[71] Roger I Bigod also founded Thetford Priory (Fig. 48), where he laid the foundation stone a few days before his death in 1107. His burial was the subject of controversy in that the monks of the Cluniac Priory at Thetford claimed that Roger asked to be buried there, but Herbert de Losinga, the first Bishop of Norwich, contested this and won his case in the Curia Regis, the king's court. Roger I Bigod was buried at Norwich Cathedral (Fig. 49), somewhere in the Presbytery, almost certainly the first lay burial in the cathedral (Fig. 50). No evidence of the tomb remains, although there was, apparently, a memorial to him in the cathedral cloister.[72] He built the original wooden castle at Framlingham, Suffolk, and the stone castle which replaced the wood was erected by Roger's son, Hugh I Bigod. The stone curtain walls were added by Roger II Bigod, and it was he who entertained King John at the castle in 1213 shortly before the First Barons' War (1215-1217), which led to Magna Carta, and, in which Roger II and Hugh II

Fig. 45. Norwich Castle (the Keep) today.

Fig. 46. Bigod Tower, Norwich Castle.

Fig. 47. Bigod Arch, the 12th century Norman entrance to the Keep.

Fig. 48. Thetford Priory, founded by Roger I Bigod.

Fig. 49. Norwich Cathedral.

Fig. 50. The Presbytery, site of the burial of Roger I Bigod.

Bigod acted as sureties.⁷³ A fine statue of Roger II Bigod, or Baron Roger le Bigod as he is sometimes known, gazes down from its position in the House of Lords Chamber, in the Palace of Westminster, on the Lords assembled, as if to remind parliament that its position, with the now democratic English state, was hard-fought, and should not be taken for granted (Fig. 51).

The Bigod family of which Isabel was a part, was powerful and ambitious, and, it is estimated that Framingham Castle held a garrison of 400 knights and men at arms.⁷⁴ Roger's second son, Hugh I Bigod, born at Belvoir Castle, Leicestershire, inherited the estate after the death of his older brother, William, a royal steward, who drowned when the "*White Ship*" sank in November 1120.⁷⁵ In a sense, therefore, Hugh I Bigod became Sheriff of Norfolk, and 1st Earl of Norfolk, by default, after

Fig. 51. Baron Roger Bigod Earl of Norfolk d. 1221.

his brother's death.⁷⁶ The ship, which sank after striking submerged rocks in the English Channel, also carried William Atheling (Adelin),, son and heir of Henry I, and many other members of the nobility,⁷⁷ and the records show that the king found this tragedy almost unbearable.⁷⁸ Henry's legitimate daughter, Matilda, was now the only direct heir to the throne, and after her first husband, the German Emperor, Henry, died, her second marriage with Count Geoffrey of Anjou led to the Angevin dynasty of kings in England.

When Henry I died after eating lampreys in Normandy in December 1135, Hugh declared that the king nominated not Matilda, but his nephew, Stephen of Blois, grandson of the Conqueror, as heir to the throne.⁷⁹ And so it was that Stephen, not Matilda, was crowned on 22 December 1135. Inevitably, conflict and civil war ensued, because Stephen and Matilda both had legitimate claims to the throne.⁸⁰ Eventually, agreement was reached that Stephen would remain king during his lifetime, and Henry, the son of Matilda and Geoffrey of Anjou, would succeed him. After Stephen died in 1154, Henry, duly became King Henry II,⁸¹ and the Angevin dynasty of English kings, Henry II, Richard I, and John, had begun. Between 1166 and 1169, Hugh I Bigod married, first, Juliane de Vere, sister of Aubrey de Vere, 1st Earl of Oxford, and second, Gundreda, daughter of Roger de Beaumont, 2nd Earl of Warwick.⁸² Hugh I Bigod's son with his first wife, was Roger II Bigod, who married Ida de Tosny, a royal ward and mistress of Henry II.[83] She was a member of another leading aristocratic family, who were Lords of Belvoir in Leicestershire.[84] By the time of his death in 1221, Roger II had amassed sufficient wealth to leave twenty-five charters, to abbeys, cathedrals, priories, nunneries, and to individuals, including a baker in Heveningham, Suffolk.[85]

Isabel Bigod married, first, Gilbert Lacy, of Ewys Lacy, Herefordshire, and second, John FitzGeoffrey, Justiciar of Ireland, and Lord of Shere, Surrey. There were three children to her first husband, and six to the second, and not surprisingly, each survivor married well, including her daughter, Joan, who continued our family line down to Margaret Butler, with her marriage to Theobald Butler "le Botiller," shown in Pedigree 5, p. 25.[86] Isabel's oldest brother, Roger IV Bigod (c.1212–1270), was still a child when his father died in 1225, so he was made a ward of William Longespée, 3rd Earl of Salisbury, his mother's son by Henry II. Roger married Isabella, the sister of Alexander II, king of the Scots, and, still underage, became a ward to his new brother-in-law. After the death of his father, Roger inherited the family estates, including Framingham Castle, becoming one of the wealthiest men in the country. He was knighted by Henry III in 1233, and became the 4th Earl of Norfolk. He was Marshal of England by 1246 because his mother, Maud Marshal-Bigod's brothers all died without children. In the 1250s, serious disagreements with the king occurred, mainly because of Bigod's debts, but when Simon de Montfort and his followers rebelled against the king, Bigod remained loyal initially, later siding with de Montfort. He outlived his sister, Isabel by 20 years, dying in 1270, childless, and he was buried in Thetford Priory. His carved and painted shield, "or, a cross gules" that is to say, "gold, [with] a red cross" is displayed in the north choir aisle of Westminster Abbey.[87] He was succeeded in 1270 by his nephew, Roger V Bigod (c.1245–1306).[88]

The Bigod earls of Norfolk and Suffolk were part of a small group of noblemen who claimed the title "earl" somewhat akin to the Anglo-Saxon "provincial governor." They were overseers of vast estates, and a great many men owed them service and rents from their tenancies. Isabel died in 1250, and was outlived by her second husband, John FitzGeoffrey, by eight years.[89] Isobel's maternal grandfather, William Marshal (c.1146–1219), 4th Earl of Pembroke, was a distinguished soldier and administrator, and after seeing action in Flanders and Boulogne, he was captured in Poitou. He was released from captivity when Queen Eleanor, the wife of Henry II, paid his ransom, and enlisted his services. He was appointed tutor to Henry the Young King following his coronation in 1170, the only king crowned during his father's (Henry II's) lifetime. After the young king died, Marshal took the boy's cloak to Jerusalem, to fulfil a vow, where he remained for two years, re-joining the court on his return home. He carried the sceptre at the coronation of Richard I, a sign of the growing power and influence of the Marshal family. He supported the accession of John after the death of his brother, Richard, in 1199, and was his loyal supporter for several years. He took part in negotiations with the French King

Philip after the loss of Normandy, whilst securing his own French lands. After a period of alienation from court life, he arranged King John's funeral at Worcester Cathedral, and in effect became guardian of the king and the kingdom. Marshal had the distinction of serving five English kings: Henry II, his sons, 'Young King Henry' Richard I and John, and also John's son, Henry III.[90] He was later to be known as "the veteran regent William Marshal".[91]

With his wife, Isabel de Clare, he had five sons and five daughters, and the girls all married into English aristocracy.[92] Marshal's widow, Isabel Bigod's mother-in-law, one of the richest heiresses in the land, died in 1220, the year after her husband, and was buried in Tintern Abbey, Monmouthshire.[93] Isabel's mother, Maud Marshal-Bigod-Warenne died in 1248, and she was also buried in Tintern Abbey, with four of her sons acting as pallbearers. Outliving both her husbands, she helped to develop the future of two of the most prestigious families in England.[94] On her death, Maud left five charters in her own name comprising estates, in Norfolk, Yorkshire, and in Ireland where the Marshal's most valuable lands were held.[95] This was clearly a very wealthy family, and, despite the challenges, the value of their estates, including the dowers received when Bigod daughters married, together with Maud Marshal's substantial inheritance, has been estimated. An approximate value for the manors and estates of Hugh II Bigod, was £1,067.[96] This equates to an annual income of well over £1m today using the retail price index methodology.[97] It was against this illustrious, aristocratic and wealthy family background on both the paternal and the maternal sides, that Isabel Bigod was to emerge, when her father, Hugh Bigod, married the Marshal's daughter, Maud.

The family connections between Margaret Butler, wife of Sir William Boleyn, and the Bigod earls of Norfolk 400 years earlier and the Mallom boys, 300 years later, can be summarised as follows: Margaret Butler was the 10th great granddaughter of Roger I Bigod, and the 7th great grandmother of Captain John Mallom. The family from Roger I Bigod to Captain John Mallom spans 22 generations, over approximately 700 years; that is an average of 32 years per generation, and Roger I Bigod was his 19th great grandfather.[98]

Ida de Tosny (Toëny, Toeni, Todeni) (c.1156–1225) is believed to have been the daughter of Ralph V de Tosny, Lord of Flamstead, Hertfordshire (d.1162), and his wife, Margaret, the daughter of Robert de Beaumont, 2nd Earl of Leicester.[99] After her father's death when she was still a child, Ida was made a royal ward, and became a mistress of Henry II, by whom she gave birth to one of his illegitimate sons, William Longespée (Longsword), later to become 3rd Earl of Salisbury.[100] William was the half-brother of Richard I and King John, and he became a military commander of considerable ability, not just because of his tall stature and the long weapons he used.[101] Little is known of the relationship between Henry and Ida, but in December 1181 the king gave her in marriage to Roger II Bigod, 2nd Earl of Norfolk, together with the Norfolk manors of Acle, Halvergate and South

Walsham as her dower, manors which had been confiscated by the king after the death of Hugh I Bigod in 1177. Roger and Ida had at least eight children, who all married well, including their son, Hugh II Bigod, 3rd Earl of Norfolk, who married Maud Marshal, in keeping with the custom that sons and daughters of high-status Anglo-Norman families would marry into the aristocracy.[102]

The Tosny or Toëny family of nobles were originally from the duchy of Normandy. Tosny, the name of the village from which the family took their name, lies a few miles south-east of Rouen, where one of the family castles stood. An earlier member of the de Tosny family of Belvoir, Adelisa, also known as Alice de Tosny, married Roger I Bigod, (c.1060–1107), Sheriff of Norfolk and Suffolk, and a royal councillor, shown in Pedigree 5, p. 25. Adelisa was one of the daughters of Robert de Tosny, an Anglo-Norman nobleman named in the Domesday Book of 1086 as Lord of Belvoir,[103] founder of Belvoir Castle, Leicestershire, and the nearby Benedictine Priory, and his wife, Adela[is].[104] She was the daughter of Osulf son of Fane, who had been Lord of Belvoir at the time of Edward the Confessor, and it is not difficult to imagine the acrimony which this change of ownership would have imposed.[105] Ida's father, Robert de Tosny, may have been one of William the Conqueror's Standard Bearers, although this is disputed and his name appears on the Battle Abbey rolls of those who supplied ships and men to William in 1066. As a result of his services at Hastings, the new king gave Robert lands in at least eleven English counties, more than half of them in Leicestershire and Lincolnshire,[106] even though he continued to hold his family estates in Normandy.[107]

The relationship between Adelisa de Tosny in the mid-late 1000s and Ida de Tosny, nearly 100 years later is complex, and historians have reached different conclusions, although the surnames clearly imply a connection.[108] However, combining recent research using extensive genealogical information derived from primary sources, and a family tree database, suggests that Ida de Tosny was the 1st cousin four times removed of Adelisa, and Ida was the 3rd cousin twice removed from her husband, Roger II Bigod.[109] The common ancestor was Roger II de Tosny (c.990–1040), in France before the family came to England. Ida's family of Norman aristocrats became owners of cross-channel estates, developing extensive and rich holdings in England in the decades after the Conquest.[110] The connection between the Tosny and the Bigod families is a good example of the way in which members of aristocratic families intermarried, and in so doing, protected and enlarged their estates, and became evermore powerful and influential. Ida de Tosny was the 8th great grandmother of Lady Margaret Butler, and the 17th great grandmother of Captain John Mallom. Captain Mallom and his distinguished and illustrious ancestors were separated by many generations and several centuries, but they are nevertheless of great fascination, partly because they were completely unexpected. Selected relationships are shown in the following table:

Admiral Horatio Nelson	2nd cousin
Margaret Butler	7th great grandmother
Sir Geoffrey Boleyn	8th great grandfather
Queen Anne Boleyn	1st cousin 7 times removed
Queen Elizabeth I	2nd cousin 6 times removed
Eleanor de Bohun	12th great grandmother
Roger Mortimer	12th great grandfather
King Edward I	14th great grandfather
Isabel Bigod	15th great grandmother
Sir Henry de Bohun	1st cousin sixteen times removed
Ida de Tosny	17th great grandmother
Archbishop Hubert Walter	18th great uncle
Roger I Bigod	19th great grandfather
William the Conqueror	20th great grandfather

Table 1: Relationships between Captain John Mallom and some of his illustrious ancestors.

References and Further Reading

1. Slatter, Howard, http://slatters.org.uk/history/bowdens/bk/f4555.htm
2. Blatchly, J. M. Suckling, (formerly Fox), Alfred Inigo, 1796–1856. *Oxford Dictionary of National Biography*. Published online 23 September 2004.
3. Clayton, Tom. Suckling, Sir John (1609–1641). *Oxford Dictionary of National Biography*. Published online 3 January 2008.
4. Socage, from Wikipedia, the free encyclopedia. https://en.wikipedia.org/wiki/Socage: *English Oxford Living Dictionaries*. https://en.oxforddictionaries.com/definition/socage.
5. The History of Parliament. http://historyofparliamentonline.org/about/latest-research/1640–1660.
6. Mosley, Charles, editor. *Burke's Peerage, Baronetage and Knightage*, 107th edition, 3 volumes. Wilmington, Delaware, U.S.A.: Burke's Peerage (Genealogical Books) Ltd, 2003. Read online at, http://www.thepeerage.com/p34266.htm#i342660
7. Roskell, J.S. and Woodger, L.S. Wodehouse, John (d. 1431), of Royden, Norf[olk]. and Crowfield, Suff[olk]. *The History of Parliament: The House of Commons 1386–1421*, ed. J.S. Roskell, L. Clark, C. Rawcliffe, 1993. https://www.historyofparliamentonline.org/volume/1386-1421/member/wodehouse-john-1431
8. Suckling, Alfred.,*The history and antiquities of the County of Suffolk*, Volume 1, p. 43. Originally published by WS Crowell, Ipswich, 1846. British History Online.
9. Collins, Arthur, and Brydges, Egerton, and Brydges, Samuel Egerton. *Collins's Peerage of England; Genealogical, Biographical, and Historical...*, Volume 5, p. 559.
10. Burke, John. *Suckling, of Woodton Hall. A Genealogical and Heraldic History of the Landed Gentry; Or Commoners of Great Britain and Ireland*. Henry Colburn, London, 1838. Volume 3, pp. 457–461: The Slatter Family History Pages. Ancestry.com, Community online. Howard Slatter, 2009.
11. Blomefield, Francis, *An Essay Towards a Topographical History of the County of Norfolk*: Volume 5. Originally published by W Miller, London, 1806: https://en.wikipedia.org/wiki/Shelton_Hall (Norfolk): The descendants of John de Shelton, at http://www.tudorplace.com.ar/SHELTON.htm : Shelton Family History, at https://sheltonfamilyhistory.wordpress.com/tag/shelton-family-tree/
12. ibid : http://www.tudorplace.com.ar/SHELTON.htm.
13. Woodger, L.S. in Shelton, Sir Ralph (1348–1414), of Shelton and Great Snoring, Norf[olk] *The History of Parliament: The House of Commons 1386–1421*. Eds J. S. Roskell, L Clark, C Rawcliffe., 1993: Calendar of Plea Rolls (CPR), 1399–1401, p. 433; E101/404/21, f. 50: PCC. i. 163: ii. 86: C219/10/4, 5 Quoted by Woodger.
14. Norfolk Churches. St Mary, Shelton, http://www.norfolkchurches.co.uk/shelton/shelton.htm
15. Hughes, Jonathan, Boleyn, Thomas, earl of Wiltshire and earl of Ormond. *Oxford Dictionary of National Biography*. Published online 4 October 2007.
16. Norton, Elizabeth, *The Boleyn Women: The Tudor Femmes Fatales Who Changed English History*. Amberley Publishing, The Hill, Stroud, Gloucestershire, GL5 4EP. Electronic edition published 2013. Part I Norfolk Origins
17. Ives, E.W. Anne [Anne Boleyn], *Oxford Dictionary of National Biography*, 23 September 2004, published online 23 September 2004. https://www.oxforddnb.com/view/10.1093/ref:odnb/9780198614128.001.0001/odnb-9780198614128-e-557?rskey=lawz8K&result=1
18. Sutton, Anne, F., *The Mercery of London: Trade, Goods and People, 1130–1578*. Ashgate Publishing Limited, Gower House, Croft Road, Aldershot, Hants, GU11 3HR. ISBN 0 7546 5331. pp. 231, 233–34, 566: Blomefield, Francis, Hundred of South Erpingham: Blickling, in *An Essay Towards A Topographical History of the County of Norfolk*: Volume 6 (London, 1807), pp. 381–409. British History Online http://www.british-history.ac.uk/topographical-hist-norfolk/vol6/pp381-409: Geoffrey Boleyn, Wikipedia, https://en.wikipedia.org/wiki/Geoffrey_Boleyn#cite_ref-21

19. Harriss G. L., Fastolf, Sir John. *Oxford Dictionary of National Biography*, 23 September 2004, online edition 23 September 2004. https://www.oxforddnb.com/view/10.1093/ref:odnb/9780198614128.001.0001/odnb-9780198614128-e-9199?rskey=7JNLlC&result=1
20. Ives, ibid.
21. Block, Joseph S., Shelton Family (*per* 1504–1558). *Oxford Dictionary of National Biography*, Published in print and online 23 September 2004. https://doi.org/10.1093/ref:odnb/70835: and https://www.oxforddnb.com/view/10.1093/ref:odnb/9780198614128.001.0001/odnb-9780198614128-e-70835?rskey=7Jonx0&result=1
22. Thurley, Simon, Tudor Ambition: Houses of the Boleyn family. Gresham College Lectures, 16 September 2020. https://s3-eu-west-1.amazonaws.com/content.gresham.ac.uk/data/binary/3334/2020-09-16_Thurley_Boleyn-T.pdf : PCC Will of Galfridus (Geoffrey) Boleyn. The National Archives, Kew, London. PROB 11//5/12.
23. Large, David M, *The Life and Family of Robert Large, Mercer, Mayor of London 1439–1440. first Employer of William Caxton.* Foundation for Medieval Genealogy, Oak House, Vowchurch, Hereford, HR2 0RB, 2008. pp. 6, 7, 9, 10, 11, 12, 13, 16, 17, 55.
24. Spelman, Diana, Personal Communication, 7 March 2022, with reference to the following: the will of Robert Suckling of Woodton Esq. [NCC 1709, 58 Famm, NRO, Norfolk], Suckling, Revd. Alfred [Inigo], The history and antiquities of the County of Suffolk with Genealogical and Architectural Notices of its several towns and villages. London, John Weale, 59 High Holborn, 1846, p 40 (online edition, https://books.google.co.uk/books/about/The_History_and_Antiquities_of_the_Count.html?id=24-PzgEACAAJ&redir_esc=y: Woodton Parish Registers on FreeREG, images checked on Ancestry: Suckling Pedigree on Ancestry [unverified]: Harvey, William, Clarenceux King of Arms. The visitation of Norfolk in the year 1563. From Harleian MSS in the British Museum, Volume I. Eds Dashwood, G.H. and Bulwer, W. E. G. L. et al. pp. 342 forwards: Will of Sir John Shelton junior, NCC Will 14 November 1558, proved 12 February 1558/9, IPM 4 March 1559: Sir Ralph Shelton, Admon 15 February 1582, IPM 25 April 1582 and 28 April 1584. Marriage with Anne Barrowe of Shipdham, Norfolk and Barningham, Suffolk, married at Shelton 16 October 1570: Henry Shelton, NCC Will dated 18 September 1635, proved 23 January 1635/6: Parish Register entries, Barningham, Suffolk, for the marriage of Robert Suckling Esq. and Mrs Sarah Shelton, 16 November 1669. Parish Register entries, Shelton, Norfolk, between November 1558–December 1661: Parish Register entries, Woodton, Norfolk, from January 1670–December 1708: Will of Lady Anne Shelton of Carhow next Norwich widow, late wife of Sir John Shelton Kt, 16 December 1556, proved 8 January 1556/7 [NCC will register Jagges 175] NRO, Norwich: Will of John Shelton Kt, 14 November 1558, proved 12 February 1558/9 [PCC 1559, Welles quire]: Will of Henry Shelton of Shelton Esq. 18 September 1635, proved 23 January 1635/6: Will of Robert Suckling of Woodton, Esq. 29 September 1707, proved 18 April 1709 [NCC 1709, 58 Famm] NRO, Norwich: Will of Geoffrey Boleyn, PCC Will proved 2 July 1463 [PCC, 1463, Godyn quire]: Geoffrey Boleyn mercer and alderman of St Lawrence Jewry, London: Will of William Boleyn, PCC Will proved 27 November 1505, [PCC 40 Holgrove]: Sir William Boleyn of Blickling (Norfolk): Rye, Walter, Norfolk Families. Issued to Subscribers only. Goose and Son, Norwich, 1913. Includes brief notes on the Boleyn Family, pp. 61–62, mentioning Sir Geoffrey Boleyn's marriage with Anne, daughter and co-heir of Thomas Lord Hoo and Hastings, their son, Sir William Boleyn, died 1505, and married Margaret Parker, daughter and co-heir of the Earl of Ormond (the grandmother of Anne Boleyn), who died insane (see Esch. Inq, Camb. and Hunts, 30-1 Henry VIII. Their son, Sir Thomas Boleyn, created Earl of Wiltshire, married Elizabeth, daughter of Thomas Howard, Duke of Norfolk, and was the father of (1) George Boleyn, beheaded for incest with his sister (2) Anne married Henry VIII, and was the mother of Queen Elizabeth, (3) Mary, married Sir William Carey…,:" : Hughes, Jonathan, Boleyn, Thomas, earl of Wiltshire and earl of Ormond 1476/7-1539. *Oxford Dictionary of National Biography*, 23 September 2004. Published online 4 October 2007. https://www.

oxforddnb.com/view/10.1093/ref:odnb/9780198614128.001.0001/odnb-9780198614128-e-2795?rskey=48DyYC&result=1 : Ives, E. W., Anne [Anne Boleyn]. c. 1500–1536. *Oxford Dictionary of National Biography*, 23 September 2004. Published online 23 September 2004. https://www.oxforddnb.com/search?q=anne+boleyn&searchBtn=Search&isQuickSearch=true: Block, Joseph S., Shelton Family (*per* 1504–1558). *Oxford Dictionary of National Biography*, 23 September 2004. Published online 23 September 2004. https://www.oxforddnb.com/view/10.1093/ref:odnb/9780198614128.001.0001/odnb-9780198614128-e-557?rskey=MHy89y&result=1

25. Hughes, Jonathan, Boleyn, Thomas, earl of Wiltshire and earl of Ormond (1476/7-1539). *Oxford Dictionary of National Biography*, published in print and online, 23 September 2004. This version 04 October 2007. https://doi.org/10.1093/ref:odnb/2795

26. The Tudor Travel Guide. Briis-sous-Forges: A Sophisticated French Education or Simply a Harlot in Exile? May 11, 2019; MacKay, Lauren, *Among the Wolves of Court, the untold story of Thomas and George Boleyn*, Bloomsbury Publishing PLC., ISBN: 9781350147058; Ridgway, Claire, The Anne Boleyn Files, Anne Boleyn's Family Tree. February 8, 2013. https://www.theanneboleynfiles.com/annes-roots/, quoting Julien Brodeau, La Vie de Maistre Charles du Moulin, Julien Brodeau, p.6: Denny, Joanna, *Anne Boleyn: A New Life of England's Tragic Queen*. First published by Portrait, 2004. ISBN 0 7499 5051 X. 2005, p. 26. Sample read online.

27. Ridgeway, Claire, The Anne Boleyn Files, 2013, https://www.theanneboleynfiles.com/annes-roots/ quoting also Denny, Joanna, *Anne Boleyn: A New Life of England's Tragic Queen*, Piatcus, 2005, p. 26.

28. Ridgeway, ibid..

29. https://www.deviantart.com/tffan234/art/Anne-Boleyn-Family-Tree-Part-1-633689618 For an account of Charlemagne, see the Wikipedia entry, with references appended, at https://en.wikipedia.org/wiki/Charlemagne, and Sullivan, Richard E., Charlemagne, Holy Roman emperor (?747–814), https://www.britannica.com/biography/Charlemagne

30. Ramirez, Janina, *Femina: A New history of the Middle Ages, Through the Women Written Out of It*. W.H. Allen, July 2022. Introductory article in *BBC History Magazine*. September 2022, pp. 71–75.

31. Crawley, Charles, Medieval Lands. Earls of Ormond (Walter/Butler). Chapter 9. Ireland. Foundation for Medieval Genealogy. 2006–2021. V4.2 updated 29 October 2021. https://fmg.ac/Projects/MedLands/IRELAND.htm#_Toc389126211

32. Cockayne, George E., *The Complete Peerage of England Scotland Ireland Great Britain and the United Kingdom, Volume II Bass to Canning*, London, The St Catherine Press, 34 Norfolk Street, Strand, 1912, p. 447: http://www.kilkennycastle.ie/en/TouroftheCastle/LordsoftheCastle/TheButlersofOrmondee/ ; Beresford, David. Walter (Butler) Theobald. *Dictionary of Irish Biography*, https://doi.org/10.3318/dib.001290.v1, Originally published October 2009 as part of the Dictionary of Irish Biography.

33. Otway-Ruthven, A. J., *A History of Medieval Ireland*. New York: Barnes and Noble, 1993, p. 67. Quoted in James Butler, 1st Earl of Ormond, in the Wikipedia entry, https://en.wikipedia.org/wiki/James_Butler,_1st_Earl_of_Ormond#cite_ref-Otway67_3-0 ;Flanagan, M. T., Butler [Walter], Theobald (d. 1205), *Oxford Dictionary of National Biography*. Published online: 23 September 2004. https://doi.org/10.1093/ref:odnb/4207

34. Flanagan, M. T., Butler [Walter], Theobald (d. 1205). *Oxford Dictionary of National Biography*. Published online 23 September 2004. https://doi.org/10.1093/ref:odnb/4207

35. Cockayne, ibid., pp. 446–450.

36. Frame, Robin, Butler, James, first earl of Ormond (c.1305–1338). *Oxford Dictionary of National Biography*. Published online: 23 September 2004. https://doi.org/10.1093/ref:odnb/50021

37. Stacey, Robert C., Walter, Hubert (d. 1205). *Oxford Dictionary of National Biography*, Published online: 23 September 2004. This version 3 January 2008. https://doi.org/10.1093/ref:odnb/28633

38. the peerage.com, http://www.thepeerage.com/p1452.htm#i14519 : http://www.thepeerage.com/

p2597.htm#i25962
39. Dryburgh, Paul, The King of Folly. An account of Mortimer's audacious escape from the Tower of London and his actions against Edward II. BBC History Magazine, August 2023, pp. 40—44.
40. Carr, Helen, Edward II dies in mysterious circumstances. BBC History Magazine, September 2022, p. 16.
41. Crowley, ibid. Earls of Hereford 1200–1373 (Bohun). https://fmg.ac/Projects/MedLands/ENGLISH%20NOBILITY%20MEDIEVAL.htm#_Toc56410509
42. Pascual, L.D., The de Bohun Dynasty: Power, Identity and Piety 1066–1399. PhD Thesis, Royal Holloway, University of London, 2014, p. 23 https://pure.royalholloway.ac.uk/portal/files/27830947/2017diazpascuallphd.pdf
43. Cockayne, ibid., volume IV, pp. 213–214. http://www.thepeerage.com/p10192.htm#i101916; Burke, John, A General and Heraldic Dictionary of the Peerages of England, Ireland, and Scotland, Extinct, Dormant, and in Obeyance. London; Henry Colburn and Richard Bentley, New Burlington Street, MDCCCXXXI, p. 64. https://archive.org/details/dli.granth.90912/page/64/mode/2up?view=theater : Crowley, ibid. Humphrey (VII) de Bohun https://fmg.ac/Projects/MedLands/ENGLISH%20NOBILITY%20MEDIEVAL.htm#_Toc56410509 : Pascual, ibid, Appendix A, p. 270, Appendix B, p. 271: Holton, G., S., Battle of Bannockburn Family History Project, Strathclyde Institute for Genealogical Studies, Centre for Lifelong Learning, University of Strathclyde https://www.strath.ac.uk/media/1newwebsite/centres/centreforlifelonglearning/bannockburn/bannockburndocuments/genealogical_Bohun.pdf; For a comprehensive account of the life and times of Edward I, see also Morris, Marc, A Great and Terrible King, first published in 2008 by Hutchinson. Windmill Books, The Random House Group Limited, 20 Vauxhall Bridge Road, London, SW1V 2SA, 2009.
44. Prestwich, Michael. Mary [Mary of Woodstock], (1278–c.1332). Oxford Dictionary of National Biography. Published in print 23 September 2004. Published online 23 September 2004. https://www.oxforddnb.com/view/10.1093/ref:odnb/9780198614128.001.0001/odnb-9780198614128-e-60121?rskey=nyB4aE&result=1
45. Orme, ibid. p. 96.
46. Hamilton, J. S. de Bohun, Humphrey, fourth earl of Hereford and ninth earl of Essex (c.1276–1322). Oxford Dictionary of National Biography, Published online 23 September 2004. This version 3 January 2008. https://doi.org/10.1093/ref:odnb/2777; Warner, Kathryn, Eleanor and Margaret de Bohun, In Edward II. 17 February 2007. http://edwardthesecond.blogspot.com/2007/02/eleanor-and-margaret-de-bohun.html
47. Pascual, L.D., ibid. p. 207.
48. Bigelow, M. M. The Bohun Wills. The American Historical Review, Vol I, No. 3 (April 1896), pp. 414–435, specifically, p. 424 (English translation).
49. Measuringworth.com. ibid.
50. Pascual, ibid, p. 270–271: Holton, ibid.
51. Prebble, John, The Lion in the North. A personal view of Scotland's history. Penguin Books Ltd., Harmondsworth, Middlesex, England. 1973, p. 102.
52. Phillips, J., R., S. Edward II [Edward of Caernarfon] (1284–1327). Oxford Dictionary of National Biography. Published in print 23 September 2004. Published online 23 September 2004. This version 03 January 2008. https://doi.org/10.1093/ref:odnb/8518
53. Rogers, Clifford J., Dagworth, Thomas, first Lord Dagworth (d. 1350). Published online: 26 May 2005. This version: 04 January 2007. https://doi.org/10.1093/ref:odnb/50128 : http://www.thepeerage.com/p10694.htm#i106939
54. Warner, ibid. http://edwardthesecond.blogspot.com/2007/02/eleanor-and-margaret-de-bohun.html
55. Richardson, Douglas. Plantagenet Ancestry: A Study In Colonial And Medieval Families, 2nd

Edition. Kimball G. Everingham, Editor. 1681 West 1000 North Salt Lake City, Utah 84116, p. 450.

56. Gillingham, John, John (1167–1216), *Oxford Dictionary of National Biography*, Published online: 23 September 2004. This version 8 April 2021, https://doi.org/10.1093/ref:odnb/14841; Gillingham, John, Richard [called Richard Coeur de Lion, Richard the Lionheart] (1157–1189). *Oxford Dictionary of National Biography*, Published online: 23 September 2004. This version 8 October 2009. https://doi.org/10.1093/ref:odnb/23498; Keefe, Thomas K., Henry II (1133–1189). *Oxford Dictionary of National Biography*, Published online: 23 September 2004. This version 3 January 2008. https://doi.org/10.1093/ref:odnb/12949; Churchill, Winston S., *The Island Race*, Corgi Books, A Division of Transworld Publishers, London, 1968. pp. 40–57: Magna Carta. Discover the history and legacy of one of the world's most celebrated documents. https://www.bl.uk/magna-carta?gclid=EAIaIQobChMI6va07sKq-QIVh6ztCh1GoAMpEAAYAyAAEgK7V_D_BwE

57. The official website of the British Monarchy. http://www.royal.gov.uk/HistoryoftheMonarchy/KingsandQueensofEngland/TheAngevins/TheAngevins.aspx

58. Schama, Simon. *A History of Britain: At the Edge of the World? 3000BC–AD1603.* BBC Worldwide Ltd., Woodlands, 80 Wood Lane, London W12 0TT. 2000. pp. 160–165.

59. Schama, ibid., p. 164.

60. Saul, Nigel, The 25 Barons of Magna Carta. Magna Carta Trust, Foundation of Liberty. https://magnacarta800th.com/schools/biographies/the-25-barons-of-magna-carta/

61. https://www.thepeerage.com/p10287.htm#i102869

62. See entry for Hugh le Bigod, 3rd Earl of Norfolk, and following, at thepeerage.com. http://thepeerage.com/p462.htm#i4613

63. Morris, Marc, *The Bigod Earls of Norfolk in the Thirteenth Century.* Boydell Press, Woodbridge. First published 2005. Paperback edition 2015, p. 1; Stewart, Peter. Origin and early generations of the Tosny family. Revised version 2012, p. 64, expresses reservations about the descent from Robert Bigod. https://www-personal.umich.edu/~bobwolfe/gentxt/Origin_and_early_generations_of_the_Tosny_family.pdf

64. Morris, ibid. Preface, p. ix.

65. Cockayne, ibid. volume IX, p. 575, and n. (a). https://www.familysearch.org/library/books/viewer/421516/?offset=0#page=589&viewer=picture&o=&n=0&q=

66. Harris, Kim, Archives Assistant, Arundel Castle, West Sussex. From Folder G1/1, a collection of hand-written documents, this page from Cartae Antiquae W: n: 7. later included in Westminster Abbey Charters 1066–c.1214. Originally published by the London Record Society, 1988. Gilbert Crispin was Abbot of Westminster (d. 1117). Other slips of paper in G1/1 include a written list of estates and manors held by Roger Bigod in Norfolk and Suffolk, and 2 slips of paper in which his wife, Adeliza was erroneously described as the daughter of Hugh Grantmesnil (d. 1098) a known companion of William the Conqueror at Hastings in 1066. Arundel Castle became the seat of the Dukes of Norfolk, the senior ducal family in the land, who succeeded the Bigod Earls of Norfolk, after Roger V Bigod died without heirs in 1306. The Castle Archives hold a small folder G1/1 of items which include the name of Roger I Bigod, as above.

67. Keats-Rohan, K., S., B. Belvoir: The Heirs of Robert and Berengar de Tosny. *Prosopon Newsletter 9*, (July 1998), p. 2.

68. Cockayne, ibid. p. 576: Morris, ibid. p. 1; Keats-Rohan, Katharine S., B. *Domesday People, A Prosopography of Persons Occurring in English Documents 1066–1166. I Domesday Book.* The Boydell and Brewer Ltd. p. 396.

69. Harris, ibid. From G1/1, Arundel Castle Archives. A hand-written note taken from Tyrells History vol 2: page 77.

70. Norwich Castle Guide. Norwich Castle around 1200 (PDF). norwich.museums.gov.uk: History of Norwich Castle, Royal Palace (1066–1345). The Home of Norman Kings. Version 3. p. 3. file:///C:/

Users/david/Downloads/History%20of%20Norwich%20Castle%20Version%203%20(1).pdf

71. Ashley, Stephen, Lions Confronted on Bigod's Tower: Proto-Armorial Decoration on the Fore-Building of Norwich Castle Keep and Elsewhere. In: Status, Identity and Authority. Studies in Early Modern Archives and Heraldry, presented to Adrian Hiles. Edited by Sean Cunningham, Anne Curry and Paul Dryburgh. London, The Heraldry Society, 2021. *Part I: Heraldry and Iconography.* Section 2. pp. 12—29.

72. Warren, Gudrun, Librarian and Curator, Norwich Cathedral, quoting Communar Rolls of Norwich Cathedral Priory, 1443—44. Norfolk Record Society, 1972, p. 43: Harper-Hill, Christopher, *English Episcopal Acta, Norwich 1070—1214*, British Academy, 1990, p. 21: *Norwich Cathedral, The Medieval Church and the Wider World, Church, City and Diocese, 1096—1996.* Eds Ian Atherton, Eric Fernie, Christopher Harper-Hill and Hassell Smith. The Hambledon Press, London, 1996, pp. 281—313, cf. The Cathedral Priory and the Laity, p. 301.

73. Cockayne, ibid. p. 577; Morris, ibid. p. 1 : *Framlingham Castle, The Bigods. Suffolk.* English Heritage. https://www.english-heritage.org.uk/visit/places/framlingham-castle/history/history/

74. Wareham, Anglo-Norman Studied XXII. *Proceedings of the Battle Conference, 1999.* Edited by Christopher Hill. The Boydell Press. Woodbridge. 2000. *Anglo-Norman Garrisons*, by John S. Moore. pp. 205—261. p. 235, quoting ref. 212, *Diceto i*, 384—5.

75. Spencer, Charles, *The White Ship. Conquest, Anarchy and the Wrecking of Henry I's dream.* William Collins, 2020, pp. 156, 265, 288. Numerous pages relate the details involved.

76. Cockayne, ibid. p. 579.

77. Spencer, ibid. pp. 158, 180—181, 185, 190, 197, 205, 223; Schama, ibid. p. 117.

78. Spencer, ibid. pp. 184—185.

79. Cockayne, ibid. p. 580; Schama, p. 117: Green, Judith A. The Descent of Belvoir. *Prosopon Newsletter* 10, (April 1999), p. 3, and footnote 27. Henry of Huntingdon, *Historia Anglorum*, ed. D. Greenway (Oxford, 1996), pp. 728—30 and n; *Histora Pontificalis*, ed. M.M. Chibnall, corrected edition (Oxford, 1986), p. 84.

80. King, Edmund, Stephen (c.1092—1154). *Oxford Dictionary of National Biography.* Published in print: 23 September 2004. Published online: 23 September 2004. This version: 23 September 2010. https://doi.org/10.1093/ref:odnb/26365

81. Keefe, Thomas K, Henry II (1133—1189). *Oxford Dictionary of National Biography.* Published in print: 23 September 2004. Published online: 23 September 2004. This version: 3 January 2008. https://doi.org/10.1093/ref:odnb/12949; Schama, ibid. p. 124: Spencer, ibid. p. 295, quoting Edmund King, Henry I, London, Allen Lane, p. 89.

82. Cockayne, ibid. p. 585.

83. Morris, ibid. p. 2.

84. Keats-Rohan, ibid. pp. 380, 396—397.

85. Morris, ibid. Appendix E, *Calendar of Bigod Charters. Charters of Roger II Bigod (1177—1220).* pp. 210—211.

86. FindaGrave, https://www.findagrave.com/memorial/69748146/isabel-bigod : https://www.thepeerage.com/p462.htm#i4612

87. Stacey, Robert C., Bigod, Roger, fourth earl of Norfolk (c.1212—1270). *Oxford Dictionary of National Biography.* Published in print: 23 September 2004. Published online: 23 September 2004. https://doi.org/10.1093/ref:odnb/2380 : https://www.westminster-abbey.org/abbey-commemorations/commemorations/roger-bigod-4th-earl-of-norfolk

88. Prestwich, Michael, Bigod, Roger, fifth earl of Norfolk (c.1245—1306). *Oxford Dictionary of National Biography.* Published in print: 23 September 2004. Published online: 23 September 2004. https://doi.org/10.1093/ref:odnb/2381

89. Cawley, Charles, MEDIEVAL LANDS. A prosopography of medieval European noble and royal families. Foundation for Medieval Genealogy. England, Earls of Norfolk 1142–1306 (BIGOD). v. 4.7, updated 12 August 2022. http://fmg.ac/Projects/MedLands/ENGLISH%20NOBILITY%20MEDIEVAL1.htm#JohnFitzGeoffreydied1258 :ibid. Earls of Norfolk, 1142–1306 (Bigod). http://fmg.ac/Projects/MedLands/ENGLISH%20NOBILITY%20MEDIEVAL.htm#_Toc56410520
90. Crouch, David. Marsham, William [called the Marshal], 4th Earl of Pembroke (c.1146–1219). *Oxford Dictionary of National Biography*. Published in print: 23 September 2004. Published online: 23 September 2004. This version: 24 May 2007. https://doi.org/10.1093/ref:odnb/18126 : https://www.thepeerage.com/p10677.htm#i106761
91. Schama, ibid. p. 165.
92. Morris, ibid. p. 26.
93. Flanagan, M., T., Clare, Isabel de, *suo jure* countess of Pembroke, (1171x6-1220). *Oxford Dictionary of National Biography*. Published in print: 23 September 2004. Published online: 23 September 2004. This version: 24 May 2010. https://doi.org/10.1093/ref:odnb/47208 : Find a Grave. https://www.findagrave.com/memorial/32004131/isabel-de_clare
94. Morris, ibid. p. 31.
95. Morris, ibid. p. 39, 213.
96. Morris, ibid. p. 36, but see also pp. 32–42.
97. Measuring Worth, Purchasing Power of British Pounds from 1270 to present. https://www.measuringworth.com/calculators/ppoweruk/
98. Lund, Ira J., Cumberland Family Tree, Version 4.10. http://www.cft-win.com/
99. Richardson, ibid. p. 425,
100. Strickland, ibid; Keefe, ibid
101. A History of William Longespée. English Monarchs. 2004–2022. https://www.englishmonarchs.co.uk/plantagenet_78.html .
102. Morris, ibid. p. 2–3, and footnote 8, p. 2 : Richardson, ibid. p. 425.
103. Keats-Rohan, K.S.B. *Domesday People: A Prosopography of Persons Occurring in English Documents 1066–1166 I*: 1999, pp. 380–381; Green, ibid. p. 2.
104. Keats-Rohan, ibid. Belvoir: The Heirs of Robert and Berengar de Tosny. *Prosopon Newsletter 9*, (July 1998), p. 2; Huffman, Joseph P., "Ralph III and the House of Tosny" (1984). Master's Thesis. 3843. Genealogies p. 99. https://scholarworks.wmich.edu/masters_theses/3843
105. Faux, David K. Descendants of Hughes I de Cavalcamp Seigneur de Conches. https://www.davidkfaux.org/files/deTosnyReport.pdf;
106. Manuscripts of His Grace the Duke of Rutland, KG. Preserved at Belvoir Castle. Vol IV. HMSO, London, 1905, p. 105. https://archive.org/details/cu31924032311023/page/104/mode/2up; Moore, James. The Norman Aristocracy in the long eleventh century: three case studies. DPhil thesis. Oxford University, 2017, p. 140.
107. Keats-Rohan, ibid.
108. Keats-Rohan, ibid. p. 1: Huffman, ibid, p. 67, quoting Frank Stenton, ref 227, Anglo-Norman England, p 623: Stewart, ibid.
109. Moore, James, "The Norman aristocracy in the long eleventh century: three case studies." D Phil Thesis, University of Oxford, 2017, pp. 20–21, 138-140, 159–163, 166–170: Lund, ibid.
110. Moore, ibid. pp. 164, 169–170.

Part 6: Descendants of Richard Mallom of Wacton

There is not a shred of evidence that Captain John Mallom left a wife, or children, or a will when he died in 1782: he had no descendants. But what happened to his younger brother, Richard, born and baptised in Wacton in 1744 (Fig. 52), who survived to adult life to be named in his father's will of 1761? It goes without saying that his ancestry is identical to that of his brother, as displayed in the Pedigrees and in the Table at the end of Part 5. In this sixth and final section of the story of the Mallom family, the focus moves 40 miles to the north west, from Wacton, to Sculthorpe, in north-west Norfolk *(see map on p.xii)*.

Mallom connections between Wacton and Sculthorpe

Despite the fact that Mallom was a rare surname in Norfolk, good reasons would be needed to claim a link between families with the name living in villages in different parts of the county, and merely postulating a connection based on the surname spelling alone would be unlikely to satisfy critical scrutiny.

Years before the death of John Mallom in 1761, part of the Mallom family left Wacton, and the name does not appear in any record in this part of Norfolk after this date. Furthermore, Wacton was unusual in having taken a census of its population in 1811, 30 years before the first national census was carried-out in 1841. Mallom did not appear in the list of names.[1] As a result, the focus moved north-west to Sculthorpe, where three Mallom sisters, aunts of John Mallom, the last owner of Wacton Hall, were buried inside Sculthorpe Church: Elizabeth in 1723, Mary in 1727, and Audrey in 1758. The inscriptions on their black marble ledgerstones, which are laid north to south, rather than the more usual east to west, have been examined and copied by Dr Julian Litten, a former Senior Curator at the Victoria and Albert Museum, London, and a national authority on funereal customs. Two ledgerstones are partly hidden behind and beneath the organ case, and without special arrangements, photography would be difficult. Nevertheless, with these three

Fig. 52. The font in Wacton Church where Richard Mallom was baptised on 6 April 1744.

burials, the Mallom family connection between Wacton and Sculthorpe is proven beyond all doubt. The key sister was Audrey, the youngest child of John and Elizabeth (Suckling) Mallom, who was baptised in Wacton in the latinised form of Etheldreda in September 1678. She married Revd. Thomas Donne, Rector of Sculthorpe, although their marriage entry has not been found. Incidentally, Etheldreda was the name of her maternal grandmother, the wife of Thomas Stone of Bedingham, so this was a family name. The ledgerstones were probably cut in King's Lynn, the nearest place to Sculthorpe where ledgercutters were working. The port facilities were ideal because the stones would have been transported from the Lowlands as ballast black marble, and taken to Sculthorpe after completion, on the inland water-courses of the Bedford Levels.[2]

In his *The Book of Sculthorpe*, Gary Windeler showed that Thomas Donne was presented as Rector of Sculthorpe by his father, Robert Donne, who was patron of the living. His cousin, Roger Donne of Wacton, was a tenant farmer of John Mallom of Wacton Hall, and his youngest daughter, Audrey, may have met her future husband through Roger Donne. Audrey and her husband the Rector lived in Sculthorpe Parsonage House and, at about the same time, Roger Donne married a Sculthorpe bride, Katherine Clench.[3] Furthermore, Thomas Donne was an Executor to the will of his brother-in-law, John Mallom, in 1728, and so there was undoubtedly close contact between the Donne family of Sculthorpe and the Mallom family of Wacton. Audrey's sister, Elizabeth Mallom, born in Bedingham in 1673, died a spinster in Sculthorpe, in 1723, when the Parish Register recorded her burial as: "Mrs Elizabeth Mallom was buried September 11th 1723." As noted, the title "Mrs" implies a woman from a high-status family, and from her will it is clear that Elizabeth was a spinster. Her memorial in Purbeck marble, includes a Latin inscription inscribed below the Mallom coat of arms, in a lozenge, with a frame of leaves incorporating a winged hour-glass. The lozenge on the ledgerstones of Elizabeth and Mary is the diamond-shaped symbol used instead of a shield or armorial by females who were spinsters or widows, entitled to bear arms.[4] A spinster (Elizabeth), took the arms of her father displayed in a lozenge, whereas a widow (Mary), would display her father's arms with her husband's arms impaled with hers (two coats of arms, side by side in one heraldic shield).[5] However, Mary's husband, James Wortley, was not arms-bearing, so the Mallom arms were displayed in a lozenge on her ledgerstone (Fig. 53).

Fig. 53. Lozenge carved on the ledgerstone of Mary (Mallom) Wortley, illustrating the Mallom coat of arms.

Sub Hoc Marmore
Sunt Depofitæ Reliquæ
ELIZABETHÆ
Filiæ Secunda JOHANNIS MALLOM
Armigeri
et ELIZABETHÆ
Uxoris ejus filiæ
THOMÆ STONE
Armigeri
et Etheldredæ Uxoris eius
Obit octavo die Septembris
1723

That is to say: "Beneath this marble are deposited the remains of Elizabeth the second daughter of John Mallom, Armiger (Arms bearer, Gentleman, Esquire) and Elizabeth his wife, the daughter of Thomas Stone, Armiger, and Audrey (Etheldreda) his wife, who died on the 8 September 1723."

The second black marble ledgerstone commemorates Audrey's sister, Mary (Mallom) Wortley, born in Wacton in 1675. Mary married James Wortley in North Creake in 1699, when James was styled 'Mr' and Mary as 'Mrs,' indicating their status. The couple had one son, John, baptised in April 1700 in Wells-next-the-Sea, buried there in February 1701. James was buried in Wells in 1710. Given her marriage, it is interesting to see that Mary's memorial was inscribed in her maiden name to mark her Mallom origins, rather in her married name, and the burial in Sculthorpe suggests that Mary came to live in the village after the death of her husband, probably to live with her sisters, at Cranmer Hall. Elizabeth's will confirms James's death by referring to her sister as "Mary Wortley, widow." Mary was one of the Executors to Elizabeth's will, and the burial entries of the two sisters in the Sculthorpe Parish Register is in the handwriting of their brother-in-law, Revd. Thomas Donne, the Rector. Mary died on 9 September 1727, and the burial took place two days later when the entry in the register recorded the event as "Mrs Mary Wortley, widow was buried September 11th [1727]." Her ledgerstone was laid next to that of her sister Elizabeth. Mary's inscription, in Latin, below the Mallom coat of arms, in a lozenge, with a frame of leaves incorporating a winged hour-glass, reads as follows:

Sub Hoc Marmore
Depofitæ Sunt Reliquie MARIÆ Tertiæ
Filiæ JOHANNIS MALLOM
Armigeri
et ELIZABETHÆ
Uxoris ejus filiæ
THOMÆ STONE

Armigeri
et Etheldredæ Uxoris eius
Obiit Nono Die Septembris
1727

That is to say: "Beneath this marble are deposited the remains of Mary, the third daughter of John Mallom, Armiger and Elizabeth his wife, the daughter of Thomas Stone, Armiger and Audrey (Etheldreda) his wife, who died on the 9 September 1727." The inscriptions on the ledgerstones of Elizabeth and of Mary were carved with the same chisel and they were probably laid at the same time.[6]

The third ledgerstone, commemorates both Revd. Thomas Donne and his wife, Audrey (Mallom) Donne, born in Wacton in 1678. Sculthorpe Parish Register recorded her burial as follows: "Mrs Audrey Donne, widow and Relict of Thomas Donne Clerk late Rector of this Parish buried November 17th 1758." Donne had been the Rector of Sculthorpe from 1705 until 1739 when he was succeeded as Rector by his bachelor son, Robert Donne, who served in the Parish from 1739 to 1765. However, it was the Curate, Revd. William Pretheroe, who officiated at Audrey's burial service, and her register entry is in Pretheroe's handwriting. This ledgerstone lies in front of the south aisle altar, in black marble laid north to south. The English inscription appears below a carved coat of arms, showing Donne impaling Mallom, and reads as follows:

Near this place lie the Remains of
The Reverend THOMAS DONNE
late of Cramner in Sculthorpe, Patron and
Rector of this Church, who departed this Life
on the 5th of June 1739 Aged 60.
Alƒo of Audrey the Youngest Daughter of
JOHN MALLOM late of Wacton Hall
in Norfolk, Esquire, Relict of the aforeƒaid
THOMAS DONNE of Cramner who
Departed this life on the last Day of
October 1758 Aged 81

These burials unmistakably confirm the connection between members of the Mallom family of Wacton, and Sculthorpe. The original Mallom interest in Sculthorpe was through Audrey (Mallom) Donne who lived with her husband, the Rector, in comfortable accommodation at Cranmer Hall, and later in the Parsonage House. Her sister, Elizabeth, was a spinster of independent means thanks to a bequest specified in her father's will of 1687.[7] In her own will, she left her brother, John Mallome of Water Acton (Wacton), £10, and the interest on £100 to her sister Katherine, wife of John Harris of Norwich, and her sisters, Mary Wortley and Audria, the wife of Revd. Thomas Donne.[8] The Executors were Thomas Donne and her sister, Mary (Mallom) Wortley, widow. She died 35 years before Audrey, probably moving to Sculthorpe in the early 1700s, and it is more than likely that she lived with her sister and brother-in-law in Cranmer Hall, Sculthorpe. Audrey's second sister, Mary (Mallom) Wortley, a widow, died in 1727, and, having buried both her son and her husband, it is quite likely that she went to live with Audrey and Thomas Donne after the death of their sister, Elizabeth, since it was not unusual for a spinster sister and a widowed sister to live with their married sister.[9] The burial arrangements for Elizabeth and Mary were supervised by Audrey, who left similar plans in her will for her own interment in Sculthorpe Church, having outlived her husband by almost 20 years.[10]

For a number of years, Thomas and Audrey Donne lived at Cranmer Hall, Sculthorpe, until his death in 1739, since the Parish Register entry for his burial records that this was his residence. He was succeeded as Rector by their son, Revd. Robert Donne, and he and his mother continued to live at Cranmer Hall until the autumn of 1747. However, on 30 October that year, Audrey signed over Cranmer Hall to her son, by which time she was in Norwich,[11] where her third sister, Catherine, had settled after having married John Harris, gent. The coincidence of the dates involved - of Audrey signing over Cranmer Hall to her son (30 October 1747)—and the death of her sister (buried 29 October 1747 at St Lawrence, Norwich), is worth noting. In addition, Audrey's will was written in Norwich, suggesting that she might have been involved in some way with the terminal care of her sister, Catherine. The will indicates that all her "wearing apparel and household furniture" was left to her niece, Martha Harris, Catherine's daughter.[12] In whatever the circumstances, Audrey (Mallom) Donne died in Norwich, in 1758, aged 81, and her remains were interred in Sculthorpe Church, at her request. Her connections with Sculthorpe remained very strong to the end of her life: she wished to be buried with her sisters in the church where her husband had been the Rector.

MARRIAGE OF JOHN MALLOM WITH ANNE HIPKIN, 1792

Almost thirty-four years after Audrey's burial, the marriage took place in Sculthorpe, on the 22 October 1792, of a young man called John Mallom, with Anne Hipkin, the Banns having been read in church on the preceding three Sundays, as required. The couple were both single and 'of the Parish.' It was a requirement of the Hardwicke Marriage Act of 1753 that one of them was resident in the parish, but the other party might move into the parish shortly before the marriage to avoid two sets of fees for the reading of the Banns.[13] John Mallom was described in the Marriage Register as 'of this Parish Singleman', so he was living in Sculthorpe. Of course, this leaves unanswered the question of where he was born, where he lived, and how was he employed before 1792, and exactly when he came to live in Sculthorpe. Anne was from a local family, but John's baptism, if there was one, has not been found, despite exhaustive searches. Is it possible that this John was related to the Malloms of Wacton? His baptismal name and surname are certainly suggestive, recalling that John was a very important baptismal name in the earlier generations of the family.

Of great additional interest in the marriage entry is the name of the first witness. The names of the fathers of brides and grooms were not yet being included in parish marriage registers, and so the name of John's father was not recorded. However, the first witness was Nathaniel Raven, the wealthy landowner and farmer of Brancaster and Sculthorpe, and the question is why he was involved in the marriage arrangements? Parish Registers in the locality were searched for a period of 20 years (1780–1800) for Raven's signature as a witness to a marriage, and it was found on 27 occasions, this being the only time he signed at a Sculthorpe marriage. No connection between either of the two families and Nathaniel Raven's family has been found, and the name Mallom does not appear in his will of 1808.[14] It is possible that John Mallom may have been in Raven's employment, although no documentary evidence to support this has been found. Nevertheless, the coincidence of Sculthorpe as the village where John Mallom was married and where Nathaniel Raven owned property and land is intriguing.

He was a member of the Raven family of Whissonsett and Horningtoft which had a Coat of Arms, and included yeomen and others who left wills.[15] This suggests influence in the area which would be consistent with the marriage of John Mallom and Anne Hipkin having had a special social significance in Sculthorpe, as would befit a descendent of the Mallom family of Wacton, which had its own grant of arms in 1685.

Were there other circumstances in which John's father, Richard Mallom, and Nathaniel Raven could have become acquainted? Raven married Sarah Money in East Raynham in 1774, and her surname is the same as that of Captain Mallom's friend, Lieutenant John Money, of Norwich. Whether there was a family connection between the two families is unknown, but is worth considering, since it could have provided a basis for Raven and Richard Mallom to meet. However, friendship between Nathaniel Raven and Richard Mallom implied by his presence as a witness at the Sculthorpe wedding would have been crucial. Richard and his son would inevitably have struggled socially, given the problems in Wacton, but the Ravens would have been in a position to give them some social acceptance in and around Sculthorpe.

Incidentally, John's surname was written with a terminal 'n' in the marriage entry, and also in the baptism entry of his first child, Sarah, in November 1792, shortly after the marriage. However, each of the remaining seven baptisms to John and Anne recorded the surname as Mallom, and so there is no doubt that these are the names of the same individuals and family, and no one named Mallon lived in the parish during the next 100 years. Anne was heavily pregnant on her wedding day, and so she and John had clearly known each other for some time, implying that he was living in or near Sculthorpe.

John and Anne Mallom raised eight children in Sculthorpe between 1792 and 1808, the second of their two sons being baptised Richard, the name of the boy's paternal grandfather. However, Richard was also a name seen in the Hipkin family: Anne had five siblings, all boys, including a younger brother baptised Richard, in Sculthorpe in 1774, and three other relatives baptised Richard in Sculthorpe or Fakenham between 1750 and 1775. John and Anne Mallom's first son was baptised William, and this was the name of Anne's maternal grandfather, William Allard. This name is not seen in the Mallom ancestry, apart from in a cousin named William Mallom, the Ship's Butcher, the son of Robert Mallom of Swaffham, and it is unlikely that he was the source of the name. At first sight, therefore, it looks as if John and Anne named their son, William, from her family, and their second son, Richard, from John's, in each case, commemorating the baptismal name of a grandfather. The evidence at least supports this suggestion. In contrast to the outcomes of the offspring of John and Phillis Mallom of Wacton, 60—70 years earlier, the children of John and Anne Mallom all survived childhood and adolescence, with the sole exception of their daughter, Dorothy, named after her mother's sister, Dorothy Hipkin, and who died as a young adult. All the other children of John and Anne married and had families of their own as will be discussed below.

Burial of John Mallom in Sculthorpe, 1810

Not long after the birth of his last child, John Mallom died in 1810, at the age of 45 years, relatively young even for the late Georgian period, and the Sculthorpe Burial Register entry gives invaluable additional information about him, as follows:

> John Mallom, the son of Richard Mallom and Mary his Wife/ late Mary Smith, Spinster/ a married man, was buried July 25th 1810, aged 45 years.

Including the name of the father or of both parents of a deceased child was common at this time, but in some parishes the tradition of naming the parents of deceased adults in burial registers was also adopted. This practice has been researched in parishes of north-west Norfolk which have burial entries for adults in which the parents were named. 35 examples were investigated and the relevant baptismal entry for each individual was traced, showing that the names of the parents were always correctly recorded in the burial entry, and the ages at death were within 2—3 years of that expected. It follows that there is no reason to doubt the parentage of John Mallom, who must have been born in about 1765 (1762—1768). From 1812 onwards, printed register books were issued for parish use, and baptisms, marriages and burials were recorded separately. In Sculthorpe, the Rector regularly included causes of death from 1814 onwards, but not before then, and so a possible cause of death of John Mallom was not included. His name did not appear in an obituary notice in Norfolk newspapers in circulation at the time, either, and so the reason for John's death remains unknown. An obituary notice might have included the place of death and the circumstances, and perhaps also a reference to his origins.[16] John Mallom was buried in Sculthorpe graveyard on 25 July 1810, and his daughter, Dorothy, was buried in the same grave following her death, in 1816. A headstone with their names and dates marked the site until it was removed when the inscription became illegible following 200 years of weather damage, and grass alone now marks the place of their burial.[17]

The inclusion of the names of John Mallom's parents in the Sculthorpe Burial Register entry suggests that they were given to the Rector by someone attending the funeral who knew the details were correct. The person most likely to have given the information to Mr Dowsing, was John's widow, Anne, who was still alive. After all, Richard and Mary (Smith) Mallom were her in-laws, and it is hard to believe that she did not know their names, even if they had died before she and John were married. No siblings of John's, other children of Richard and Mary, have been found, so perhaps Richard had died when he was still quite young, at which point his son was left to fend for himself as best he could. There is no sign that Richard Mallom left a will, even if he had inherited anything from his brother, Captain Mallom. On the other hand, had he survived, Richard would have been 66 years old in 1810, and so he may have been present at his son's funeral, in person: the details of his later life are completely unknown.

SEARCHES FOR THE MARRIAGE OF RICHARD MALLOM WITH MARY SMITH

Recalling that the burial register entry of John Mallom shows that his parents were Richard and Mary (Smith) Mallom, very extensive searches have been carried-out throughout Norfolk, including by a professional genealogist, in every one of the more than 700 parishes with surviving records.[18] Additional searches for the marriage of Richard and Mary have been made in the Phillimore Marriage Registers for Norfolk,[19] Boyd's Marriage Indexes, 1538–1850, and in a Norfolk Marriage Index compiled by Patrick Palgrave-Moore, the leading authority on Norfolk families and their records. This is an index of marriages which took place between 1538–1812, by Hundred, covering the whole of Norfolk, using all available sources. In addition, 42 individuals who registered an interest in the surnames Mallom, Mallon, Smith, Smyth and variants, were contacted through the Norfolk Transcription Archive, but none had any information about the Mallom-Smith marriage.[20] The Buxton Papers, a collection of documents held in the Department of Manuscripts at Cambridge University, was examined, since the names of John Mallom of Aslacton and George Smith of Topcroft, Norfolk were included. However, the reference was to John Mallom's will and a clause of the will of George Smith.[21] The Nelson Society was unable to help in the quest.[22] All the Norfolk parishes with available records have been searched between 1758–1775, and the Mallom-Smith marriage has not been found.

During the searches, note was taken of surname variants. Particular care was taken with the name Mallow(s) because of the similarity in some handwriting of the terminal letters 'w' and 'm,' and the surname Hallam and variants was also considered. The following are examples: John, son of Richard and Mary Murlon of North Elmham was baptised in July 1766, and so a possible contender for John, son of Richard and Mary Mallom. The Murlons baptised six other children between 1761 and 1779, and Mary died in 1784, whereupon Richard remarried. However, the origin of this Richard was found in nearby Stanfield, where he was baptised in May 1731, and his wife was Mary Taylor, not Mary Smith. In Guist, a Richard Mallon was living during the 1770s, but his wife was Elizabeth, and there was no sign of an earlier or a later marriage. Other members of the Mallon family of Guist included William, who married Sarah Lockett in 1820. They had a grandson, Richard Mallon, who married Beatrice H M Forster, the daughter of Thomas Forster, Gentleman, in February 1886, in Swaffham. Richard became a carpenter, a timber merchant and poultry appliance manufacturer in Swaffham.[23] The presence in Swaffham during the 19th century of families named Mallom and Mallon who were not related, might have led to confusion unless their origins had been thoroughly researched. A John Malum was baptised in June 1764 in Aldeby, but his parents were John and Susannah. The name of Richard Marham appeared in Yaxham, where a widower with the name was buried in 1770. It is likely that he was baptised in nearby Great Dunham to Thomas and Ann, in 1762, since there was no marriage or burial for him there. A man with the same name also appeared in Shipdham, where he was buried in 1788. However, his wife was named Ester. A number of other surname variants including Mullon, Mallone, Mallen, Mileham, Marham, Marlum and Mallow(s) were investigated, without finding any credible candidates for our Mallom family. The name of Richard Mileham appeared in the Death Duty Register in Norwich, in 1816, the year he was buried as a widower, aged 73 years, and so born c.1743. However, he was part of a settled family living in Norwich, and so he was not considered further.

These searches were based on the assumption that Richard Mallom married his bride in church, something which all his forebears had done, and which would be expected given the status of the family. One plausible candidate for Richard Mallom has been found, and only one, and he was the son of John and Phillis Mallom of Wacton Hall, baptised in Wacton Church on 6 April 1744, as described earlier. The dates and family names all appear to be appropriate, including the use of the name John in Richard's son. Despite the exhaustive searches, however, no record of John's baptism, has been found. It is worth noting that no baptisms of other children to Richard and Mary (Smith) Mallom, have been located, either, suggesting that the relevant register has not survived, or that Richard and/or his wife died young, or that their children were not baptised at all. It is true that some marriages were informal. However, a church ceremony gave written evidence of the union, and it follows that the widow and any children could subsequently inherit an estate without further proof. In other cases, the church ceremony acted as a public statement confirming a recent private arrangement.[24]

In an attempt to overcome some of these irregularities, and bigamy, parliament introduced "The Clandestine Marriages Act," long title "An Act for the Better Preventing of Clandestine Marriage," also known as Lord Hardwicke's Marriage Act, in 1753.[25] A form of clandestine marriage for Richard and Mary is unlikely, and no evidence of this has been found.[26] The Act specified that marriages should be conducted in an Anglican Church, except in the case of Jews and Quakers. Quaker Meeting Houses would have been in existence in the 1760s, although there is no evidence that Richard Mallom was married in one. Most non-conformist chapels came into existence later, including the branches of the Methodist church, but in any case, the 1753 Act means that their marriages would have been conducted in the parish church.[27]

Infants were not always baptised in the Established Church, and even after the emergence of non-conformist churches and chapels, some infants may not have been presented for baptism, although this is difficult to investigate. Others, especially the sickly, may have been baptised at home and the event not recorded in the Parish Register. Infants of Quaker families were not baptised at all, and those of a Baptist persuasion would be baptised as teenagers or later, if they were so inclined.[28] The possibility of a late baptism of John has been excluded by checking the sources up to 1775.

During our period of interest, two families named Smith lived in Sculthorpe, including Thomas and Elizabeth Smith, who baptised three children during the mid-1740s, one of them, a daughter, Mary, baptised in June 1746. No marriage or burial for her has been found for her in Sculthorpe, and so it is just possible that she was the Mary Smith who married Richard Mallom in the early 1760s. The problem is the lack of an entry in the Parish Register, and the fact that hers was a common name, with several examples of marriages and burials in nearby villages during the period 1745–1765. If a church ceremony took place, it should have been included in the register because two of the recent Rectors of Sculthorpe, Revd. Thomas Donne and his son, Revd. Robert Donne, were close relatives of Richard Mallom, his great aunt, Audrey Mallom having married Thomas Donne. However, no record of the Donne-Mallom marriage has been found, either, and omissions from the registers of other members of the Mallom families have also been noted. Richard was entitled to expect certain social favours because of the status of his forbears, but nevertheless, no record has been found stating that Richard and Mary Mallom lived in or near Sculthorpe. Gentry families named Smyth/Smith, had property dealings with Sculthorpe during the mid-1700s, including the family of George Smyth of Topcroft Hall, gent, and his widow Mary, and the family of Offley Smith of Harlestone, gent.[29] However, Mary, the daughter of George and Mary Smyth, married William Stone in Topcroft and not Richard Mallom, who, in any case, may not have been an attractive prospect for such a family, given the events in Wacton and Aslacton. Six girls baptised 'Mary' were born to Smith families, in Long Stratton, Woodton, Carleton Rode and Aslacton, between 1739 and 1755, and an estimated at least 200 baptisms of 'Mary Smith' took place in

Norfolk between 1740 and 1755, the most likely period for the future bride of Richard Mallom to have been born. However, based on information derived from searches in commercial family history websites, none of these women married a man called Richard Mallom.

According to the burial entry of their son, John, in Sculthorpe in 1810, Richard Mallom's wife was described as a spinster called Mary Smith before their marriage. In the light of this, a series of searches was made in the wills of men and women named Smith who lived in and around Aslacton where John and Phillis Mallom and their two sons, John and Richard, moved in 1754. In the mid-1800s, the Bunwell Brick Works, formerly owned by John Mallom, passed into the hands of the Smith family, notably Robert Smith (1828–1886), the son of James Smith, farmer and bricklayer.[30] Could Richard have met and married the daughter of an earlier member of this family, called Mary, such that her name might appear in one of their wills, either in her maiden or her married name? Ten wills and/or administrations were examined, but Mary's name did not appear in any of them.[31] Clearly, this would have been relevant only if Mary had been a member of a Smith family who owned assets sufficient to leave in a will, and this seems not to have been the case, based on these examples.

SEARCHES OUTSIDE NORFOLK

Searches were also undertaken for the marriage of Richard Mallom with Mary Smith and the baptism of their son, John, beyond the boundaries of East Anglia, using commercially available family history software, and in correspondence with County Record Offices and Family History Societies. Some examples of possibilities include the baptism of John to Richard and Mary Malam in October 1762 in Audlem, Cheshire. However, there were eight baptisms to Richard Malam, most of these with his wife, Mary, between 1762 and 1783, together with marriages of men and women named Malam in the same village during the 19th century. These baptisms coincided with the time when John, son of Richard and Mary Mallom, was born, excluding the Cheshire family as plausible contenders. In the same county, a Richard Malone was buried in 1808, but his mother was Elizabeth. Between 1680 and 1760, three infants baptised 'Richard Mallom' were identified, including the 1744 son of John and Phillis Mallom in Wacton. The other two were baptised in Chester-Le-Street, Durham, in 1740, and in Chilton Foliat, Wiltshire, in 1752. Both were part of settled families in their areas, with other siblings having been baptised in each parish: Richard of Chilton Foliat was buried in 1752. [32]

Several Lincolnshire villages had families named Mellam, Malam, Malan, Malham and Mullham, some of which included individuals named John, but none of them with the correct parents' names. In Milton, Berkshire, a Richard Malam, born in February 1764, was buried in March 1799. A son named John was baptised in Milton, in August 1771, to Richard and Mary Mal(l)am. Children of this couple were baptised between 1764 and 1786, but with no obvious connection to

Norfolk. Nevertheless, John, the son of Richard and Mary Malam, was a possible contender for our John Mallom of Sculthorpe, because of the name and the names of his parents, and the year of his birth, and so he was examined in detail. He left a will in Milton, in February 1835, in which he was described as a gentleman, with a valuable estate, and bequests to his wife, Mary, and his children. The will indicated a connection with Kent, where Mallam's marriage was found, in August 1814, to Mary Smith, in Westerham, Kent, by Licence. This, however, is not the John Mallom who married Anne Hipkin in Sculthorpe, although the discovery of Mary's maiden name, is intriguing.[33]

Families named Meallam/Mallam included men named Richard, in Ardington, Berkshire, between 1781 and 1809, but without a wife named Mary or a son named John. A Richard Mallam paid 4/9 Land Tax in Limpsfield, Surrey, in 1804, and the surname Mallam appeared in other Surrey parishes paying Land Tax, although none fitted our Richard Mallom of Wacton, Norfolk. Younger sons of gentry families sometimes moved from their home counties to London in the hope of making sufficient money to return home more prosperous. However, London Metropolitan Archives found no evidence to suggest our Richard Mallom moved to London. Poll Books and Electoral Registers for London, 1538–1893 included no relevant names. London Apprentice Abstracts included four examples of a John Mallom, three from Surrey and one from Berkshire, but none of them had a father named Richard, and Lambeth Palace Library had no record of our Richard's marriage. The Oxfordshire Wills Index 1576–1857 included a Richard Mallam, Yeoman, of Bampton, Oxfordshire, in 1773. There were two sons, John and Joseph, and John was an Executor to the will written in 1767, in which he inherited property. There was no marriage record of a Richard Mallam and a Mary Smith in Oxfordshire, and no record of a baptism for a John Mallom between 1762 and 1768 in Oxfordshire, either.[34] In the Index to Death Duty Register 1796–1903, the surname Mallam, Mallon, Mellon and Malin occurred, including a Richard Mallam in 1817, of North Street, Chelsea.[35]

These negative searches mean that the marriage record of Richard and Mary, if there was one, is unlikely to have survived. However, it is possible that Richard Mallom and Mary Smith formed a liaison but were never married in a church ceremony, and by its nature, this can never be proven. Assuming their son, John, who was born in about 1765, was baptised, the event may well have taken place in the church were his parents were married, and the register or its pages, has not survived. On the other hand, it is abundantly clear that John Mallom lived his life, married, had children, died and was buried. and so, he was definitely born. The challenge encountered in locating the marriage of his parents, has meant that the search for circumstantial evidence to support the hypothesis described in this section, became very important.

Whereabouts of Richard Mallom after the death of his parents

When his mother died in May 1754, Richard had just had his tenth birthday: he was still a child. His father was a widower living in financially constrained circumstances, and could hardly be described as well-able to look after himself and his family even while his wife was at his side, but now she had died, things were very different. Had he remained in Aslacton, Richard would have witnessed within the next few years, his older brother leave Norfolk to join his regiment, and the death of his father. The family home in Aslacton would be sold, leaving him orphaned and homeless, although he was old enough to know that he had relatives living in Sculthorpe, and that his great aunt Audrey (Mallom) Donne lived in comfort in the Parsonage House. What became of him? Is it possible that Richard remained in the Aslacton area, finding somewhere to live and work on his late father's estate? He was the son of a gentleman who had mounting debts, but although his needs were considerable, it would have been difficult for Richard, as the son 'from the big house in Wacton' to work and live as a farm labourer, for example. And difficult also for the estate workers to accept him on those terms. In short, crossing the social divide to this degree in mid-Georgian England, would have been unusual. It should also be born in mind that one of the witnesses at the marriage in Sculthorpe, of his son, John, in 1792, was Nathaniel Raven, the farmer and landowner, and this courtesy does not suggest that Richard had adopted the lifestyle of an agricultural labourer. With little to keep him in Aslacton but memories, some of them arguably not very pleasant, Richard would have had to find somewhere else to live. It is unlikely that he went to Norwich to live with his older cousin, Martha Harris, although the city would have offered him employment opportunities and social contacts. Richard undoubtedly grew-up in difficult circumstances, and although he could have been styled 'gent' he may have wished to avoid this, and live the early part of his adult life in relative obscurity.

However, at some point after the death of his mother, in 1754, it is much more likely that he was sent off, still a child, with his teenage brother, John, to live with his great aunt Audrey, in Sculthorpe. Later, in Sculthorpe, Richard and his son, John, would have found the friendship, support and encouragement of the wealthy landowner, Nathaniel Raven, crucial to their social acceptance in the area. Raven would not have acted as witness at John's marriage unless there had been a close connection between the men, not forgetting that Richard Mallom was the son of a gentleman.

Richard Mallom did not join a regiment of the British Army, or the Navy, and he did not go up to Cambridge or Oxford University.[36] Did he follow the example set by his brother, by enlisting in either the East or the West Norfolk Militia, recalling that the Mallom brothers were related by marriage to Sir Armine Wodehouse of Kimberley, Colonel of the East Norfolk Militia from 1759?[37] It was to Wodehouse that his brother, John, wrote, asking for a recommendation to George Townshend, but there is no mention of the name of Richard Mallom in the published Musters of the East Norfolk Militia which subsequently became the 4th Battalion Norfolk Regiment.[38] The list of Officers from 1759 to 1898 would be expected to include his name, although Musters were missing in the key years between 1760 and 1779. However, lists of Appointments to Officer posts were shown between 1774 and 1778, by which time Richard Mallom would have been 34 years old and eligible for promotion to the equivalent rank of that achieved by his brother in the 63rd Regiment of Foot. His name was not included. As far as the West Norfolk Militia is concerned, no comprehensive published history has been found.[39] Some surviving County Regimental Returns for the West Norfolk Militia, which include names without locations, have been published for the years 1780–1876, but these are probably too late to include Richard's name.[40] Militia Ballot Lists for a few selected parishes in North Erpingham Hundred, Norfolk, have also been published, but these do not include the name of Richard Mallom, either.[41] Had he enlisted in one of the Norfolk Militias, Richard would have been able to live at home, at least, during peacetime, a significant advantage for a married man.[42]

The search for additional documentary evidence of a move by Richard to the Sculthorpe area of north-west Norfolk where his relatives had been living, led to the examination of the following documents: Sculthorpe maps for 1766, 1767, 1796 and 1822 showed no evidence of an owner/occupier named Mallom.[43] The Sculthorpe Enclosure map of 1829 likewise showed no Mallom landowners.[44] Sculthorpe Manor Court Records were searched from 1789–1843 without finding reference to Mallom.[45] Equivalent searches were also made in the Manors of nearby Fakenham, Dunton cum Doughton, South Creake, and Houghton St Giles, none of which included the name of Mallom.[46] Similarly, fourteen books of rentals, for the years 1771 - 1785 (apart from 1773) for the manors of Sculthorpe, Gressenhall, Whissonsett, Fakenham and Barsham did not include the name Mallom, either.[47] Searches were also made in the Poll Lists for Norfolk, 1765–1810,[48] in the Survey of Glebe Lands of Sculthorpe, 1796,[49] and in the Papers of Daniel Jones of Cranmer Hall, Sculthorpe, for the period 1750–1783.[50] None of these documents included the name of Mallom or a surname variant.

Between January 1752 and Michaelmas (29 September) 1763, Cranmer Hall was rented to Colonel the Hon. George Townshend.[51] His tenancy ended in 1763 when Townshend succeeded to his late father's title and returned to the family seat at Raynham Hall.[52] Was it at Cranmer Hall that Townshend heard of the Mallom family difficulties, either from Audrey or from Robert Donne, before her brother, John Mallom died in 1761? A comment about this was included in the letter from Sir Armine Wodehouse to Townshend in May 1770, concerning Lt John Mallom, as noted in Part 2: "…the Circumstances of his Family are well known to you…" As we have seen, it is more than likely that John's sponsorship by Townshend's brother, Charles, also originated in discussions at Cranmer Hall. Did Richard Mallom also benefit from this extensive social network in some way?

The three Mallom sisters who were buried in Sculthorpe Church were the great aunts of Captain John and Richard Mallom, and so the 2nd great aunts of Richard's son, John, who died in 1810. Descendants of John and Anne (Hipkin) Mallom lived in Sculthorpe throughout the 19th and most of the 20th centuries, and the baptismal name Richard was used on six occasions, including in a son and four of the grandsons of John and Anne Mallom. This suggests a definite wish to preserve the name in memory of Richard Mallom of Wacton, from whom all the Mallom families of Sculthorpe were descended.

2ND MARRIAGE OF ANNE (HIPKIN) MALLOM, 1811

Her husband's death left Anne (Hipkin) Mallom a widow with eight children, three of whom were under the age of 10 years, and so it is not surprising that she remarried. This second marriage gave Anne's children a step-father, and additional security during difficult times, well before there was any form of Social Security or Widow's Pension. The register entry recorded the details of the marriage on 4 February 1811, in Sculthorpe, as follows "John Bastard, Single Man of this Parish and Anne Mallom of the same, Widow." The ceremony was conducted by the Revd. Horatio Dowsing, who had buried her first husband the previous year. The couple had one child, a son, James, in Sculthorpe, but he died in early infancy (lived February-May, 1815). John Bastard died in 1829, and his widow, Anne—Hipkin-Mallom-Bastard went to live with her daughter, Elizabeth, and her son-in-law, William Parker, in Burnham Westgate, as shown in the censuses of 1841 and 1851. Anne died in 1858 and was buried in Burnham Sutton cum Ulph on 15 January 1858, aged 87 years, outliving her first husband, John Mallom, by nearly 50 years.

DESCENDANTS OF JOHN AND ANNE (HIPKIN) MALLOM OF SCULTHORPE

John and his wife had eight children, all baptised in Sculthorpe, and 51 grandchildren, many of whom were baptised in the village (Fig. 54). Sculthorpe had two village censuses, the first in 1821 and the second in 1831, the latter, ten years before the first official national census. The Parish of Sculthorpe was quite

Fig. 54. Sculthorpe Church and its font where baptisms, marriages and burials of members of the Mallom and Large families took place from the late 1700s onwards.

innovative in this respect, and in 1821 the population of the village, including males, females and children, was 466. By 1831, it had risen to 619, and during the years covered by these records, many of the grandchildren of John and Anne Mallom were born. Seven of their eight children survived to adult life to marry and have their own children, the sole exception being Dorothy, who died 1816. Anne was pregnant with her daughter, Sarah, when she and John were married in Sculthorpe, and Sarah subsequently married Ransom Bell in Sculthorpe in 1818. They had seven children between 1818 and 1832, all baptised in Sculthorpe.

John and Anne's second daughter, Anne Mary, was baptised in Sculthorpe in June 1794, and she married Martin Large, my 2nd great grandfather, in Sculthorpe, in April 1818, when the Mallom and the Large families collided. The bride's name was recorded as Mary Mallom, whereas she was baptised as Anne Mary Mallom. However, a younger sister was subsequently baptised Anne in December 1802, and it is likely that the older sister became known as Mary following this. Martin Large was baptised in April 1797, in nearby Houghton St Giles, the seventh of the eight children of John and Ann (Mitchell) Large, and through his marriage, John and Anne (Hipkin) Mallom became my 3rd great grandparents. Families named Large lived in Sculthorpe for more than 100 years during the 19th and 20th centuries, and so the surnames Mallom and Large feature regularly in parish records.

Their third daughter, Dorothy, was baptised in Sculthorpe in June 1796. She contracted Pulmonary Tuberculosis, and died in 1816, aged 20 years of 'Pulmonary Consumption.' Dorothy Mallom was buried in the same grave as her father, when her name on their shared headstone was Dotty.

The next child born to John and Anne Mallom was William (1798–1876), who married Mary Rayner from Thornage, in North Barsham in 1822, but returned to Sculthorpe where their five children were baptised. During his long life, William Mallom appeared at the Petty Sessions in Fakenham in June 1864, when he accused Henry Simmonds of Sculthorpe of stealing 11 partridge eggs from the estate of Sir W[illoughby] Jones, Bart., of Cranmer Hall. The defendant, an old offender, was fined £1 with 10s 6d. costs.[53] William was a labourer who became the Parish Clerk, an important role in the parish, a position which he held for 40 years as recorded in the burial register entry and inscribed on his gravestone, when he was buried in January 1876:

> In memory of/ William MALLOM/ 40 years clerk/ of this parish/ who departed/ this life/ January 22nd/ 1876/ aged 76 years/ Mary/ the beloved wife of/ William/ MALLOM/ who departed/ this life/ December 7 1868/ aged 71 years/ But if we hope for that we see not then do we/, with patience wait for it. Romans [8, verse 25]/. I know that my Redeemer liveth Job [19 v 25].

His death was significant enough to be reported in *The Norfolk Chronicle* when the words "deeply regretted" were included.⁵⁴ Two of the daughters of William and Mary, Ann and Mary were spinster dressmakers, who lived together in Sculthorpe. Mary's name appeared as an Occupation Voter in the Polling Register for Sculthorpe in 1900, when she was living in Fakenham Road.⁵⁵ William and Mary's third daughter, Hannah, born in 1828, moved to London, where she married Samuel Shepherd in Clerkenwell in 1863. Their son, Samuel Mallom Shepherd, was born in Dulwich, retaining the memory of his Norfolk Mallom ancestry.

Meanwhile, in Sculthorpe, the next child born to John and Anne Mallom was their son, Richard, baptised in 1800, and who married Frances Finch in the village in 1827, where they baptised seven children between 1830 and 1845, including their youngest child, a son, Richard (1845–1879), named after his father and his great grandfather. Young Richard subsequently moved north east to Beeston Regis, now a suburb of Sheringham, but never married. The names of the two brothers, William and Richard, sons of John and Anne Mallom, both appeared in 1839, in a list of Sculthorpe Tithe Apportionments: William Mallom was listed for three plots, a garden with 20 perches of land, a cottage with 2 perches and a second garden with 20 perches of land, all owned by John Harper. Richard had half an acre of allotment-arable, owned by Colonel Sir J[ohn] T[homas] Jones Bart., the Lord of the Manor of Cranmer Hall, Sculthorpe. 20 perches is equivalent to 505.9 square metres, and there are 160 perches to the acre, so these were small plots, used for domestic purposes. The oldest daughter of Richard and Frances Mallom was Marianne (Mary Anne), and she married James Parker in Sculthorpe in 1849, and moved to South Creake, where their second daughter was born. The family subsequently moved to Ashwicken and later to West Dereham, where further daughters were born. The next youngest son of Richard and Frances Mallom, was John, who married Mary Anne Britten English in Sculthorpe in 1866, where he was a publican, as was her father.

Branches of the Mallom family leave Sculthorpe

John and Mary Anne Mallom moved to Bath the year after the birth of their first daughter, where he worked as a coachman and domestic [servant]. Here, they had four more children. The first was Charles William Mallom, born in 1869 in Weston, Somerset, who became a coachman, and by 1911, at the age of 31, was still living with his parents. Albert Mallom, born in 1871, married Amy S E Lavis and they had five children, including Albert d'Arcy Mallom (1913–2004), and Bertrude John Mallom, born in Bath in 1871, but registered as Bertrude John Mellem.⁵⁶ Bertrude was the name of a Frankish Queen Consort of the early 7th century, later used as a name for both boys and girls. In December 1875, John Mallom's name appeared in *The Bath Chronicle*, in a report from the County Magistrates' Office, where he was charged with assaulting his wife by trying to throw her down stairs and striking her with a hot iron, evidently during an attack of Delirium Tremens, a severe state of confusion due to alcohol withdrawal, often known as DTs. Mallom's heavy drinking was probably a legacy of his former occupation in Sculthorpe, and he was sent to prison for one month.[57]

Anne was the fourth daughter of John and Anne (Hipkin) Mallom, and she married Charles Twiddy in North Barsham in 1828. They had eight children, all baptised in Houghton St Giles, her husband's home parish, where the baptism entries of his children record that he was a shoemaker, and later the publican of The Buck Inn in Houghton St Giles.

Hannah, Anne's younger sister, was the seventh child of John and Anne Mallom, and she married Robert Grimmer of Dunton, in Dunton in 1830, where each of their nine children was baptised.

The youngest child of John and Anne Mallom was their daughter, Elizabeth, who was born in Sculthorpe, but who moved to South Creake, where she married William Parker in 1836, the family later moving to Burnham Westgate, where four of their five children were born and raised. Their youngest son, Charles, was baptised in the Docking Primitive Methodist Circuit, but died in 1852, aged 4 years. Living with the family in Back Lane, Burnham Westgate in 1841 and in 1851, as we have seen, was Anne Bastard (formerly Hipkin-Mallom), Elizabeth's mother. Anne died in 1858, and was buried in the churchyard of Burnham Sutton cum Ulph, having married her first husband, John Mallom in Sculthorpe in 1792. The only alternative at this time for a widow with few means would have been to go into the Docking Union Workhouse, on Heacham Road, a disappointing outcome for the great granddaughter by marriage of John Mallom of Wacton Hall.

FAMILY OF MARTIN AND ANNE MARY (MALLOM) LARGE

Martin and Mary, as she was known, had ten children baptised between 1818 and 1838, including my great grandfather, Thomas Large (1830–1915). The first two children, John and William, were baptised in Houghton St Giles, after which the family moved to North Barsham, where the other children, Anne, Richard, Elizabeth, Sarah, Thomas, Martin, Mary Anne and Richard, were baptised. The baptism of two boys as Richard would be consistent with the parents' wish to commemorate the name of the boys' great grandfather, Richard Mallom of Wacton. When their mother died in 1857, the entry in the North Barsham Burial Register recorded her name as Ann Mary Large aged 60 years, a minor discrepancy given her baptism in 1794, but which confirms that she was indeed the wife of Martin Large, and the daughter of John and Anne (Hipkin) Mallom. In April 1863, Martin Large married Esther Marriot, , his second wife, originally from nearby Wighton. He was buried in North Barsham in 1865.

It is worth recalling that my great grandfather, Thomas Large, was the 1st cousin of the children of his uncles and aunts on the Mallom side of the family, in addition to those on his father's side. Thomas would have known some of his Mallom cousins, despite growing up in North Barsham, because, by 1851, he was living as an unmarried lodger with Isaac Vertigan, in Sculthorpe. In 1891, he was still living in Sculthorpe, with his wife, and in 1911, as a widower, he was living in the Sculthorpe Almshouses. He was therefore familiar with the village both as a young adult, in middle age, and again in old age, where he would have had regular opportunities to meet his cousins, knowing that his mother was a member of the Mallom family. Village celebrations to mark the harvest and other festivities would have brought different branches of the family together, as are described in novels of the period, although the details of their relationships were probably rather vague to them. Martin and Anne Mary (Mallom) Large were the grandparents of my own grandfather, whom I remember very well because our lives overlapped. In fact, today, some young children know their great grandparents as well, although this was not often the case in previous generations. My grandfather never met his grandfather, Martin Large, because he died well before his grandson was born. It is interesting to speculate whether Martin might have met his wife's grandfather, Richard Mallom, had their lives overlapped.

John and Anne (Hipkin) Mallom had a total of 51 grandchildren, and many great grandchildren. Brief mention may be made of the following since they hold some special interest distinguishing them from the others: their grandson, William (1833–1914), the son of Richard and Frances (Finch) Mallom, married Elizabeth Dye in Sculthorpe in 1859. They moved north east to Cromer, where William became the gamekeeper at Cromer Hall, living at the Gamekeeper's Lodge in Hall Road, as shown on the censuses of 1881, 1891 and 1901, and at South Lodge, Hall Road, in 1911, when he was described as Lodge Keeper, Retired Gamekeeper. His name was also included on the Poll of Electors of Cromer, between 1885 and 1912. In 1901, Cromer Hall was visited by Arthur Conan Doyle, author of the Sherlock Holmes stories while he was convalescing from typhoid fever contracted in South Africa. A story emerged that it was at Cromer Hall that he heard tell of 'Black Shuck,' the Hell Hound of Norfolk, thought by some to have been the model for his famous story 'The Hound of the Baskervilles' which was published the following year. And the coachman who drove Conan Doyle and his friend, Bertrum Robinson, to Cromer Hall, where he heard the story of the devilish dog, is said to have been called Baskerville. This story is almost certainly apocryphal, but there was a branch of a family named Vaskerville, living in Wells-next-the Sea, 20 miles west of Cromer, in the 1860s.[58]

William Mallom's nephew, Richard William (1872–1949), was born to Fanny Mallom, William's sister, before she married his father, William Overman Davey, although Richard retained his Mallom surname. Did this perhaps suggest that his mother had heard faint whispers of her Wacton ancestry, because the boy was the second great grandson of Richard Mallom of Wacton, and given the same baptismal name? By 1891, Richard was a carpenter's apprentice, a trade he pursued throughout his life. He married Laura Elizabeth Owen in Sculthorpe in 1896, and the couple had one child, a daughter, baptised Ethel Minnie. Richard avoided military service in both the South African War and the Great War, the

Fig. 55. Headstone of Laura Elizabeth and Richard William Mallom in Sculthorpe Graveyard.

Fig. 56. Minnie (Mallom) Woodhouse arriving at St Peter's Church Dunton-cum-Doughton, with Revd. Derrick Wood to play for Evensong, in the late 1960s.

latter because of his age. The Military Service Act, passed in January 1916, introduced conscription on all single men aged between 18 and 41, whilst exempting the medically unfit, clergymen, teachers and certain classes of industrial worker.[59] Carpenters were not in a reserved occupation and so were not exempt from service. However, Richard Mallom was 44 years old in 1916, and so he was not conscripted. He saw many of his near contemporaries go off to war from Sculthorpe, including his distant cousin, David Large, a conflict from which many of them failed to return. He was admitted as a Carpenter and Joiner to the Amalgamated Society of Carpenters, Cabinet Makers and Joiners in 1919, when the Branch Meetings were held in nearby Fakenham.[60] He and Laura were buried in Sculthorpe graveyard, where the headstone, inscribed with the surname Mallom, is the last in Sculthorpe with the family name. Indeed, it is the last such in the whole of Norfolk, and has a special significance because of this (Fig. 55).

Richard and Laura Mallom's daughter, the last member of the Sculthorpe Mallom family to bear the surname at birth, was Ethel Minnie (1896–1980). She was the 2nd great granddaughter of John and Anne (Hipkin) Mallom, and she married John Manning Woodhouse in 1927. She trained as a dressmaker, and they lived in Sculthorpe where she was very active within the community and as organist at Sculthorpe Parish Church for 60 years (Fig. 56). She was known in the village as "Aunt Minnie," and a brass plaque on the organist's bench marks her many years of service.[61] There were no children, and John and Minnie were buried together in Sculthorpe graveyard.

The marriage of John Mallom with Anne Hipkin gave rise to a great number of descendants, many of whom lived all their lives in or near Sculthorpe, but since just two of their eight children were male, few of their later descendants bore the surname Mallom. John Mallom died two years after the birth of his youngest child, Elizabeth, born in 1808, and so did not live to witness the births or baptisms of any of his grandchildren, something which today, most of us would take for granted. In contrast, his widow, Anne, who lived into her late 80s, would have enjoyed the births, baptisms and marriages of her grandchildren, and the births and baptisms of some of her great grandchildren.

As is recognised through widely available national statistics and discussions within families, the number of children born to couples fell during the 19th and 20th centuries, and today, most of us are not members of families which have ten or more children. In Norfolk, for example, numbers of births fell from 14,000 in 1851 to 11,000 in 1911, and the number of infant deaths fell from 2,200 in 1871 to 1,200 in 1911.[62] In other words, although fewer children were born, more of them survived, and the tendency for couples to have big families, gradually diminished.

For purposes of comparison, the frequency of the name Mallom and other surnames found in this study living in the mid-20th century have been taken from the 1939 Register.[63] The surname Mallom remained very rare in this spelling, both in Norfolk and also in England and Wales (which includes Norfolk), as shown in Table 2, p. 208. As far as Norfolk is concerned, this is not surprising, given that only two of the children of John and Anne Mallom in Sculthorpe were male. The surname variant, Mallon, has also been included in the table. However, in 1939, Mallon, too, remained very rare in Norfolk, although much more common than Mallom elsewhere in England and Wales, probably from its origin in Ireland.

Other family names found in this study were more numerous, sometimes much more so at the time the 1939 Register was taken, both in Norfolk, and also in other parts of England and Wales. With some exceptions, especially those of Mallon and Phillips, the frequency of the surnames in Norfolk was generally parallel with numbers of the same surnames in the rest of England and Wales. The name Phillips, on the other hand, was much less common in Norfolk than might be expected in comparison with the numbers in England and Wales.

The rarity of the surname Mallom in the last century supports the general contention that examples of the name found in different parts of Norfolk in the 18th and 19th centuries may well have been part of the same family, especially when convincing evidence is included in the support.

To bring the question of the frequency of the surname Mallom up to date, a search was made using the online BT Phone Book of the name in Norfolk, and in England and Wales in 2018, exactly 200 years after the marriage in Sculthorpe of Anne Mary Mallom with Martin Large. No one called Mallom, and only one example of Mallon, was found in Norfolk,[64] although the reduction in the use of BT land lines, needs to be taken into account. The contrast with the position during the previous 400 years is obvious.

Surname	Number in Norfolk	Number in England and Wales
Mallom	1	18
Mallon	2	691
Wodehouse	16	93
Shelton	30	5,537
Suckling	58	1,565
Large	296	4,906
Phillips	315	78,599
Walpole	326	1,703
Nelson	511	16,916

Table 2: Frequency of the surname Mallom compared with other surnames in the study, shown in order of frequency in Norfolk, and in England and Wales, from the 1939 Register.

Concluding Comments: the importance of circumstantial evidence

Family history research can be straight-forward when records of baptisms, marriages and burials are readily available, and major pitfalls are avoided. The absence of a marriage record of Richard Mallom and Mary Smith, and the baptism record of their son, John, is inconvenient, and has resulted in the extensive searches, in part, to exclude alternative candidates. However, it should be borne in mind, as Patric Dickinson, then Clarenceux King of Arms, commented:

> … in genealogical research there is always yet another source one can tackle but the work tends to get ever more laborious and the law of diminishing returns applies once the more obvious categories of records have been exhausted. [65]

Nevertheless, the evidence supporting the proposal that John Mallom of Sculthorpe was the son of Richard and Mary (Smith) Mallom, and hence the grandson of John Mallom of Wacton Hall, is very persuasive, and has been reviewed by Patrick Palgrave-Moore, the leading expert on Norfolk's Family History and its records, and Founder of the Norfolk and the Cambridgeshire Family History Societies. It was agreed that with Richard orphaned comparatively young, it seems certain that he was packed off to Sculthorpe to live with his great aunt. He would have been brought up as a gentleman, but in reduced circumstances, and as such, his status in the county would have been known. Nevertheless, he and his son John would have struggled socially, although there would have been friends, such as the Ravens, who knew their background and gave them at least some social acceptance. The friendship with the Raven family was crucial to the case:

> From the information I have received and questions answered, I am of the opinion that the descent from Wacton to Sculthorpe is correct. I am happy to say that what evidence there is, is sufficient to state that your descent from Wacton is correct. In fact, to imagine an alternative scenario seems

almost unthinkable.⁶⁶

Richard and Mary's choice of the name John for their son would be expected, given that the name had clearly been favoured by the Norwich-Booton-Bedingham-Wacton family for several generations, often as the first-born son of the family, and it would have been surprising had any other name been chosen. Furthermore, the proven connection between Wacton and Sculthorpe for the Mallom family as shown by the three Mallom ledgerstones inside Sculthorpe Church, the presence of Nathaniel Raven as a witness at John and Anne's 1792 marriage in Sculthorpe, and the preservation of the name Richard in six of their descendants, adds to the supporting evidence. And the interval between the birth of Richard in Wacton in 1744, and the subsequent birth of his son, John, in about 1765, is also perfectly appropriate. All this, together with the complete absence of a plausible alternative candidate for Richard Mallom, helps to confirm, beyond reasonable doubt, that John was indeed the son of Richard Mallom as stated in the 1810 burial record: he was the nephew of Captain Mallom. In other words, there is more to establishing relationships than simply finding records in Parish Registers, Transcripts, or Censuses, important though these are for family history research. Some couples were satisfied with informal relationships as they are today rather than having a marriage ceremony, although given his background, it is likely that Richard would have chosen to marry his bride in church as his forebears did and as his son would do in 1792.

The hypothesis that Richard Mallom, the father of the John who was buried in Sculthorpe in 1810, was himself the son of John and Phillis Mallom of Wacton, Norfolk, is also consistent with the philosophical principle known as 'Ockham's Razor.' In summary, this proposes that the simplest solution, or the simplest answer that requires the fewest assumptions, is generally the correct one. Ockham wrote "pluralitas sine necessitate non est ponenda," in other words, "entities should not be multiplied unnecessarily."⁶⁷ Circumstantial evidence which helps to confirm the case, while eliminating other potential contenders, is also crucial, as it has been in this piece of research.

And so, on the basis of all the evidence, the hypothesis that Richard Mallom was my 4th great grandfather is shown to be correct beyond reasonable doubt, and his older brother, Captain John Mallom, the main subject of this research, who achieved distinction with the British Army during the American War of Independence, was my 5th great uncle (or 4th great grand uncle).⁶⁸ Clearly, the ancestry of Captain Mallom and his brother, Richard applies to all the descendants of Richard Mallom, whatever their surnames happen to be. No attempt has been made to discover exactly how many living individuals this involves, although it is likely to be considerable, given the number of children born to Richard's son, John and his wife, Anne (Hipkin) Mallom in Sculthorpe. All the 4th great grandchildren of Richard Mallom have as their ancestors those shown in Table 3, p. 210, created by adding the number 6 to each of the names shown in Table 1, p. 179, because

Admiral Horatio Nelson	2nd cousin 6 times removed
Margaret Butler	13th great grandmother
Sir Geoffrey Boleyn	14th great grandfather
Queen Anne Boleyn	1st cousin 13 times removed
Queen Elizabeth I	2nd cousin 12 times removed
Eleanor de Bohun	18th great grandmother
Roger Mortimer	18th great grandfather
King Edward I	20th great grandfather
Isabel Bigod	21st great grandmother
Sir Henry de Bohun	1st cousin 22 times removed
Ida de Tosny	23rd great grandmother
Archbishop Hubert Walter	24th great uncle
Roger I Bigod	25th great grandfather
William the Conqueror	26th great grandfather

Table 3: Table of Relationships showing the connections between the 4th great grandchildren of Richard Mallom of Wacton and the individuals included in Table 1 p. 179.

6 generations separate us from him. We each have sixty-four great grandparents, and Richard Mallom was one of them.

A great many other distinguished ancestors may be discovered using published genealogies and other records, such as Burke's Peerage, first published in 1826, and now available in an online edition.[69]

All the findings presented here have come from traditional historical records, and none from DNA genealogy. The latest estimate is that about 30 million individuals in the world have been included on the databases of the companies which offer DNA testing, a tiny fraction of the world population, and relatives who have not been tested obviously do not appear. Nevertheless, despite the various challenges involved in the technology and interpretation of results, DNA genealogy is set to transform the way many people look into their family history, especially when used in combination with historical records.[70] For example, the search for long-lost parents of those adopted or separated from their parents soon after birth, those conceived by sperm donation who are anxious to know the identity of their father and whether they have any close relatives, and the search for living relatives by those who feared their families had been lost in the Holocaust and other atrocities. The discovery of the remains of Richard III under a car-park in Leicester in 2012, proven by DNA testing of descendants of his mother, has brought the technology fully into the public eye,[71] and in 2016, Prince Philip's DNA was used to confirm that remains found in Ekaterinburg, Russia, were those of his relatives, the Romanov Imperial family, who were murdered by the Bolsheviks in 1918.[72] A group of 10 British soldiers, killed in northern France in 1914, have also been identified and reburied with full military honours after DNA was recovered from the remains and matched with known living descendants.⁷³

On the other hand, the individuals who appear in this account have been found without resorting to genetic testing, and it is unclear whether the findings derived from paper records would have been significantly altered by tests based on samples of saliva or blood. And whilst not wishing to minimise the fascination of coming across unexpected discoveries such as occurred here, the British geneticist, Adam Rutherford, has proposed that virtually everyone with predominantly British ancestry, who was born during the 1970s, is descended between 21 and 24 generations from Edward III.⁷⁴

The issue for those hoping to demonstrate this for themselves is finding the records which can help to confirm the claim.

References and Further Reading

1. Bristow, M., Wacton Census 1811, GENUKI, UK and Ireland Genealogy, abstracted from PD 496/91 held at NRO. Norwich.
2. Litten, Julian. Personal Communication, 21 December 2013.
3. Windeler, Gary. *The Book of Sculthorpe*, Halsgrove, 2003, p. 107.
4. Pine, Leslie Gilbert, Hogarth, Frederick. In, Coat of Arms, Heraldry, Arms of Ladies. *Encyclopaedia Britannica* online, 2018. https://www.britannica.com/topic/heraldry#ref19957
5. Pine and Hogarth. ibid. https://www.britannica.com/topic/heraldry#ref20017
6. Litten, Julian. Personal Communication, 3 September 2012.
7. Will of John Mallom of Wackton, gentleman, [ANF will 1687-89, no 101]. NRO. Norwich.
8. Will of Elizabeth Mallom of Sculthorpe, singlewoman, [ANF will 1721-23, no 261]. NRO. Norwich.
9. Litten. Personal Communication, 9 February 2017.
10. Will of Audry Donne of the city of Norwich, widow, [NCC will 1759 8 Gooch on GS 0166918]. NRO. Norwich.
11. Deed of release of dower in an estate in Sculthorpe: 1) Audry Donne of Norwich, widow of Thomas Donne of Sculthorpe; 2) Robert Donne of Sculthorpe her son, [NRS 14338]. NRO. Norwich.
12. Will of Audry Donne of the city of Norwich, widow, [NCC will 1759 8 Gooch on GS 0166918]. NRO. Norwich.
13. https://en.wikipedia.org/wiki/Marriage_Act_1753: Hannah Verge, Archivist at NRO, Norwich. Personal Communication, 13 February 2017.
14. Raven, Nathaniel, of Brancaster 1808. ANF will register, 1808–1810 (1808) fo. 176 no. 104. NRO. Norwich.
15. Raven of Whissonsett. Pedigree. NRS vol 13, *East Anglian Families*, p 178–181. NRO, Norwich.
16. *The Ipswich Chronicle* (first published in 1720), *Norwich Mercury* (first published in 1727), *Bury and Norwich Post* (first published in 1782), and *Norfolk Chronicle* (first published in 1800), were the only newspapers in circulation in Norfolk in 1810, the year John Mallom died in Sculthorpe, and which might have included an obituary notice.
17. I am grateful to Revd. Clive Wylie and Richard Land for confirming my suspicion that the headstone to John Mallom and his daughter, Dorothy, was removed since the Sculthorpe Graveyard Book was compiled; Dorothy Mallom was 20 years old when she died in August 1816, having been born and baptised in June 1796, according to the relevant Parish Register entries. Some published transcriptions have recorded her age at death as 17 years, relying on the Burial Register entry, alone, which was incorrect.
18. Searches covered the available Parish Registers, Archdeacons and Bishops Transcripts, Marriage Licence Bonds, Wills, relevant Manor Court Records, Maps and Rentals, and also the Parish Registers in Suffolk, looking for their marriage. Many of the Registers are now available online, courtesy of FamilySearch.org, Ancestry.co.uk and FindmyPast.co.uk, and many of these have been indexed by FreeREG.org.uk, which has extensive coverage of the Norfolk parishes, and from the database held by the Norfolk Family History Society. Staff of these organisations have been very helpful in the searches. Where original parish records are not available online, they have been checked at Norfolk Record Office, so that the whole county of Norfolk has been thoroughly searched for the marriage, between the years 1758–1775.
19. Rosier, M.E., (compiler), *Index to Parishes in Phillimore's Marriages*. ISBN 095114653X, Huntingdon, Family Tree Magazine, 1988. Norfolk Marriages volumes held by Norfolk Family History Society, Norwich. Courtesy of Paul White, Norfolk Family History Society, Norwich.
20. Rivett, Andrew and Lowe, Geoff, The Norfolk Transcription Archive. http://doun.org/transcriptions/ (Note: this is no actively updated).

21. The Buxton Papers. Department of Manuscripts and University Archives, Cambridge University, Cambridge, UK. Dr Peter Meadows, Personal Communication, 9 December 2013 and 2 January 2014: http://www.lib.cam.ac.uk/deptserv/manuscripts/Buxton/boxesind.htm
22. Gangou, Paul, Committee Member and South East Regional Secretary, The Nelson Society. Personal Communication, 8 September 2017.
23. Alefounder, Peter, Personal Communication, 10 January 2012: http://www.shepherdhuts.co.uk/page10.htm
24. Chater, Kathy, *How to Trace your Family History. The Complete Practical Handbook for all Detectives of Family History*. Anness Publishing Ltd, 2003, 2007. Hermes House, 88-89 Blackfriars Road, London SE1 9HA. p. 64.
25. Clandestine Marriages Act 1753. https://en.wikipedia.org/wiki/Clandestine_Marriages_Act_1753: Lemmings, David, Marriage and the law in the eighteenth century: Hardwicke's Marriage Act of 1753. Published online, 11 February 2009, https://www.cambridge.org/core/journals/historical-journal/article/abs/marriage-and-the-law-in-the-eighteenth-century-hardwickes-marriage-act-of-1753/5F09D8E8F36375AA132AD2F74FA58B53#: For the text of the Act, see "1753: An Act for the Better Preventing of Clandestine Marriage. 26 Geo. II. c. 33," http://statutes.org.uk/site/the-statutes/eighteenth-century/1753-26-geo-2-c-33-prevention-of-clandestine-marriages/
26. England, Clandestine Marriages, 1667–1775. https://search.findmypast.co.uk/search-world-records/england-clandestine-marriages
27. England and Wales, Quaker Birth, Marriage, and Death Registers, 1578–1837. https://www.ancestry.co.uk/search/collections/7097/: Results for England and Wales Non-Conformist Marriages, https://search.findmypast.co.uk/search-world-records/england-and-wales-non-conformist-marriages: England, Norfolk Non-Conformist Records — FamilySearch Historical Records, https://www.familysearch.org/search/record/results?count=20&q.anyPlace=Norfolk&q.givenName=Richard&q.surname=Mallom&f.collectionId=1666142
28. Parish Register transcriptions and family history. http://essexandsuffolksurnames.co.uk/history/sources/parish-registers/baptisms/: Baston, Stuart, Birth-Baptism intervals for Family Historians. Cambridge Group for the History of Population and Social Structure. Department of Geography. University of Cambridge. UK. 2015. Online at https://www.familysearch.org/wiki/en/Birth-Baptism_Intervals_for_Family_Historians
29. Conveyance of Estate in Sculthorpe by 1) Mary Smyth of Topcroft, widow (of George), and Offley Smyth of Harlestone, gent, 2) Daniel Jones of Fakenham, gent, messuages, lands and tenements in Sculthorpe. [NRS 14331]. NRO. Norwich.
30. Herne, John. Brickmaking in Bunwell: Bunwell Heritage Group, 2011, ibid.
31. Lettice Smith of Aslacton, NCC admon 1767, no 55; Thomas Smith of Aslacton, wheelwright, ANF will 1831 no 29.; Mary Smith of Bunwell, ANF admon 1794-97, no 10.; James Smith of Bunwell, yeoman, NCC will 1833, 421 Cubitt.; John Smith of Bunwell, bricklayer, ANF will 1829, no 97.; Robert Smith of Carlton Road, yeoman, ANF will 1746-48 no 166.; Martha Smith widow of Carleton Road, ANF will 1762-3 no 104.; Robert Smith of Carleton Rode, yeoman, ANF will 1807 no 69.; William Smith of Carleton Rode, ANF admon bond 1826 no 19.; James Smith of Great Yarmouth, bricklayer, NCC will 1777, 366 Yallop. Abstracts of wills and administrations held at NRO, Norwich, by Diana Spelman, 16 July 2018.
32. Findmypast.co.uk.
33. PCC Will of John Mallam of Milton Berkshire, Gentleman. PROB 11/1853/103
34. Will of Richard Mallam, Yeoman, 1773. Oxfordshire Wills Index ref. 216.164;142/3/48, Oxford History Centre, St Luke's Church, Temple Road, Cowley, Oxford OX4 2HT: Chris Hawkins, History Assistant, Oxfordshire History Centre. Personal Communication, 7 July 2015.
35. FndmyPast.co.uk: Ancestry.co.uk: Staff at the East Surrey Family History Society. Personal

Communications 12 July 2015, 27 August 2015: Staff at the London Metropolitan Archives, Personal Communications, 8 July 2015, 22 July 2015: Emily Rumble, Archives Assistant, Lambeth Palace Library, Personal Communication, 10 July 2015.

36. Jones, Heather. Library Assistant, National Museum of the Royal Navy. Personal Communication, 10 September 2013: ACAD-A Cambridge Alumni Database. venn.lib.cam.ac.uk/Documents/acad/2016/search-2016.html: Oxford University Alumni, 1500–1886, Ancestry.co.uk.
37. https://collection.nam.ac.uk/detail.php?acc=1998-11-1-1. Portrait by David Morier, National Army Museum, London.
38. Harvey, Colonel Sir Charles, The History of the 4th Battalion Norfolk Regiment (Late East Norfolk Militia). List of Officers in the Regiment. London, Jarrold and Sons, 1899: WO 13/1586. Musters for the 2nd East Norfolk Militia, Dec 1780–Dec 1801 (Musters with gaps): WO 13/1590. Musters Dec 1800–Dec 1801: WO 68/123 Digest of services of the East Norfolk Militia 1803–1908.
39. Newby, Pat. List of Officers in the West Norfolk Militia encamped at Caister, (Great) Yarmouth. Norfolk Newspapers; *Norfolk Chronicle* 27 July 1782. In GENUKI. UK and Ireland Genealogy. Norfolk Origins. July 2005: NRO, Norwich: TNA, London: Norfolk Family History Society, Personal Communication, 25 November 2018: National Army Museum: Personal Communication, 27 November 2018. http://www.origins.org.uk/genuki/NFK/norfolk/newspapers/nfkchron/1782/0727.shtml
40. WO 13/1560-85. TNA, London: Gibson, Jeremy and Medlycott, Mervyn, Some Georgian "Censuses." The Genealogists' Magazine, 23, 2 (June) 1989.
41. Gibson, Jeremy and Medlycott, Mervyn, Militia Lists and Musters, 1757–1876. *A Directory of Holdings in the British Isles*. Genealogical Publishing Company, 1990. Norfolk Lists, pp. 27-28: *The Norfolk Ancestor*. The Magazine of the Norfolk Family History Society, December 2010, pp, 232–233.
42. Gibson and Medlycott, ibid. p. 9.
43. Sculthorpe Maps, 1766 [Hayes and Storr, No 88], 1767 [Hayes and Storr, No 176], 1796 [NRS 21390], 1822 [Hayes and Storr, No. 6]. NRO. Norwich.
44. Sculthorpe Enclosure map, 1829 [C/Sca 2/246]. NRO. Norwich.
45. Sculthorpe Manor Court Book 1789–1843 [MS 19783]. NRO. Norwich.
46. Fakenham Rectory Manor Court Book, 1746–1783 [MS 19655], 1784–1817 [MS 19656]; Fakenham Rectory Manor Account Book, 1779–1792 [MS 19663]; Fakenham Lancaster Manor Book of Rentals 1748–1768 [MS 19690], 1769–1774 [MS 15401], 1774–1790 [MS 15402], 1791–1806 [MS 15403], 1806–1819 [MS 19691]; Dunton cum Doughton Manor Court Book, Manor of Dunton, 1747–1870 [MS 20688], checked 1755 and 1762; South Creake, Abbotts late Bodhams Manor in South Creake Court Book, 1756–1905 [FOS 218] checked 1756–1810; Houghton St Giles Court Book of the Manors of Houghton Roos otherwise Sydneys, Houghton Lexhams and Gaunts Hall and Gurneys in Houghton, 1746–1787 [MS 19755] and 1788–1812 [MS 19756].
47. Rentals [MS 19740]. NRO. Norwich.
48. Poll Lists for Norfolk, 1765–1810. Norfolk Poll Book, 1768, 1802, 1806: Norfolk Voting Registers. Transcription—Voters and Occupiers Names, Freeholds, Residences for 1768. GENUKI UK and Ireland Genealogy. Transcribed by Mike Bristow, 2014. http://www.genuki.org.uk/big/eng/NFK/Voting/Norfolk
49. Survey of Glebe Lands of Sculthorpe, 1796. [NRS 21389]. NRO. Norwich.
50. Papers of Daniel Jones of Cranmer Hall, Sculthorpe, 1708–1783 (period 1750–1783). NRO, Norwich.
51. Lease of Cranmer Hall from Daniel Jones to George Townshend dated 11 January 1752, the term of the lease to last till Michaelmas 1763 and the rent £33-6-0 a year. Box RAS D2/9, Raynham

Hall, Norfolk. Anthony Smith (Archivist at Raynham Hall Seat of the Townshend Family). Personal Communication, 9 November 2016.
52. Windeler, Gary. The Book of Sculthorpe, Halsgrove, 2003, p. 108–9.
53. *Norfolk Chronicle*, 4 June 1864.
54. *Norfolk Chronicle*, Saturday 29 January 1876. https://www.britishnewspaperarchive.co.uk
55. North Western Division of Norfolk. Fakenham Polling District (District H) - Parish of Sculthorpe. Occupation Voters. 1900.
56. Bath Record Office. 2 May 2017.
57. *The Bath Chronicle*, Thursday, December 2, 1875. County Magistrates' Court. British Newspapers online.
58. Literary Norfolk. www.literarynorfolk.co.uk/cromer_hall.htm: Pete Golland, Library and Information Assistant. Norfolk and Norwich Millennium Library, Norwich. Personal Communication, 6 August 2018.
59. Conscription: the First World War. Conscription introduced. UK Parliament. https://www.parliament.uk/about/living-heritage/transformingsociety/private-lives/yourcountry/overview/conscription/
60. Record Transcription: Britain, Trade Union Membership Registers. MSS.78/ASCJ/2/2/10. findmypast.co.uk
61. Land, Richard, great nephew of "Aunt Minnie." Personal Communication, 5 March 2014: Windeler, ibid, pp. 62, 63, 80, 87, 125, 126.
62. GB Historical GIS / University of Portsmouth, Norfolk RegC through time | Statistics |, A Vision of Britain through Time. Including maps, statistical trends and historical descriptions. Norfolk. Norfolk RegC. https://www.visionofbritain.org.uk/unit/10107337/theme/VITAL
63. 1939 Register. https://www.findmypast.co.uk/1939register
64. BT Phone Book online, https://www.thephonebook.bt.com/person/.
65. Dickinson, P.L., Clarenceux King of Arms, College of Arms, London, UK. Personal Communication, 19 February 2019.
66. Palgrave-Moore, Patrick, FSA. Founder of the Norfolk and Cambridgeshire Family History Societies. Personal Communication, 9 December 2021
67. Courtenay, W. J., William of Ockham (c. 1287–1347). Philosopher, theologian and political theorist. *Oxford Dictionary of National Biography*, 27 May 2010. Online edition: Ockham's razor. https://en.wikipedia.org/wiki/Occam%27s_razor
68. Churchill, Else, Genealogist, Society of Genealogists, London. Personal Communication, 23 May 2022
69. Burke, John, General and Heraldic Dictionary of the Peerage of England, Ireland and Scotland. 1831. https://archive.org/details/dli.granth.90912/page/n1/mode/2up?view=theater
70. Holton, Graham, S., Editor, with contributions by John Cleary, Michelle Leonard, Iain McDonald, and Alasdair F. Macdonald. *Tracing your Ancestors using DNA. A guide for Family and Local Historians.* Pen and Sword Books Ltd, 47 Church Street, Barnsley, South Yorkshire. 2021. ISBN 978 1 52673 309 2. This publication provides a comprehensive and up-to-date review of the challenges, ethics and opportunities of DNA testing.
71. https://kriii.com/about-the-centre/an-incredible-discovery/: Holton, G. S., ibid. pp. 216–217.
72. BBC World: Europe, Bones confirmed as Tsar's remains http://news.bbc.co.uk/1/hi/world/europe/51920.stm
73. Soldiers killed during WW1 named via DNA from relatives. BBC News report, 22 March 2014. https://www.bbc.co.uk/news/uk-26690387: And from the Battle of Fromelles in northern France in July 1916, of many casualties, 159 of 250 Australian remains were identified by DNA

testing of descendants. See Holton, G. S., ibid. pp. 218–219.

74. Rutherford, Adam, Issue of Edward III of England. From Wikipedia, the free encyclopedia. https://en.wikipedia.org/wiki/Issue_of_Edward_III_of_England. Quoting Martha Greengrass, " Family Fortunes: Adam Rutherford On How We Are All Related to Royalty." Waterstones Blog, 14 September 2017, https://www.waterstones.com/blog/family-fortunes-adam-rutherford-on-how-were-all-related-to-royalty: Rutherford, ibid, *A Brief History of Everyone Who has Ever Lived*, Weidenfeld and Nicholson, 2017. pp. 143–146, 147, 148–149, 152–153, 191.

Index

See Pedigrees 1–5, pp. 21–25, for Mallom family connections, and Table 1, p. 179, for relationships between Captain John Mallom and some of his illustrious ancestors.

Page numbers in *italics* refer to illustrations.

Adye, Captain Stephen Payne, Deputy Judge Advocate at Court Martial Panels, 1777–1778, **122**, **126–127**.

Aetheling, William, (Adelin), son and heir of Henry I, drowns in the *White Ship* disaster in November, 1120, **175**.

Amyas, John, of Hingham, Attorney in the 1732 case between John Mallom and his sister, Elizabeth, her husband, Thomas Ekins and Robert Suckling concerning the management of her legacy, **64**; in the case of George Bedel, **77–79**; leaves bequest to Robert Mallom, **78**.

Arms, Coat of, granted to John Mallom of Wacton Hall, **54–57**; blazon of, **55**; illustration of *55*, *56*.

Aslacton, Mallom home in, description of in Sales particulars, 1761, **92–94**, **97–98**.

Aslacton, marriage of John Mallom with Phillis Phillips, **27–28**; church in, *28*; burials and ledgerstone of Mallom family, **28–29**, *90*.

Bacon, Sir Edmund, MP for Thetford, hustings attended by John Mallom and others, 1728, **74**.

Balfour, Lieutenant-Colonel, Commandant of Charleston, S. Carolina, letter to London, carried by Captain Mallom, **139–140**, **142–144**, **150**.

Bastard, John, bachelor, marries Anne (Hipkin) Mallom, widow, in Sculthorpe, 1811, **201**; their son, James, dies in infancy, **201**; death 1829, **201**.

Beachamp, Joan de, descendant of Roger Mortimer, 1st Earl of March, grandmother of Margaret Butler, wife of James Butler, 4th Earl of Ormond, **166–167**.

Bedell, George Esq., Lord of the Manor of Woodrising, Roman Catholic, death, 1715, **76–77**; High Court of Chancery cases between 1715–1743, concerning John and Robert Mallom, amongst others, **77–78**; Elizabeth Mallom to receive £150 per annum for life, **77**.

Bedingham, Stone family of, **49**; marriage of Elizabeth Stone with Revd. William Copping, then with John Mallom, **49**; leases of 1663 and 1672 concerning property and land in, **49**, **61**; marriage of Mary Mallom with Merchant Berry in, **70**; Revd. Joseph Parsons, Vicar of, **70**.

Berry, Merchant, marries Mary Mallom, daughter of John and Elizabeth (Suckling) Mallom, burial in 1766, aged 96, **70**.

Bigod, Hugh I, son of Roger Bigod, inherits the estates of Belvoir, Leicestershire after his older brother, William, drowns in the *White Ship* disaster in November 1120, becomes Sheriff and 1st earl of Norfolk, father of Roger II Bigod, **172, 175**.

Bigod, Hugh II, 3rd Earl of Norfolk, acts as surety at Magna Carta, 1215 (with Roger II Bigod), marries Maud Marshal, daughter of William Marshal, 1st Earl of Pembroke, **171–172, 178**.

Bigod, Isabel, daughter of Hugh II Bigod, 3rd Earl of Norfolk, and his wife, Maud Marshal, daughter of William Marshal, and his wife, Isabel de Clare, marries (second) John FitzGeoffrey, Justiciar of Ireland and Lord of Shere, Surrey, **172, 175, 176, 177**.

Bigod, Robert, a poor Norman knight, progenitor of the Norfolk Bigod families whose estates become the greatest in East Anglia, **171**.

Bigod, Roger I, marries Adelisa (Alice) de Tosny, daughter of Robert de Tosny of Belvoir, Leicestershire, builds the keep of Norwich Castle *173*, the wooden castle of Framlingham, Suffolk, and founds Thetford Priory *174*, burial in Norwich Cathedral *174*. Loyal to William Rufus and Henry I, later aligning with Robert Curthose in revolt against William Rufus, oldest son of William the Conqueror, **172**.

Bigod, Roger II (aka Baron Roger le Bigod), marries Ida de Tosny, a royal ward and mistress of Henry II, acts as surety at Magna Carta, 1215 (with Hugh II Bigod), statue in the House of Lords Chamber, Westminster, **51**, leaves 25 charters in his will to abbeys and cathedrals, **176–177**.

Bigod, William, son of Hugh I Bigod, drowns in the *White Ship* disaster in November 1120, **175**.

Blackstock's Farm, skirmish at, when Lieutenant Money, Captain Mallom's friend and fellow officer, is killed, **137**.

Bohun, Eleanor de, daughter of Humphrey de Bohun, 4th Earl of Hereford, and his wife, Elizabeth Plantagenet, daughter of Edward I, niece of Edward II, marries James Butler, 1st Earl of Ormond, 6th great granddaughter of William the Conqueror, **165, 166, 167–169**.

Bohun, Humphrey de, 4th Earl of Hereford, Hereditary Constable of England, marries Elizabeth Plantagenet, daughter of Edward I and Eleanor of Castile, acquires Loch Maben Castle and lands of Robert the Bruce, leads assault at Bannockburn, June 1314, when taken prisoner, later opposes the king, killed at Boroughbridge in March 1322, burial at the Dominican Friary, York, **161, 165, 167–168**.

Bohun, Sir Henry de, 1st cousin once removed of Humphrey de Bohun, killed in single combat with Robert the Bruce at Bannockburn, June 1314, **168**, *169*.

Boleyn, George, brother of Queen Anne Boleyn, **162**.

Boleyn, John, of Salle, Norfolk, progenitor of the Norfolk Boleyn families, living in the late 13th century, **162**.

Boleyn, Lady Anne, of Blickling, Norfolk, daughter of Sir William Boleyn, sister of Sir Thomas Boleyn, Queen Anne's father, marries Sir John Shelton, aunt of Queen Anne Boleyn, 2nd wife of Henry VIII, care of Princess Mary at Hatfield House, Hertfordshire, **162**.

Boleyn, Mary, sister of Queen Anne Boleyn, "The Other Boleyn Girl," **162**.

Boleyn, Queen Anne, 2nd wife of Henry VIII, 1st cousin seven times removed of Captain Mallom, **159**, **161**, **162**, **163**, **164**, 164.

Boleyn, Sir Geoffrey, Freeman of London, Mercer, Alderman and Lord Mayor, 1457–1458, **162–163**.

Boleyn, Sir Thomas, brother of Lady Anne Boleyn, marries Elizabeth Howard, daughter of the 2nd Duke of Norfolk, parents of Queen Anne Boleyn, **162**, **163**.

Buckton, Sir Peter de, supporter of Henry IV, whose retinue includes Thomas Mallom, archer, **39**.

Burke's Peerage, first published in 1826, online edition of, value in tracing names of distinguished ancestors, **210**.

Butler, James, 1st Earl of Ormond (Ireland), marries Eleanor, daughter of Humphrey de Bohun, 4th Earl of Hereford and Lady Elizabeth Plantagenet, daughter of Edward I, **165**, **166**, **169**.

Butler, Lady Margaret, daughter of Thomas, 7th Earl of Ormond, marries William Boleyn, son of Sir Geoffrey, 7th great grandmother of Captain Mallom, **159**, **163**, **165**, **166**, **167**, **176**.

Butler, Theobald, son of Hervey Walter, becomes Chief Butler (botellier) of Ireland to Henry II, later a hereditary office, hence the family name, **165**.

Butler family, earls of Ormond, original surname of Walter, from Hervey Walter of Dereham, Norfolk, late 12th century, **165**.

Buxton, John, Norfolk Gentleman and Architect, of Channonz Hall, Tibenham, in letters to his son, Robert, 1719–1729, mentions John Mallom between 1725–1728, **73–74**.

Buxton Papers, University of Cambridge, **194**.

Calendar Act of 1750, adjustment in dates of baptism, **30**.

Cambridge University, Gonville and Caius College, **30**, **40**, **61**, **63**. Corpus Christi College, **68**.

Camden, Battle of, August 1780, **135–136**, **145–148**, 136.

Campbell, Captain Alexander, aide to General Sir William Eskine, accused of treachery, found not guilty, **126**.

Charleston, S. Carolina, 1st siege of, 1776, **115**; 2nd siege of, 1780, **129**; 63rd Regiment of Foot in, **128**, **130**, **132–133**, **134**, **135**, **138**, **144**, **145**, **147**, **149–151**.

Cley-next-the-Sea, Mallom family of, **34**; administration of Margaret Malham of, 1594 **39–40**.

Clinton, Lieutenant General Sir Henry, **115–116**, 115; commands the failed attack on Charleston, South Carolina, June 1776, **116**; retakes Charleston in 1780, **129**.

College of Arms, London, Pedigree of the Mallom family showing origins in Yorkshire, **37**.

Copping, Revd. William, Rector of Bedingham, marries Elizabeth Stone, 1663, **42—43**;

indenture agreement with Thomas Stone, his father-in-law, and William Stone, his brother-in-law, concerning lands and property, 1663, **42—43**; death, 1666, **43**; administration of his assets granted to his mother, Susan Copping, **44**; memorial in the chancel of Bedingham Church, 44; legal ramifications following his death, **44**, **51—52**.

Copping, Susan, Court of Chancery case in 1676, **51—52**.

Cornwallis, Charles, 1st Marquess, Lieutenant General under Sir Henry Clinton, **116**, 116; failed siege of Charleston, 1776, **115—116**; leading role in the Long Island and New York campaigns, **116**; returns to America for the Southern Campaign, successful second siege of Charleston 1780, **128—129**; his dispatch to London carried by Captain Mallom, January 1781, **138**; surrenders British forces to General George Washington at Yorktown, October 1781, **150**.

Court Martial Panels, John Mallom serves on, in New York, Head of Elk, Maryland, Army Headquarters in Philadelphia, Mount Holly in New Jersey Province, Stony Point Camp in New York, with Presidents and members of, **121—128**.

Cranmer Hall, Sculthorpe, tenancy of Hon. George Townshend, 1762—176, residence of Revd. Thomas Donne and his wife, **114**, **200**, until 1747, **189—191**, **200**, **202**, **203**; residence of Sir Willoughby Jones, Bart., **202**, and later, of Sir John Thomas Jones, Bart., **203**, 111.

Cromer Hall, 1901, where Richard Mallom, formerly of Sculthorpe, was the game keeper; visit by Arthur Conan Doyle, author of the Sherlock Holmes stories, **205**.

Cunningham/Cunnynghame, Colonel Sir David Bart., Commanding Officer of 57th Regiment of Foot when John Mallom enlisted in 1761, **107—108**.

DNA testing, value in genealogy, relevance in the story of Richard III; Prince Philip's DNA used to confirm that remains found in Ekaterinburg, Russia, were those of his relatives, the Romanov Imperial family, and of British soldiers killed in France, 1914, **210—211**.

Donne, Revd. Thomas, Rector of Sculthorpe (1705—1739), presented by his father, Robert Donne, the patron of the living, **188—191**.

Donne, Roger, cousin of Robert, tenant farmer of John Mallom of Wacton Hall, **188**.

Edward I, King of England, **165**, **167**, **168**, **169**, **43**.

Ekins, Thomas, husband of Elizabeth Mallom, 1731, **64**; Prison Surgeon in Norwich, 1733—1734, **65**; Freeholder in Shotesham, **65**; will of 1742, proved in Norwich, **65**.

Elizabeth I, Queen of England, 2nd cousin six times removed of Captain Mallom, **163—164**, 164.

Eutaw Springs, Battle of, **135**, **146—147**, 146.

Fastolf, Sir John, of Caister Castle, Norfolk, purchased by Geoffrey Boleyn, Queen Anne's great grandfather, **162**, **163**.

Finch, Heneage, Lord Chancellor, Court of Chancery, 1676, case involving John Mallom and his wife, Elizabeth, **51**.

Fisher, Corporal John, charged with rape, found guilty and sentenced to death on 7 March 1778, with others, **125**.

Fisher, John, Drummer, charged with desertion and joining the enemy, found guilty, sentenced to death by hanging "… on a tree by the road …" on 22 June 1778, **126**.

George II, King of England, 27, cartoon of, by George Townshend, 113.

Germain, Lord George, Secretary of State for the Colonies in London, later 1st Viscount Sackville, **129, 138–144**.

Grant Lieutenant General, Francis, Commander of the 63rd Regiment of Foot, **124, 130**.

Great Moulton, Church of St Michael's and All Angels, baptism of John Mallom, 1742, **27**, 27.

Great Yarmouth, Mallom family of, 1577–1610, **34**.

Henry I, King of England, dies after eating lampreys in Normandy, December 1135, deathbed nomination of Stephen of Blois as his heir, grandson of the Conqueror, **175**.

Herring, Thomas, Fellow of Corpus Christi College, Cambridge, Tutor of John Mallom, ordained Deacon, 1716, Priest, 1719, Doctor of Divinity, 1728, Chaplain to George II, Bishop of Bangor, Archbishop of York, Archbishop of Canterbury, 1747–1757, **68**.

Hethersett, village 4 miles north of Wacton, where Elizabeth (Suckling) Mallom lived briefly as a widow, and where she died, 1758, **75**.

Hipkin, Anne, marriage with John Mallom in Sculthorpe, 1792, **191–194, 198, 201**; 2nd marriage, with John Bastard, in Sculthorpe, 1811, **201**; descendants of, **201–207**, death and burial of, 1858, **201**.

Holwell, Private Daniel, charged with desertion, found not guilty, 1 September 1777, **123**.

Howe, General Sir William, 5th Viscount, Commander-in-Chief of British land forces in America, **116**, 116, failed siege of Boston, **116**; followed by successful attack on New York, from July 1776, **117–118**; advance from Staten Island to Gravesend Bay, Long Island, New York, August 1776, **116–117**, 117, with flat–bottomed boats, 117, 118, capture of New York city, held by the British, **117**.

Howes, John, Barrister, case against John Mallom concerning allegation of interest owed, **94–95**.

John, King of England, **165–166, 170, 171**.

Kemp, Revd. Thomas, son of Sir Robert Kemp, 3rd Baronet of Ubbeston, Suffolk, marries Anna Mallom, daughter of John and Elizabeth (Suckling) Mallom; Rector of Flordon, burial in the Kemp vault in Gissing Church, 1761, **69–70, 100**.

Large, Martin, marries [Anne] Mary Mallom, son–in–law of John and Anne (Hipkin) Mallom, in Sculthorpe, 1818, **202**; of their 10 children, the first 2 were baptised in Houghton St Giles, the others in North Barsham, including Thomas Large, the author's great grandfather, **204**; 2 sons baptised Richard, in memory of their great grandfather, Richard Mallom, of Wacton, **204**.

Large, Robert, Mercer, Warden of the Mercer's Company of London, Mayor of London, 1439–1440, master of his apprentice, William Caxton, **36**.

Large, Thomas, son of Martin and [Ann] Mary (Mallom) Large, baptism in North Barsham, 1830, lodger in Sculthorpe with Isaac Vertigan, 1851, widowed, 1895, living in Sculthorpe Almshouses, 1911, **205**.

Laud, William, Archbishop of Canterbury, licences Revd. John Mallom of Booton as a Preacher, **40**; indenture between William Copping of Woodton, and Thomas Stone & William Stone of Bedingham, December 1663, land and property identified within, explanation of, **42–43**.

Lease and Release between John Mallom, his wife, Elizabeth, and George Copping of Woodton, 1672, details of land and property in Woodton, **50–51**.

Ledgerstone lozenges, armorial of spinster or widowed females entitled to bear arms, **188**, 188.

Leslie, General Alexander, Letter Book, includes campaign correspondence from Balfour to Germain, 1781, **143**.

Magna Carta, Runneymede, 1215, **161**, **171**; Bigod earls witness to, **159**, **172**.

Malham village, Yorkshire, **37–39**, 38.

Mallam families of Great Yarmouth, 1577–1610, **34**.

Mallom, Ann[a] (1705-1748), daughter of John and Elizabeth (Suckling) Mallom, **69**; marries Revd. Thomas Kemp, Rector of Flordon,1739, **69**, **100**; left £2000 on Kemp's death, 1734, **69**; burial in Gissing, 1748, **69**.

Mallom, Anna (1734–34), daughter of John and Phillis Mallom, baptism and burial in Wacton, **28**.

Mallom, Anne (1802–1885), daughter of John and Anne (Hipkin) Mallom, baptism in Sculthorpe, marries Charles Twiddy, shoemaker, in North Barsham, 1828, baptises 8 children in Houghton St Giles, **204**.

Mallom, Anne Mary (1794–1857), daughter of John and Anne (Hipkin) Mallom, also known as Mary Mallom, birth and baptism in Sculthorpe, marries Martin Large in Sculthorpe, 1818, **202**, **207**; her 10 children including 2 sons, baptised Richard, **204–205**; grandchildren of, **205–206**; burial in North Barsham as Ann Mary Large, 1857, **204**.

Mallom, Audrey (Etheldreda) (1678–1758), daughter of John and Elizabeth (Stone–Copping) Mallom, baptism in Wacton, **56**; marries Revd. Thomas Donne, Rector of Sculthorpe, **188**; lives at Cranmer Hall, Sculthorpe, **191**, 111, and later in Parsonage House, **188**; death in Norwich, **191**; burial and ledgerstone in Sculthorpe Church, **190**.

Mallom, Catherine (1671–1747), daughter of John and Elizabeth (Stone–Copping) Mallom, baptism in Bedingham, **56**; marries John Harris, 1688, **191**; burial in Norwich, **191**.

Mallom, Charles (1616–16), son of Richard Mallom, baptism and burial in St Peter Mancroft Church, Norwich, **32**, 33.

Mallom, Dorothy (1796–1816), (Dotty), daughter of John and Anne (Hipkin) Mallom of

Sculthorpe, death, 1816, burial with her father, **193–194**, **203**.

Mallom, Elizabeth (1673–1723), daughter of John and Elizabeth (Stone–Copping) Mallom, baptism in Bedingham, 66, **188**; spinster, moves to Sculthorpe, **188**; will, 1723, **188**; burial in Sculthorpe Church, 1723, **188**, ledgerstone in Sculthorpe Church, **189**.

Mallom, Elizabeth (1731–37), daughter of John and Phillis Mallom, baptism in Wacton, burial in Aslacton, **28**; ledgerstone inscription, 29.

Mallom, Elizabeth (1739–39), daughter of John and Phillis Mallom, baptism in Wacton, burial in Aslacton, **28**; ledgerstone inscription, 29.

Mallom, Elizabeth (1808–1879), youngest child of John and Anne (Hipkin) Mallom, baptism in Sculthorpe, marries William Parker in South Creake in 1836, of their 5 children the first was baptised in North Creake, the others in the Burnhams, where Elizabeth's mother, Anne (Hipkin) Mallom, later moved to live with them in Burnham Westgate, **204**.

Mallom, Elizabeth, (1697–1757), daughter of John and Elizabeth (Suckling) Mallom, **63**; marries Thomas Ekins 1731, **64**; case in the High Court of Chancery against her brother, John Mallom, **64–65**; death and burial in Norwich, 1797, **65**.

Mallom, Elizabeth, marries John Smith, Swaffham in 1803, but her origins unclear, **103**.

Mallom, Ellen (1618–), daughter of Richard Mallom, baptism in St Peter Mancroft Church, Norwich, **32**, 33.

Mallom, Ethel Minnie (1896–1980), daughter of Richard William and Laura Elizabeth (Owen) Mallom and 2nd great granddaughter of John and Anne (Hipkin) Mallom, baptism in Sculthorpe, marries John Manning Woodhouse in 1927, lived in Sculthorpe, known as "Aunt Minnie", buried with her husband in Sculthorpe Graveyard, **206**, 206.

Mallom, Frances (1752–1815), daughter of Robert Mallom of Swaffham, 1st cousin of Captain Mallom, death in Norwich, 1815 and burial in Swaffham, **103**.

Mallom, Hannah (1805–1891), daughter of John and Anne (Hipkin) Mallom, baptism in Sculthorpe, marries Robert Grimmer of Dunton, 1830, 9 children baptised in Dunton, 1831–1851, **204**.

Mallom, Hannah (1828–1887), daughter of William Mallom, baptism in Sculthorpe, 1828, moves to London and marries Samuel Shepherd in Clerkenwell, 1863; their son, Samuel Mallom Shepherd, retains his ancestry in his Mallom name, **203**.

Mallom, James (c.1746–1831), son of Robert Mallom of Swaffham, 1st cousin of Captain Mallom, **101**; marries Eleanor Ollet in Swaffham, 1770, and baptises 8 children between 1788–1813, including a son, James, described as "an idiot," **102–103**.

Mallom, John (1650–1687), great grandfather of Captain Mallom, marries Elizabeth, daughter of Thomas Stone of Bedingham, gent, **42**, **49**; controversy surrounding lease between Mallom and Elizabeth his wife, with George Copping of Woodton, 1672, **42–43**, **49–51**; purchase of Wacton Hall from Henry Reve, 1672, **51**, **53**; Coat of Arms granted, 1685, **54–56**, 56, will, 1686, leaves his estate and property to his son, John, **60**; death, 1687, **58**; burial in Wacton Church with his wife, Elizabeth, ledgerstone in the Chancel floor, 58.

Mallom, John (1671–1728), son of John and Elizabeth (Stone–Copping) Mallom, baptism in Bedingham, **56**; school in Wymondham, **30**; Gonville & Caius College, Cambridge, where he fails to graduate, **30**, **61**; marries Elizabeth Suckling, daughter of Robert Suckling of Woodton, 1692, **62**; name on the Voting Registers for Norfolk, one of four freeholders in Wacton, 1714–1715, **78**; acquires the advowson of Stratton St Mary as part of his marriage settlement, **63**, sold to Gonville and Caius College, Cambridge, 1725, **63**; children of, **63–71**; legal cases against his brother, Robert, **66–68**, **78–82**; will of 1719, probate 1728, **71–72**; appears in the Letters of John Buxton, Norfolk Gentleman and Architect to his son, 1725–1728, **73–74**; death, 1728, **75**; burial in Wacton Church alongside his wife, Elizabeth, ledgerstone in the Chancel floor, 75.

Mallom, John (1695–1695), son of John and Elizabeth (Suckling) Mallom, baptism and burial in Wacton, **63**.

Mallom, John (1700–61) (father of Captain Mallom), baptism in Wacton, **27**; Corpus Christi College, Cambridge, 1689, **30**, failure to graduate **68**; marries Phillis Phillips in Aslacton, 1728, **31**; pastel portrait of, **31**, 31, High Court of Chancery case against his sister, Elizabeth, her husband, Thomas Ekins and Robert Suckling of Woodton, his father-in-law, concerning her legacy, 1732, **64**, purchase and sale of property in Norwich, **64**; name on the Voting Register in the Poll of Knights for Norfolk, 1734, **78**; acquires Bunwell Brick Works with his wife, 1734, **82**; Commissioner of the Peace, 1738–1756, **98**; interest in horse–racing and his horse, *Foxhunter*, 1739, **91**, **100**; High Court of Chancery cases involving his brother, Robert, concerning their father's will, 1742–1743, **78–81**; move to Aslacton, 1754, **92**; death of his wife, Phillis, 1754, **90**; her ledgerstone in Aslacton Church, **90–91**, 90; Wacton Hall advertised "to be Let" with description of the estate, 1756, **88–90**; last High Court Case, 1759–1761, **94–96**; surrender of the estate to Eleanor Collin of Brancaster, 1761, **89**; sale of Wacton Hall to John Ramey, of Great Yarmouth, 1760–1762, **89**; description and sale of Aslacton home, 1761, **92–93**; will, 1761, **96–97**; death and burial in Aslacton, 1761, **91**; meetings of creditors in Diss, 1764 & 1765, **97–98**; Aslacton home "to be Let" 1780, and 1821, **97**.

Mallom, John (1732–34), son of John and Phillis Mallom, baptism and burial in Wacton, **28**.

Mallom, John (1738–39), son of John and Phillis Mallom, baptism in Wacton, burial in Aslacton, **28**.

Mallom, John (1740–42), son of John and Phillis Mallom, baptism in Wacton, **28**.

Mallom, John (1742–82), son of John and Phillis Mallom, birth in Wacton, **21**; baptism in Great Moulton, **27**; education, **30**; guardianship to his father, 1756, **92**; acquires Bunwell Brickworks, 1761, **91**; named in father's will, 1761, **28**; enlists in the 57th Regiment of Foot, 1761 sponsored by Charles Townshend MP, **107**; regiment in Gibraltar, 1757– 1763; then in Menorca, where he was promoted to Lieutenant in June 1767, **107**; posted to Dublin, 1768–1776, **108**, **114**; writes to Sir Armine Wodehouse, April 1770, appealing to General George Townshend for favours, **108–109**; 57th Foot moves to Kilkenny, 1775, **114**; sails for North Carolina, February 1776, **115**; failed attack on Charleston, South Carolina, June 1776, **115–116**; sails to Staten Island, New York, August 1776, **116**; 57th Foot takes part in attack from Staten Island for Gravesend Bay, Long Island, August 1776, in flat–bottomed boats 118; storms Redbank, and helps take New York, **117**; attack on Paulus Hook Fort on the western side of the Hudson River, **117–118**; supervises the reinforcement of defences, October

1776–January 1777, **119**, 119; and submits account for payment, **120**, 120; serves on 5 Court Martial Panels, February 1777 to June 1779, in New York, Maryland, Philadelphia, New Jersey and New York, when punishments include the death penalty, **121–128**; promotion to Captain 63rd Foot, September 1777, **123–124**; sees action in the Northern and the Southern Campaigns of the war, when 63rd Foot occupies Charleston, **128–129**, 129; Musters of Captain Mallom's Company, June 1777 to December 1781, **130–137, 145, 147**; witness at the Court Martial of Captain Hayes St Leger, Charleston, 1780, **133–135**, Battle of Camden, August 1780, when many of Mallom's Company suffer Revolutionary Fever **135–136**, 36, Battle of Eutaw Springs, September 1781, **146–147**, 146, death of his friend, Lieutenant John Money, at Blackstock's Farm, South Carolina, 1780, involving Colonel Banastre Tarleton, the most hated British Officer, **137, 142**, 137, carries dispatches from Cornwallis to London, January 1781, **138**; writes letter of thanks to Cornwallis, **140**; described as an Officer of Merit by Lieutenant Colonel Nisbet Balfour, **139**; *The London Gazette*, and provincial newspapers announce Mallom's arrival in England during February 1781, **142–143**; 63rd Foot based in Charleston, 1780–1781, **145**; absence from his Company noted on Muster 10 for December 1781, **145**; his whereabouts after the voyage to England, **147–149**; death of Captain Mallom, February 1782, arguably in Charleston, South Carolina, **150–152**; replaced by Captain William Marshall, 1st March 1782, **150**.

Mallom, John (1744–), son of Robert Mallom of Swaffham, 1st cousin of Captain Mallom, **101**.

Mallom, John (1841–1882), son of Richard and Frances (Finch) Mallom, grandson of John and Anne (Hipkin) Mallom, baptism in Sculthorpe, 1827, marries Mary Anne Britten English in Sculthorpe, 1866; publican in Sculthorpe, **203**; moves to Bath working as a Coachman and Servant, summoned to Court for injuring his wife in a drunken state, sentenced to 1 month in prison, report in *The Bath Chronicle*, **203–204**.

Mallom, John (c.1765–1810), son of Richard and Mary (Smith) Mallom, marries Anne Hipkin in Sculthorpe, October 1792, **191–192**; baptises eight children in Sculthorpe, 1792–1808, **193**; death and burial in Sculthorpe, 1810, age 45 years, register entry identifies his father as Richard Mallom, and mother as Mary (Smith) Mallom, **193**; children of, **201–204**; 51 grandchildren of, **201**.

Mallom, Margaret (1615–), daughter of Richard Mallom, baptism in St Gregory's Church, Norwich, **32**.

Mallom, Mary (1610–), daughter of Richard Mallom, baptism in St Gregory's Church, Norwich, **32**, 32, marries John Read, citizen and mercer of Norwich, master of Thomas Mallom, **34**.

Mallom, Mary (1675–1727), daughter of John and Elizabeth (Stone–Copping) Mallom, baptism in Wacton, **56**; marries James Wortley, 1699, **189**; death, 1727, **189**; burial and ledgerstone in Sculthorpe Church, 188.

Mallom, Mary (–1758), daughter of John and Elizabeth (Suckling) Mallom, confusion over baptismal names, **70**; marries Merchant Berry, Bedingham, 1736, **70**; death and burial, Hempnall, 1758, **70**.

Mallom, Phillis (1735–38), daughter of John and Phillis Mallom, baptism in Wacton, burial in Aslacton, **28**, ledgerstone inscription, 29.

Mallom, Revd. John, son of Richard Mallom of Norwich, grocer, education in Norwich under

Mr Stonham, **40**; Gonville and Caius College, Cambridge, 1624–31, **40**; ordained in Norwich in 1632, **40**; made Priest, 1633, **40**; appointed Rector of Booton, 1634, **40**; licensed as a preacher by William Laud, Archbishop of Canterbury, 1635, **40**; acquires the deeds of Oak Farm, Booton, 1638, **40**; marries Katherine Mann, daughter of Timothy Mann, gent, of Binham, 1640, **40**; executor of the will of John Read in 1652, **40**; financial and property interests in Norwich, Cambridge and Essex, **41**; death, 1662, **41**.

Mallom, Richard (1612–), son of Richard Mallom, baptism in St Gregory's Church, Norwich, 1612; **32**; made free, 1633, **34**.

Mallom, Richard (1744–), son of John and Phillis Mallom, baptism in Wacton, April 1744, **28**, **187**, **52**; education, **30**; named in father's will, 1761, **28**; marries Mary Smith, **193–194**, searches for the marriage entry, **194–198**; whereabouts after the deaths of his parents, **199–201**; father of the John Mallom who marries Anne Hipkin in Sculthorpe, 1792, **192**.

Mallom, Richard (1800–1867), son of John and Anne (Hipkin) Mallom, baptism in Sculthorpe, marries Frances Finch in 1827, baptises 7 children in Sculthorpe 1830–1845, including a son, Richard in 1845, appears in list of Sculthorpe Tithe Apportionments, 1839, with brother, William, and rents half an acre of allotment owned by Colonel Sir John Jones Bart, Lord of the Manor of Cranmer Hall, Sculthorpe, **203**, **205**.

Mallom, Richard, of Norwich, grocer, born between 1581–84, marries Mary Ward, daughter of John Ward of Norwich, **32**; made free, 1605, **34**; buried in St Peter Mancroft Church, Norwich, 1636, **33**,33.

Mallom, Richard William (1872–1949), nephew of William Mallom and great grandson of John and Anne (Hipkin) Mallom of Sculthorpe, marries Laura Elizabeth Owen in Sculthorpe, 1896, **205**; trains as a Carpenter, admitted as a Carpenter and Joiner to the Amalgamated Society of Carpenters, Cabinet Makers & Joiners, 1919; their daughter, Ethel Minnie, was the last child baptised with the surname Mallom in Sculthorpe, 1896; burial in Sculthorpe Graveyard, headstone inscription includes his wife, who died, 1939, **206**, 206.

Mallom, Robert (1693–1697), son of John and Elizabeth (Suckling) Mallom, baptism in Woodton and burial in Wacton, **63**.

Mallom, Robert (1703–1785), son of John and Elizabeth (Suckling) Mallom, baptism in Wacton, uncle of Captain John Mallom, **66**; boarding school in Wymondham, and school in Norwich under Mr Wingfield, **67**; trains as a Legal Clerk to Mr Sayer Attorney in Harlestone, **67**; contracts smallpox, when care paid by his brother, **67**; moves to Yoxford, Suffolk, bound for 5 years to Mr Wychingham, Attorney, **67**; moves to Swaffham as Articled Clerk to Mr Youngs, **67**; marries Mary Dusgate in Swaffham, 1742, **67**; lengthy court cases against his brother, John, concerning the annuity left to him by George Bedell Esq., **66–68, 76–81, 94–96**.

Mallom, Robert (1743–1815), son of Robert Mallom of Swaffham, 1st cousin of Captain Mallom; announcement of death in *The Norfolk Chronicle*, 1 April 1815, **103**.

Mallom, Sarah (1698–1745), daughter of John and Elizabeth (Suckling) Mallom, baptism in Wacton, **63**; marries Daniel Youngs, Freeman of Norwich, in Bracon Ash, 1732, **66**; death and burial in Norwich, **66**.

Mallom, Sarah (1737–37), daughter of John and Phillis Mallom, burial in Aslacton, **28**, ledgerstone inscription, 29.

Mallom, Sarah (1792–1836), daughter of John and Anne (Hipkin) Mallom, birth and baptism in Sculthorpe, **192**; marries Ransom Bell in Sculthorpe, 1818; their 7 children all baptised in Sculthorpe, including a son, Richard, **202**.

Mallom, Sarah, daughter of John and Elizabeth (Suckling) Mallom, **65–66**; marries Daniel Youngs in Bracon Ash, 1732, **66**, **100**; burial in Norwich, 1745, **66**.

Mallom, surname variants of, in Norfolk Lay Subsidy Rolls, 1327 & 1332, **35–36**; and Poll Tax returns, 1377, 1379 & 1381, **35**.

Mallom, Susan (1620–23), daughter of Richard Mallom, baptism and burial in St Peter Mancroft Church, Norwich, **32**, 33.

Mallom, Susanna, marries William Buck in Bedingham, 1742; baptises 8 children in Hempnall, **70–71**; her origins unclear.

Mallom, Thomas (1613–), son of Richard Mallom, baptism in St Gregory's Church, Norwich, made free as a Mercer of Norwich, 1637, **33**.

Mallom, Thomas (–1748), son of Robert Mallom of Swaffham, 1st cousin of Captain Mallom, **101**.

Mallom, Thomas, archer, muster in York, 1400, **39**; Hundred Years War **39**; retinue of Sir Peter de Buckton, supporter of King Henry IV, **40**.

Mallom, William (1753–), son of Robert Mallom of Swaffham, 1st cousin of Captain Mallom, **101**.

Mallom, William (1798–1876), son of John and Anne (Hipkin) Mallom, baptism in Sculthorpe, 193; marries Mary Rayner in North Barsham, 1822, **202**; 2 daughters baptised in Sculthorpe, **202**; witness at Petty Sessions, 1864, **203**; Parish Clerk of Sculthorpe for 40 years, **203**; death and burial in Sculthorpe, 1876, headstone inscription includes his wife, Mary, who died, 1868; obituary notice in *The Norfolk Chronicle*, **202–203**.

Mallom, William (1833–1914), son of Richard and Frances Mallom, grandson of John and Anne (Hipkin) Mallom, baptism in Sculthorpe, marries Elizabeth Dye in Sculthorpe, 1859, moves to Cromer as gamekeeper at Cromer Hall, name on the Poll of Electors of Cromer, 1885–1912, **205**.

Mallom, William, (1753–1777), son of Robert Mallom of Swaffham and 1st cousin of Captain Mallom, **101**; Ship's Butcher on the East India Ship "Nassau," **101**; will, 1775, leaves possessions to brother, Robert Mallom of Swaffham, butcher, **101**.

Mallom apprenticeships in Norwich, **34**.

Mallom families in medieval Yorkshire recorded on a Pedigree held at The College of Arms, London, **37**.

Mallom family estates in Tibenham, Bunwell, Wacton, (Great) Moulton, Stratton, Taseburgh, Hempnall, Booton, Witchingham, and Kerdiston in Reepham, **82**.

Mallom family of Cley-next-the-Sea (1592–98), **34**; administration of Margaret Malham of Cley, **34**.

Malloms as Freemen of Norwich, **32, 34, 36**.

Malloms in Yorkshire, surname variants, Malham, Malhamdale, Skipton, Clapham, **37–39**.

Malloms paying Lay Subsidy Tax, Norfolk, 1327, 1332, **35**.

Malloms paying Poll Tax, Norfolk, 1377, 1379, 1381, **37–39**.

Mann, Katherine (–1685), daughter of Timothy Mann of Binham, wife of Revd. John Mallom of Booton, mother–in–law of John Mallom of Wacton Hall, **40**; death, 1685, **59**; burial in Wacton Church, ledgerstone in the Chancel floor, 59.

Mann, Timothy, of Binham, gent, 1663, bequests to his Mallom grandchildren, John and Timothy, **40**.

Manor Court Records near Sculthorpe, Fakenham, Dunton cum Doughton, South Creake, Houghton St Giles, **200**.

Marsh, John, of Haberdashers Hall, London, in the estate of George Bedell of Woodrising, **77–78**.

Marshal, William, 4th Earl of Pembroke and Marshal of England, soldier and administrator, captured at Poitou, but released when Queen Isabella wife of Henry II, paid his ransom, carries the sceptre at the coronation of Richard I, supports King John, arranging his funeral at Worcester Cathedral, known as the veteran regent or "The Marshal," father of Maud, who marries Hugh II Bigod, **171, 176–177**.

Matilda, daughter of Henry I, marries (second) Geoffrey of Anjou, leading to the Angevin dynasty in England, **169, 175**.

Mercers Company of Norwich, members and freemen of, **33**.

Militia, East and West Norfolk, musters of, **199–200**.

Money, Lieutenant John, son of Revd. Thomas and Margaret Money of Norwich, friend and fellow–officer in the 63rd Foot of Captain Mallom, **124, 131, 133, 137**; aide–de–Camps to General Cornwallis, **141**; killed in action at Blackstock's Farm, November 1780, **141**; commemorative poem published in *The Norfolk Chronicle* on 17 March 1781, **142**; letter from his mother, Margaret Money, to Earl Cornwallis, March 1781, enquiring as to his fate, mentions his friend, Captain Mallom, **141**.

Mortimer, Roger, 1st Earl of March and Baron of Wigmore, Herefordshire, leads a revolt against Edward II, imprisoned in the Tower of London, romantically involved with Isabella, Edward's queen, executed at Tyburn, November 1330, **166–167**.

Nelson, Horatio, later Admiral Lord Nelson, 2nd cousin of Captain Mallom, **159**, 161.

Norfolk Poll Lists, 1765–1810, searches of, for Richard Mallom, **200, 203, 205**.

North, Lord George, Prime Minister of Great Britain, 1770–1782, later 2nd Earl of Guildford, **138, 141**.

Norwich, city of, **30**; Mallom baptisms in, **32–33**; Mallom apprentices in, **33—34**; Mallom family origins in, **34**; Malloms as freemen of, **36–37**; property bought and sold in, **41**, **78**. Thomas Ekins, Surgeon of, **65**; Robert Mallom, school in, **67**; life in, **67**; convalescence in **78**; signs document concerning annuity in, **67**; Shire elections in, **71**, **78**; Assizes in, 1738, **78**; Mary Tawell, widow of, loan to John Mallom, 1744, **95**, newspapers of, advertising sale of Mallom home in Aslacton, **97**; Frances Mallom of, **103**; Roger Bigod (also known as Roger bigot) seizes castle in, **172**; Herbert de Losinga, bishop of, **172**; burial of Bigod in, **172**; castle in, **173**; Audrey Mallom living in, **191**; her death in, **191**; family of Lieutenant John Money of, **142**, **193**.

Norwich Castle, built by Roger I Bigod, **172**, 173, Bigod Tower of, 173, Bigod Arch of, 173.

Norwich Cathedral, 174, Presbytery of, 174, burial site of Roger I Bigod, **172**.

Norwich, churches in, where members of the Mallom family were baptised and/or buried, St Gregory's, **32**, **33**, **34**, 32; St Peter Mancroft, **32–33**, 33.

Ockham, William of, Ockham's Razor, philosophy concerning complex problems, **209**.

Palgrave—Moore, Patrick, Norfolk Genealogist and Antiquarian, Index of Norfolk Marriages, **13–14**, **33**, **194**, **208**.

Parsons, Revd. Joseph, Vicar of Bedingham from 1725–1774, omission of baptism entries of Mary and Susanna Mallom, daughters of John and Elizabeth (Suckling) Mallom, **70**.

Peebles, John, Lieutenant, later Captain in the 42nd Regiment of Foot, fears competition with Lieutenant John Mallom, for a captaincy, **124**; member with Mallom, of a Court Martial panel, February—March, 1778, **125**.

Paulus Hook Fort, New Jersey, Lieutenant John Mallom's work on, **117–121**, 119 and 120.

Paulus Hook Monument, in Jersey City, New Jersey, erected, 1903, 121.

Phillips, Phillis, daughter and surviving child of Robert Phillips of Tibenham, **27**; marries John Mallom in Aslacton, 1728, **27–28**, **76**; acquires Bunwell Brickworks from her father, 1734, **82**; death, 1754, and burial in Aslacton Church, **90**; ledgerstone inscription in the Chancel floor, with Mallom arms impaled with arms of Phillips. **28–29**, 28, 29, and 90.

Ramey, John, Esq., Barrister, Mayor of Great Yarmouth, purchase of Wacton Hall from John Mallom, 1760–1762, absentee landlord, **89**, **93**.

Raven, Nathaniel, marries Sarah Money in East Raynham, 1774, **192**; witness at the marriage of John Mallom and Anne Hipkin, 1792, **192**, **199**; Coat of Arms of, **192**; significance for Richard Mallom, **208**.

Reve, Augustine, inherits Wacton Hall and other estates from his brother, Sir Edmund Reeve, Chief Justice of the Common Pleas; pays tax for 18 hearths for Wacton Hall and its estate, **53**.

Reve, Henry, son of Augustine Reve, inherits Wacton Hall estate from his father, and sells to John Mallom, 1672, **43**, **51**, **53**.

Reynard, Private Benjamin, charged with leaving his camp and plunder, found guilty, sentenced to 1000 lashes, **127**.

Richard I, The Lionheart, King of England, **166, 170, 176–177**.

Schools, in Norwich, in Thetford, in Wymondham, and in Wacton, **30**.

Sculthorpe, censuses of, 1821, 1831, **201**.

Sculthorpe Church, *201*; burials with ledgerstones of Elizabeth Mallom, 1723, Mary (Mallom) Wortley, 1727, *188*, and Audrey (Mallom) Donne, 1758, **188–190**.

Sculthorpe documents, in the search for evidence of Richard Mallom, maps 1766, 1767, 1796, 1822, Enclosure Map of 1829, Manor Court Records 1789–1843, books of rentals 1771–1785, Glebe lands 1796, papers of Daniel Jones, 1750–1783, **200**.

Shelton, John de, born c. 1140, Lord of the Manor of Shelton, ancestor of Elizabeth Suckling, **62**.

Shelton, Lords of the Manor of, **62–63**; ancestry of, **62, 159–161**; Sir John Shelton marries Lady Anne Boleyn, **162**; stained glass window commemorating the couple in Shelton Church, *162*.

Shelton, Ralph, son of Sir Ralph Shelton, takes part in the siege of Malo with John of Gaunt, Duke of Lancaster, 1378, **161**.

Shelton, Sarah, marries Robert Suckling, Captain Mallom's great grandparents, **160–161**.

Shelton, Sir John, 21st Lord of Shelton, marries Lady Anne Boleyn of Blickling in *c*.1497 in Shelton Church, commemorated in a stained-glass window in Shelton Church, *162*; Sheriff of Norfolk and Suffolk, 1504, created Knight of the Bath at the coronation of Henry VIII, June 1509, comptroller of the household of the Princesses Mary and Elizabeth, **161–162**.

Shelton, Sir John de, 1st Lord of the Manor of Shelton, born, 1140, **161**.

Shelton, Sir Ralph, 14th Lord of Shelton, knighted by Edward III at Crecy, 1346, **62, 161**.

Singh, Prince Frederick Victor Duleep, first owner of the John Mallom portrait, **31–32**.

Smith, Mary, husband of Richard Mallom, mother of John Mallom of Sculthorpe, **193**; searches for her marriage entry, **194–198**.

Smith/Smyth, George, of Topcroft Hall, gentry family with property dealings in Sculthorpe, **194, 196**.

Smith family, owners of Bunwell Brick Works, which passed to John and Phillis Mallom of Wacton, and later to their son, John (Captain) Mallom, **197**.

Snow, Private Patrick, charged with desertion, February 1777, found guilty and sentenced to 300 lashes, **122**.

Socling, Thomas, admitted to certain estates, 1348, ancestor of Elizabeth Suckling, **62**.

Stewart, Corporal John, charged with desertion and joining the enemy, February 1777, found guilty and sentenced to death, **123**.

St Leger, Captain Hayes, member of Court Martial Panel with John Mallom, June 1779, **127**; Court Martial of, in Charleston, May 1780, accused of disrespectful behaviour towards Major James Wemyss, acquitted, **133–135**; fatally wounded during the Battle of Eutaw Springs, September 1781, **135**.

Stone, Elizabeth, marries Revd. William Copping, Rector of Bedingham, 1663, **42**, **43**, **44**; and after his death, John Mallom, 1670, son of Revd. John Mallom of Booton, **49**; death, 1684, burial in Wacton Church with ledgerstone in the Chancel floor, 58.

Stone, Henry, of Wotton near Bedingham, Executor of the will of John Mallom, 1686, **60**.

Stone, Thomas, of Bedingham, gent, **42–43**, born Good Friday 1603, hearth tax paid, 1664, father-in-law of John Mallom of Wacton Hall, **42**, **49**, will, 1688, with bequests to his Mallom grandchildren, **60**; death of, **60**.

Suckling, Catherine (1725–1767), marries Revd. Edmund Nelson, mother of Horatio, later Admiral Lord Nelson, niece of Elizabeth (Suckling) Mallom, Captain Mallom's grandmother, great niece of Prime Minister, Sir Robert Walpole, **160**.

Suckling, Elizabeth (1670–1728), daughter of Robert Suckling Esq., of Woodton and Sarah, daughter of Maurice and Elizabeth Shelton of Wooton Hall, **62**; marries John Mallom of Wacton Hall in Woodton Church, 1692, **62**, 63; move to Hethersett after the death of her husband, **75**; death 1728, **75**; burial in Wacton Church alongside her husband, **75–76**, ledgerstone in the Chancel floor, 75; administration of, 1729, **75**.

Suckling, Revd. Alfred Inigo, clergyman and antiquary, **159–160**.

Suckling, Revd. Maurice, brother of Elizabeth (Suckling) Mallom, Rector of Barsham and Woodton, Prebendary of Westminster Abbey, **160**.

Suckling, Robert Esq., of Woodton (1641–1708), father-in-law of John Mallom of Wacton Hall, **62**; pays tax on 16 hearths, **62**; will, 1707, proved in 1709; case against John Mallom, his son-in-law, **64–65**; estate and wealth distributed among his surviving nine children, except his married daughters, including Elizabeth, wife of John Mallom, **71**.

Tarleton, Colonel Banastre, promotion to Lieutenant Colonel aged 23 years, brilliant tactical military leader, **130**; tended John Money's wounds at Blackstock's Farm, November 1780, **142**, regarded by the Americans as brutal and vicious, their most hated opponent, **135**, 137.

Thetford, Ancient House Museum, holds the pastel portrait of John Mallom of 1728, **31**.

Thetford Priory of, Founded by Roger I Bigod, Curia Regis controversy, **172**, 174.

Tibenham, birth place of Phillis Phillips, future wife of John Mallom of Wacton Hall, **27**; home of John Buxton at Channonz Hall, **73**; land in the estate of John Mallom, 1761, **92**; James Lincoln of, Executor of will of John Mallom, 1761, **96**.

Tosny, Adelisa or Alice de, daughter of Robert de Tosny, Lord of Belvoir, Leicestershire, wife of Roger I Bigod, **178**.

Tosny, Ida de, royal ward and mistress of Henry II with whom she had a son, William Longespée (Longsword), later 3rd Earl of Salisbury, wife of Roger II Bigod, 2nd Earl of Norfolk, mother of Hugh II Bigod, 3rd Earl of Norfolk, who marries Maud Marshal, **166**, **176–**

177, 178.

Tosny, Robert de, Anglo–Norman nobleman, Lord of Belvoir, Leicestershire, possible standard–bearer of William the Conqueror, name appears in Battle Abbey Rolls, lands in 11 English counties as reward for service to the Conqueror, **172, 178**.

Tosny family (Toëny), noble family from the duchy of Normandy, Tosny the name of the village of origin, a branch of which moved to Belvoir, Leicestershire, **178**.

Townshend, General George, later of Raynham Hall, Norfolk, seat of the Townshend family, **108**; MP for Norfolk, **108**; receives letter from Sir Armine Wodehouse concerning Lieutenant Mallom, April 1770, **110**; baptism sponsored by George I, **112**; joins the British army, 1743, sees action in Quebec as a Brigadier, **112**; appointed Lieutenant–General, 1772, **112**; caricaturist and cartoonist, **112, 113**; Lord Lieutenant of Ireland, 1767, **114**; tenant of Cranmer Hall, Sculthorpe, Norfolk, **114**, 111; death at Raynham Hall, 1807, **114**.

Townshend, Rt. Hon. Charles Townshend, MP, sponsor of John Mallom, **107, 113**; trains as a lawyer, called to the Bar, 1747, MP for Great Yarmouth, 1747, Charismatic parliamentarian, Chancellor of the Exchequer to William Pitt, 1766–1767, proposes the Townshend Acts, imposing trade restrictions and taxation on the American Colonies leading eventually to war, death, 1767, **114**.

Twiddy, Charles, husband of Anne Mallom and son–in–law of John and Anne (Hipkin) Mallom, shoemaker and publican of the Buck Inn, Houghton St Giles, **204**.

Uniforms, worn by officers of 63rd Regiment of Foot, 115 and 129.

Wacton, population census of 1811, **187**.

Wacton, village of, **56–57, 60, 63**, church and baptisms, **27–28**, 57; burials in church with ledgerstones, 58, 59, 75.

Wacton Hall, original building from 13th century, **53**, purchased by John Mallom, 1762, **51, 53–54, 56**, 88, 89, description of, **88–90**, let to tenants, 89, sale of, **89–90**, Mallom home, **62–63, 67, 76–77, 82**, recent renovations of, **53**.

Wacton Hall Farm, description of and sale of, advertised in the *Ipswich Journal*, 1756, **88**, 88.

Walpole, Sir Robert, 1st Prime Minister of Great Britain, **27**.

Walter, Hervey, of Dereham, Norfolk, progenitor of the Butler family, earls of Ormond (Ireland), **165**.

Walter, Hubert, brother of Theobald, raised in the household of Ranulf de Glanville, chief justiciar of Henry II, Dean of York, Bishop of Salisbury and Archbishop of Canterbury, crowns John, King of England, May 1299, death and burial in Canterbury Cathedral, 1205, **165**.

Ward, Mary, daughter of John Ward of Norwich, gent, marries Richard Mallom, grocer, **32**.

Washington, General George, negotiations with General Sir William Howe, 1776, **116**, involvement in the war, **126**, surrender to by Lord Cornwallis, of the British, 19 October 1781, **149**.

Wemyss, Major James, accuses Captain St Leger of disrespectful behaviour and demands his Court Martial, **133**; taken prisoner at the Fishdam skirmish in November 1780, **135**; returns to England carrying dispatches to London, spring 1781, **135**; known as the second most hated British Officer by the Americans, **135**.

William I, The Conqueror, **171, 172, 178**.

Wodehouse, Anne, daughter of Sir Thomas Wodehouse of Kimberley, Norfolk, marries Colonel Robert Suckling, grandmother of Elizabeth (Suckling) Mallom, 2nd great grandmother of Captain Mallom, **160**.

Wodehouse, John, Constable of Castle Rising, 1402, Esquire of Body to Henry V, 1413–1422, MP for Norfolk, **160**.

Wodehouse, P.G., author, **108**.

Wodehouse, Sir Armine, 5th Baronet of Kimberley, Norfolk, 111, MP for Norfolk, distant relative of Lieutenant John Mallom, **108, 132**; receives letter from Mallom, April 1770, **108–109**; writes to General Townshend on behalf of Mallom, May 1770, **110**; Colonel of the East Norfolk Militia, **112**.

Woodton, village and church, **62**; 63, memorials in, **57**; home of the Suckling family, **62**; baptism of Mallom children, in, 1693–1697, **63–64, 65–66**.

Yorkshire, medieval, Mallom families in, **37–39**; Malham village and origin of the surname, **37–38**; Malhamdale Poll Tax 1379, **37–39**; York Minster Library, examples of, **38**; early Yorkshire Charters of, **37**; Kirkby Malhamdale near Skipton, **37–38**; Feet of Fines of, **38**; Stephen de Malgham, 1420, **37**; Richard Malhom, 1420, **38–39**; Kirkby Malham Muster Roll, 1539, in which Rob't Malhom enlists with a bill. **39**.

Yorktown, surrender of British forces at, October 1781, **149**.

Youngs, Daniel, husband of Sarah Mallom, 1732, Mercer Freeman of Norwich, 1730, **66**.

Milton Keynes UK
Ingram Content Group UK Ltd.
UKHW022306181124
451388UK00001B/23